THE TURNING POINT IN
CHINA'S
ECONOMIC DEVELOPMENT

Ross Garnaut & Ligang Song eds

THE TURNING POINT IN CHINA'S ECONOMIC DEVELOPMENT

Ross Garnaut & Ligang Song eds

Asia Pacific Press at
The Australian National University

Co-Published by ANU E Press and Asia Pacific Press
The Australian National Unversity
Canberra ACT 0200
Email: anuepress@anu.edu.au
Website: http://epress.anu.edu.au

National Library of Australia Cataloguing in Publication entry

The turning point for China's economic development.

Bibliography.
Includes index.
ISBN 0 7315 3763 7
ISBN 1 920942 76 9 (Online document)

1. Industrialization - China. 2. China - Economic policy.
3. China - Economic conditions. 4. China - Commercial
policy. I. Song, Ligang. II. Garnaut, Ross.

338.951

This work is copyright. Apart from those uses which may be permitted under the Copyright Act 1968 as amended, no part may be reproduced by any process without written permission from the publisher.

Editors: Bridget Maidment and Jan Borrie
Cover design: Annie Di Nallo Design

First edition © 2006 ANU E Press and Asia Pacific Press

Contents

Tables	vii
Figures	x
Symbols	xii
Abbreviations	xiii
Acknowledgments	xvi
Contributors	xvi

1	The turning point in China's economic development **Ross Garnaut**	1
2	Continued rapid growth and the turning point in China's development **Ross Garnaut and Yiping Huang**	12
3	Growth accounting after statistical revisions **Xiaolu Wang**	35
4	Quadrupling the Chinese economy again: constraints and policy options **Justin Yifu Lin**	53
5	China's interaction with the global economy **Nicholas R. Lardy**	75
6	Global imbalance, China and the international currency system **Fan Gang**	87
7	Who foots China's bank restructuring bill? **Guonan Ma**	103
8	Keeping fiscal policy sustainable in China: challenges and solutions **Jinzhi Tong and Wing Thye Woo**	128
9	Employment growth, labour scarcity and the nature of China's trade expansion **Cai Fang and Dewen Wang**	143
10	The impact of the guest-worker system on poverty and the well-being of migrant workers in urban China **Yang Du, Robert Gregory and Xin Meng**	172
11	China's growth to 2030: demographic change and the labour supply constraint **Jane Golley and Rod Tyers**	203
12	Changing patterns in China's agricultural trade after WTO accession **Chen Chunlai**	227

13	Village elections, accountability and income distribution in rural China	256
	Yang Yao	
14	China's resources demand at the turning point	276
	Ross Garnaut and Ligang Song	
15	Economic growth and environmental pollution: a panel data analysis	294
	Bao Qun and Shuijun Peng	
16	Harmonising the coal industry with the environment	314
	Xunpeng Shi	
17	Growth, energy use and greenhouse gas emissions in China	335
	Warwick McKibbin	
	References	360

Tables

2.1	Average wage rates by region, 1999–2006	31
2.2	Average annual wage rates for agriculture, manufacturing, construction and finance, 1978–2004	32
3.1	Average GDP growth rate in 1992–2004 by different sources	41
3.2	Changes in GDP structure, 2004	43
3.3	Estimation result: Prais-Winsten Regression AR(1)	48
3.4	Sources of TFP growth, 1952–2005	50
4.1	Oil production and consumption in China, 1990–2020	55
4.2	The saving rate of Japan and the 'small dragons', 1961–81 and 1982–2002	59
4.3	Banking structure in China, 1994–2004	61
4.4	Profitability and non-performing loans of the big four banks and shareholding banks in China, 2002–2004	63
4.5	Profitability and non-performing loans in the banking sector in some Asian countries, 1997–2002	64
4.6	The structural changes of Chinese export composition, 1998–2004	67
4.7	Main indicators of state-owned enterprises during 1997–2004	72
6.1	Trade balance between China and its neighbouring economies, 1999–2005	90
6.2	Asymmetry in asset value changes by devaluation	97
7.1	The big four Chinese banks in the Chinese banking system, 2002–2005	107
7.2	Announced direct foreign investment in Chinese banks, 2002–2006	114
7.3	Outside fund sources of the non-financial corporate sector, 1998–2004	117

A7.1	Estimating the cost of China's bank restructuring, by early 2006	127
8.1	Comparative perspectives on the size of the national debt, 1995 and 2003	131
8.2	Per capita net tax payments for different cohorts in JRW's base case simulation	139
8.3	The ratio of per capita net tax payments of future generations to the zero-age generation in 2002 under different retirement age assumptions	140
9.1	GDP and employment growth in China, 1991–2005	145
9.2	Employment growth in urban and rural areas, 1991–2004	147
9.3	Numbers of workers laid off and registered unemployment, 1998–2005	150
9.4	Urban unemployment rates in large cities, 1996–2005	151
9.5	Revealed comparative advantage indices of export and import commodities, 1994–2004	156
9.6	Macroeconomic contribution of net exports to economic growth, 1978–2004	159
9.7	Employment increments driven by trade growth, 1991–2005	160
9.8	Distribution of manufacturing employment by region, 1993–2002	161
9.9	International comparison of manufacturing wage costs, 1995–2002	169
10.1	Summary statistics	177
10.2	Poverty rate, poverty gap and per capita income/expenditure	180
10.3	Working status and working hours of migrants and urban residents	182
10.4	Selected results from tobit estimation of hours worked for urban residents and real and predicted hours for migrants	186
10.5	Real and predicted work hours for rural migrants	186
10.6	Selected results from per capita household income equation	189
10.7	Real and predicted per capita income and poverty rates	191
10.8	Marginal effects from probit estimation of Equation 5	195
10.9	Real and predicted proportion of migrants who are unhealthy	196
A10.1	Summary statistics for wage/salary earners and self-employed	201
A10.2	Dibao and CBN poverty lines by province, 2002	202
11.1	Baseline birth rates in China and Japan, 1997–2030	211
11.2	Baseline age and gender-specific labour-force participation rates in China and Japan	211
11.3	Baseline population structure in China, 1997–2030	212
11.4	Baseline labour-force structure in China, 1997–2030	212
11.5	Baseline real GDP and per capita income projections to 2030	217

11.6	The Chinese population under alternative demographic scenarios, 2000–2030	217
11.7	Economic effects of faster Chinese population growth to 2030	220
11.8	Economic effects of increased aged labour-force participation, 2010–2030	221
12.1	Comparison of agricultural product coverage	231
A12.1	China's agricultural exports by commodity groupings, 1992–2005	250–51
A12.2	China's agricultural imports by commodity groupings, 1992–2005	252–53
A12.3	China's revealed comparative advantage indices (NER), 1992–2005	254–55
13.1	First election in the sample villages and adoption of the OLVC in the sample provinces	262
13.2	The effects of elections on public and administrative expenditure	268
13.3	Village elections and income distribution	270
13.4	Village elections and income distribution	272
14.1	China's shares of energy and metal products in investment, exports and outputs, 1997 and 2000	283
15.1	Six indicators of environmental pollution	299
15.2	Simultaneous estimation results on water pollutants and solid pollutants	302
15.3	Simultaneous estimation results on air pollutants	303
15.4	GDP per capita; the five highest cities in 2000	304
15.5	Summary of some empirical results on EKC estimations	305
15.6	Average trends of China's regional industrial structural change, 1996–2000	308
16.1	Western European coal industry subsidies, production and import prices, 2000	319
16.2	China's coal production and consumption, 1995–2004	330
17.1	China's share of global energy consumption and carbon dioxide emissions, 1990–2030	336
17.2	China's shares of global consumption of fossil fuel energy components, 1990–2030	339
17.3	Shares in global consumption of non-fossil fuel energy components, 1990–2030	340

| A17.1 | Overview of the G-cubed model | 359 |

Figures

2.1	Quarterly real GDP growth and inflation in China, 2000–06	14
2.2	Changing composition of GDP, 2000–05	14
2.3	Growth of fixed-asset investment and retail sales, January 2000–June 2006	16
2.4	Growth of exports and imports, January 2000–June 2006	16
2.5	Share of state sector in total assets for selected industries, 2005	17
2.6	Growth of labour costs is a global phenomenon in rapidly growing economies	22
2.7	Changing correlation between wage and inflation, 1985–2005	22
2.8	Profit growth and profit margins in the Chinese industry, January 2001–June 2006	24
2.9	Profit margins of selected industries, 2000–06	24
2.10	China's export prices, January 2005–May 2006	26
2.11	Labour productivity growth and increases in real wages in China, 1998–2005	26
2.12	The share of employees' earnings in total industrial value-added, Q1 2000–Q1 2006	28
2.13	Recent decline in rural employment, 1991–2005	28
2.14	Declines in agricultural employment, 1991–2005	29
2.15	Changes in China's labour force, 1990–2020	29
2.16	Improving levels of education of the Chinese population, 1982–2020	30
3.1	China's GDP, revised and unrevised, 1991–2005	37
3.2	GDP growth rate, revised and unrevised, 1991–2005	37
3.3	Adjustment of GDP data at the provincial level, 2004	39
3.4	GDP structure after the statistical revisions, 2004 and 2005	43
3.5	GDP components by expenditure, 2004	44
4.1	Changes in government appropriation for education, 1991–2003	57
4.2	Regional income disparity, 1978–2000	68
5.1	Applied tariff rates, China and other emerging markets, 2004	78
5.2	China's import tariff revenue as a percentage of the value of imports, 1978–2004	78
5.3	Imports as a percentage of GDP in China, 1978–2005	79
5.4	Share of US trade deficit by region, 1985 and 2005	83
6.1	China's import and export growth and trade balance, 2003–2006	89

6.2	China's trade surplus as a percentage of GDP, 2004	89
6.3	China's bilateral trade balance, 2004	91
6.4	China's current account balance and increase in foreign exchange reserves, 1997–2005	93
6.5	Speculations: error and omission and current transfer, 1997–2006	93
6.6	Inflation: China and United States differential, 1997–2005	98
6.7	China's real wage and labour productivity changes, 1994–2004	98
9.1	Urban unemployment rate in China, 1990–2004	149
9.2	Ratio of job vacancies to job seekers, first quarter of 2001 to fourth quarter 2005	152
9.3	Share of trade in GDP in China, 1978–2004	153
9.4	Changing components of China's trade, 1980–2004	155
9.5	Per capita income versus population age structure	164
9.6	Predictions for labour supply and demand in non-agricultural sectors, 2004–10	166
9.7	Changes in population dependence, 1949–2048	167
10.1	Hours worked per day and days worked per month/week	183
10.2	Hours worked per month	184
10.3	Real and predicted hours worked per month	187
10.4	Real and predicted per capita income	190
10.5	Age distribution of urban residents and migrants	194
A10.1	Distribution of starting year for the current job	202
11.1	China's and India's projected populations and labour forces, 1995–2035	205
11.2	Growth scenarios for China's population and labour force, 1995–2035	218
11.3	Four scenarios for the Chinese non-working-aged (60+) dependency ratio, 1995–2035	218
11.4	Chinese real GDP, departures from the baseline, 1995–2035	220
11.5	Chinese real wage and per capita income, departures from the baseline, 1995–2035	221
A11.1	The demographic sub-model	226
12.1	China's revealed comparative advantage indices (NER) of the whole agricultural sector, 1992–2005	233
12.2	China's revealed comparative advantage indices (NER) of agricultural products by commodity groups, 1992–2005	235
12.3	China's revealed comparative advantage indices (NER) for agricultural products by factor intensity of production, 1992–2005	235

12.4	China's agricultural trade, 1992–2005	236
12.5	China's agricultural exports by categories, 1992–2005	237
12.6	China's agricultural imports by categories, 1992–2006	238
12.7	Shares of China's agricultural exports by commodity groups, 1992–2001 and 2002–05	240
12.8	Shares of China's agricultural imports by commodity groups, 1992–2001 and 2002–05	240
12.9	Shares of China's agricultural exports by factor intensity of production, 1992–2001 and 2002–05	241
12.10	Shares of China's agricultural imports by factor intensity of production, 1992–2001 and 2002–05	242
12.11	China's exports of spinach and cabbage to Japan, 1992–2005	246
13.1	Introduction of village elections in the sample villages, 1987–2002	261
13.2	Shares of public expenditure and administrative costs in village spending, 1986–2002	264
13.3	Fees and income transfer, 1987–2002	264
13.4	Trend of the Gini coefficient in the sample villages, 1987–2002	265
13.5	Histograms of the Gini coefficients in 1987, 1999 and 2002	265
14.1	Total energy consumption intensity: China, Japan and Korea	281
14.2	China's coal consumption in comparison with East Asian economies	281
14.3	Steel demand and economic growth in Northeast Asia	282
14.4	Long-run investment shares of GDP: China, Japan, Korea and India, 1965–2004	284
14.5	Steel consumption per capita with urbanisation	284
14.6	Shares of petroleum consumption in the world: Japan, Korea, China and total Northeast Asia, 1960–2005	286
14.7	China's shares of incremental world demand for four metals, 1995–2005	286
14.8	World copper consumption per capita, 1905–2005	287
14.9	The copper price of the world in 2004 US dollars, 1895–August 2006	287
14.10	China's shares of demand growth for four metals, 1995–2005	288
14.11	Energy production and consumption in China, 1989–2005	289
14.12	Growth rates of demand for petroleum: Northeast Asia and the world, 1961–2005	289
14.13	Crude oil price adjusted for inflation, 1946–July 2006	291
15.1	The impact of pollution control variables	310
15.2	The impact of factor inputs	312

16.1	World coal consumption, 1990–2030	317
16.2	Coal production and consumption in the United Kingdom, 1980–2004	320
16.3	Average prices of fuels purchased by major United Kingdom power producers, 1990–2006	321
16.4	United States' coal real price, 1977–2003	323
16.5	United States' coal production, 1977–2003	325
16.6	Economic logic of environmental regulations	326
16.7	Different emissions per unit of coal consumption	326
16.8	Outputs of coal, electricity, cement and steel, 1995–2004	330
16.9	Coal production and air pollution emissions, 1997–2004	332
17.1	China's total energy consumption and supply, 1980–2003	336
17.2	Energy consumption by source in China, 1980–2003	341
17.3	Projections of energy consumption in China, 1990–2025	342
17.4	Projections of carbon dioxide emissions by fuel type in China, 1990–2030	342
17.5	Global carbon dioxide emissions from fossil fuels, 1990 and 2030	344
17.6	Labour-augmentative technical change for uniform productivity scenario, 2002–2100	347
17.7	Labour-augmentative technical change by sector in differential productivity scenario, 2002–2100	349–50
17.8	Projection of Chinese carbon emissions, 2002–2026	351
17.9	Projection of Chinese real GDP growth, 2002–2026	352
17.10	Response of emissions to a carbon tax in each country, 2007–2058	354
17.11	Response of GDP to a carbon tax in each country, 2007–2055	354

Symbols

..	not available
n.a.	not applicable
-	zero
.	insignificant

Abbreviations

ABC	Agricultural Bank of China
ADB	Asian Development Bank
ADBC	Agricultural Development Bank of China
AEC	ASEAN Economic Community
AMC	asset management corporation
APEC	Asia Pacific Economic Cooperation
APPCDC	Asia Pacific Partnership for Clean Development and Climate
ASEAN	Association of Southeast Asian Nations
BOC	Bank of China
BVAR	Bayesian vector autoregression
CANET	China Academic Network
CAR	capital adequacy ratio
CBC	Construction Bank of China
CBRC	China Banking Regulatory Commission
CERD	Chinese economy with regional details
CES	constant elasticity of substitution
CESG	cultural, educational and sports goods
CET	constant elasticity of transformation
CGAP	Consultative Group to Aid the Poorest
CIA	Central Intelligence Agency
CNY	Chinese yuan
CNNIC	China Internet Network Information Centre
CPC	Communist Party of China
CPI	consumer price index
CRN	China Research Network
CSRC	China Securities Regulatory Commission
DFN	Deutsche Forschungsnetz [German Research Network]
DPP	Democratic Progressive Party
EEFSU	Eastern Europe and the former Soviet Union
EEM	electronic equipment and machinery
ETE	electronic and telecommunications equipment
FDI	foreign direct investment
FPC	Funding the Poor Cooperation
FTA	Free Trade Agreement
GATT	General Agreement on Tariffs and Trade
GDP	gross domestic product

GLS	generalised least squares
GTAP	Global Trade Analysis Project
HRS	Household Registration System
HSBC	Hong Kong and Shanghai Banking Corporation
ICBC	Industrial and Commercial Bank of China
LDC	less developed country
LIR	labour insurance regulations
MCA	Ministry of Civil Affairs
MFI	microfinance institution
MFN	most-favoured nation
MNE	multinational enterprise
MOF	Ministry of Finance
MOFERT	Ministry of Foreign Economic Relations and Trade
MOFTEC	Ministry of Foreign Trade and Economic Cooperation
NBS	National Bureau of Statistics
NGO	non-governmental organisation
NATO	North Atlantic Treaty Organisation
NIE	newly industrialised economy
NPC	National People's Congress
NPL	non-performing loans
NRC	net relative change
NSSF	National Social Security Fund
NYSE	New York Stock Exchange
OECD	Organisation for Economic Cooperation and Development
PAYGO	pay-as-you-go
PBOC	People's Bank of China
PECC	Pacific Economic Cooperation Council
PEO	Pacific Economic Outlook
PPI	producer price index
PRC	People's Republic of China
RCA	revealed comparative advantage
RCC	rural credit cooperative
RCCU	Rural Credit Cooperative Union
RCF	rural credit foundation
RFI	rural financial institution
RIETI	Research Institute of Economy, Trade and Industry
RMB	Renminbi

RPI	retail price index
RPS	rural postal savings
SARS	Severe Acute Respiratory Syndrome
SASAC	State-Owned Asset Supervision and Administration Commission
SCO	Shanghai Cooperative Organisation
SCORES	China Society for Research on Economic Systems
SITC	Standard International Trade Classification
SME	small and medium enterprise
SEZ	special economic zone
SOB	state-owned bank
SOCB	state-owned commercial bank
SOE	state-owned enterprise
SSF	social security fund
TFP	total factor productivity
TIFA	Trade and Investment Framework Agreement
TRQ	tariff-rate quota
TVE	township and village enterprise
UHIDS	Urban Household Income Distribution Survey
UMLS	Urban Minimum Living Security Program
UNCTAD	United Nations Conference on Trade and Development
VAR	vector autoregression
VAT	value added tax
VECM	vector error correction model
WHO	World Health Organization
WTO	World Trade Organization
XUAR	Xinjiang Uighur Autonomous Region

Acknowledgments

The China Economy and Business Program gratefully acknowledges the financial support for China Update 2006 from the Australian government's development agency, AusAID, and the assistance provided by Rio Tinto through the Rio Tinto-ANU China Partnership.

Contributors

Bao Qun is with the School of Economics, Nankai University, China.
Cai Fang is with the Institute of Population and Labour Economics, Chinese Academy of Social Sciences.
Chen Chunlai is with the Crawford School of Economics and Government, The Australian National University.
Fan Gang is with the National Economic Research Institute, China Reform Foundation (NERI-China), Beijing, China.
Ross Garnaut is with the Division of Economics, Research School of Pacific and Asian Studies and the China Economy and Business Program, The Australian National University.
Jane Golley is with the School of Economics, The Australian National University.
Robert Gregory is with the Research School of Social Sciences, The Australian National University.
Yiping Huang is with Citigroup, Global Markets Asia Limited.
Nicholas R. Lardy is with the Institute for International Economics in Washington, DC.
Justin Yifu Lin is with the China Center for Economic Research at Beijing University.
Guonan Ma is with the Bank for International Settlements in Hong Kong.
Warwick J. McKibbin is with Division of Economics, Research School of Pacific and Asian Studies, The Australian National University.
Xin Meng is with the Division of Economics, Research School of Pacific and Asian Studies, The Australian National University.
Shuijun Peng is with the School of Economics, Nankai University, China.
Xunpeng Shi is with the Crawford School of Economics and Government, The Australian National University.

Ligang Song is with the Crawford School of Economics and Government and the China Economy and Business Program, The Australian National University.

Jinzhi Tong is with the School of Economics, Xiamen University, China.

Rod Tyers is with the School of Economics, The Australian National University.

Dewen Wang is with the Institute of Population and Labor Economics, Chinese Academy of Social Sciences.

Xiaolu Wang is with the National Economic Research Institute, China Reform Foundation (NERI-China), Beijing, China.

Wing Thye Woo is with the Department of Economics, University of California at Davis.

Yang Du is with the Institute of Population and Labour Economics, Chinese Academy of Social Sciences.

Yang Yao is with the China Center for Economic Research at Beijing University.

1

The turning point in China's economic development

Ross Garnaut

'All roads lead to Rome', they said, two thousand years ago on the Western peninsular of the Eurasian continent. Or, at the Eastern end, 'All roads lead to Changan'.

This year in China, all roads lead to the turning point in economic development.

There is now a persistent tendency for growth to exceed the 7.2 per cent per annum that would realise the authorities' ambitions to quadruple turn of the century output by 2020; for labour to become scarce and more expensive in rural and urban areas; and for surpluses in external payments to argue for exchange rate appreciation. There is rapid progression towards the point where the number of workers falls, especially of younger unskilled workers who have driven the rapid growth of industrial China over the past one and a half decades. Focus on the labour market identifies the importance of breaking down barriers to rural-urban migration and other inhibitions against employing increasingly scarce and valuable human resources in their most productive uses. Analysis of the rural economy notes that China has become a net importer of agricultural products, reflecting the change in comparative advantage that accompanies sustained rapid economic growth. A look at the natural resource based industries discovers that urbanisation, and the shift towards more capital-intensive industrial structure, has made Chinese economic growth the source of profound change in the global balance of supply and demand for minerals and energy. Contemporary global environmental problems are inextricably linked to Chinese growth and structural change. And environmental concerns are beginning to influence policy and resource allocation, as they have

The Turning Point in China's Economic Development

in other countries as incomes have risen in the process of economic growth, but at lower measured incomes than in other economies.

The theme of this year's review of recent developments in and research on the Chinese economy selects itself. China has or is fast approaching reached the turning point in its economic development, at which 'surplus' labour from agricultural employment in the countryside ceases to be available to drive the growth of the modern economy; so that labour becomes scarce and valuable; forcing large real wage increases and real exchange rate appreciation; which generate structural change towards more capital-intensive and technologically sophisticated industrial structure at the relative expense of labour-intensive manufacturing and agriculture; and changes fundamentally the character of China's interaction with the international economy.

Thirty years ago, Ryoshin Minami published an important book on postwar Japanese economic development, *The Turning Point in Economic Development: Japan's Experience* (1973). Minami applied to the Japanese case the theory of the turning point formulated by Lewis (1954), and elaborated in an East Asian context by Fei and Ranis (1961, 1963, 1964a, 1964b, 1966).

In the Lewis model of economic development, rapid economic growth in its early stages is driven by the presence of 'surplus' labour in the traditional, rural economy, and its movement into more productive modern employment in urban areas. The apparently infinitely elastic supply of unskilled labour from the countryside allows rapid modern sector growth to proceed for a considerable while without putting upward pressure on wages. Over time, the withdrawal of 'surplus' labour from agriculture increases per capita land and other resource endowments enough to raise the marginal productivity of labour and therefore of incomes and wages in the rural sector. The labour supply from rural areas to the modern economy becomes inelastic: higher wages must be offered to induce additional movements of labour into the rapidly growing modern economy. From this point, wages in both rural and urban areas rise more rapidly the faster the rate of economic growth.

The 'turning point in economic development' is the point at which surplus labour in the countryside dries up, and real wages begin to rise. Other major economic changes occur around this point. Demand for agricultural products grows more rapidly than supply, and there is a tendency for net imports of agricultural products to rise. Industrial structure becomes more capital-intensive, having implications for demand and net imports of minerals and energy. The prospects for continued rapid growth beyond the turning point depend on the economy's success in structural change towards industries which can expand profitably despite higher labour costs. This places a premium on flexibility in the allocation of capital and labour resources, on the efficiency of financial markets in allocating scarce capital to its most productive uses, and on education and the accumulation of labour skills.

One feature of the turning point is that the higher wages complicate non-inflationary management of monetary policy. Wages must rise by one process or another, in terms of both domestic and international purchasing power. The adjustment can occur in a non-inflationary way through appreciation of the exchange rate. Or the adjustment can be achieved through monetary accommodation of the pressures for increased wages, with high and potentially destabilising inflation, but without the inflation being accompanied by correspondingly large currency depreciation. The real exchange rate appreciation, whether achieved through nominal exchange rate appreciation or inflation, moderates what would otherwise have been a powerful tendency towards external trade and current payments surpluses.

Real exchange rate appreciation at the turning point makes standard technology, labour-intensive exports less competitive. These industries were the mainstays of internationally oriented growth in its early stages. This can appear to be a threat to the continuation of rapid growth. In reality, it is resistance to structural change that is the threat to growth.

There is some risk that the Chinese authorities are misjudging the nature and consequences of current internal pressures for structural change. They are seeking to reduce the rate of economic growth below the rates in excess of 10 per cent towards which they have been tending. The attempts at reduction in the rate of growth have been motivated by concern for the emergence of inflation. The preferred instruments have been direct controls and tightening of access to credit, aimed at reducing the level of investment. To the extent that these measures are successful, they will reduce the growth in domestic demand further below the economy's growth in productive capacity and increase the external payments surplus. The surplus is already huge and growing at an extraordinary rate. It is already the source of considerable tension in China's foreign economic relations, especially with the United States. And it will, sooner or later, become a source of unwanted and destabilising monetary expansion and inflation.

Whether the upward adjustment of real wages is secured through inflation or exchange rate adjustment, it will lead to measured income and output 'catching up' with other countries more quickly than a simple comparison of growth rates would suggest (Garnaut 2002:9–13). Thus, at the point at which labour became scarce and wages began to rise rapidly, each of the East Asian economies that had secured successful economic development before China experienced rapid movement towards the average incomes and output, conventionally measured, of the developed countries. For example, at the extremes of rapid catching up, Hong Kong per capita incomes expressed in US dollars doubled between 1971 and 1973. Korean per capita incomes expressed in US dollars roughly doubled in three years from the mid 1970s. Singapore per capita incomes expressed in US dollars increased by about three quarters between 1971 and 1974 (Garnaut 2002:10).

The 'turning point' will not be as sharp in China as it was in Japan, Hong Kong, Singapore, Taiwan and Korea. Greater size and geographic and economic diversity, and more daunting internal barriers to the movement of people, goods, services and capital, mean that labour scarcity will spread more slowly from the main centres of economic dynamism in China. The upward adjustment in the real exchange rate will occur over a decade or two, rather than a few years.

Nevertheless, the adjustment will be fast enough significantly to affect China's place in the global economy and society over the next two decades. Justin Yifu Lin (Chapter 4), shows that the Chinese official goal of quadrupling output over the next two decades—implying compound growth at 7.2 per cent per annum—is achievable, so long as some important structural weaknesses are corrected If the weaknesses are removed, the official target might be exceeded by a significant margin. The most important barriers to continued strong growth are associated with weaknesses in financial institutions, and in the continuation of economically inefficient state-owned enterprises in major roles. Thus reforms of the financial sector and of state-owned enterprises will be major determinants of future economic success.

Xiaolu Wang (Chapter 3) demonstrates that, following the large, upward adjustments in official figures late in 2005, China's national accounts data converted at current exchange rates, measure GDP at 18 per cent and per capita output at 4.1 per cent of United States levels. The Purchasing Power Parity (PPP) data measure GDP at 69 per cent and per capita GDP at 17.6 per cent of United States' levels. Wang's careful analysis of the corrections to the national accounts in late 2005 raises questions about whether the December 2005 revisions of the national accounts are the last such changes. It is likely that the present starting point for estimating the future size of the Chinese economy may turn out to be higher than the current official data suggests.

The rapid increase in the real exchange rate that follows the turning point in economic development leads to convergence over time in national accounts and PPP measures of output. The accelerated 'catching up' that was observed in Japan, Korea and other successful East Asian economies beyond the turning point, for this reason, is apparent in the conventional national accounts and not the PPP measures of output. The PPP data is therefore the appropriate base for comparison when differential growth rates are applied to the estimation of how long it will take a developing country to catch up with an economy at the frontiers of global productivity and incomes.

It is well within the bounds of possibility—in the absence of domestic or international political instability seriously disrupting the process of economic reform and growth—it is likely that average growth rates will turn out to be significantly higher than the official objective for much of the next two decades.

Chinese wages and consumption could be expected to grow substantially more rapidly than per capita output.

The following chapters, embodying the results of some of the best recent research on the Chinese economy, by analysts based in Australia, China and the United States, provide important background to the generalisations that I have presented in this introductory chapter.

Ross Garnaut and Yiping Huang (Chapter 2) examine recent macroeconomic performance in the context of the theory of the turning point in economic development. The past year has been good for Chinese growth by the conventional measures of performance. Growth has risen above 10 per cent, the highest for about a decade, while maintaining low inflation. Growth continues to be unusually dependent on investment. There is less anxiety now than a year ago that the high investment rates will be a source of vulnerability in the near term—although a fear that excessive investment levels will be inflationary and destabilising continues to haunt the policy community. There is, however, recognition that, sooner rather than later, consumption must come to carry a much heavier load in supporting domestic demand growth.

Savings continue to rise from extraordinarily high levels. Thus even unprecedentedly high and rising investment rates leaves savings well in excess of investment. The consequence is a huge and rising trade surplus. Imports are growing rapidly—at a faster rate than in any other substantial economy—but exports are expanding faster still. The current account surplus is augmented by earnings on China's rapidly growing net foreign assets. With continued capital inflow, this has taken Chinese foreign exchange reserves beyond Japan's, to first rank in the world.

The small (1.9 per cent) appreciation of the yuan in mid 2005 has been followed by a low rate of currency appreciation—1.8 per cent against the US dollar to 18 August 2006—under the more flexible exchange rate system introduced at that time. This has been far too little to dent the external payments imbalances. The expansion of real domestic demand and imports has become an urgent matter. It is important for the quality and the value to China of relations with major trading partners, especially the United States. It is also important for domestic reasons: such expansion would be achieved with much less risk to currency appreciation, in the absence, and to remove a source of inflationary and destabilising monetary expansion.

The greater part of Chapter 2 examines the evidence of growing labour scarcity in rural and urban areas. Real wages in dynamic industrial cities have been drawing attention for some time. Over recent times, awareness of labour scarcity and rising wages has become widespread. It is driven by continued rapid economic growth in the cities, and in rural areas by emigration. The labour scarcity and pressures for rising wages will intensify rapidly. The absolute size of the labour force is growing slowly and will soon become negative; emigration has taken pressure off rural resources and raised the income levels that are necessary to attract more migrants; the labour force itself will soon be ageing, reducing the supply of young unskilled workers who have provided much of the requirements of rapidly growing labour-intensive industries; and rapidly increasing per capita investments in education are reducing the proportion of the labour force that is available for low-skill employment in manufacturing, construction and urban services.

Nicholas Lardy (Chapter 5) and Fan Gang (Chapter 6) discuss the external dimensions of China's contemporary economic challenge, in particular the large and increasing United States' current account deficit, the large and increasing Chinese current account surplus, and the immense and expanding US bilateral deficit with China. They approach the issues from different directions, and at first sight reach contrasting positions on the appropriate international policy response to the imbalances. But a closer look reveals some important common elements both in analysis and prescription, with recognition that each of China and the United States must accept part of the responsibility for adjustment, and that the correction of the imbalances will require some Chinese currency appreciation. At this stage, they maintain vastly different views on proportions of adjustment for which each country will have to accept responsibility, but over time this gap, too, will be reduced by increased knowledge about emerging structural changes in China.

Lardy analyses the bilateral imbalances in United States-China economic relations that has generated high levels of bilateral tension, and the multilateral imbalances in which China plays an important role. He dismisses some of the standard American and Chinese positions in the arguments about whether the imbalances should be the focus of policy concern and correction. There will be no solution to problems of United States deficits that do not involve adjustment on the American side. However, there are still powerful reasons why large appreciation of the yuan is required—much larger than is currently considered a possibility by anyone in China.

Fan (Chapter 6) takes a different view on United States-China imbalances, but draws some similar conclusions about desirable adjustments in Chinese policy. Fan notes that the fact that the United States dollar is the international as well as a national currency loosens the application of the normal fiscal and monetary disciplines on that country. That tempts it into more expansionary policies than it would otherwise choose, for which the whole world pays some price. One consequence is an extraordinary current account deficit with the whole world. It looks like a deficit in trade with China, but this view ignores the fact that China's manufactured exports draw components from the whole of Asia, and that as a result many other Asian countries run bilateral surpluses with China.

Fan's long-term solution would be the use of an international currency, or failing that, and pending the emergence of the conditions under which it could play a role, an Asian currency. The political environment for Asian monetary cooperation is currently favourable, with China and Japan sharing perspectives and objectives in relation to it. An Asian currency would take pressure from the bilateral relationship between China and the United States, but would not remove the need for adjustment within the United States.

Fan comments that a large part of the recent surpluses in the Chinese balance of payments is the result of speculative capital inflow that could be temporary. The structural part—the current account surplus—has grown a great deal last year and this because policy has been geared to bringing overinvestment to heal, reducing imports as a result. This part of the analysis is undoubtedly correct: tightening credit exacerbates external payments surpluses, which would now be somewhat lower if there were had been no attempt to reduce investment.

What, then, is the rationale of Chinese attempts to slow economic growth by tightening credit and reducing investment? At one level, it is driven by a view that the 'natural' or non-inflationary rate of growth of the Chinese economies is well below the recent 10 per cent plus levels—perhaps near the official 'target' of 7.2 per cent per annum, or perhaps a bit above 8 per cent. For those who hold this view, the recent increases in wages are evidence of overheating, requiring a monetary policy response. An alternative view, more easily reconciled with contemporary Chinese reality, is that with China's high levels of investment, and the rapid lift in productivity that is being driven by continued reform and integration into the international economy, the 'natural' rate of growth may well be 10 per cent per annum or higher. Within this view, rapid increases in real wages are a normal accompaniment of rapid growth at the turning point in economic development. If attempts are made to hold growth rates below the 'natural' levels, the main consequence will be unnecessarily to delay rises in Chinese living standards. At least in the short term, they exacerbate external trade and payments surpluses. The payments surpluses lay the basis for inflationary expansion of domestic money supply.

Wang (Chapter 3) mentions another reason why the authorities have sought to reduce investment levels: it is feared that they will generate excess capacity, generating financial and other sources of instability. Wang observes that the current evidence points less ambiguously to underconsumption than to overinvestment.

Guonan Ma (Chapter 7) and Jinzhi Tong and Wing Thye Woo (Chapter 8) discuss one of the critical determinants of the sustainability of strong economic growth in China: the problems of bad loans in the banking system, who will be required to meet the cost of managing the problem, in particular its cost to the budget, and the compatibility of the fiscal burden with future economic stability.

Ma's authoritative assessment of the bad loans problem draws some strong conclusions about the cost to be borne by elements of Chinese society, and by foreign purchasers of shares in Chinese banks. The eventual cost may reach 30 per cent of GDP. Credible corrective action has been taken since the late 1990s, but greater transparency is required in future action if the resolution of the banking problem is to maintain community support. The largest problems are in the state-owned banks in which taxpayers are the repository of responsibility, although foreigners have been prepared to share a substantial part of the burden as the price of buying equity in the franchise value of the banks. To date, taxpayers have carried 85 per cent of the costs, and foreigners the balance. The increasing role of direct foreign investment has raised the quality of the banking system, and reduced the risk of continuing deterioration in asset quality.

Tong and Woo focus on the interaction between Chinese demography and fiscal policy, and the intergenerational distributional consequences of current budget policies. The fiscal burden of the banking system problem is highlighted. The correction of the current extent of the banking system problem is consistent with manageable future fiscal burdens. However, a failure to arrest now the systemic weaknesses that have generated the current problems could tip the balance towards fiscal instability.

Cai Fang and Dewen Wang (Chapters 9), Yang Du, Robert Gregory and Xin Meng (Chapter 10) and Jane Golley and Rod Tyers (Chapter 11) are situated in the labour market, which is at the centre of the turning point in China's economic development.

Cai and Wang explore the links between China's integration into international markets, and growing demand for labour and wages in rural China. In the early twenty-first century, Chinese trade policy adjustments on entry into the World Trade Organization (WTO), and the rapid restructuring of business ownership away from state-owned and collective enterprises had been expected to place downward pressure on employment. The opposite turned out to be the reality. Rapid expansion of self employment and private enterprises outweighed the loss of jobs in state-owned and collective enterprises. However you look at it, urban employment grew strongly and unemployment fell through the early twenty-first century. Agricultural employment growth eased, but only because it was a buffer, that absorbed more labour during the weaker labour demand conditions during and in the years following the Asian financial crisis. One factor behind buoyant labour market conditions was the shift in the structure of Chinese production and exports towards China's comparative advantage in labour-intensive products, and away from comparative disadvantage in natural-resource based products, in the years of deepening integration into the international economy that followed entry into the WTO.

China is now moving quickly towards a declining labour force, and especially the young and unskilled component of the labour force. On modest assumptions about future growth, and relatively low employment elasticities of output, China is heading rapidly towards severe labour shortages at current real wage levels and economic structure. The consequence will be rising wages and evolution of industrial structure towards more capital-intensive production. The labour shortage that had been apparent in the heartland of internationally oriented growth in 2003—in the Pearl River delta—is now apparent in provinces that are sources of migrant labour. Chinese wages are rising much more rapidly than other countries, and will improve the competitive position of other Asian developing countries in global markets for labour-intensive products. The growing scarcity of labour will place pressure on artificial barriers to labour mobility and increase demands for labour rights in many forms.

Du, Gregory and Meng draw attention to the remarkable fact that China is the only country to have a system of 'guest workers' for its own citizens. There are about 120 million migrant workers in China's urban areas—about one third of the urban labour force, and likely to double in number over the next 10 to 20 years. These are not poor in income terms. But they and their families are denied a range of basic services. Their average incomes are reasonably high because they work much longer hours than urban residents, and go back to the villages if they fall on hard times in the cities. The balance of advantages is likely to shift against the guest worker system over time, for reasons of equity and efficiency, amongst other things because it inhibits the rural–urban migration that can raise incomes in the village and expand the labour available for higher value activities in urban areas.

Golley and Tyers (Chapter 11) use the well-known GTAP model to explore the relationship between demographic change, income levels and employment. It deepens our perspective on the role that the Chinese Government's anti-natal policy in the reform era has played in establishing the conditions for growing labour scarcity that are important in the contemporary Chinese economy. It models the effects of a range of adjustments in policy and response to them, concluding that higher fertility will not necessarily lead to greater economic welfare.

Chen Chunlai (Chapter 12) begins with an application of the theory of comparative advantage to China's situation. Chen notes that rapid economic growth in an economy with China's resource endowments can be expected to expand net imports of agricultural products and turn the country into a net importer. Trade liberalisation and deepening integration into the international economy can be expected to expand net imports of land-intensive agricultural products, and to expand net exports of labour-intensive products. Detailed empirical analysis demonstrates that the restructuring of Chinese agricultural production and trade has been proceeding rapidly along the lines suggested by theory since China entered the WTO in late 2001.

Yang Yao (Chapter 13) explores an important but so far little discussed dimension of the turning point in economic development: the emergence of greater popular participation in governance with the increase in incomes, education and the self confidence of ordinary Chinese. Yao's careful examination of village elections since their first introduction in 1987 and extension in 1998 shows that the village election has improved village governance and the welfare of the villagers.

Ross Garnaut and Ligang Song (Chapter 14) discuss the increase in Chinese demand for energy and metals that has accompanied rapid economic growth, urbanisation and the shift in industrial structure towards more capital-intensive activities. Growth and structural change have caused China to be by far the most important source of growth in global demand for these products over the early years of the twenty-first century. This has changed the balance between supply and demand in global markets, to the point where continued economic growth is likely for many years to keep world prices well above the levels of the last quarter of the twentieth century.

Bao Qun and Shuijun Peng (Chapters 15), Xunpeng Shi (Chapter 16) and Warwick McKibbin (Chapter 17) explore the important relationship between environmental amenity and economic growth. Economic growth in China in itself places pressure on global and local environmental conditions. It also increases concern for the environment, and causes people to be prepared to allocate more of their potential increase in incomes and consumption to environmental improvement.

Bao and Peng (Chapter 15) show that Chinese valuation of environmental amenity in relation to other dimensions of material welfare is rising, at measured income levels that are low compared with those that have triggered a big increase in concern for environmental amenity in other countries. However, there is room for acceptance of considerable further deterioration of environmental amenity before improvement becomes imperative.

Shi (Chapter 16) discusses the vexed question of the coal industry's contribution to the environmental impact on China's growth. While the intense and increasing use of coal is a source of huge negative environmental impact, the experience of Europe and North America, and the conditions in China, make it likely that coal will play a large part in China's energy future. This places a large premium on technological and other developments that reduce the negative impact of coal use.

McKibbin (Chapter 17) concludes with incisive analysis of one of the great international issues of our times, affecting the future condition of humanity in fundamental ways. China's contribution to global climate change is immense, and will grow in future. China is already the world's second largest source of carbon dioxide emissions, and is expected to account for a quarter of the growth in global emissions in the years ahead. There is no solution to global warming problems that does not encompass China and other large and rapidly growing developing economies. McKibbin suggest expedients that hold out prospects for improving the trade-off between economic growth in China and global environmental amenity.

2

Continued rapid growth and the turning point in China's development

Ross Garnaut and Yiping Huang

China's rapid economic growth continued strongly over the past year. Earlier concerns about overheating and inflationary pressures have eased, despite some acceleration of growth. The debate about whether China's unprecedented investment share of GDP is consistent with sustained rapid growth has subsided somewhat, although policymakers are still concerned about risks of overcapacity in certain industries as the investment share is a bit higher this year than last. There is increasing recognition that current or moderately higher investment shares could be sustained for long periods, and also that, sooner or later, consumption must grow much more strongly than over the past decade. The rate of growth in consumption has in fact increased over the past year. The small currency appreciation and change towards a more flexible exchange rate regime in mid 2005 has been followed by a small additional appreciation, and a sharp increase in China's trade and current account surpluses and in the level of foreign exchange reserves. It is now clear that a large deficiency in real domestic expenditure relative to rapidly growing productive capacity requires early correction.

Over the past year there have been stronger signs of emerging scarcity of labour, especially in the rapidly growing and relatively rich coastal provinces. The signs include rates of increase in real wages—high by historical standards in China or elsewhere. These lead us to ask whether China has reached what in the literature has been called 'the turning point in economic development' (see Chapter One, this volume). Chinese economic growth in the reform era has been associated with the transfer of large amounts of labour from agriculture to non-agricultural employment, increasingly from rural to urban areas. At first, the presence of large amounts of 'surplus labour' in the countryside made rapid growth in demand for unskilled labour in industrial and a range of urban employment consistent with relatively stable wages in rural areas and towns. This supported continuing competitiveness of labour-intensive export industries.

Has the growth in labour demand pushed China into the 'turning point', at which surplus labour is no longer available, and at which continued rapid growth is associated with large and continuing increases in labour costs? If so, how will this affect the structure of the Chinese economy and its interaction with the international economy, and China's prospects for sustaining growth? We take up these important questions later in the chapter.

Overview of macroeconomic development

China continued its remarkable macroeconomic performance during the past year. While economic growth gradually accelerated, inflation remained very mild (Figure 2.1). Quicker pace of GDP expansion during recent quarters, rising from 9.8 per cent in the third quarter of 2005 to 11.3 per cent in the second quarter of 2006, caused some concerns about overheating risks. However, the unusually low CPI, staying consistently below 1.5 per cent during the past four quarters, did not appear to support the case for drastic policy tightening. Economists and government officials are divided on the inflation outlook. Some warn that deflation is the key risk as the overinvestment problem continues to deteriorate, while others fear that inflation rates will rise rapidly, fuelled by increasing wage rates and high commodity prices.

Composition of GDP evolved further (Figure 2.2). Consumption, especially private consumption, shrank further in relative terms. Share of investment edged up to 43.4 per cent in 2005 from 43.2 per cent in 2004. More importantly, the share of net exports rose to 4.5 per cent from 2.5 per cent. In fact, net exports contributed more than half of GDP growth in 2005. The current account surplus equalled 7.1 per cent of GDP in 2005, compared with 3.5 per cent in the previous year. Remarkably, these data imply that China's national saving rate had come to exceed 50 per cent.

From the beginning of 2006, especially following implementation of the 11th Five-Year Plan, the authorities stepped up efforts to rebalance economic growth, with increasing consumption relative to investment and increasing domestic demand relative to external demand. Policymakers took steps to consolidate industries with high risks of overcapacity, to caution commercial banks on loan expansion and to tighten monetary conditions in order to cool down investment.

Figure 2.1　**Quarterly real GDP growth and inflation in China, 2000–06** (per cent year/year)

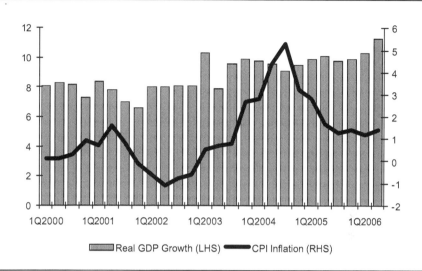

Source: CEIC Data Company.

Figure 2.2　**Changing composition of GDP, 2000–05** (per cent of GDP)

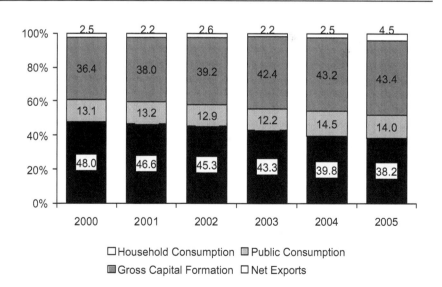

Source: CEIC Data Company.

They also sought to stimulate private consumption, by increasing the threshold for personal income tax, abolishing agricultural taxes and encouraging development of easier access to consumer credit.

However, the ratios that have been the concern of policymakers have not moved in the preferred directions. Fixed-asset investment grew by 31.3 per cent in the first half of 2006, compared with 27.2 per cent in 2005, and growth accelerated in recent months (Figure 2.3). Consumer spending accelerated slightly, but its growth remained lower than investment.

Both export and import growth rates fell somewhat, but the trade surplus expanded. It was 54.9 per cent higher in the first half of 2006 than in the corresponding period of the preceding year (Figure 2.4). This, together with continued inflows of foreign direct investment and other capital, contributed to rapid accumulation of foreign exchange reserves, which increased by US$123 billion during the first six months of 2006. At US$941 billion at the end of June 2006, China's reserves were the largest in the world.

Macroeconomic policies began to shift towards modest tightening bias from the beginning of the year. Calls for further tightening intensified following publication of very strong second quarter economic data. The People's Bank of China (PBOC) quickly raised the reserve requirement ratio by another 50 basis points, only a month after the first hike and three months after increase in base lending rates by an average of 27 basis points. These policy measures caused some renewed fear in international financial markets of rapid slowdown of the Chinese economy, with significant implications for the rest of the world, especially the global commodity markets. As with similar concerns over recent years, they will be disappointed.

So far, the policy tightening has been modest and selective. It is possible that the authorities may introduce more tightening policies, but it is very unlikely that the economy would slow significantly. With a savings ratio of around 50 per cent, a slowing of investment would not serve a good macroeconomic purpose at this time.

Given that investment continues to grow much faster than consumption, to many government officials and investors overcapacity is the key risk. In March, the State Council issued an official document addressing the concern about overcapacity in some sectors. It specifically claimed that the iron and steel, electrolysis aluminum, calcium carbide, iron alloy, coke and automotive sectors had already suffered overcapacity problems while the cement, coal, power and textile sectors could see overcapacities soon.

Interestingly, overcapacity risks are likely to be larger in industries dominated by the state sectors (Figure 2.5). In the coal mining and power sectors, for instance,

Figure 2.3 **Growth of fixed-asset investment and retail sales, January 2000–June 2006** (per cent year/year)

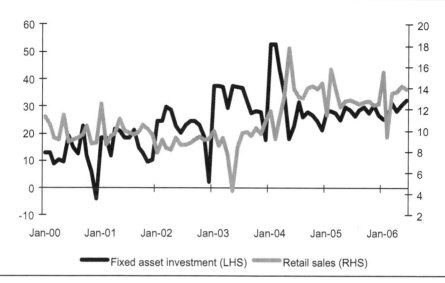

Source: CEIC Data Company.

Figure 2.4 **Growth of exports and imports, January 2000–June 2006** (per cent year-on-year)

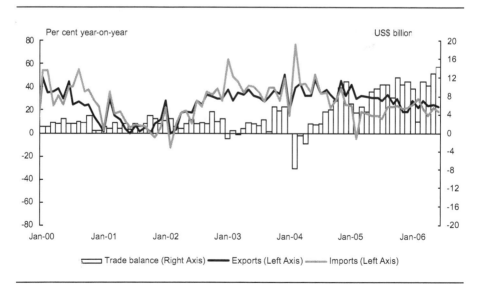

Source: CEIC Data Company.

shares of the state sector in total assets are well above 80 per cent. The only two sectors with even higher state sector shares are tobacco and extraction of oil and gas.

More importantly, for an open and dynamic economy like China, there are many tricks in the definition of overcapacity. While the government has successively warned about overcapacity risks in electronics, personal computers, mobile phones, automobiles, and building materials over the past ten years, most excess capacity appears to be temporary, and rapidly growing demand including the expansion of exports has quickly absorbed the so-called overcapacity.

The turning point in economic development?

When economic reforms began in the late 1970s, China enjoyed significant potential comparative advantages in labour-intensive activities. It was the world's most populous country with a total population of close to 1 billion. In 1978, more than 80

Figure 2.5 **Share of state sector in total assets for selected industries, 2005** (per cent)

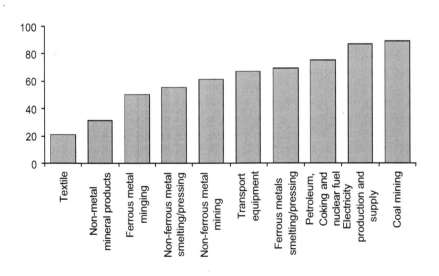

Source: National Statistics Bureau of China and Citigroup estimates.

per cent of the population was involved in the agricultural sector and most of these workers were underemployed. Arable land area per agricultural worker was less than one hectare, only about 10 per cent of the world's average.

The serious underemployment problem in the agricultural sector and potential productivity gain from transferring labour from agriculture to the non-agricultural sector offer a live case of the Lewis dual sector development model (Lewis 1954). The model assumes that developing countries have dual economies with both a traditional agricultural sector and a modern industrial sector. As labour productivity is so low in traditional agricultural areas people leaving the rural areas would have virtually no impact on output. The 'capitalist' industrial sector develops by drawing labour from a non-capitalist 'subsistence' agricultural sector. The existence of 'surplus labour' in the subsistence sector ensures that during an extended period of rapid modern sector growth, wages remain steady, because the supply of labour to the modern sector exceeds demand at this wage rate. The surplus of output over wages is captured by the owners of businesses as profit.

Development in China was broadly consistent with the insights from the Lewis model during the first twenty-five years of China's economic reform. From the mid 1980s, surplus labour moved to rural non-agricultural activities established by large number of township and village enterprises (TVEs). By 1990, rural non-agricultural employment had already reached 109 million, which was about 23 per cent of the total rural labour force. This number further increased to 185 million in 2005, or 38 per cent of the rural labour force.

From the early 1990s, as urban reforms and growth gathered momentum, farmers began to move into the cities for employment in manufacturing, construction and service industries. This happened despite the official household registration system (HRS) continuing to restrict labour mobility. By 2004, the total number of migrant workers in the cities had risen to over 100 million.[1]

Continuous supply of vast numbers of unskilled workers at very low wages fuelled boom in the labour-intensive industries in China. The unusually low labour costs pushed up returns on capital, enhanced Chinese products' international competitiveness and improved most companies' cash flows. Cheap labour and huge domestic market potential are the top two reasons most commonly identified as attractions for foreign investors into China.[2]

In recent years, however, much of the coastal region was surprised by the emergence of labour shortages. This raised the questions of whether the 'unlimited' supplies of labour had come to an end, and whether China had reached a turning point in economic development at which rising wages begin to undermine competitveness of labour-intensive industry, and at an extreme whether the associated reductions in returns on investment would reduce the rate of capital accumulation and economic growth.

The turning point in China's economic development can have very important implications for China's economic structure and also for global markets. Faster growth of wage rates following the conclusion of the era of 'unlimited' supplies of labour, for instance, could eventually increase consumption, force major appreciation of the real exchange rate (either through currency appreciation or inflation), squeeze profit margins, force industrial upgrading, shift China's export specialisation away from labour-intensive products, and raise export prices. China's comparative advantage could be expected to shift to more capital or technology-intensive sectors. This would also induce further global restructuring.

Has China, after a quarter century of reform and rapid growth, arrived at the turning point? We first take a quick look at the latest labour shortages in China. We then examine the impacts of recent increases in labour costs on profitability and inflation. Finally, we glance into the future.

Recent labour shortages

Many China watchers were surprised when reports about shortages of unskilled labour emerged in early 2004, especially in the relatively dynamic coastal region (Huang 2004). According to some reports, early that year, migrant workers in various cities of Zhejiang province fell by 10–20 per cent from a year earlier. Other reports estimated on limited data that there was a shortage of about 2 million workers in the municipalities of Guangzhou, Shenzhen and Dongguan in Guangdong province. Fujian Provincial Bureau of Statistics said that labour shortage was the reason why the average capacity utilisation rate only reached 80–85 per cent.[3] These were scattered observations and might not be consistent with one another. But the new challenge was clear—many employers had difficulties recruiting workers.

At first sight, these shortages of unskilled workers were somewhat odd, given that there were still more than 300 million farmers in agriculture and a serious underemployment problem in the countryside seemed to remain. In retrospect, labour shortages at first reflected short-term changes in demand and supply relations. It was probably more about slow adjustment to faster growth of demand in the urban sector, instead of a decline in supply. There were probably a number of reasons why supply did not keep pace with demand at that particular period of time. First, rising food prices, which reached 15 per cent year-on-year in mid

2004, increased income in the countryside and living costs in the cities. In fact, rural income rose by 10.6 per cent and urban consumer prices also increased by 3.6 per cent during the first half of 2004. This probably reduced the attractiveness of migrating to coastal provinces. As a result, the decline in the rural labour force slowed to –0.1 per cent in 2004 from –0.3 per cent in the previous two years, but picked up again to –0.5 per cent in 2005.

Second, there was no efficient nationwide information network for labour demand and supply. Labour-exporting provinces did not have information about recent rapid growth in demand for migrant labour in Zhejiang, Guangdong and some other provinces. Many large employers increased efforts to recruit directly in labour-exporting provinces.

Third, there were problems of skill or age mismatch. While there was still a huge unskilled surplus labour pool in the countryside, employers in the cities increasingly looked for workers with 2–3 years' experience. In fact, many employers targeted a special segment of the labour force in their recruitment—females aged between 18 and 25. The total number of that special group in rural areas was probably no more than 70 million. And by 2004, the pool had probably been nearly exhausted, given that the total number of migrant workers had reached 100 million. Therefore, employers had to relax their age preferences if they wanted to hire more.

And, finally, though some of the migrant workers had lived in the cities for more than ten years, most of them were still denied entitlement to pension funds, medical care and education benefits due to discrimination within the household registration system. While government policies began to require employers to pay the benefits for their employees, implementation was still at a primitive stage and differed vastly among regions. Naturally, migrant workers would prefer to work in the regions where the social welfare policies were better implemented, such as in the Yangtze River Delta. Of course, the cost of labour to employers was higher when and where the expanded benefits were being paid.

Labour shortages that occurred in parts of China two years ago were temporary and could be eased by the development of labour markets. It is probably too early to conclude that China has entered a new phase of general labour shortage. But the labour shortage sent an important message to investors—that the old era of easy and abundant access to labour at low rates was coming to an end, that the total cost of labour was starting to rise, and that costs may soon start to rise quickly. In other words, the so-called 'unlimited' labour supply was probably passing into history. Going forward, the supply curve of labour was likely to be upward sloping.

As a response to the shortage problems in 2004, many employers tried various ways to attract or keep their workers. Some reimbursed employees' home-return trips during the Chinese New Year holiday in 2004. Others offered renminbi100 per head for referring new employees. Many raised workers' wages from renminbi1000 per month to renminbi1200–1400. As companies began to pay for regular social welfare contributions for their employees, payrolls could rise by 40–50 per cent, including pensions (20 per cent of the payroll), health insurance (6 per cent), unemployment (2 per cent), work injury (1 per cent), maternity (0.8 per cent), and housing (5–10 per cent).[4]

Rising labour costs are a normal phenomenon in rapidly growing economies. Between 1975 and 2004, real manufacturing wages, measured in US dollars per hour, grew by 5.9 per cent per annum in Korea, 6.6 per cent in Taiwan, 5.8 per cent in Singapore and 5.1 per cent in Japan. Interestingly, Korea's unit labour cost rose from 5.2 per cent of that in the United States in 1975 to 49.7 per cent in 2004 (Figure 2.6). China's current unskilled labour cost, which is estimated at US$1.3 per hour, is about 5.6 per cent of the cost in the United States. Will it take more or less years for China's labour cost to rise to half of the labour cost in the United States, than it did in Korea?

Labour costs, inflation and profitability

What has been the impact of the recent increases in labour costs on the Chinese economy? Normally, higher wages are likely to push up production costs and, therefore, either reduce profit margins or force technological upgrading. Higher labour incomes often also contribute to stronger consumer spending and generate stronger inflationary pressures. Experience over the last couple of years in China, however, has not provided strong evidence of such impact, although some new trends have started to emerge.

Chinese nominal wage rates have been growing strongly since the early stage of economic reform (Figure 2.7). Until very recently, however, nominal wage and inflation rates moved together closely, implying that real wages rates were far more stable. This relationship, however, broke down after the East Asian financial crisis. Between 2000 and 2005, nominal wage rates jumped by 14.5 per cent per annum, but consumer prices increased by only 1.3 per cent. This means that the real wage rate rose by 13.2 per cent a year. Clearly, while labour shortages became an issue in early 2004, real wage pressures started earlier, probably from as early as 1999. But wage growth has not caused an inflation problem in recent years.

When wage rates began rising alongside skyrocketing commodity prices but sluggish finished goods prices, most economists predicted a significant squeeze of profit margins for Chinese producers. Some even argued that the Chinese economy was heading to a hard landing. Contrary to the popular concerns, however,

The Turning Point in China's Economic Development

Figure 2.6 **Growth of labour costs is a global phenomenon in rapidly growing economies** (US costs =100 per cent)

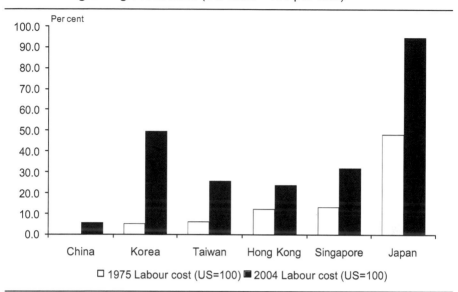

Source: United States Department of Labor.

Figure 2.7 **Changing correlation between wage and inflation, 1985–2005** (per cent)

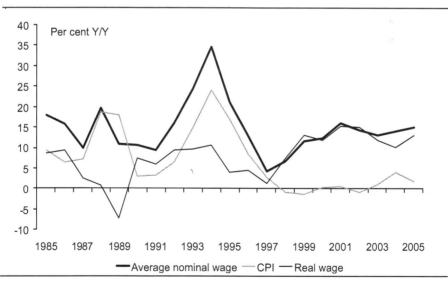

Source: CEIC Data Company.

total industrial profits have continued to grow rapidly for the past years (Figure 2.8). Even profit margins, measured by annualised profit/asset ratios, showed no sign of a significant squeeze. In fact, the current ratio, at around 6 per cent, is still close to the highest level of the current economic cycle.

Nonetheless, disaggregated data reveal differential stories for individual sectors. Of the total 34 sectors we examined, only one industry, petroleum processing and coking, suffered negative profit margins, –2.4 per cent in 2004 and –7.5 per cent during the first five months of 2006. Petroleum and natural gas extraction, non ferrous metals mining and processing, and tobacco processing enjoyed double-digit and rising profit rates. Profitability of most other industries remained largely stable. That of textile and electronic industries started to fall recently (Figure 2.9). The situation was similar in some other industries, such as chemical materials, timber products and furniture and rubber products. Therefore, margin squeezes are happening in selected areas.

Why have returns on investment held up so strongly despite the rapid rate of increase in unskilled wages? One reason is rapid growth in total factor productivity. A second has been a shift from more to less labour-intensive activities within each industry. Across sectors, more labour-intensive industries have shrunk relative to less labour-intensive industries. The more labour-intensive sectors (for example textiles, garments and parts of the electronics sector) are now showing signs of falling or more slowly growing returns on capital (Figure 2.9). Finally, while the cost of unskilled labour has increased, continued upgrading of the education and skill levels of the population has reduced the cost of human capital, and high savings have kept low and perhaps reduced the cost of other forms of capital. This has provided some benefit to all industries, and larger benefits towards the capital-intensive end of the spectrum.

Recent rises in labour costs have led to formulation of a new hypothesis that China could soon become an exporter of inflation. It is debatable whether export prices from one country could be a source of inflation in another country, as inflation within each country is a monetary phenomenon and should be a consequence of individual economies' monetary policies. The logic of the above hypothesis is that since China is an important exporter to global markets, higher Chinese prices could push up prices for products in markets where Chinese exports dominate. This would occur whether China chose monetary policies that achieved the required appreciation of the real exchange rate as labour becomes scarce through domestic inflation, or whether it chose policies that achieved the real appreciation through currency appreciation.

Figure 2.8   **Profit growth and profit margins in the Chinese industry, January 2001–June 2006**

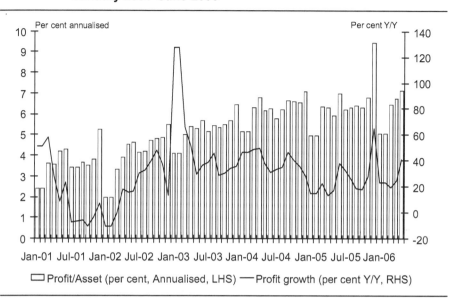

Source: CEIC Data Company.

Figure 2.9   **Profit margins of selected industries, 2000–06** (per cent)

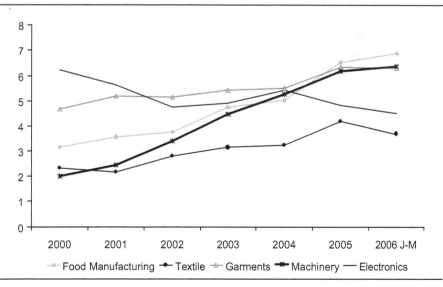

Note: 2006 J-M are based on first five months' year-on-year growth data.
Source: CEIC Data Company.

For now, however, there is no clear evidence that China's export prices have started to rise. In fact, the index measured by United States' import prices from China shows a year-on-year decline by 1.3 per cent during the past year (Figure 2.10). Of course, in China as in countries that earlier trod along the path of export-oriented industrialisation, continued export growth is associated with increases in the quality of exports within each category of exports, and upgrading from lower value to higher value versions of similar items. It is notoriously difficult to take such matters into account in assessment of the true inflationary situation for export industries.

Of the many reasons why China's rising labour costs have shown limited general negative effects on profitability, inflation or export prices, the most important is productivity growth. If labour productivity grows faster than real wages, then producers should be able to absorb rising costs comfortably. Growth in labour productivity may take the form of technological progress, changes in product mix or increase in capital intensity. In Chinese industry, labour productivity grew much faster than real wages between 1998 and 2003. In 2004 and 2005, however, real wages outpaced productivity (Figure 2.11). This suggests that we might soon begin to see a larger impact of higher labour costs on profits, inflation and export prices in China, especially for the most labour-intensive products.

The share of employees' earnings in total value-added basically tells a similar story (Figure 2.12). In the period 2000–04, labour cost's share declined consistently, implying declines in labour cost per unit of output. But the share took a drastic upturn from the beginning of 2005. It will be interesting to see whether this important structural change signals the beginning of a new paradigm.

That an international investment response to rising labour costs in China has already commenced is evident in statements from major global exporters of textiles, garments, electronics and other labour-intensive goods in 2006. The Managing Director of Fung and Fung in Hong Kong, for example, in August 2006 is reported on Bloomberg business news services as saying that rising labour costs were causing them to shift the sourcing of labour-intensive products and components from coastal China, to the inland of China, South Asia and Southeast Asia.

A glance into the future

Experiences of the past couple of years suggest that China's economic development has reached an important turning point—the ending of so-called unlimited labour supply—even though the impact of rising labour costs on inflation and profitability are limited in extent. Such changes in the labour market can be expected to accelerate significantly in the coming years.

Figure 2.10 **China's export prices, January 2005–May 2006**

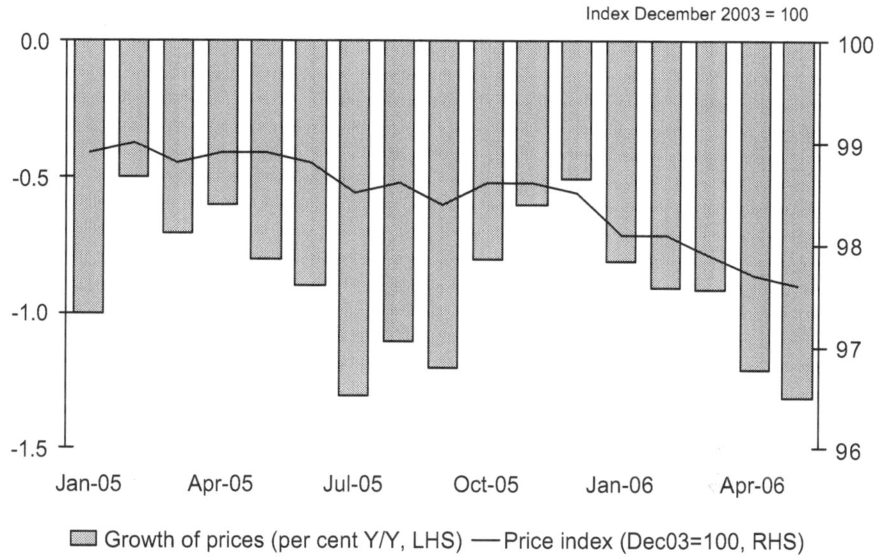

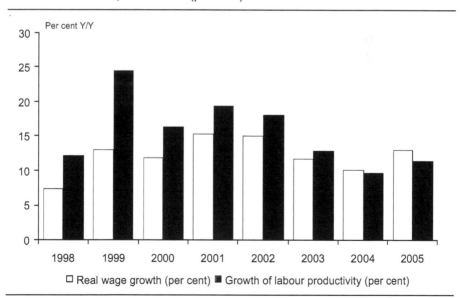

Source: CEIC Data Company.

Figure 2.11 **Labour productivity growth and increases in real wages in China, 1998–2005** (per cent)

Source: CEIC Data Company.

A closer look at the supply and demand for relatively unskilled labour suggests that there is likely to be a considerable tightening in the market in the period ahead—larger and earlier than has featured in the general discussion of China's economic prospects, within China or abroad. The balance between supply and demand for and the cost of skilled and managerial labour will not be subject to as much tension, where supplies are being expanded rapidly by formal education, on-the-job training and experience, and the demonstration effects through the ubiquitous presence of foreign enterprises.

Growth of China's total labour force has already slowed markedly, from 3 per cent per annum in the 1980s to 1 per cent in the period 2000–05, as the effects of the one-child policy of the reform period have moved through into the working-age population. Until recently, migration of workers to meet the requirements of strong urban employment growth slowed growth of rural employment only moderately. Between 2000 and 2005, however, the rural labour force declined by 0.9 per cent (Figure 2.13). This raises productivity of rural labour at home, and can be expected to put strong upward pressure on rural labour costs. This raises the supply price of migrant labour to urban areas.

The opposing changes in agricultural versus non-agricultural (inclusive of urban and rural non-agricultural) employment were more profound (Figure 2.14). These changes are likely to accelerate in the coming years. Over time, as the rural labour force shrinks and the urban labour force expands, a given rate of increase in urban labour demand represents a continuously increasing proportion of the pool of rural labour from which migrants are drawn, both because the denominator is shrinking, and the numerator is increasing. Higher and higher wages can be expected to recruit the same number of workers, and yet the required number of additional workers will increase each year.

Looking ahead, according to the Asian Demographics Ltd, China's total labour force may also start to decline from 2010 (Figure 2.15). Between 2009 and 2020, the number of Chinese workers may decline by an average of 4.3 million workers a year, or 0.6 per cent per annum.

The decline in supply of labour will be more dramatic for unskilled labour, due to the combination of a decline in the total labour force and improving education levels of the population. The number of people with education up to completed primary school had already declined from 645 million in 1990 to 494 million in 2004 (see Figure 12.6). According to Asia Demographics Ltd, this number can be expected to fall further to 268 million by 2020. The absolute numbers of unskilled workers available for labour-intensive tasks in industry, construction and services will fall much more rapidly than the labour force in total, at a time when the absolute

Figure 2.12 **The share of employees' earnings in total industrial value-added, Q1 2000–Q1 2006** (per cent)

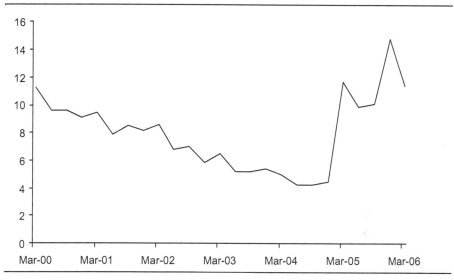

Source: CEIC Data Company.

Figure 2.13 **Recent decline in rural employment, 1991–2005** (per cent of total employment)

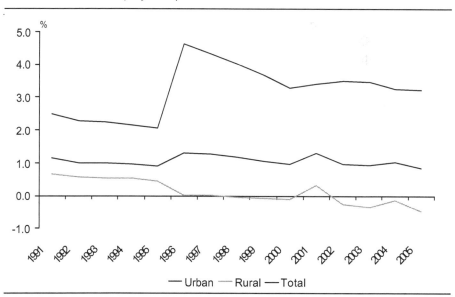

Source: CEIC Data Company.

Figure 2.14 **Declines in agricultural employment, 1991–2005** (per cent of total employment)

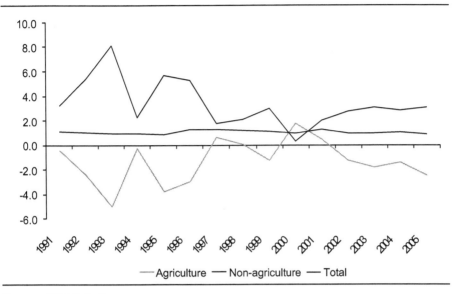

Source: CEIC Data Company.

Figure 2.15 **Changes in China's labour force, 1990–2020**

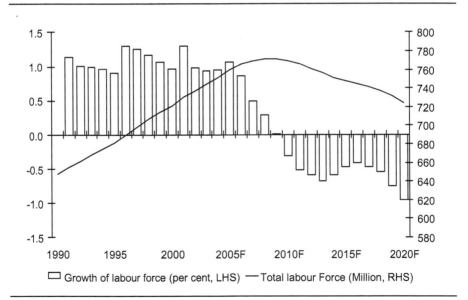

Source: Asia Demographic Limited.

Figure 2.16 **Improving levels of education of the Chinese population, 1982–2020**

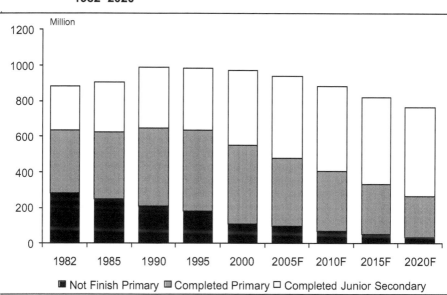

■ Not Finish Primary ▨ Completed Primary ☐ Completed Junior Secondary

Source: Asia Demographic Limited.

size of the annual increase in demand for labour will be rising rapidly—unless it was moderated by rapidly rising wages.

Recent official wage data also support the view that China is moving toward the turning point. On average, urban wages increased faster than GDP during the past five or six years, pointing to rising share of labour compensation in GDP. More interestingly, although wages are still quite low in the labour-exporting provinces, such as Sichuan, their growth has been faster than in typical labour-importing provinces, such as Guangdong and Shanghai (Table 2.1). The supply price of labour from the inland regions to the coastal cities is rising, at the same time as demand growth is placing upward pressure on urban wages.

Sector-wise, wage growth has been led by mining and financial industries. Wages for agricultural and construction workers grew at a similar pace. Construction workers are mostly temporary migrant farmers, and their wages reflect the rising opportunity cost of labour from rural areas (Table 2.2).

The quality of education is rising, as increasing education expenditure is allocated to a student population that is declining at the lower levels and growing only

Table 2.1 **Average wage rates by region, 1999–2006ᵉ** (yuan constant 1999 prices and per cent per annum growth)

	Beijing	Liaoning	Shanghai	Zhejiang	Hubei	Guang Dong	Sichuan	Ningxia
1999	14,450	8,037	16,690	11,208	6,972	12,311	7,246	7,477
2000	16,317	8,889	18,428	13,044	7,546	13,875	8,414	8,679
2001	19,194	10,199	20,962	16,082	8,556	15,686	9,919	10,476
2002	21,788	11,911	22,406	18,365	9,604	17,747	11,097	11,731
2003	24,477	13,130	25,144	20,461	10,426	19,616	12,128	12,994
2004	27,504	14,163	26,658	21,630	11,082	20,783	13,132	13,967
2005	31,079	16,025	29,301	23,454	12,793	22,078	14,464	16,292
2006E	36,845	18,729	32,354	25,461	14,729	23,661	16,071	19,062
Growth 1999–2006ᵉ	14.3	12.8	9.9	12.4	11.3	9.8	12.1	14.3

Note: 2006ᵉ are estimates based on the first quarter data. Beijing, Shanghai, Guangdong and Zhejiang are from the dynamic coastal region; Liaoning from the old industrial Northeast; Hubei from central China; and Sichuan and Ningxia from the Southwest and West respectively.
Source: CEIC Data Company.

slowly at higher levels of education. This expansion of the stock of human capital will facilitate the rapid diversification of Chinese industrial structure into more technologically complex activities.

Concluding remarks

The recent labour shortage probably signaled the beginning of the end to the 'unlimited' supplies of labour. It came earlier than was economically necessary because of imperfections in labour markets, and improvements in the market can ameliorate these effects for a while. But there will be no avoiding the implications of the supply curve for labour becoming steeply upward sloping.

Average real wages grew by 13 per cent per annum during the past five years.

So far, wage inflation has had limited impacts on profitability, inflation and export prices. The key factor contributing to muted macroeconomic implication in the near term was rapid economy-wide growth of productivity. Structural change towards more capital-intensive processes and industries also played an important role.

This may change soon, as, according to our estimation, real wage growth had already outpaced improvement in labour productivity in 2004 and 2005. The share of workers' compensation in total industrial value-added also surged from 2005.

Table 2.2 **Average annual wage rates for agriculture, manufacturing, construction and finance, 1978–2004** (yuan constant 1999 prices and per cent per annum increase)

	Agriculture	Mining	Manufacture	Construction	Wholesale and Retail	Finance
1985	2,895	4,365	3,666	4,491	3,320	3,805
1986	3,244	4,857	3,947	4,755	3,554	4,189
1987	3,297	4,797	4,090	4,858	3,663	4,206
1988	3,108	4,768	4,152	4,756	3,778	4,222
1989	2,859	4,894	3,910	4,458	3,416	3,842
1990	3,075	5,424	4,137	4,758	3,628	4,185
1991	3,189	5,679	4,419	5,113	3,824	4,353
1992	3,317	5,823	4,781	5,563	3,999	5,133
1993	3,231	5,871	5,297	5,979	4,238	5,917
1994	3,594	5,965	5,461	6,240	4,509	8,557
1995	3,835	6,268	5,628	6,299	4,625	8,031
1996	4,072	6,518	5,673	6,283	4,687	8,452
1997	4,216	6,683	5,803	6,509	4,739	9,520
1998	4,464	7,140	6,965	7,351	5,783	10,484
1999	4,832	7,521	7,794	7,982	6,417	12,046
2000	5,164	8,307	8,716	8,701	7,162	13,425
2001	5,679	9,482	9,668	9,382	8,104	16,101
2002	6,381	10,987	10,971	10,251	9,372	19,083
2003	6,867	13,482	12,313	11,310	10,779	22,128
2004	7,217	16,000	13,307	12,109	12,254	25,585
Growth 2000–04	8.7	17.8	11.2	8.6	14.4	17.5

Source: CEIC Data Company.

More importantly, demographic transition implies that China may soon face much more serious supply constraint in the labour market, especially for unskilled workers, in rural as well as urban areas.

With these developments, we are likely to see major transition in the pattern of Chinese economic growth. The dynamic coastal regions will graduate surprisingly quickly from labour-intensive activities and re-specialise in capital- or technology-intensive sectors of the production process. In the absence of currency appreciation, inflation rates would start to rise. Higher real wages would lead to higher rates of increase in consumer spending. Rising opportunity cost of labour in the countryside and wages in towns would be helpful in containing the increase in income inequality—a source of growing tension and concern. It would also increase the self confidence and bargaining power of labour, and lead to pressures for improved conditions of work across a wide range of issues, and in the absence of thoughtful management responses, to increased industrial unrest.

A few factors may also cushion the economic impact of the turning point. Productivity growth is likely to remain strong in the Chinese economy. Reform of the household registration system, which has been carried out in some provinces this year, reduces transaction costs of migration and can increase potential supply to the urban economy (see Du, Gregory and Meng, Chapter 10).

How would growing labour scarcity and higher wages affect Chinese economic growth and relations with the international economy?

Growth need not slow, until China is approaching the frontiers of global productivity and incomes—and in the best of circumstances that approach is a couple of decades away. With falling labour supply and rising wages, China will rely on continued capital intensification—human capital and capital in other forms— and total factor productivity growth. Capital intensification will continue to be supported by high savings rates and the value that society places on education— although the quality of policy in the education sector will affect outcomes. Total factor productivity growth is already reasonably high (see Wang, Chapter 3), and will be encouraged by continuation of high levels of direct foreign investment, and by structural change driven by rising labour costs themselves. The condition for continued rapid productivity growth is that China is structurally flexible, investing heavily in the infrastructure, human capital and other capital required to support profitable knowledge-based industries, and accepting the decline of labour-intensive industries and processes as they are rendered obsolete in a labour-scarce economy. Inevitably, these developments will make much larger demands on the free flow of economic and other information, and free movement of people within China and across its borders.

The diversification of Chinese exports away from simple labour-intensive goods, towards technologically complex and capital-intensive goods and services, has already begun. At first, this reduces protectionist resistance to Chinese export growth in the rest of the world, which, within the manufacturing sector, is strongest in labour-intensive goods. Global markets are deeper for more complex manufactures, which will assist adjustment to rapid Chinese export growth. However, the scale of the increase in Chinese trade will be so large in absolute terms that areas of trade that are now subject to minimal protectionist intervention will come to be seen as sensitive in much of the rest of the world. For China and its trading partners, to give in to these pressures would be to forgo opportunities for continuing improvement in material conditions. This adds to the importance of ensuring now that we have an effective, rules-based international trading system.

China's rapidly growing trade and current account surpluses are currently a source of tension with trading partners. In themselves, rising wages and consumption will help to correct the imbalances, but too slowly and incompletely to reduce the urgency of accelerated adjustment in the nominal exchange rate. Timely appreciation will ease the path for rapid growth of the wider range of manufactured exports that will accompany the turning point. It will also ensure that the increase in real costs through the turning period does not take the form of destabilising inflation.

Monetary policy choices will determine whether the increased scarcity of labour, as China goes through the turning point, comes out as a stronger currency or as inflation. Either way, the cost of labour-intensive Chinese goods, but possibly not other Chinese exports, will rise. Either way, Chinese incomes, as measured by standard national accounts and converted at current exchange rates, will rise much more rapidly relative to other countries than simple comparisons of growth rates across countries would suggest. China will move towards the average incomes of the high-income countries much more rapidly than is generally expected. That has been the case with all other successful Northeast Asian economies at and beyond the turning point of economic development. China will not be a special and different case.

Acknowledgments

The authors are indebted to Ligang Song for analytic contributions to our discussion of the turning point in economic development. The views expressed in this chapter are those of the authors and do not necessarily represent views of the organisations they are associated with.

Notes

1 According to the Research Center for Rural Economy under the Ministry of Agriculture, however, total number of migrant workers reached 98 million at the end of November 2003 and has been growing at 5 per cent year-on-year since then. In addition, a survey of 2600 firms in 26 cities by the Ministry of Labour and Social Security shows the number employed migrant labour up 13 per cent in 2004 from a year ago.
2 'Manufacturers attracted to China with low wages, WTO admission', Washington Post, 27 November 2001.
3 For reports in the Chinese media, see, for instance, an article on *Southern Weekend* on 15 July 2004, at http://finance.tom.com/1001/1002/2004715-74213.html
4 These estimates are from Zhai Fan, formerly an official of the Ministry of Finance.

3

Growth accounting after statistical revisions

Xiaolu Wang

This chapter examines the size, per capita level, structural characteristics and growth rate of the Chinese economy after the new statistical revisions recently released, as a result of the countrywide economic census at the end of 2004 and other surveys in 2005 and 2006. New growth accounting analyses are carried out to assess the contribution of factors and productivity to China's economic growth. The greater size of the economy indicated by the new statistics has new implications for the driving forces of growth.

The first section of the chapter reviews the revisions of GDP statistics and looks at the economic implications of the size and per capita levels of the Chinese economy, and discusses issues relating to the economic growth rate. The second section discusses the structural characteristics of the Chinese economy indicated by the revised statistical data, and the implications for future growth. The third section carries out a growth accounting analysis to examine the contribution of factors and productivity changes to economic growth, and is followed by a conclusion.

How large is the Chinese economy after statistical revisions?

China carried out a new economic census on 31 December 2004, covering all economic activities in secondary and tertiary industries. The census indicated that the size of the Chinese economy was seriously understated in previous statistics, due mainly to incomplete statistical systems for the services sector, indicating that values were missing from small enterprises in that sector. Total

GDP data for 2004 and earlier years up to 1978 were revised and published by the National Bureau of Statistics in 2006 (National Bureau of Statistics 2006a), however, major revisions have been made to the data since the early 1990s (a nationwide census for tertiary industries was carried out in 1993). According to the new statistical revisions, the Chinese economy in 2004 was 16.8 percentage points larger than previously reported. At the provincial and sectoral levels, some revised data for 2004 are also available in the *China Statistical Monthly* (National Bureau of Statistics 2006b), and allow comparisons between the revised and unrevised data (see National Bureau of Statistics 2005c) in different dimensions.

A comparison between the revised and unrevised GDP data (1991–2005, current prices) is shown in Figure 3.1. Figure 3.2 shows the official revisions of the GDP growth rates for the same period.

According to the new statistics, the average economic growth rate for the period 1993–2004 was 9.9 per cent, rather than the previously announced figure of 9.4 per cent. The growth rate remained the same into 2005, while in the first six months of 2006, GDP growth reached 10.9 per cent (Zheng 2006).

In 2005, China's total GDP was 18,232 billion yuan, or US$2,229 billion (World Bank 2006). In terms of economic size, China's economy surpassed the United Kingdom and France in 2005 and is now ranked fourth in the world. According to the World Bank's Purchasing Power Parity (PPP) measure, China's GDP was US$8,573 billion in 2005; that is, 3.85 times as large as stated above, and more than twice that of Japan. The PPP measure ranks China in second place globally, after the United States (World Bank 2006).

In terms of per capita GDP, China is still a poor country, although not as poor as previously stated. In 2005, GDP per capita in China was RMB13,944 or US$1,704. According to the World Bank's PPP measure (based on Ren and Chen's study, 1995) China's GDP per capita was US$6,556, making it already a middle-income country.

There have been some concerns about a possible upward bias of the World Bank's estimations because the differences in quality between products in China and industrial countries have been ignored. There are other studies that derived similar or different results to the World Bank's estimations. Garnaut and Ma (1993) and Garnaut and Huang (1994) compared consumption of food, steel, energy and other goods in China and other economies and concluded that the real GDP of China should be adjusted by a factor of three. Wu (1997) reviewed different PPP estimates and suggested China's GDP was three times higher than the market-exchange rate converted level. Wu also pointed out that the PPP measure indicated only the Chinese people's standard of living, and should not be interpreted as

Growth accounting after statistical revision

Figure 3.1   **China's GDP, revised and unrevised, 1991–2005** (trillion yuan)

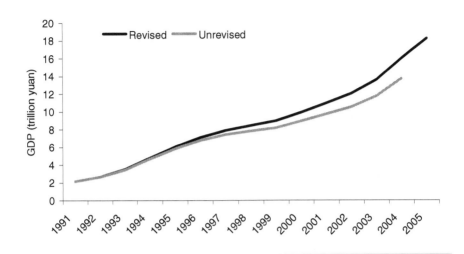

Sources: National Bureau of Statistics of China, 2006a. *China Statistical Abstract 2006*, China Statistics Press, Beijing. National Bureau of Statistics of China, 2005c. *China Statistical Yearbook*, China Statistics Press, Beijing.

Figure 3.2   **GDP growth rate, revised and unrevised, 1991–2005** (per cent)

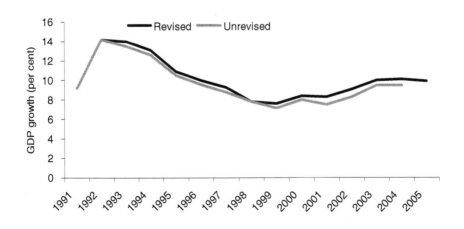

Sources: National Bureau of Statistics of China, 2006a. *China Statistical Abstract 2006*, China Statistics Press, Beijing. National Bureau of Statistics of China, 2005c. *China Statistical Yearbook*, China Statistics Press, Beijing.

representing China's economic power in the world market. Other estimates of China's PPP measure include Maddison (1998) and Heston et al. (2002). In a late estimation, Heston et al. (2002) estimated that China's GDP per capita (PPP) in the year 2000 was US$3,843. This was about 4.5 times greater than the figure derived from the 2000 exchange rate using unrevised statistical data.

It should also be taken into account that many studies were carried out some time ago and relative domestic prices between China and other countries have since changed, especially with China's process of internationalisation, this, therefore, might reduce the factor for China's GDP conversion. If we take a possible range of 3.0 to 3.8 for a reasonable conversion factor, then GDP per capita in China in 2005 might have been in the range of US$5,000–6,500, and its total GDP in the range of US$6,600–8,600 billion. In any case, China's GDP in PPP measures is larger than that of Japan (US$3,943 billion) but significantly smaller than the United States ($12,409 billion).

The statistical revisions have also changed the relative position of different regions in terms of economic development. In Figure 3.3, all 31 provinces (including five autonomous ethnic regions and four municipalities administrated at the provincial level) are ranked by their economic size according to the revised data. Of the top 11 provinces, nine are in the east coast areas, whereas, of the bottom 10 provinces, nine are in the west. The middle 10 provinces are located mainly in the central and northeast areas.

Figure 3.3 shows how much the data were revised upwards or downwards for each province. GDP was adjusted upwards by 41 per cent for Beijing and by more than 10 per cent for several provinces including Guangdong, the largest province in terms of economic size, and Ningxia, a less developed autonomous region in western China. Downward adjustments were made to 11 of the 31 provinces. Of those, Heilongjiang and Hubei, two provinces at the middle level in economic development, each lost more than 10 per cent. In general, the more advanced east coast region and the underdeveloped western region gained, respectively, by 4.4 and 3.8 per cent, while the central region, which was at the middle level of economic development, lost 2.1 per cent of its GDP.

Such figures might puzzle many readers, since GDP was revised upwards by 16.8 per cent in 2004, but the aggregate of provincial GDP was increased by only 2.7 per cent. This is because, for a long period, the National Bureau of Statistics believed that GDP at the provincial level was overstated, therefore they made their own adjustment to the national GDP according to various economic surveys, without adjusting the provincial data. For example, the National Bureau of Statistics had announced that the unrevised 2004 GDP was RMB13,687 billion, whereas

Growth accounting after statistical revision

Figure 3.3   **Adjustment of GDP data at the provincial level, 2004** (billion yuan)

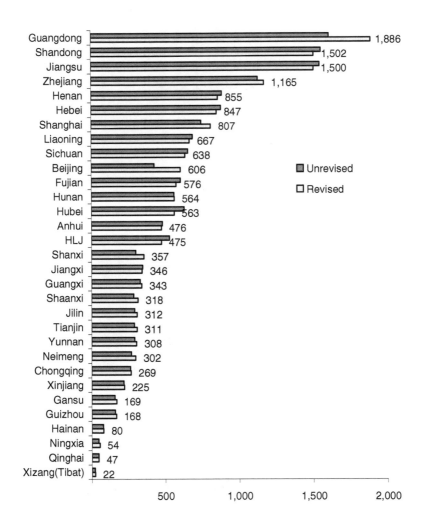

Note: Data in the chart are revised figures. Unrevised data are not shown due to space limitations.
Sources: National Bureau of Statistics of China, 2006a. *China Statistical Abstract 2006*, China Statistics Press, Beijing. National Bureau of Statistics of China, 2005c. *China Statistical Yearbook*, China Statistics Press, Beijing.

the provincial sum was RMB16,324 billion. The latter is 19 per cent greater than the former. After the new statistical revision, the two figures are closer, although still inconsistent. The revised GDP in 2004 was RMB15,988 billion for the national total and RMB16,760 billion for the provincial sum. The latter is still 5 per cent greater. In 2005, the announced total GDP and the published provincial sum of GDP were RMB18,232 billion and RMB19,657 billion, respectively. The latter is 7.8 per cent greater than the former.

Was the unrevised GDP data at the provincial level more reliable? The answer is no. First, data for individual provinces changed largely after the economic census. Only in the aggregate was the total change small, because the upward and downward changes offset one another. Second, while the previous data for tertiary industries in most provinces were found to be understated, data for secondary industries were overstated in a number of provinces. This was the reason for the National Bureau of Statistic's previous downward adjustments.[1] Comparing the new 2005 data for GDP structure at the provincial level with the unrevised data in 2004 (revised 2004 data are not available at this stage), one finds that the size of secondary industries in current prices shrank by 6 to 7 per cent in Heilongjiang and Hubei, although both claimed GDP growth of more than 11 per cent (data from National Bureau of Statistics 2006a, 2005c). In a few other provinces, the changes for secondary industries were too small to be consistent with their economic growth rates, indicating that the previous data on secondary industries were over-reported.

In terms of growth statistics, there is still a large gap between the growth rates of the national GDP and the provincial average. In 2005, based on the new statistical data announced by the National Bureau of Statistics, the GDP growth rate was 9.9 per cent, whereas the weighted provincial average was 12.9 per cent—three percentage points higher than the former. This inconsistency still exists.

It is too early to judge whether some local governments still intend to overstate their economic performance after the national economic census. There are, however, some other likely reasons for the lower growth rates stated by the National Bureau of Statistics at the national level. One is how the data are deflated. The author constructed an alternative GDP deflator to compare with the implicit GDP deflator used by the National Bureau of Statistics. Four price indexes are used. They are Consumer Price Index (CPI), ex-factory Price Index of Industrial Products (PIIP), Producer Price Index of Farm Products (PPIF; Purchasing Price Index of Farm Products is used for the period before 2001) and Fixed Investment Price Index (FIPI). These are the major price indexes provided by the National Bureau of Statistics, and cover the main (although not all) areas of economic activity.

Price indexes at the national and provincial levels are calculated separately. Different weights for the four indices are taken for sensitivity tests, and the results are very close.[2]

Interestingly, comparisons between the National Bureau of Statistics' deflator and the alternative deflator show significant differences. For the period from 1996 to 2005, the National Bureau of Statistics' price index was generally higher than the alternative index by an average of 1.2 percentage points. For the earlier period, from 1978 to 1995, however, it was generally lower than the latter by an average of 0.9 percentage points.

The alternative deflators at the national level and for each province are used to derive the national and provincial GDP growth rates to compare with the official growth rates. Revised and unrevised GDP data in current prices for the period from 1992 to 2005 are used. The results are shown in Table 3.1 and they indicate significant inconsistency between the official growth rates at the national level and those at the provincial level—the latter is 2.4 percentage points higher than the former (unrevised data). The alternative deflator gives more consistent growth rates between the national total and provincial aggregate. For unrevised GDP data, there is a 1.4 percentage point difference between them and, for revised data, the gap was further reduced to 0.3 percentage points.

Table 3.1 shows an alternative growth rate that is higher than the official rate, based on the revised GDP data. The alternative states a growth rate of 10.7 per cent for the 1992–2004, 0.5 percentage points higher than the official rate. In contrast, when unrevised data are used, the alternative rate is lower than the official one. Therefore there are greater changes in growth rates after the data

Table 3.1 **Average GDP growth rate in 1992–2004 by different sources**

	National total	Provincial sum	Inconsistency
Official (unrevised)	9.7	12.1[a]	2.4
Official (revised)	10.2	n.a.	n.a.
Alternative (unrevised)[b]	9.4	10.8[c]	1.4
Alternative (revised)[b]	10.7	11.0[c]	0.3

Notes: [a] Weighted average using the shares of provincial GDP in aggregate as the weights. [b] Calculated by the author using GDP in current prices and the alternative deflator. [c] Calculated by the author from the deflated sum of provincial GDP using the alternative deflators at the provincial level.
Sources: National Bureau of Statistics of China, 2006a. *China Statistical Abstract 2006*, China Statistics Press, Beijing. National Bureau of Statistics of China, 2005c. *China Statistical Yearbook*, China Statistics Press, Beijing.

revision. In the official statistics, the average growth rate in the 1992–2004 period was revised upwards from 9.7 per cent to 10.2 per cent, an increase of 0.5 percentage points. By the alternative calculation, however, the average growth rate should be revised from 9.4 per cent to 10.7 per cent, an increase of 1.3 percentage points.

Again, the growth rate change in the alternative calculation is more consistent with the findings from the economic census. According to the outcome of the census, the economy in 2004 was 16.8 per cent larger than reported earlier, whereas a 0.5 percentage point upward revision of the growth rate from 1992 to 2004 makes the total GDP only 6 per cent larger. Using the alternative growth rates, one can find that the total GDP was 16 per cent larger after the data revision.

Is the alternative GDP growth rate for China suggested in this chapter reliable? This might need further confirmation in future studies. Nevertheless, for the first half of 2006, the National Bureau of Statistics reported a further speed up of GDP growth, at a rate of 10.9 per cent. A high growth rate of more than 10 per cent might be expected for the near future.

The structure of the Chinese economy

Major changes occurred to the size of the services sector after the statistical revision. Table 3.2 shows minor increases in value-adding in primary and secondary industries after the revision (by 0.7 per cent and 2 per cent, respectively), but a major increase in tertiary industries (by 49 per cent). The previous data showed an unbalanced structure in the Chinese economy, with an obviously low proportion of the services sector and a high proportion of the industrial sector in GDP, compared with most other economies with either the same or higher levels of development. After the data revision, the share of tertiary industries in GDP is now closer to the common pattern, although it is still low. It increased from 32 per cent to 41 per cent. Meanwhile, the share of the secondary sector decreased from 53 per cent to 46 per cent in 2004 (Figure 3.4).

Another abnormality of the GDP structure was the very low proportion of private consumption and very high ratio of capital formation. The statistical revision did not make any positive change to this picture, rather, the share of private consumption in GDP in 2004 dropped by 1.6 percentage points, from 41.4 per cent to 39.8 per cent. Government consumption increased by three percentage points, and capital formation decreased by one point (Figure 3.5). Private consumption dropped further, by 1.6 percentage points, to 38.2 per cent in 2005, which was the lowest in at least the past half a century.

Table 3.2 **Changes in GDP structure, 2004** (billion yuan)

	2004 unrevised	2004 revised	Change (per cent)
Primary	2,081	2,094	0.7
Secondary	7,241	7,386	2.0
Tertiary	4,366	6,507	49.0

Sources: National Bureau of Statistics of China, 2006a. *China Statistical Abstract 2006*, China Statistics Press, Beijing. National Bureau of Statistics of China, 2005c. *China Statistical Yearbook*, China Statistics Press, Beijing.

Figure 3.4 **GDP structure after the statistical revisions, 2004 and 2005** (per cent of GDP)

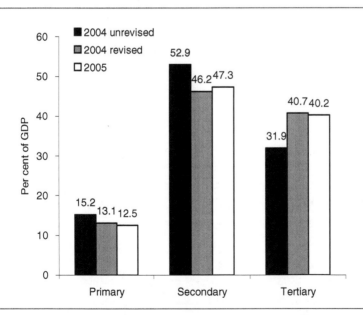

Sources: National Bureau of Statistics of China, 2006a. *China Statistical Abstract 2006*, China Statistics Press, Beijing. National Bureau of Statistics of China, 2005c. *China Statistical Yearbook*, China Statistics Press, Beijing.

Figure 3.5   **GDP components by expenditure, 2004** (per cent)

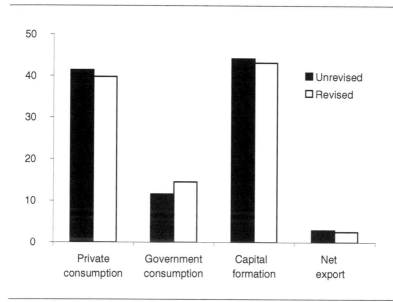

Sources: National Bureau of Statistics of China, 2006a. *China Statistical Abstract 2006*, China Statistics Press, Beijing. National Bureau of Statistics of China, 2005c. *China Statistical Yearbook*, China Statistics Press, Beijing.

The relatively weak consumption growth resulted in deficiency in aggregate demand, pushing up net exports and fuelling high investment. While strong investment lifts up aggregate demand in the short run, it also creates rapid growth of production capacity in the longer term. With slower consumption growth, overcapacity appears later in some industrial sectors, and further generates upward pressure on net export and downward pressure on prices. While economic growth rate remained high, CPI decreased from 3.9 per cent in 2004 to 1.7 per cent in 2005, and then to 1.5 per cent in the first half of 2006. Meanwhile, the share of net export in GDP increased from 2.5 per cent in 2004 to 4.5 per cent in 2005 when renmimbi moderately appreciated in the middle of the year. The export pressure has resulted in more trade disputes.

Insufficient consumption demand also leads to inefficient use of resources. In 1999, total amount deposited in banks and other financial institutions were 10,878 billion (1.2 times GDP), and the loan-deposit ratio was 86.2 per cent. In 2005, the total amount deposited grew to 28,717 billion (nearly 1.6 times GDP), and the loan-deposit ratio dropped to 67.8 per cent. Although total loans increased at a real annual rate around 10–11 per cent (by different deflators), a greater proportion of bank deposits became unused.

Foreign exchange reserves also mounted. According to the State Administration of Foreign Exchange, reserves achieved an historical high of US$ 941 billion at the end of June 2006,—the highest amount worldwide. A large part has been invested in US treasury bonds. Whether China needs this amount of reserves and whether this is an efficient use of foreign exchange is now a controversial issue.

Private consumption is depressed by a few factors: employment uncertainty, incomplete social security systems, the high prices of social services (mainly medical services and higher education) and real estate. The rapid increase in income disparity is also responsible (Wang 2005). In the past 20 years, the Gini coefficient increased from 0.27 (in 1985) to 0.45 (in 2004). While incomes for high income earners increased rapidly, those of low-income earners changed slowly, or even decreased. This had a negative impact on private consumption because rich people are able to save far more than poor people. In addition, the incomplete taxation system taxes poor people more than the rich, because the latter have much greater chances for tax evasion.

All of the above indicate necessities for improvement in the social security system, public services and the taxation system. For the sustainability of long-term economic growth, institutional reform for a better-managed public service sector, with more efficiency, more transparency and more public monitoring, is essential.

Growth accounting after statistical revision

China has managed to maintain a very high economic growth rate during the past 28 years, since the beginning of its economic reform in the official data, at an average of 9.7 per cent. This growth was, however, criticised by some researchers as being unsustainable, and as being driven mainly by heavy investment or input growth (for example, Krugman 1994; Young 2000). Meanwhile, many other researchers found moderate productivity changes but the major source of growth was the increase in inputs. What is the overall picture after the statistical revisions? In this section, I attempt to provide a preliminary answer to this question via growth accounting analysis, based on the newly revised statistical data.

Considering the continued increases in the education levels of the labour force in China, and the new phenomenon of labour-supply shortage, human capital is expected to play a more important role in China's economic growth. For this reason, a Lucas-style growth model (Lucas 1988) is used for growth accounting

$$Y_t = A_0 K_t^a H_t^{(1-a)} H_{a(t)}^b X_{1t}^{g_1} X_{2t}^{g_2} \ldots X_{nt}^{g_n} \quad (1)$$

where Y_t is real GDP of the year 't'; K_t is capital stock; H_t is education-enhanced labour force, or stock of human capital; H_a is the average education level of the labour force; X_{it} represents other variables that might effect total factor productivity growth; a and 1-a are, respectively, the elasticities of capital and human capital with respect to GDP under the restriction of constant returns to scale; b catches the possible externality of average education on growth, as a source of TFP changes; g_i represents the effect of the '*i*th' factor on TFP growth; and A_0 is a constant that presents the initial level of TFP.

The model is estimated empirically in a logarithm form, with and without the restriction on constant returns to scale. To impose the restriction, the model is transformed as follows

$$\ln y_t = C + a \ln k_t + b \ln H_{a(t)} + \Sigma(g_i \ln X_{it}) \quad (1')$$
where $y_t = Y_t/H_t$, $k_t = K_t/H_t$, and i=i(1, 2, ...n).

National-level data for the 54-year period from 1952 to 2005 are used (National Bureau of Statistics 2005c, 2005d, 2006a). Two sets of GDP data—that is, revised and unrevised—are used and deflated to 1978 prices using the implicit National Bureau of Statistics GDP deflator. Capital stock is calculated based on historical data of total investment in fixed assets and the price index for fixed investment, using the Perpetual Inventory Method. To avoid shortage of data on various categories of capital stock, an overall depreciation rate of 5 per cent is used. For the initial capital stock in 1952, the author took RMB70 billion, based mainly on Chow (1993).[3]

Human capital (H_t) is defined as total labour force times years of schooling. The accumulation of H_t for each year from 1952 to 2005 is calculated from graduation and one education period of lagged enrolment data, from primary to postgraduate education. The calculation used the information from the 1964, 1982, 1990 and 2000 national population censuses. Incomplete school education (that is, the differences between graduation and period of lagged enrolment) is assumed to have an average length of 50 per cent of the corresponding education period. Vocational education, adult education, special education, overseas study and informal training programs are also calculated. Human capital depreciation is calculated based on the death rate of the population and the calculated average years of schooling of the population (not of the labour force) with a time lag.[4] The initial human capital stock in 1952 was projected as an average of 1.3 years of schooling of the total population. This is based on 1964 national census data on education and detailed education data between 1952 and 1964.

A number of variables are tested for X_is, that is, sources of TFP growth other than the externality of education. They are marketisation, urbanisation, foreign trade, foreign investment and research and development. Marketisation has been found to have a positive effect on factor allocation and possibly on technological innovation. Urbanisation can increase TFP as it transfers inefficiently used labour and other resources from rural to urban sectors, thus increasing efficiency. Foreign trade exploits comparative advantages in the economy, and might also lead to technological transfers. Foreign investment can bring new technology and management skills into the country. Research and development directly promotes technological innovation.

For marketisation in the period under investigation, the shares of non-state enterprises (that is, private enterprises, foreign-funded enterprises and shareholding companies) in the values of industrial output are used as a proxy (NSE). Urbanisation is defined as the ratio of urban to total population. Because its impact on TFP is mainly in the reallocation of resources—that is, a short-term effect—the changes in the urbanisation ratio (Ud) were used in this study. To present the level of foreign trade (or economic openness), the sum of total export and import values as a ratio to GDP is used (TRY). For foreign investment, the ratio of Foreign Direct Investment (FDI) (converted at the official exchange rate) to total investment in fixed assets is used (FI). Data for overall research and development activities are not available; instead, government expenses on research and development as a proportion of GDP are used (GRY).

There are also some possible drags of TFP growth. In this context, one factor being considered commonly is inefficient use of government resources. In China, government expenses on administration and the operating costs of government departments accounted for a large proportion of total government expenditure. In this study, the ratio of these government expenses to GDP is used (GAY) to test the possible effect on TFP.

Normally, there are time lags between investment in and utilisation of industrial capital, and between the graduation of students and when they become skilled employees. For this reason, and to avoid possible bi-causal problems, one-year lagged variables of K, H, and H_a are used in the equations. The Prais-Winsten regression method is used for auto-correlation. The results are reported in Table 3.3.

Table 3.3   **Estimation result: Prais-Winsten Regression AR(1)**

Dep. var	$\ln Y_t$ Equation 1 (unrestricted)	$\ln y_t$ Equation 1' (unrestricted)	$\ln y_t$ Equation 2 (restricted)	$\ln y_t$ Equation 2 (old GDP)	$\ln y_t$ Equation 3 (restricted)
$\ln H_{t-1}$	0.600 (2.340*)				
$\ln K_{t-1}$	0.449 (6.626**)				
$\ln k_{t-1}$		0.454 (7.223**)	0.431 (7.289**)	0.413 (6.995**)	0.385 (5.760**)
$\ln H_{a(t-1)}$	−0.212 (−0.454)	−0.103 (−0.886)			
EV					0.559 (2.987**)
NSE	0.334 (2.452*)	0.318 (2.369*)	0.258 (1.844')	0.251 (1.816')	0.309 (1.741')
Ud	8.555 (4.893**)	8.405 (4.936**)	7.663 (4.628**)	7.792 (4.659)	7.100 (4.629**)
TRY	0.875 (2.880**)	0.880 (2.899**)	0.846 (2.753**)	0.818 (2.841**)	0.816 (2.618*)
GAY	−5.778 (−2.527*)	−5.914 (−2.676**)	−5.489 (2.396)	−5.213 (−2.460*)	−8.282 (−2.992**)
GRY					13.242 (1.501)
C	−2.667 (−1.255)	−2.214 (−5.629**)	−2.454 (−9.459**)	−2.536 (−10.071)	−2.618 (−8.794**)
Adj. R^2	0.989	0.964	0.961	0.960	0.962
DW (original)	1.721	1.559	1.335	1.382	1.183
DW (transformed)	1.876	1.843	1.776	1.767	1.469

Note: Figures in parentheses are t-ratios. Those with ' are significant at the 10 per cent level, with * are at the 5 per cent level and with ** are at the 1 per cent level.

The restricted and unrestricted models obtained significant results and very similar estimates (Equations 1 and 1'). Adjusted R^2s are high, and the Durbin-Watson statistics are acceptable at the 5 per cent level. Both models indicate a 0.45 elasticity of capital. The unrestricted model shows an increasing returns-to-scale character in the economy, with the elasticity of human capital being 0.60 and significant at the 5 per cent level. The restricted model implies a 0.55 elasticity of human capital, but the externality of average human capital stock (H_a) in both models becomes negative (but insignificant). Both models show significant positive effects of marketisation (NSE), urbanisation (Ud) and foreign trade (TRY) on economic growth, and both show negative and significant effects of government administration expenses on growth. Omitting H_a results in only slight changes in estimates. The elasticity of capital becomes 0.43, and other TFP-related coefficients are slightly lower (Equation 2). Foreign investment (FI) was omitted from Equations 1 and 2 because of its low t-ratios.

The non-positive externality of H_a is worth further investigation. Some evidence has shown possible misallocation of China's educational resources. These resources might be under-allocated in vocational education and over-allocated in regular secondary education. Most high schools aim to provide only as many candidates as possible for universities with high examination marks. Three-quarters of the junior and senior high school students, however, have to be employed without entering tertiary education, and mostly without any job training. To test the possible different growth effects between vocational and regular education, the author calculated new graduates' years of schooling from secondary vocational schools as a ratio of that from the whole secondary schools, from 1952 to 2005. This new variable (EV) is included in Equation 3 in Table 3.3. Government expenses (GRY) on research and development as a ratio of GDP are also included. EV is significant at the 1 per cent level, implying an additional contribution of vocational education to TFP. The estimate of GRY is also positive, and large, but the t-ratio is below significance level (t=1.501). These effects are, however, not confirmed because the Durbin-Watson statistics fall into the undetermined interval, although they likely do exist.

Using the estimates and statistical data, the effects of marketisation, urbanisation and economic openness (trade) on TFP growth are derived in Table 3.4. The table shows that the sum of these effects made no positive contribution to TFP growth during the pre-reform periods, but contributed about two percentage points during all the sub-periods of economic reform since 1978. The calculation results in Table 3.4 suggest that trade played a more important role in the latest period (1998–2005),

Table 3.4 **Sources of TFP growth, 1952–2005** (per cent, annual average)

	Marketisation	Urbanisation	Trade	Administration expenses	Sum (new data)	Sum (old data)
1952–57	−0.83	0.21	0.05	−0.85	−1.43	−1.36
1958–67	−0.90	−0.68	−0.29	0.60	−1.27	−1.28
1968–77	0.29	0.18	0.18	0.04	0.70	0.69
1978–87	0.45	0.52	1.44	−0.26	2.15	2.11
1988–97	0.73	0.49	0.73	0.59	2.53	2.46
1998–2005	0.31	−0.19	3.17	−1.33	1.96	1.91

Sources: Calculated from the estimates and statistical data in National Bureau of Statistics of China, 2006a. *China Statistical Abstract 2006*, China Statistics Press, Beijing. National Bureau of Statistics of China, 2005c. *China Statistical Yearbook*, China Statistics Press, Beijing. National Bureau of Statistics of China, 2005d. *China Compendium Statistics 1949–2004*, China Statistics Press, Beijing.

and government administration and operation costs deducted 1.3 percentage points from TFP growth for the same period. This suggests inefficient and inadequate uses of public financial resources, highlighting the importance of reforming public financial systems to make governance more efficient and transparent.

Note that the above results on TFP growth imply a rate higher than the 2 per cent TFP growth that might be derived from a conventional production function method using only capital and labour as inputs. This is because growth of human capital stock is faster than growth of the labour force, resulting from expansion of education scales. In the past 27 years, from 1978 to 2005, average years of schooling of the labour force increased by nearly four years, from 5.3 to 9.2 years per person. Human capital growth rate is higher than the growth rate of the labour force by 2.1 per cent, on average (author's calculation). This is evidence that human capital accumulation, rather than simple expansion of the size of the labour force and reallocation of labour between different sectors, is becoming more and more important for economic growth.

As shown in Table 3.3, estimates based on the unrevised statistical data of GDP are very close to those based on the new data. This induces a similar calculation of the contribution to TFP (see the last column of Table 3.4). However, as shown in the first section of this chapter, the revised GDP growth rate for the period 1992–2004 was only 0.5 percentage points higher than the old one. It could be 1.3 percentage points higher if an alternative (probably more reasonable) deflator is used. This implies that TFP could be close to one percentage point higher than has been estimated here.

Conclusion

China is now the fourth largest economy in the world, according to the exchange-rate measure of GDP, or the second largest, according to the PPP measures. After the statistical revision, its size is nearly 17 per cent larger than stated earlier. For the period 1992–2004, the economic growth rate was officially revised upwards by 0.5 percentage points, to an average of 9.9 per cent. There are, however, reasons to believe that the real growth rate might be even higher, and has risen further in 2006.

Meanwhile, China is still a poor country in per capita terms, although not as poor as previously thought. In 2005, China's per capita GDP increased to US$1,700 (and it is likely to be US$5,000–6,500 by different PPP measures).

There was understatement as well as overstatement of economic achievement in Chinese statistics. The new economic census revealed that the size of the tertiary industry sector has been seriously under-reported. According to the new statistics, the share of tertiary industries in 2005 was 40.2 per cent, which is closer to the normal range for developing countries than had been indicated by the earlier data.

The data revision did not, however, change the structural abnormality in terms of savings and consumption—that is, very high saving rates and a low proportion of private consumption in total GDP. In 2005, private consumption accounted for only 38.2 per cent of GDP, a 50-year low. This pushed up investment, creating over-capacity in industry and pressure on exports. This indicates a need for sustainable growth in the long run to encourage private consumption by job creation, improving social security systems to cover low-income earners, and improving public services.

Using the revised data, growth accounting in this study found that human capital is now playing an important role in China's economic growth. Further developing the education system—especially improving vocational education—can be an important measure for human capital accumulation, and therefore for sustaining rapid growth in the future.

The study also found at least two percentage points of TFP growth in nearly three decades, a result mainly of marketisation, urbanisation and economic openness. Government spending on research and development probably made a positive contribution to TFP, although this needs further confirmation.

An important finding of this study is the negative and significant impact of government administration and operating costs. To sustain economic growth, reform to improve governance of public financial systems will be essential.

Acknowledgments

This chapter was completed during the author's visit at the Asian Development Bank Institute. The author thanks the institute for its support, and Ross Garnaut and Ligang Song at the Australian National University for their valuable comments and encouragement.

Notes

1 Two directions of biases in GDP statistics existed previously. One was that output data at the local level in various localities were seriously, and arbitrarily, over-reported, under the influence of local governments. This problem was reported widely in the media and noticed not only by the National Bureau of Statistics, but by a number of academics, including the author and his colleagues (see, for example, Wang and Meng 2001). This was also the reason why the National Bureau of Statistics made downward adjustments to the raw data when it was calculating GDP at the national level. Another indication of bias was the missing values from tertiary industry due to the incomplete statistics system for that sector. This problem is rarely recognised because it relies on inside knowledge of the methodologies for data collection and calculation. Seemingly, even National Bureau of Statistics staff did not fully recognise this before the economic census.
2 For the default deflator (Deflator 1), the weights are taken as CPI 0.4, PIIP 0.3, PPIF 0.1, FIPI 0.2. For Deflator 2, the four price indexes are weighted equally (each 0.25). For Deflator 3, the weights are CPI 0.6, PIIP 0.2, PPIF 0.1, FIPI 0.1. GDP in constant prices, derived using these three deflators, gives very close results in average growth rates for the period 1992–2005. They are 10.76 per cent, 10.83 per cent and 10.68 per cent, respectively. The reason for giving the CPI a greater weight in Deflators 1 and 3 is to make up the defect that PIIP and PPIF reflect only price changes in the primary and secondary industries at the producer side, whereas CPI covers price changes in the services sector. An available price index that the author did not use is the Purchasing Price Index for Raw Materials, Fuel and Power. The reason for its exclusion is that its impact is already included in other indexes, and it might result in an over-weighting of these products.
3 Chow (1993) calculated that capital stock in the non-agricultural sectors was 58.3 billion yuan in 1952 (1952 price), of which fixed capital stock was 31.6 billion. He estimated a 45 billion yuan capital stock in the agricultural sector, including non-fixed capital. Based mainly on these calculations, and considering that capital stock might be more or less underestimated due to incomplete data, the author took a total of 69 billion yuan fixed capital stock in 1952 at the 1952 price. In an earlier study, the author estimated a RMB160 billion capital stock in 1952 (Wang 2000), which should include non-fixed capital stock (and might be a bit too large). Therefore, it is inconsistent with later figures sourced from fixed investment. Nevertheless, I should mention that the 1952 capital stock consists only of a very small part of total capital for later periods (less than 10 per cent in 1980, and less than 1 per cent in 2002), therefore its variation does not have a significant impact on the result of growth accounting.
4 This might result in overestimation of the overall human capital stock, because retired person years are not deducted. However, comparing the result with the national census data in several key years, average years of schooling from the former are lower than the latter. This might result from 1) possible overstatement of education levels in the censuses, and 2) underestimating the years of schooling of those quitted. The calculation therefore seems acceptable.

4
Quadrupling the Chinese economy again: constraints and policy options

Justin Yifu Lin

Since reforms started at the end of 1978, China has become the most dynamic economy in the world. Between 1978 and 2004, China's GDP growth rate averaged 9.4 per cent per annum and the international trade growth rate 24.6 per cent (National Bureau of Statistics of China 2005). In 2004, China's per capita GDP reached 10,561 yuan and is targeted to quadruple between 2000 and 2020 (National Bureau of Statistics of China 2005). To reach this target, the annual average GDP growth rate needs to be kept at more than 7.2 per cent for 20 years.

From an engineer's point of view, the long-term growth of an economy depends on the increase of inputs, especially capital, the relocation of inputs from the low value-added sectors to high value-added sectors, and technological innovation. Among these, technological innovation is the key. Without a continuous stream of technological innovation, high levels of investment leads to diminishing returns to capital, depressing the incentives to save and obstructing the accumulation of capital (Schultz 1964).

There are two methods for technological innovation: invention and technological borrowing. While the main source of technological innovation for industrial countries is invention, developing countries could borrow new technologies from industrial countries in addition to inventing technologies themselves, as there is a technological gap between industrial and developing countries. Developing countries could potentially benefit from this gap by borrowing technology from industrial countries by way of licensing, imitating and so on, and achieve a higher rate of technological innovation than that of industrial countries. In fact, a reliance on technological borrowing is one of the main reasons why China has been able to maintain dynamic growth during the past two decades (Hayami 1997). The contrasting growth performance in China before and after the reforms in 1978 also supports the idea that technological borrowing is an engine of growth in low-income countries (Lin et al. 1994).

Potentially, developing countries can achieve dynamic economic growth by borrowing technology from industrial countries and can substantially narrow the income gap or even catch up with industrial countries. Only a small number of economies in East Asia have, however, narrowed the gap and converged to the level of per capita income in industrial countries. Whether or not a developing country can benefit from the technological gap and realise the convergence of income depends on the relationship between the developing country's development strategy and its endowment structure (Lin 2003). The failure of most developing countries to converge with industrial countries in terms of economic performance can be explained largely by their governments' inappropriate development strategies, that is, the comparative advantage defying (CAD) strategy, which attempts to encourage firms that ignore the comparative advantages of their industry or technology (Lin 2003).

For the newly industrialised economies in Asia, and recently China, the success of these economies in converging with industrial countries in terms of economic performance can be explained largely by their governments' appropriate development strategies, that is, the comparative advantage following (CAF) strategy. Such a strategy attempts to facilitate a firm's choice of industry or technology according to the economy's comparative advantage (Lin 2003a). When the government in a developing country chooses a CAF strategy, the economic growth rate can be much greater than that in an industrial country to utilise large potential gains from trade (Lin et al. 2006), leading to convergence.

In spite of rapid growth in the past two decades, China is still a developing country and there is a gap to close before it becomes an industrial country. Limited per capita inputs (resources) and the incomplete transition from a centrally planned economy introduce many constraints on China in reaching the targeted quadrupling of the economy between 2000 and 2020, including institutional weakness and potential macroeconomic instability. There are 12 issues that be associated with potential barriers to China quadrupling GDP by 2020: energy and land resources; education; capital; technological progress; an inefficient financial (banking) sector; market segmentation and local protection; sustainability of export growth; income distribution; employment; corruption; economic fluctuations; and state-owned

Energy and land resources

China's oil production continued to rise between 1990 and 2003: 31 million tonnes more oil were produced in 2003 than in 1990 (Table 4.1). If this momentum were maintained, oil production in China would reach 188 and 213 million tonnes in 2010 and 2020, respectively. For China to quadruple its GDP by 2020, there must, however, be a rapid expansion of industries such as car manufacturing, civil aviation and shipping. Therefore, demand for oil in China is bound to grow dramatically in the future, out of all proportion to the largest conceivable expansion of oil production.

In 2003, China overtook Japan to become the world's second largest importer of oil after the United States. Conservatively estimated, this oil demand will reach

Table 4.1 **Oil production and consumption in China, 1990–2020** (million tonnes)

	Production (million tonnes)	Consumption (million tonnes)
1990	138.3	110.3
1991	141.0	117.9
1992	142.0	1,290.0
1993	144.0	140.5
1994	146.1	149.5
1995	149.0	160.7
1996	158.5	174.4
1997	160.1	185.6
1998	160.2	190.3
1999	160.2	207.2
2000	162.6	230.1
2001	164.8	232.2
2002	166.9	246.9
2003	169.3	275.2
2010	188.0	345.5
2020	212.8	466.6

Note: Oil production in 2010 and 2020 are projected values, derived from a linear regression on the basis of the data for 1990–2003. The total amount of oil production from 2003 to 2020 is estimated to be 3.28 billion tonnes, slightly above total oil reserves.
Source: BP, 2004. *Statistical Review of World Energy*. Available from http://www.bp.com/statisticalreview2004.

345.5 and 466.6 million tonnes in 2010 and 2020 respectively, with a gap in oil supply of 157.5 and 253.8 million tonnes respectively. Thus, oil security will be an important issue in China's attempts to achieve its quadrupling target.

There are several responsible strategies for resolving the oil-supply issue and supporting sustainable development: importing oil through various channels; greatly expanding collaborative ties in petroleum exploitation with countries from Africa, Southeast Asia and eastern Europe; actively developing new energy forms such as nuclear, wind and solar energy; gradually loosening controls on energy prices and resorting to the market for energy distribution; promoting corporations and enterprises to enhance energy efficiency through market mechanisms, in conjunction with favourable energy policies.

China, with its population of more than 1.2 billion, has per capita natural resource endowments that are well below the world average. Official statistics show that China has a land area of 96 billion hectares, making it the third largest country in the world. The land area per capita, however, is only 0.1 hectare, much lower than the world average. Based on the projections by Chinese and overseas scholars for China's future grain demand, 99.6 and 112 million hectares of arable land would be needed in 2010 and 2020 respectively for China to supply food for itself. The lowest estimate (5 per cent of the total grain supply imported) is that in 2020, to meet its grain demand, there will be a gap in arable land supply of up to 10.1 million hectares. The most conservative official estimate published (10 per cent of total grain supply imported) indicates that this gap in arable land supply will be 4.7 million hectares in 2020.

As discussed by Chen (this volume, Chapter 12), as China's agriculture is integrated more deeply into the world economy, there will be a powerful tendency for China to specialise more in production of labour-intensive and in imports of land-intensive agricultural products. However, the amount of grain and other land-intensive agricultural products that it is efficient for China to import will be less the more efficient is Chinese production.

China should accelerate technological upgrading for food production, enhance the variety, quality and economic benefits of agricultural products, push forward innovations in the promotion of agricultural technologies and the trade systems of agricultural products, promote further international cooperation in agriculture and related fields, and introduce more advanced agricultural techniques and new breeds. China should also aim to establish an excellent mechanism for the planning and management of land use, and remove such planning and approval from local control. To avoid inefficiency, China's central government should take control of the approval of land planning and use.

Education

The overall situation of educational development in China is satisfactory. There is still, however, a discrepancy between China and mid-level industrial countries, and current educational development cannot fully meet the needs of economic development in the era of diversification into more technologically efficient processes and products. Remaining problems and difficulties include the low overall educational levels and the comparatively high rates of illiteracy and semi-illiteracy among the whole population.

By 2000, Chinese 25 years or older had received an average of 5.48 years of education, in contrast with 7.33 years in the Philippines and 6.42 in Jordan. The percentage of Chinese 25 years old or older who had received higher education was only one-tenth that of the figures for Jordan and the Philippines. In the meantime, the rate of return on human capital investment in China is highly profitable (Heckman 2002; Zhang et al. 2005).[1] In addition, there are still large discrepancies between education levels in rural and urban areas.

If China successfully quadruples its economy between 2000 and 2020, the per capita GDP in 2020 is expected to catch up with that of Greece in 2000, namely US$16,501 (calculated by the purchasing power parity [PPP] method). Therefore, we can use the education level of Greece in 2000 as a benchmark for China's education level in 2020. To enhance the education level of Chinese in 2020 to

Figure 4.1 **Changes in government appropriation for education, 1991–2003** (per cent of GDP)

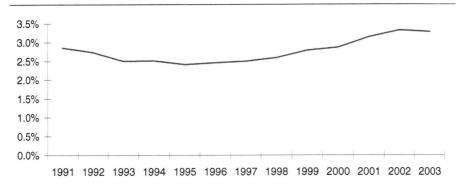

Source: National Bureau of Statistics of China, 2005a. *China Statistical Yearbook 2005*, China Statistics Press, Beijing.

close to that of Greece in 2000, the mean years of education for Chinese will have to increase by approximately 60 per cent in the coming decade. The percentage of people with higher education experiences is expected to undergo a sixfold rise accordingly. This will be an enormous challenge for China.

To implement the strategy of reinvigorating the country through science and education, the central government has been intensifying support for education since the 1990s. As illustrated in Figure 4.1, the ratio of annual fiscal educational outlay to GDP has been increasing, from 2.4 per cent in 1995 to 3.3 per cent in 2002. This ratio is, however, overshadowed by a mean level of 4 per cent for all developing countries—far behind that of industrial countries, whose ratios range from 5–6 per cent. Hence, under-funding of the education system is an important reason for the overall low mean education attainment of Chinese residents.

The central government must further intensify its support for education, accelerate the universality of compulsory education, especially in rural and less-developed areas in the midwest of China, construct a multi-channel funding system for education, vigorously develop higher education to meet the needs of national integrated innovation capabilities and of future industrial structure upgrading, and promote vocational education to increase the total supply of skilled workers.

Capital

To quadruple the Chinese economy between 2000 and 2020 successfully, the annual average GDP growth rate needs to be kept at more than 7.2 per cent for 20 years. According to the Solow decomposition, in order to realise this growth rate, China's annual average capital accumulation growth rate must be 8.1 per cent, supposing that the annual average growth rate of total factor productivity (TFP) is 4 per cent, the annual average growth rate of labour supply is 1 per cent and the annual average capital share is 31 per cent. Furthermore, if we take the rise of investment prices into account, the annual average increase in the capital stock must be at least 13 per cent. There are, however, some challenges in achieving this growth rate in capital.

First, the potential for further increases in the saving rate in China is limited. Since 1992, China's average saving rate has reached a high of 41.3 per cent, lower only than that of Singapore, but far more than that of Japan and other East Asian economies since the 1980s. Some scholars might argue that the Chinese economy corresponds with that of the 'small dragons' (Korea, Taiwan, Singapore and Hong Kong) between 1961 and 1980, and that, as the small dragons all experienced a rise in the saving rate after 1980 (Table 4.2), China will also witness

Table 4.2 **The saving rate of Japan and the 'small dragons', 1961–81 and 1982–2002**

	Saving rate during 1961–81 (per cent)	Saving rate during 1982–2002 (per cent)
Japan	35.1	30.7
Hong Kong	27.7	32.9
Taiwan	-	30.0
Korea	16.9	33.4
Singapore	15.1	45.6

Sources: Data for Japan, Hong Kong, Korea and Singapore from the World Bank's *World Development Indicators*; data for Taiwan from the Asian Development Bank.

a rise in its saving rate in the future. This argument might be true, but it is very difficult for China to make further sustainable increases in its saving rate because the current rate has surpassed the peak of the saving rates of all East Asian countries other than Singapore.

Second, the potential for an increase in foreign direct investment (FDI) is also limited. Although FDI flowing into China during 1992–2003 grew at the high rate of 31.2 per cent on average, this has slowed to 7.5 per cent since 2000. As a result, the ratio of FDI to capital formation in China has declined from 12.2 per cent in 1992–2003 to 9.9 per cent in 2000–03. Obviously, the growth of FDI in China is on a downward trend. In fact, the wave of increased FDI, mainly between 1992 and 1997, was simply a temporary burst resulting from deregulation policy in China, and had no dynamics to sustain it. It would be difficult for China to experience such a golden age in FDI again.

Furthermore, China faces serious inefficiencies in transforming domestic savings into investment. Based on data from the *China Statistical Yearbook* (National Bureau of Statistics of China various years), the domestic saving rate in China was 38.2 per cent between 1978 and 1992, but the capital formation rate was just 32.2 per cent. Since 1992, the domestic savings rate has increased to 41.3 per cent, but the capital formation rate is only 36.2 per cent. There is a gap of 5–6 per cent between the savings rate and the capital formation rate.

In conclusion, owing to the capital supply from domestic savings and because FDI has no potential to increase further, China must spare no effort to enhance its efficiency in investment and make full use of its high savings. Otherwise, investment growth is in danger of slowing down, increasing the difficulty of quadrupling the economy by 2020.

Technological progress

China is at the intermediate stage of industrialisation, and there is a significant lag in equipment and technology levels in traditional industries, meaning that many mature and general technologies from industrial countries could have great applicability in China. Consequently, we should import as many technologies as possible, in association with indispensable independent research and development to fit these technologies to local needs.

The current institutional system in China is, however, far from suitable for borrowing technology to achieve technological innovation. The majority of China's scientific manpower is distributed to national research institutions, which is kept away from industrial circles, and scientific research is out of line with application. Technologies from abroad have gradually become the primary source of techologies in China. The crucial industries that drive rapid economic growth after the reform and open-door policy depend heavily on importing production lines, while other pillar industries, such as the communication and automobile industries, are built by foreign direct investment or joint ventures. A wide gap exists between national research institutions and the manufacturing system. The lack of an enterprise-wide capability to digest and absorb imported technologies has resulted in the development of technology falling into a vicious circle of 'importing lagging behind reimporting'. Besides, some firms still ignore the existing comparative advantage of the economy in their entry/choice of industry/technology. In a situation where domestic enterprises' innovation is lacking and overall international competetiveness in technology is weak, China's economic development would be severely limited. Unless technical innovation can be improved, there will be an inadequate supply of technology to keep up with the accelerated structural adjustment and industrial upgrading.

The Chinese government must, therefore, encourage firms to utilise the existing comparative advantage of the economy in their choice of technology to benefit the technological gap between China and industrial countries. Meanwhile, the Chinese government should accelerate the process of reforming technological institutions; it should establish a multi-channel funding system for technological innovation; improve enterprises' technological innovation and absorption abilities; construct technology centres in large and medium-sized enterprises; speed up the formation of an effective operation mechanism that is favourable to technological innovation and the conversion of scientific achievement; strengthen coordination and cooperation between research institutes and universities; and encourage enterprises to actively increase their investment in technological innovation.

Table 4.3 Banking structure in China, 1994–2004 (per cent)

	ICBC	ABC	BOC	CBC	State-owned commercial banks total	Other commercial banks	Foreign banks
Assets							
1994	28.5	13.6	19.9	15.1	77.1	5.2	n.a.
2002	18.8	11.8	11.5	12.2	54.3	17.1	1.1
2003	17.8	11.8	11.0	12.0	52.6	18.6	1.4
2004	17.0	12.0	10.4	11.7	51.1	19.4	1.5
Loans in RMB							
1994	29.9	14.5	8.9	12.5	65.8	4.1	n.a.
2002	21.5	14.2	8.0	12.8	56.4	17.6	0.3
2003	20.0	13.9	8.3	12.7	54.9	19.4	0.3
2004	19.5	14.1	7.8	11.8	53.2	21.5	n.a.
Deposits in RMB							
1994	29.4	17.2	7.3	13.3	72.5	5.4	n.a.
2002	22.6	14.1	8.3	14.6	59.6	20.0	0.1
2003	21.0	13.9	8.6	13.8	57.3	20.7	0.2
2004	19.9	14.2	8.8	13.3	56.1	23.1	0.2

Note: ICBC = Industrial and Commercial Bank of China; ABC = Agricultural Bank of China; BOC = Bank of China; CBC = Construction Bank of China.
Sources: *Almanac of China's Finance and Banking*, 1995, 2003, 2004, 2005.

Inefficient financial (banking) sector

As the previous discussions about capital, land, energy and education show, the resources that can be used to support the Chinese economy to grow further are limited, so improving the efficiency of resource allocation should be the key factor in sustaining rapid economic growth in the future. The financial system will play an extremely important role in this process. The Chinese financial system is, however, dominated by a large but inefficient banking system, which presents a serious challenge for China.

Although financial markets have undoubtedly developed since they were established in the early 1990s, they are very small relative to the banking sector. In 2004, the 'negotiable market capitalisation' on the equity markets was only 6.6 per cent of the total bank loans and 8.5 per cent of GDP (National Bureau of Statistics 2004). In terms of fund flows, the capital raised by listed companies through initial public offerings (IPOs) or state-owned enterprises (SOEs) was only 7.9 per cent of the changes in total loans (a proxy of new loans), while the ratio for corporate bonds issued was even smaller, that is, 1.7 per cent. We can, therefore, safely conclude that the financial system in China is dominated by the banking sector.

The banking sector is further dominated by the 'big four banks', although their dominance has declined since the mid 1990s. As Table 4.3 shows, the big four banks made more than 65 per cent of the total loans made in RMB by the whole banking system in 1994, and this number was still larger than 53 per cent in 2004. The ratio of assets of the big four banks to the total assets of all banking institutions was about 77 per cent in 1994, and 51 per cent in 2004. In terms of deposits, the dominance of the big four banks was even more prominent. The big four obtained more than 72 per cent of all deposits in RMB in 1994, and 56 per cent in 2004. The ratios for assets, loans and deposits of the other commercial banks in 2004 were about 19 per cent, 22 per cent and 23 per cent respectively.

The big four banks have, however, been operating at extremely high costs compared with the shareholding banks and international standards. Profitability is usually measured as returns on average assets (ROA) and returns on average equity (ROE). The ROA and ROE of the big four banks in 2002 were about 0.2 per cent and 3.5 per cent, while for the 10 shareholding banks, the figures were 0.3 per cent and 9.1 per cent respectively (Table 4.4).

The gap between the big four and the shareholding banks in 2003 was narrowed sharply by the reform of the Bank of China (BOC) and the Construction Bank of banks. How the reform and financial support from the central government since

Quadrupling the Chinese economy again

the end of 2003 will improve the performance of the BOC and the CBC needs to be the subject of future research.

Compared with international cases, the inefficiency of the banking system in China is even more worrying (Table 4.5).

The most serious problem facing China's banking system, however, is the huge amount of non-performing loans (NPLs). The ratio of NPLs to total loans for the big four banks combined was 16 per cent in 2004 (even after the reform of the BOC and the CBC), 5 per cent for the 12 shareholding banks and 1.3 per cent for

Table 4.4 **Profitability and non-performing loans of the big four banks and shareholding banks in China, 2002–2004** (per cent)

	ROA			ROE			NPLs		
	2002	2003	2004	2002	2003	2004	2002	2003	2004
ICBC	0.14	0.05	0.04	3.35	1.42	1.39	25.69	21.24	18.99
ABC	0.11	0.06	0.05	2.15	1.40	1.85	36.65	30.66	26.73
BOC	0.34	0.93	0.62	4.31	13.56	10.23	22.50	16.28	5.12
CBC	0.15	0.68	1.30	4.01	15.26	25.40	15.28	9.12	3.92
State-owned commercial banks total	0.18	0.38	0.45	3.54	8.29	10.99	21.41	19.74	15.57
Everbright	0.09	0.12	n.a.	2.15	3.31	n.a.	13.12	7.50	-
BC	0.18	0.52	0.09	3.88	17.06	2.60	18.53	12.60	2.91
CITIC Industrial	0.45	0.41	0.07	15.03	11.79	1.74	10.81	7.85	5.96
Huaxia	0.45	0.38	0.37	21.73	13.12	11.15	5.97	4.23	n.a.
Minsheng	0.47	0.46	0.51	15.61	17.77	18.07	2.04	1.29	1.31
Guangdong Development	0.15	0.15	0.03	5.58	6.96	1.84	n.a.	n.a.	n.a.
Shenzhen Development	0.30	0.24	0.15	11.68	10.41	6.39	10.29	8.49	n.a.
China Merchants	0.54	0.51	0.57	16.56	13.01	16.07	5.99	3.15	2.87
Fujian Industrial	0.30	0.44	0.37	7.81	14.75	12.61	3.47	2.49	2.50
Pudong Development	0.57	0.48	0.47	17.10	15.68	15.13	3.38	1.92	n.a.
Hengfeng	n.a.	0.37	0.43	n.a.	5.60	9.11	7.67	4.77	3.49
Subtotal including BC	0.32	0.40	0.25	9.07	12.92	8.25	9.50	7.92	4.93
Foreign banks in China	n.a.	n.a.	n.a.	n.a.	n.a.	n.a.	6.19	2.87	1.34

Note: ICBC = Industrial and Commercial Bank of China; ABC = Agricultural Bank of China; BOC = Bank of China; CBC = Construction Bank of China; BC = Bank of Communication.
Sources: *Almanac of China's Finance and Banking*, 1995, 2003, 2004, 2005. China Banking Regulatory Commission (http://www.cbrc.gov.cn), People's Bank of China (http://www.pbc.gov.cn).

Table 4.5　**Profitability and non-performing loans in the banking sector in some Asian countries, 1997–2002** (per cent)

	1997	1998	1999	2000	2001	2002
ROA (ROE)						
Hong Kong	18.7	11.0	18.2	18.8	15.7	15.6
	(1.8)	(1.0)	(1.6)	(1.6)	(1.4)	(1.4)
India	17.0	9.7	14.2	10.9	19.2	19.6
	(0.9)	(0.5)	(0.7)	(0.5)	(0.9)	(1)
Indonesia	−3.8	n.a.	n.a.	15.9	9.7	21.1
	(−0.3)			(0.3)	(0.6)	(1.4)
Japan	−18.6	−19.2	2.7	−0.7	−10.4	−14.5
	(−0.6)	(−0.7)	(0.1)	(0)	(−0.5)	(−0.6)
South Korea	−12.5	−80.4	−34.0	−7.0	15.8	13.1
	(-0.6)	(−3.0)	(-1.5)	(−0.3)	(0.7)	(0.6)
Taiwan	11.2	9.5	6.9	5.1	4.0	−5.2
	(0.9)	(0.8)	(0.6)	(0.4)	(0.3)	(−0.4)
NPLs						
Hong Kong	1.3	4.3	6.3	5.2	4.9	3.7
India	n.a.	7.8	7	6.6	4.6	2.2
Indonesia	0.3	11.8	8.1	13.6	9.9	4.5
Japan	2.7	5.1	5.3	5.8	9.2	7.4
South Korea	2.9	4.8	12.9	8.0	3.4	2.5
Taiwan	2.4	3.0	4.0	5.2	6.2	4.1

Source: Allen, F., Qian, J. and Qian, M., 2006. *China's Financial System: past, present and future*, Working Paper, University of Pennsylvania.

foreign banks in China. At the end of 2005, the total for NPLs was still 1.3 billion yuan—7.2 per cent of GDP for that year and 8.6 per cent of the total outstanding loans, with 10.5 per cent for the big four banks, 4.2 per cent for the 12 shareholding banks and 1 per cent for foreign banks in mainland China. The figure of 8.6 per cent is still much higher than the corresponding number in other Asian countries, except during and immediately after the East Asian financial crisis.

As we look into the immediate future, more and more foreign banking institutions will enter the Chinese market, introducing cheap foreign capital and advanced management technology. The banks that might be affected the most are the big four banks. If the foreign banks attract a large share of deposits due to better service and greater efficiency, and if NPLs in the domestic banking system continue to accumulate, the ratio of NPLs in the big four banks—even in the domestic banking system—might increase again, instead of declining, as is the current trend, and could result in the bankruptcy of individual banks. This could even spark a crisis in the banking sector that could severely disrupt economic growth and social stability.

To avoid this disastrous possibility, it is necessary for the government to invest capital in the big four and other banks to reduce NPL stock, to help improve the performance of the domestic banking system in the short term. The huge foreign reserves can fund this solution. Such actions can, however, create severe problems of incentives for the banks to accumulate new NPLs. The government must, therefore, commit not to do this again, although it is hardly possible for the government not to bailout banks in financial distress in the future.

Deeper reforms in the financial system are required in the long term. The most important reform is to adjust banking composition by allowing free entry for new regional banks so as to allocate savings more efficiently in the economy. As Lin et al. (2006c) argue, only by improving the allocation efficiency of investments can the financial system reduce its exposure to financial crisis.

One main reason for the huge stock of NPLs in the big four banks is that they have made a dominant part of their loans to large state-owned enterprises (SOEs), but it is the non state-owned businesses that have been the most active part of the economy. Such businesses have mostly followed the comparative advantage of endowments in the Chinese economy and usually have been small or medium-sized firms. As small and medium-sized regional banks have greater comparative advantage than large banks and financial markets to serve such businesses, developing small and medium-sized regional banks to provide more efficient and convenient services to the non-state-owned sector can fundamentally improve the performance of the banking sector and the whole financial system and support economic growth.

Local protection and market segmentation

It is well known that in China's labour, capital and goods markets there is serious segmentation, which distorts price signals and impairs the market mechanism for resource allocation. Since the mid 1980s, China's market segmentation has been characterised mainly as preventing local goods or basic raw materials from flowing into other regions. However, segmentation began to extend into the labour and capital markets as the buyers' market came forth in the mid 1990s.

The segmentation in China's labour is the result of local government motivations to deal with the emerging problems of employment and social stability. The segmentation in China's capital market is rooted in local government ambitions to accelerate regional economic development for its own sake. In the past, when market segmentation was at its peak, many local governments even discriminated in favour of newly set-up endemic firms against acquired local firms and, at the same time, they took all kinds of action to restrain local firms from investing in other regions.

Now, in order to avoid policy constraints from the central government against local protection and market segmentation, more and more local governments are beginning to implement more implicit measures such as technical barriers and repeated check-ups for their own sake.

Obviously, local protection and market segmentation will handicap the process of trade liberalisation and the integration of markets and will impair the development of society and the economy to a large extent. This will be more damaging as China moves beyond the turning point of economic development at which labour becomes scarce, when, more than ever, continued rapid economic growth requires resources to move to where they are most productive.

To quadruple the Chinese economy between between 2000 and 2020, the Chinese central government must take measures to overcome local protection and market segmentation. These measures include shifting the government's functions into the role of providing mainly public goods and services; restraining the revenue of local governments to match their social obligations; constructing a scientific, normative and quantifiable system of achievement evaluation to assess and regulate local government behaviour; and upgrading infrastructure to enhance the linkages between different economic regions in China.

Sustainability of export growth

From 1980 to 2002, China's total exports rose from US$18 billion to US$438 billion (Table 4.6), with an average growth rate of 15 per cent. China's rising exports have put many other countries under tremendous pressure. Since 1996, China has been the leading target of international anti-dumping campaigns. Since China entered the World Trade Organization (WTO) in 2001, there have been 1,800 cases of anti-dumping, 250 of them against China. With 14 per cent of global anti-dumping actions, China ranks first in the world for cases directed against it.

China's comparative advantage will change with the upgrading of its factor endowment and economic growth. There will be an increasing overlap in trade between China and industrial countries because of the structural adjustment of China's export composition has been driven by changes in its comparative advantage. In the next decade, there will be more and more cases of anti-dumping measures against Chinese exports.

Table 4.6 **The structural changes of Chinese export composition, 1998–2004** (US$ billion and per cent)

	1998	1999	2000	2001	2002	2003	2004
Total exports	183.7	194.9	249.2	266.1	325.6	438.2	593.3
Primary products	20.5	19.9	25.5	26.3	28.5	34.8	40.6
Industrial finished products	163.2	175.0	223.7	239.8	297.1	403.4	552.8
Share of primary products (per cent)	11.2	10.2	10.2	9.9	8.8	7.9	6.8
Share of industrial finished products (per cent)	88.8	89.8	89.8	90.1	91.2	92.1	93.2

Source: National Bureau of Statistics of China, 2005a. *China Statistical Yearbook 2005*, China Statistics Press, Beijing.

Meanwhile, since most developing countries are adjusting their development strategies and will adopt a comparative advantage following (CAF) strategy, international competition in exports of mainly labour-intensive products between China and other developing countries will intensify. As labour becomes more scarce and valuable, China's comparative advantage will shift into more capital-intensive and technologically complex production. China's production and exports will need to shift in that direction if strong export growth is to be sustained. Successful transition of industrial structure will ease competition from other developing economies shifting to export-oriented strategies.

It has been demonstrated that when China's exports increase by 10 per cent, the growth rate of GDP rises by 1 per cent, and the contribution of exports to economic growth is remarkable (Lin and Li 2003). Therefore, it is necessary for China to maintain sustainable export growth in the future in order to quadruple the economy successfully between 2000 and 2020.

China should play a more active role in the international division of labour, requiring the government to adjust its development strategy in accordance with China's comparative advantage. As international competition has become fiercer, there will be an increase in new protectionism obstacles and anti-dumping cases initiated against Chinese exports. The following measures should be taken immediately: the development of new products and the improvement of services that are consistent with the evolution of China's comparative advantage; cultivating new markets abroad; the establishment of joint ventures or branches abroad;

carrying out exchanges and dialogue with industrial-country counterparts; quick responses to anti-dumping cases against China.

Income distribution

Since the mid 1980s, the average income gap between urban and rural areas has increased. China's urban–rural average income ratio reached its highest point of 2.6 in 1994, but began to decrease after 1995; it was 2.2 in 1997, a 38 per cent reduction from 1994 (Figure 4.2). The gap increased again, however, after 1997. In 2000, the ratio of the average income of urban people to that of rural people increased by 25 per cent relative to that in 1997. If we take government subsidies for health care and education received by urban people into account, the urban–rural income gap would be even larger. At the same time, the income differentials among urban residents and regional income disparity are also widening.

The rise in the urban–rural average income gap will hamper human capital investment by rural people, and in turn impair human capital accumulation in China, because most Chinese are rural residents. Human capital accumulation is another engine for economic growth (Lucas 1998). Rapid human capital accumulation is essential for China to maintain sustainable economic growth in

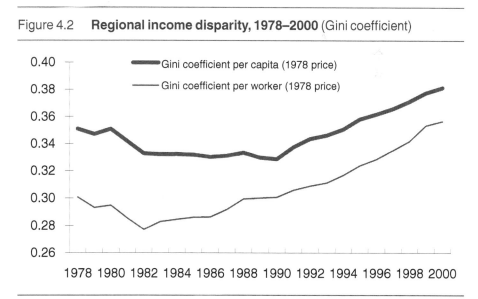

Figure 4.2 **Regional income disparity, 1978–2000** (Gini coefficient)

Sources: National Bureau of Statistics of China, various years. *China Statistical Yearbook*, China Statistics Press, Beijing, and produced statistics for all provinces.

the future. China's widening income gap is likely to trigger social instability after 2010 if the government finds no effective solution to end the disparity.

The Chinese government should take effective measures immediately to end the income disparity, including: adjusting development strategies so that more and more people can find a formal job and can share equally the benefits brought by economic development; redistributing income by a fiscal transfer payment system so as to reduce the gap between rich and poor; reforming and improving the tax system, such as by imposing a property estate tax, luxury tax and estate tax; avoiding a regressive tax system; reforming the Household Registration System (the *hukou* system) and treating peasants working in urban areas equally as urban residents.

Employment

Until recently, China has been faced with tremendous employment pressures. Growth in excess of the objective of 7.2 per cent has helped to ease the pressure in recent years.

The maintenance of 7.2 per cent per annum or higher rates of growth increasingly will require a better educated and trained labour force, to support a more sophisticated industrial structure.

Economic development and upgrading of industrial structures require more and more workers with relatively higher levels of educational attainment. Success in this endeavour will help to ensure that the requirements for unskilled workers will provide employment for rural workers with low levels of educational attainment.

China is now facing an imbalance in employment structures, which needs to be corrected.

Corruption

According to Transparency International's *Global Corruption Report 2005*, China is one of the countries suffering relatively severe corruption—and corruption ratings in China are thought to have deteriorated since the early 1980s. There are two kinds of corruption in China: rent-seeking and resource-losing corruption. Rent-seeking corruption was pervasive during the period when a two-track system for price-setting was being initiated.

After most product prices were gradually liberalised, the discrepancy between the prices of means of production set by state plans and the prices of goods set by the market narrowed on a large scale. As a result, this kind of corruption faded away. Considerable amounts of resources (including land, funds and licences) are still under the control of the government. Currently, most rent-seeking corruption comes from the land market through illegal land licensing, arbitrarily reducing the price of land for private interest, and by changing the purpose of land use to permit significant trading of land on the illegal market. What is worse, a lot of arable land is appropriated by local governments secretly and fraudulently.

Resource-losing corruption involves the private appropriation of state assets. For example, up to the end of 2000, 51 per cent of firms under reform (*gaizhi*) (32,140 firms) did not repay their loans. These unpaid loans, which amounted to 185 billion yuan, which accounted for 32 per cent of all loans to firms and represented as much as 2.1 per cent of that year's GDP. That so many loans were not repaid cannot be attributed only to the low efficiency of state-owned enterprises; there must already have been resource-losing corruption in the reform of state-owned enterprises.

Corruption does not produce any goods and services by itself. It merely redistributes wealth from the public to a few monopolists, acts as a drain on assets owned by the State to some special interest group, or illegally transfers public resources to private use. Corruption might generate the wrong signals for resource allocation and reduce the rate of capital accumulation, thereby undermining economic development. Moreover, too much corruption can lead to social turbulence in the future.

In order to eliminate the scourge of corruption, much effort should be devoted to increasing government transparency, strengthening supervision of the appointment and promotion of officials, and ensuring fair competition among different parties seeking public resources.

Economic fluctuations

In the past two decades, China has experienced rapid growth accompanied by periodic economic fluctuations. In the years of rapid growth, the annual growth rates of GDP reached as high as 13–15 per cent; while during the years of slow-down, the annual growth rates of GDP were only 4 per cent. Since the end of 1978, China has experienced five economic cycles. Each cycle is self-propelling: vigour leads to disorder, disorder leads to retrenchment, retrenchment leads to stagnation, and stagnation leads to decentralisation.

There is no doubt that the international economy has to pay a great deal for cyclical fluctuations in economic growth. It is not unreasonable to fear that one day the national economy might suddenly collapse. Should this happen, China could not realise its goal of quadrupling the economy by 2020. It is worth examining as an example of the challenges of macroeconomic instability the policy responses to the boom conditions that emerged in 2003.

In 2003, China's growth rate of GDP reached 9.1 per cent, and can be attributed to a surge in investment that focused mainly on three industries: the real estate sector, automobile manufacturing and the construction material industry. The investment growth rate in the real estate sector was 29.7 per cent, in automobile manufacturing 87.2 per cent, and in the construction material industry 96.5 per cent for steel, 92.5 per cent for electrolytic aluminium and 121.9 per cent for cement.

The investment growth rate jumped from 11.8 per cent in 2002 to 26.7 per cent in 2003. The fundamental reason for this rapid investment growth lies in the fast expansion of bank loans. In recent years, the Chinese government decided to list the four big state-owned banks, so that they could meet the challenges from the admission of foreign banks to operate on RMB business. Banks not only needed to increase the statutory capital ratio to 8 per cent, as required by the Basel Agreement, but needed to decrease the bad debt ratio from 23 per cent in early 2003 to 15 per cent in order to be listed. The simplest way to reduce the bad debt ratio is to extend credit so as to enlarge the denominator. As a result, banks were active in lending their money to huge investments such as projects in the real estate sector, automobile manufacturing and the construction material industry.

Had the rapid investment growth in these sectors continued in this economic cycle, the consequences would have been even more severe than in 1992. China's economy went through a heated investment period in 1993–96, leaving behind long-term shortages and signalling a period of over-production. What is worse, because the investment surge in this round is higher than before and focuses mainly on a few industries, there will be greater oversupply and deflation after the completion of these investments. Government tightening of policies after credit expansion will always lead enterprises to incur serious losses, which will turn latent and probable credit risk into real bad debt, thus further enlarging the bad debt ratio. The ever-growing bad debt ratio could not be controlled even if the savings rate in China was maintained at high levels in the future.

The credit expansion and contraction caused by direct governmental control on credit and investment is the unique cause of China's macroeconomic fluctuation. It is therefore urgent for the Chinese government to loosen direct controls on credit and investment to create a sound development environment. This cannot happen without thorough reform of the financial system. The fundamental solutions are to accelerate financial reform, realise market interest rates, commercialise

Table 4.7 **Main indicators of state-owned enterprises during 1997–2004**

Main indicators	1997	1998	1999	2000	2001	2002	2003	2004
Consolidated number of enterprises (10,000 units)	26.2	23.8	21.7	19.1	17.4	15.9	14.6	13.6
Profit-making enterprises (per cent)	34.1	31.3	46.5	49.3	48.8	50.1	47.4	48.0
Return on total assets (per cent)	2.3	2.1	2.7	3.3	3.3	3.6	3.5	4.5
Profit margin on net assets (per cent)	1.7	0.4	2.1	4.9	4.6	5.7	6.7	9.6
Profit margin on sales (per cent)	1.2	0.3	1.7	3.8	3.7	4.4	3.0	6.1
Assets–liabilities ratio (per cent)	67.1	65.5	65.4	66	65	64.8	65.9	65.7
Ratio of unhealthy assets to equity (per cent)	22.6	24.8	27.5	31.4	31.2	31.2	28.5	-

Source: *Finance Yearbook of China*, 2005.

the banking system, and regulate investment, consumption and bank deposits via interest rates to enable efficient enterprises to attract investments.

The main hurdle for financial reform lies in protection of state-owned enterprises, because at present the survival of many such enterprises depends on the support of cheap bank loans. The reform of state-owned enterprises has thus become the key to developing the economy and quitting the traditional economic cycle.

State-owned enterprises

State-owned enterprises play a vital role in China's economy, so reforming them will affect China's long-term growth (Garnaut , Song). Such reform has been far from successful; indeed, more serious problems have begun to emerge, including low profitability, high asset–liability ratios, increasing losses of the state-owned enterprises, and the drain of state-owned assets.

By the end of 2004, 136,000 or nearly half of all state-owned enterprises were making a loss (Table 4.7). In the eight years to 2004, the average return to total assets of the state-owned enterprises was only 3.2 per cent, far below the interest rate for the same period, 5 per cent. At the same time, the assets–liability ratio rose continuously from 30 per cent in 1980, to 40 per cent in 1985, 60 per cent in 1990 and recently to more than 65 per cent, on average.

If we take into account the ratio of non-performing assets to equity, which remained at a high of nearly 30 per cent recently, China's state-owned enterprises are in danger of insolvency. Meanwhile, the loss of state-owned assets has become more serious. According to the report of the National Audit Office of China in 2000, the total losses of state-owned assets were up to 22.08 billion yuan in 1,290 state-owned enterprises, 3.4 per cent of the total assets of these enterprises.

The root cause for the various problems in the state-owned enterprises is policy burdens resulting from China's CAD strategy in favour of heavy industries. These burdens can be divided into strategic policy burdens and social policy burdens. The former refers to the high production costs of the state-owned enterprises resulting from implementation of the government's development strategy for entry into heavy industries or the capital-intensive sector. State-owned enterprises following that strategy will enter or invest in the industries and production sectors that are not in accordance with the comparative advantages of China's economy, resulting in the enterprises in these sectors being non-viable.

Social policy burdens are the additional social functions assumed by the state-owned enterprises, such as worker redundancies and providing schooling, medical services and pensions to employees. State-owned enterprises can use policy burdens as an excuse to bargain for more government support and, because it is hard for the government to shun such responsibility, the firm's budget constraints become soft (Lin and Tan 1999).

Moreover, when a developing country adopts a catch-up strategy, the government cannot know how large subsidies need to be due to information asymmetry. Firms in the priority sector will have incentives to use their viability problem as an excuse and use resources to lobby government officials not only for more *ex ante* policy favours, such as access to low-interest loans, tax reductions, tariff protection and legal monopolies, but for *ex post* administrative assistance, such as more preferential loans or tax arrears. The economy will be full of rent-seeking activities and corruption. When soft budget constraints exist, firms will face no pressure to improve productivity and efficiency will be low.

In essence, the problems undermining China's long-term growth—including energy and land resources, education, capital, technological progress, the inefficient financial (banking) sector, market segmentation and local protection, sustainability of export growth, income distribution, employment, corruption and economic fluctuations—all originated from the problems in the state-owned enterprises. Therefore, substantial reform of these enterprises is essential for Chinese economic growth and development in the future.

Since the root causes for various problems with the state-owned enterprises are policy burdens, which resulted from China's CAD strategy, it is natural to conclude that the prerequisite for successful state-owned enterprise reform and for China successfully quadrupling its economy between 2000 and 2020 is to cancel the CAD strategy and release the state-owned enterprises from policy burdens.

Conclusions

This chapter's discussion of the problems that could block sustained, rapid economic growth suggest that there are solutions. If further reform succeeds in correcting the largest weaknesses, of state-owned businesses and of financial institutions including banks, the government's ambition of at least 7.2 per cent will be easily met. Indeed, in these circumstances, China would look forward to doing better than quadrupling of GDP in 20 years. At the beginning of the reforms, Deng Xiaopeng expressed that China would quadruple the volume of its economic output between 1980 and 2000. In the event, the quadrupling was achieved three to four years ahead of time. With active measures to remove barriers to growth under each of the 12 headings listed above, there is every reason to expect, again, China to achieve its objective well ahead of time.

Acknowledgments

I am grateful for the helpful comments of Ross Garnaut and Ligang Song and the capable assistance of Zhang Pengfei, Pan Shiyuan, Xu Zhaoyang, Sun Xifang, Li Feiyue and Ren Min.

Note

[1] The high profits from human capital investment might have some bearing on the low education levels.

5

China's interaction with the global economy

Nicholas R. Lardy

A key element of Deng Xiaoping's economic reform strategy was to abandon the Maoist ideal of national self-sufficiency and start reaping the gains available from participating in global trade. The result has been an expansion of China's trade that has outpaced the growth of its domestic economy and far exceeded the growth of global trade for almost three decades. Since reforms were launched, imports and exports as a share of China's economy have expanded greatly and China's share of global trade has grown tenfold. In 2004, China surpassed Japan to become the world's third largest trading economy, a remarkable achievement given that China's economy is only two-fifths the size of Japan's.[1] This chapter analyses two issues: China's bilateral trade with the United States and China's exchange-rate policy.

The origins of China's trade surplus with the United States

China's ever-growing bilateral trade surplus with the United States has, appropriately, received increasing attention in recent years as China's global trade and current account surpluses have increased. In 2005, after rising modestly for several years, China's global trade surplus tripled to more than US$100 billion. Meanwhile, its current account surplus soared to US$161 billion—more than 7 per cent of GDP—making China, in dollar terms, the world's second largest surplus country, only slightly behind Japan.[2] In the first half of 2006, China's trade surplus expanded by about 50 per cent and it was on track to become the world's largest current account surplus country.

China's bilateral surplus with the United States increased steadily in the 1990s and, by 2003, China moved into the unenviable position of being the single largest source of the overall United States balance of trade deficit. By 2005, the United States bilateral deficit with China reached US$202 billion, accounting for a record 26 per cent of the total United States global trade deficit of US$782 billion. As a result, many, including some in the United States Congress, see China as having replaced Japan as the principal mercantilist trader in Asia and the major source of lost United States jobs, particularly in manufacturing.

The United States bilateral trade deficit with China presents a complex and multifaceted challenge. The analysis below takes up five potential explanations for the deficit: restrictive United States export licensing; suggestions that China restricts access to its domestic market and pursues a mercantilist trade strategy; China's low-wage advantage; China's role in Asian production networks; and the undervaluation of the Chinese currency. These five alternative explanations are not mutually exclusive; indeed, several of them might be in play at the same time.

Restrictive United States export licensing

Chinese government officials regularly assert that the bilateral trade imbalance would be substantially less if the United States approved more high-technology exports to China. Yet, because of the liberalisation of export controls over the years, very few products now require licences for export to China, so the value of potential exports for which licences are sought is quite small—and the Department of Commerce approves the majority of applications. In the 2005 fiscal year, for example, United States exporters applied for licences to export products to China valued at US$3 billion. The department approved licences covering US$2.4 billion, or 80 per cent of the total. It returned applications covering US$590 million if, for example, they were incomplete, and denied licences covering US$12.5 million in potential sales (Department of Commerce, forthcoming).

That means that if the Department of Commerce had approved all of the licences rejected in the 2005 fiscal year, United States exports to China would have increased by only US$12.5 million and the bilateral trade deficit would have been a mere 0.006 per cent smaller. If it had approved the rejected and returned applications, the bilateral deficit would have been reduced by only 0.3 per cent.[3] In sum, the frequent claim by Chinese officials that liberalising export licensing would significantly reduce the bilateral trade deficit does not seem plausible.

How open is the Chinese economy?

The most common reason given by China's critics for the large and growing United States–China trade imbalance is that China is pursuing a mercantilist trade strategy, systematically restricting access to its market while aggressively supporting exports by national firms. Certainly the flood of Chinese goods into the United States, particularly into the stores of mass merchandisers such as Wal-Mart, Target, Circuit City and Best Buy, suggests, to many observers, that China's high rate of economic growth is explained in large part by its recent export boom. But the appearance of huge volumes of Chinese goods in United States retail outlets is not sufficient to demonstrate that the Chinese economy is relatively closed to imports.

Several analytical approaches are required to examine this issue. First, of course, any evaluation of China's openness based on its trade position must be on the basis of its global trade balance or its global current account position, rather than its bilateral trade balance with the United States. There is no economic basis for preferring balanced bilateral trade; indeed, the presumption is the opposite.

For most of the reform period, China's global current account surplus has been relatively modest. For example, from 1993 to 2002, China's current account fluctuated between a deficit of 2 per cent and a surplus of 4 per cent of GDP, but the average position was a surplus of only 1.6 per cent. This was about half of Japan's average surplus of 2.9 per cent of GDP during the decade 1984–93, when its global surpluses loomed largest relative to the size of its economy. As already noted, however, China's current account position has risen sharply since 2002 and it now has become a major contributor to global economic imbalances.

Second, the Chinese government has materially reduced barriers to imports. For example, the average level of applied import tariffs dropped from more than 50 per cent in 1982 to less than 10 per cent in 2005. Compared with many developing countries, China's average import tariff rate is relatively low. China's applied import tariff rate in 2004 was 10.4 per cent, compared with rates in India, Mexico, Brazil and Indonesia of 29.1, 18, 12.4 and 6.9 per cent, respectively (Figure 5.1). Moreover, import tariff exemptions in China are so widespread that the effective tariff ratio—that is, import tariff revenue collected relative to the value of the imports—is much lower than the average applied tariff. For example, the total value of import tariffs collected as a share of the value of imports fell from about 15 per cent in the mid 1980s to only 2.2 per cent in 2004 (Figure 5.2). The effective tariff protection provided to domestic firms in China is among the lowest of any developing country.[4]

Similarly, the number of goods that the Chinese government has subjected to an import licensing requirement or a specific numerical limit, such as an import quota, has dropped precipitously. At the peak in the late 1980s, the government imposed a licensing requirement on almost half of all goods imported into China. By the eve of China's entry into the World Trade Organization (WTO) in 2000, the authorities had reduced this share to less than 4 per cent and, under the terms of China's

Figure 5.1   **Applied tariff rates, China and other emerging markets, 2004**
(per cent)

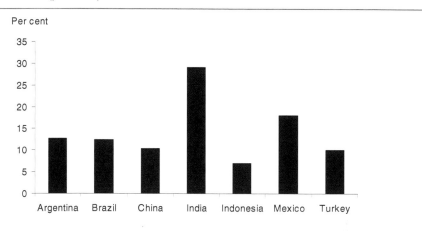

Source: World Trade Organization, 2005. *Online Statistics, Trade Profiles*. Available online at <stat.wto.org/CountryProfile/WSDBCountryPFHome.aspx?Language=E> (accessed 22 November 2005).

Figure 5.2   **China's import tariff revenue as a percentage of the value of imports, 1978–2004**

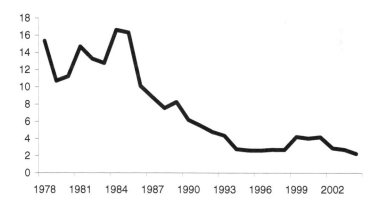

Sources: National Bureau of Statistics of China, 1982. *China Statistical Yearbook 1981*, Hong Kong Economic Information Agency, Beijing:353; National Bureau of Statistics of China, 1985. *China Statistical Yearbook 1985*, Statistical Publishing House, Beijing:494; National Bureau of Statistics of China, 2000. *China Statistical Yearbook 2000*, China Statistics Press, Beijing:258, 588; National Bureau of Statistics of China, 2005. *China Statistical Yearbook 2005*, China Statistics Press, Beijing:272, 626.

accession to the WTO in 2001, the government eliminated all remaining licensing requirements in 2005. Similarly, the government eliminated all import quotas by 2005, except those that were part of a tariff rate quota arrangement. China agreed to such arrangements for a handful of agricultural products as part of the market-opening measures it made when it joined the WTO (Lardy 2002:75–9).

Third, the extent to which an economy is open can be measured by examining the ratio of imports to GDP. This ratio has soared in China, from 5 per cent in 1978 to 30 per cent in 2005 (Figure 5.3). Thirty per cent is roughly twice the ratio of imports to GDP in the United States and more than three times the ratio in Japan. It is also higher than other geographically large developing countries such as Argentina, Brazil and India. Indeed, only geographically small economies, such as Taiwan and South Korea, have import ratios as high, or higher than China.

Finally, throughout the 1990s, China was the fastest growing export market for United States firms—a trend that accelerated from 2000 to 2005, as exports of United States firms to China rose by 160 per cent while exports to the rest of the

Figure 5.3   **Imports as a percentage of GDP in China, 1978–2005**

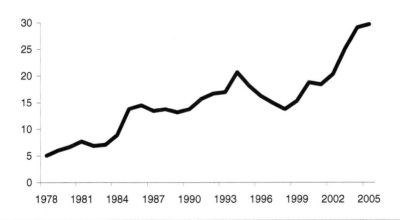

Sources: World Trade Organization, 2005. *WTO Online Statistics, Time Series*. Available online at <stat.wto.org/StatisticalProgram/WSDBStatProgramHome.aspx?Language=E> (accessed 28 November 2005); National Bureau of Statistics of China, 2005. *China Statistical Yearbook 2005*, China Statistics Press, Beijing:51; National Bureau of Statistics of China, 2006. *Table of GDP at Current Prices*. Available online at <www.stats.gov.cn/tjdt/zygg/P020060109431083446682.doc> (accessed 9 January 2006); International Monetary Fund, 2002. *IMF International Financial Statistics Yearbook 2002*, International Monetary Fund, Washington:354–5; State Administration of Foreign Exchange of China, 2006. *Table of Exchange Rates of RMB*. Available online at <www.safe.gov.cn/0430/tjsj.jsp?c_t=3> (accessed 27 February 2006).

world rose by only 10 per cent. Indeed, China alone accounted for one-quarter of the global export expansion of United States firms during that period.

In summary, it is difficult to sustain the charge that China's trade regime (as opposed to its exchange-rate policy, about which see below) reflects the traditional mercantilist approach of restricting imports. Except for very recent years, China's global current account surplus has been modest, its import tariffs are among the lowest of any developing country and the magnitude of its imports relative to the size of its economy is growing rapidly and is relatively high.

That is not to say that expanding trade has not been an important source of economic growth; it has been, but not because net exports, in an accounting sense, have been a major driver. Net exports have contributed positively to growth in only about half of the years between 1978 and 2005. Net exports fell—meaning that trade reduced economic growth—in almost as many years as they rose. Rather, trade's contribution to China's economic growth has been indirect, through its influence on China's domestic market structure. Increased openness to trade has greatly increased competition in the domestic market, which in turn has stimulated domestic firms to become more productive.

China's low-wage advantage

Some observers argue that a huge United States bilateral trade deficit with China is inevitable since it is impossible for United States firms to compete with firms with access to low-wage Chinese labour. There is no doubt that wages in China are very low compared with wages in the United States: the average monthly wage in manufacturing establishments in urban areas is only about US$120 (Banister 2004); wages in manufacturing outside urban areas and for unskilled labour are even lower. Taking into account bonuses, incentive pay and fringe benefits, the total average hourly labour cost in manufacturing in urban areas in China is about US$1, compared with almost US$30 in the United States (Bureau of Labor Statistics 2005).

Focusing simply on the level of wages or even on total labour costs, however, is misleading. Wages in China are low primarily because productivity is low. The World Bank, for example, calculates that average value added per United States manufacturing worker in 1995–99 was 28 times the Chinese level (World Bank 2002:64–6). The average unskilled Chinese worker might earn about only one-thirtieth the wage of his or her United States counterpart, but since the productivity of a Chinese worker on average is only a small fraction of that of an American worker, the Chinese firm will not be able to sell the good in question for one-thirtieth of the United States firm's price.

Moreover, wages are only one component of the overall cost of producing any good. Low wages are more likely to be a source of comparative advantage in industries where labour is a larger share of total costs—for example, shoes and apparel—than in industries such as semiconductor fabrication, in which wages are only 5 per cent of total production costs. Thus China's imports of semiconductors and microprocessors soared from US$3 billion in 1995 to US$90 billion in 2005, when China imported two-fifths of global production of these products. On the other hand, wages constitute about 20 per cent of the cost of producing apparel in the United States (Hufbauer and Yee Wong 2004:43). Firms operating in China clearly do have a comparative advantage in these products, as reflected in their high market share in countries that do not impose quotas or otherwise restrict apparel imports.

A comparison of wages in China with those in other developing countries also confirms that wages alone do not determine a nation's competitiveness. Countries in South Asia and in sub-Saharan Africa all have wages and total labour costs that are even lower than those prevailing in China, but few firms in these countries are large exporters to the United States. For many of these countries, the productivity gap *vis-à-vis* United States workers is even greater than for Chinese workers, reflecting low levels of educational attainment and other factors. In addition, many of these countries, unlike China, have failed to provide an attractive environment for foreign investors or to invest in the physical infrastructure necessary to support large volumes of international trade. India, for example, continues to impose many restrictions on inward foreign direct investment and is currently investing only one-seventh as much as China in infrastructure.

In short, the low wages of Chinese workers provide an advantage for Chinese firms in international trade, but not one that is insurmountable in many sectors where the United States maintains a comparative advantage. United States wages are among the highest in the world, but the United States remains the world's second largest exporter after Germany, another high-wage country. United States policy should be directed towards further enhancing the productivity advantage of United States workers, in order to maintain high wage rates in the United States, rather than trying to compete with Chinese exports of labour-intensive products.

China's critical role in Asian production networks

The single most persuasive explanation of the growing United States bilateral deficit is that it reflects the consolidation in China of the final assembly stage of Asian production networks. In the past two decades, the production process for a growing range of manufactured goods has become increasingly disaggregated on a geographic basis. Each country serves as the location for the portion of the production process in which it has the strongest comparative advantage. Higher-income, more technologically advanced countries have come to specialise in producing high value-added parts and components, while China, given its large pool of labour available for work in unskilled, labour-intensive operations, has increasingly become the location of choice for the final assembly of a broad range of goods, especially electronic and information technology products.

Joint ventures and wholly foreign-owned firms carry out a large portion of this assembly. Cumulative direct foreign investment in China by the end of 2005 was US$610 billion, with almost two-thirds concentrated in the manufacturing sector. Most of this investment originates in other Asian economies and is in processing and assembly operations.

Goods that are assembled from imported parts and components now account for almost 60 per cent of China's total exports and about 65 per cent of the goods China exports to the United States. When these goods are exported from China to the United States, their entire value is counted by United States Customs as imports from China. In fact, on average, about two-thirds of the value of these so-called 'processed exports' originates outside China, mostly in other Asian countries. The key point is that the geographic disaggregation of the production process for an ever-growing volume of traded goods means that the significance of bilateral trade data is much diminished today compared with an earlier era, when most production was organised vertically rather than horizontally.

China's rise as the point of final assembly for a broad range of goods is reflected in the sharp decline in the past two decades in the share of the US bilateral trade imbalance that originates in Hong Kong, Taiwan, South Korea and Japan. As these countries have moved manufacturing capacity to China—and, in the case of Japanese cars, to the United States—the share of the United States trade deficit that they account for has fallen by three-quarters, from more than 50 per cent in 1985 to less than 14 per cent in 2005, while China's share has risen from nothing to one-quarter (Figure 5.4). Between 1985 and 2005, the United States global trade deficit as a share of GDP more than doubled, reflecting a further deterioration of the United States savings–investment balance. But the share of this deficit accounted for by the combination of China, Hong Kong, Taiwan, South Korea and Japan declined by one-quarter.

Undervaluation of the Chinese currency

The fifth potential explanation for the growing United States bilateral trade imbalance with China is the undervaluation of the Chinese currency, the renminbi. It is important to note that China has had a growing trade surplus with the United

Figure 5.4   **Share of US trade deficit by region, 1985 and 2005** (per cent)

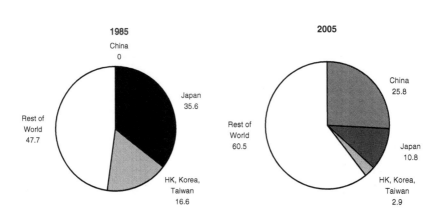

Source: US Department of Commerce, 2006. *US International Transactions Accounts Data, Table 2. US Trade in Goods*, Bureau of Economic Analysis, International Economic Accounts. Available online at <www.bea.gov/bea/international/bp_web/simple.cfm?anon=71&table_id=2&area_id=3> (accessed 30 June 2006).

States since the mid 1980s, but at least until 1994, by almost every available measurement, the renminbi was substantially overvalued rather than undervalued. Nonetheless, there can be little doubt that the increasing undervaluation of the Chinese currency since 2002 has exacerbated the underlying structural imbalance in bilateral trade—that is, China's emergence as the main point of final assembly in Asian production networks.

This means that even if the United States global trade deficit shrinks, the United States is likely to continue to have a large bilateral deficit in its trade with China.[5] After all, the bilateral deficit grew steadily as Asian manufacturers relocated to China starting in the second half of the 1980s, even as the United States global trade deficit fell from its peak of US$160 billion or 3.4 per cent of GDP in 1987 to a low of US$77 billion or 1.3 per cent of GDP in 1991. Consequently, a policy focusing on achieving a sustained reduction in the bilateral trade deficit with China will almost certainly fail. The US government should focus instead on policies that reduce China's global current account surplus.

China's currency regime

Given China's fixed peg to the US dollar, the renminbi depreciated on a real trade-weighted basis after February 2002, when the value of the dollar began to depreciate significantly *vis-à-vis* major floating currencies such as the euro, the Canadian and Australian dollars and the British pound. As a result, China's current account surplus, which had averaged only 1.6 per cent of GDP in the decade to 2002, rose moderately to 3 per cent of GDP in 2003 and to 3.6 per cent in 2004. The underlying global surplus in those years, however, was undoubtedly somewhat higher than the actual one. Since economic growth was extremely rapid, demand for imported raw materials and capital goods was growing at an above-average rate, meaning that China's global trade and current account surpluses were smaller than they otherwise would have been. In addition, starting in 2002 the full effects of the depreciation of the renminbi would raise exports and constrain imports, were not yet reflected fully in the trade balance. In 2005, as domestic demand in China softened somewhat and the effects of the renminbi's real depreciation were reflected more fully in the trade account, China's trade surplus tripled to just more than US$100 billion and the current account reached US$161 billion—7.2 per cent of GDP.[6]

In July 2005, Chinese authorities launched a reform of the exchange-rate regime that had several components: revaluing the renminbi by 2.1 per cent against the US dollar; announcing that the currency could fluctuate by up to 0.3 per cent a day and that its value would be determined increasingly by supply and demand in the market; and asserting that the renminbi would be managed against a basket of currencies rather than being pegged simply to the dollar. Since that time, the central bank has introduced a number of technical reforms that provide a more suitable market infrastructure for a flexible exchange regime.

At least through the first half of 2006, however, these reforms did little to alleviate China's large and growing external imbalance. In part, this is because the initial currency revaluation of 2.1 per cent was far too small. With fellow economist Morris Goldstein, I estimated in 2003 that the extent of undervaluation on a real trade-weighted basis was in the range of 15–25 per cent (Goldstein and Lardy 2003). By the summer of 2005, the undervaluation was more likely in the range of 20–40 per cent (Goldstein 2005).

In addition, the potential for the currency's value to move by as much as 0.3 per cent a day was theoretical—massive intervention continued to prevent the currency from appreciating. In the five months from July to December 2005, the authorities purchased an average of US$19 billion a month in foreign exchange, almost exactly the pace of intervention that occurred in the first six months of the year. As a result, the cumulative additional appreciation of the renminbi against the dollar was only 0.8 per cent. Finally, there is little evidence of pegging to a basket of currencies. China's exchange-rate system remains a heavily managed peg to the dollar, and at a little changed dollar rate (Goldstein and Lardy 2006:13).

China's large external imbalance poses a major risk to the global economy—and so does that of the United States. As a result of its large and growing current account deficits of recent years, the United States' international financial position has been transformed. Whereas until the mid 1980s the United States was a net creditor country, it has become a large net debtor. These debts now exceed one-quarter of US GDP, and, if the current account imbalances of recent years are not reduced to a more manageable level, US net debt to the rest of the world will continue to rise. Most observers believe this path is not sustainable because the foreign appetite for holding dollar-denominated assets will eventually be satiated. In addition, these large and growing US external deficits are a major cause of trade protectionism in the Congress and elsewhere in the United States.

Ultimately, the adjustment of the current large external imbalances must involve a depreciation of the US dollar, an improvement in the US national savings–investment balance, requiring that domestic demand grow more slowly than domestic output, thus making room for expanding US net exports, and a more rapid growth of domestic demand than domestic output in the rest of the world, thus leading to expanding net imports, the counterpart of expanding US net exports (Mussa 2005:175–207).

China has a key role in this process. As the world's second largest surplus country, China must allow its currency to appreciate against the dollar and it must take steps to allow a transition to a growth path driven more by domestic consumption than by further increases in its external surplus.

China is the prime candidate to lead in allowing its currency to appreciate, for several reasons. It has a huge and rising external surplus, reflecting the substantial undervaluation of its currency. In addition, the dollar has already depreciated substantially against the world's major floating currencies, but needs to depreciate by an additional 25–30 per cent in order to reduce global imbalances to a sustainable level. A substantial portion of this additional adjustment must come from Asia, where in recent years several countries, in addition to China, have intervened in the markets to prevent their currencies appreciating—thus limiting the overall depreciation of the dollar. At least in some Asian countries, appreciation has been avoided because of a concern about a loss of national competitive position to

China in third-country markets. Thus, if China were to allow its currency to appreciate significantly it likely would lead to the desired general appreciation of Asian currencies against the dollar.[7]

Moreover, if China were to continue to intervene in the market, thus allowing its currency to appreciate only at the glacial pace evident since the summer of 2005, it would increase the risk of stimulating a protectionist response in the United States and perhaps elsewhere.

Acknowledgment

This chapter is adapted from Chapter 4 of Bergsten et al. 2006.

Notes

1 As measured by the sum of imports and exports China became the world's third largest importer in 2003.
2 Japan's current account surplus in 2005 was US$164 billion.
3 These calculations ignore the fact that the licensing data are for the 12 months ending September 2005, while the trade data are for calendar year 2005.
4 When the ratio of import duties to the value of imports in China averaged 2.7 per cent in 1996–98, the ratios for Argentina, Brazil, India, Indonesia, Mexico and Turkey, respectively (for slightly varying multiple-year periods from 1996 to 2002), were 7.8, 8.4, 18.2, 1.2, 1.9 and 1.8 per cent. World Trade Organization, 2006. *Country Profiles*. Available online at <http://stat.wto.org?CountryProfiles.htm> (accessed 25 January 2006).
5 Obviously, a major US recession that massively reduced imports across the board would constitute an exception to this forecast.
6 GDP growth in 2005 moderated only slightly to 9.9 per cent compared with 10.1 per cent in 2004. However, since the contribution of net exports to growth in 2005 was at an all-time high, in the neighbourhood of one-quarter, domestic investment and/or consumption demand must have slowed significantly.
7 It should be noted that if other Asian countries were to allow their currencies to appreciate, the overall trade-weighted appreciation of the renminbi would be substantially less than its nominal appreciation against the dollar.

6

Global imbalance, China and the international currency system

Fan Gang

The US dollar has been volatile in recent decades and many observers believe it will lose a lot of its international value sooner or later. The central importance of the dollar is due to the fact that it is not just a currency for the United States—more than half of all dollar bills in circulation are held outside the borders of the United States, and almost half of United States Treasury bonds are held as reserves by foreign central banks. The US dollar is supposed to be the anchor that stabilises the global currency market. Instead, today, it is a major source of instability.

US fiscal deficits have been running high under the Bush Administration, reaching almost 3 per cent of GDP. The current account deficit is around 7 per cent of GDP, while more volatility is widely expected. The situation is challenging for the central banks of Japan, China, Korea, Taiwan and Singapore, which collectively hold about US$2.8 trillion worth of United States Treasury bonds as part of their reserves. The moment that they reduce their purchases, the value of the dollar will slip. Yet, the more they buy, the more they are exposed to a potential free-fall of the US dollar.

China has been blamed, not only by US congressmen who are understandably not familiar with either the complicated currency issues or domestic politics in any other country, but by many economists and business strategists. It has been said that the global imbalance and currency instability exists because the RMB was not revalued.[1]

How much revaluation of the RMB would be required to remove the US deficit of US$700 billion, or at least the United States-China trade deficit of US$200 billion (including Hong Kong)? Five hundred or 1,000 per cent? Of course, no one would ask for that magnitude of revaluation. Smart people would say 30–50 per cent, with the unspoken intention of suggesting another 30–50 per cent after some initial moves, then the same again and again.

This is not really a new phenomenon. It has been happening since the 'Nixon shock' in the early 1970s, and with the Plaza Accord in the 1980s. The convenient targets of blame then were the 'gold standard', the deutschmark and the Japanese yen. Now it is the turn of the Chinese renminbi.

So the question is, what are the real causes of the global imbalance and currency instability?

In this short chapter, I first take a look at what is really going on with the Chinese economy and trade balance, try to identify the sources of the current imbalance, then, as a concluding remark, rethink the possibilities of reforming the global currency system.

China's trade balance

China registered a record high trade surplus of US$101 billion and a current account surplus of US$146 billion, or about 5 per cent of GDP, in 2005.[2] Although this would apparently put more of the blame on China for the global financial imbalance and currency instability, we should look into the situation in more detail. For many reasons, 2005 was a special year for China, with the country facing a slowdown in aggregate demand after overheating in the previous two years. This was evident from the fact that the growth rate of imports was 17.4 per cent in 2005, decidedly lower than the almost 36 per cent in 2004 and 39 per cent in 2003, while the growth of exports also slowed to 28 per cent from 35 per cent in the previous year (Figure 6.1).

Except for 2005 (and maybe 2006, if my expectation is correct that China will be in a slowdown phase for some time), in most of the past 27 years, China's trade was more or less balanced, with small surpluses in some years and small deficits in others. In 2004, for example, China registered a surplus of only about US$30 billion, or about 2 per cent of GDP (Figure 6.2), as it had already been under fierce pressure for a revaluation. The previous record high trade surplus of US$43 billion occurred in 1998 when China was in a slowdown/deflation period and everyone in the world was guessing when China would devalue, while the US government was pressing China not to do so.

China's trade imbalance with the United States and the new supply chain in Asia

Why did China's trade become balanced? China not only exported, it imported—and it imported a lot. In most years, China's imports grew by double digits and, during 2003 and 2004, imports grew by almost 40 per cent per annum.

Figure 6.1 **China's import and export growth and trade balance, 2003–2006** (per cent per annum and US$ billion)

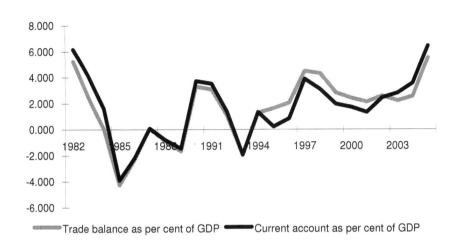

Source: National Bureau of Statistics of China.

Figure 6.2 **China's trade surplus as a percentage of GDP, 2004**

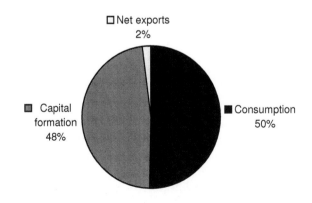

Source: National Bureau of Statistics of China.

But, if it was importing so much, why did China still run large trade surpluses with the United States? The problem here is that China imported a lot, but not from the United States. Imports came largely from rest of the world, particularly from Asian economies.

Table 6.1 shows how China ran trade deficits with almost all Asian economies except Hong Kong, which has been a major trade outlet for mainland China.

What happened in Asia was a newly emerged production–supply chain, with China as a centre of assembly and manufacturing. Figure 6.3 shows how this worked and how many things with a label 'Made in China' are really 'Made in Asia'. This is also reflected in the fact that more than 50 per cent of China's exports are from reprocessing and manufacturing sectors, of which the value-adding in China counts for only 10–20 per cent of total prices.

Table 6.1 **Trade balance between China and its neighbouring economies, 1999–2005** (US$ billion)

	1999	2000	2001	2002	2003	2004	2005
Taiwan, China	−15.6	−20.5	−22.3	−31.5	−40.4	−51.2	−58.1
Korea	−9.4	−11.9	−10.9	−13.0	−23.0	−34.4	-41.7
Japan	−1.4	0.1	2.2	−5.0	−14.7	−20.9	−16.5
Malaysia	−1.9	−2.9	−3.0	−4.3	−7.9	−10.1	−9.5
Thailand	−1.4	−2.1	−2.4	−2.6	−5.0	−5.7	−6.2
Russia	−2.7	−3.5	−5.3	−4.9	−3.7	−3.0	−2.7
Philippines	0.5	−0.2	−0.3	−1.2	−3.2	−4.8	−8.2
Singapore	0.4	0.7	0.7	−0.1	−1.6	−1.3	0.1
Indonesia	−1.3	−1.3	−1.1	−1.1	−1.3	−1.0	−0.1
India	0.3	0.2	0.2	0.4	−0.9	−1.8	−0.8
Brunei	0.0	−0.1	−0.1	−0.2	−0.3	−0.2	−0.2
Mongolia	−0.1	−0.1	−0.1	−0.1	−0.1	−0.2	−0.2
Laos	0.0	0.0	0.1	0.0	0.1	0.1	0.1
Myanmar	0.3	0.4	0.4	0.6	0.7	0.7	0.7
Pakistan	0.2	0.2	0.2	0.7	1.3	1.9	2.6
Bangladesh	0.7	0.9	0.9	1.0	1.3	1.8	2.3
Vietnam	0.6	0.6	0.8	1.0	1.7	1.8	3.1
Hong Kong, China	30.0	35.1	37.1	47.7	65.2	89.1	112.3
Total	−0.7	−4.5	−2.9	−12.5	−31.8	−39.2	−23.0
Total deficit	−33.8	−42.7	−45.4	−58.9	−102.1	−134.6	−144.2
Total surplus	33.0	38.2	42.5	46.4	70.3	95.4	121.2
World	29.2	24.1	22.56	30.4.	25.5	31.9	101.9

Sources: United Nations, WTO, PC-TAS; The Ministry of Commerce of PRC.

What Figure 6.3 does not show is another relationship: more than 50 per cent of China's exports are produced in China by foreign companies, including United States-owned companies. This fact is relevant to currency issues because one of the factors that determine the currency balance is labour costs, the major considerations for foreign investors or outsourcing companies.

Where did China's large foreign exchange reserve come from?

One of the striking phenomena central to the global imbalance problem is the surge of foreign exchange reserves, which increased by more than US$200 billion per annum in 2003, 2004 and 2005.

In 2004, for example, China's foreign exchange reserves increased by US$210 billion. This of course included the current account surplus of US$35 billion, but the rest—as much as US$175 billion—was from capital inflows. The capital that had been accumulated in other countries included US$50 billion of foreign direct

Figure 6.3 **China's bilateral trade balance, 2004** (US$ billion)

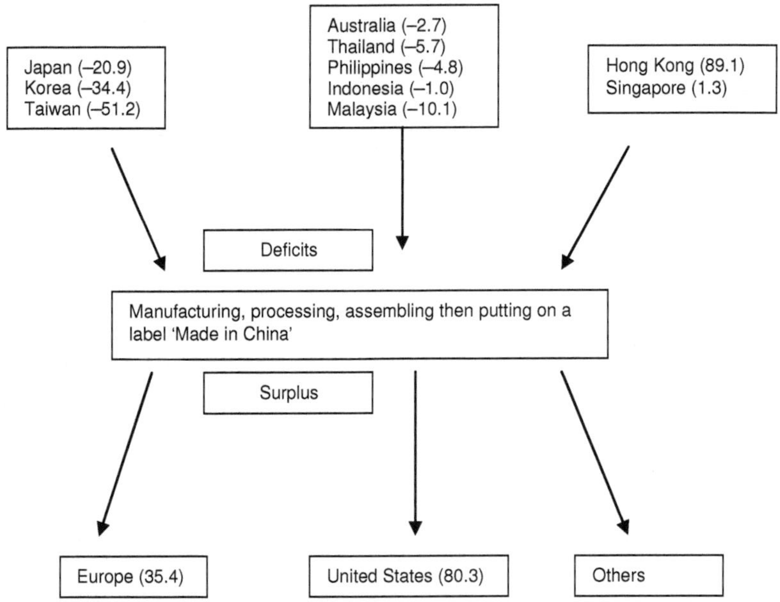

```
Japan (–20.9)         Australia (–2.7)        Hong Kong (89.1)
Korea (–34.4)         Thailand (–5.7)         Singapore (1.3)
Taiwan (–51.2)        Philippines (–4.8)
                      Indonesia (–1.0)
                      Malaysia (–10.1)
                          ↓
                       Deficits
                          ↓
   Manufacturing, processing, assembling then putting on a
   label 'Made in China'
                          ↓
                       Surplus
                          ↓
   Europe (35.4)      United States (80.3)      Others
```

Source: United Nations, World Trade Organization, PC-TAS; The Ministry of Commerce of PRC.

investment (FDI) (assuming it all came in cash and goods bought in the Chinese domestic market), and US$20 billion in increases of foreign debt and foreign security investment (Figure 6.4). Other inflows came into the economy through various channels, motivated by speculation on the revaluation of the RMB.

For example, the 'error and omission' item in China's capital account turned from negative (outflow) to positive (inflow) in 2001 as market sentiment turned from RMB devaluation to revaluation. It has been increasing steadily ever since. Also, we can see that in the current account the 'current transfer' item, which includes remittances between family members and movements between personal bank accounts, increased more rapidly after 2001 (Figure 6.5).

This situation changed slightly in 2005 and almost 50 per cent of the increase in foreign exchange reserves can be explained by the current account surplus. Capital inflows fell to US $100 billion due to calming of speculation on the RMB revaluation, particularly after China's foreign exchange regime was changed back to 'managed floating'.

The fundamental issue here is that the foreign exchange reserves in one country might not represent all of that country's national savings, but could be capital inflows from other countries, driven by market forces, including speculation.

National savings and global imbalance

The so-called global imbalance is often interpreted as the result of Chinese over-saving and American overspending. While there might be a case for American overspending, there is not necessarily a situation of over-saving in China in the sense of the international balance of payments.

Chinese do save a lot, often up to 40 per cent of GDP, but as a nation, they spend a lot too. China might not spend much on consumption (only 60 per cent of GDP), but it invests up to 40 per cent (45 per cent in 2004) of its GDP in industrial capacities, housing and public infrastructure.

Therefore, China, as a nation, buys a lot in the international market, particularly a lot of investment goods. As a result, China has pushed up resource and commodity prices on the international market in recent years.

This means that China's high saving rate might have little to do with the global imbalance—it saves, but it spends those savings on domestic investments. Sometimes China overspends, too: during 2003–04, it over-invested and therefore the economy overheated.

What is really relevant to the global imbalance problem is not the total savings of the nation, but the savings in foreign assets; that is, the current account surplus owned by the Chinese nationals.

Figure 6.4   **China's current account balance and increase in foreign exchange reserves, 1997–2005**

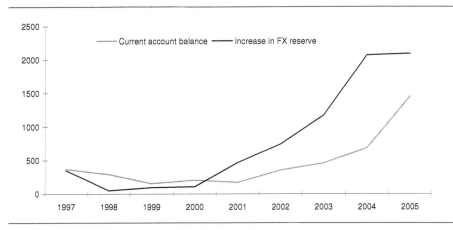

Source: National Bureau of Statistics of China.

Figure 6.5   **Speculations: error and omission and current transfer, 1997–2006**

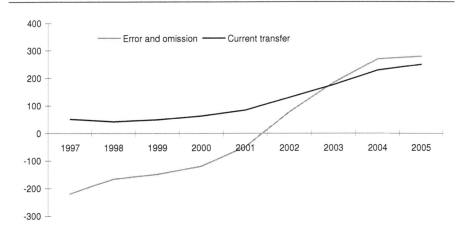

Source: National Bureau of Statistics of China.

It is important to understand that net national savings are not equal to the increase of foreign exchange reserves: increases in reserves include capital inflows, which might be the result of foreign savings (or the wealth that was saved before), not national savings. Only those parts contributed by the current account surplus are national net savings related to the international imbalance.

From this point of view, China did not have significant net national savings in past years—normally less than US$30 billion per annum. The large scale of global imbalances measured by the US trade deficits of up to US$600 billion per annum should be explained by the sum of current account surpluses of all economies everywhere, some of them (including almost all economies in Asia) running a surplus against China.

From this perspective, we can see the following. If the United States wants to blame someone for its trade deficits, it should blame every country that has a surplus, and therefore contributes to the matter directly (having a surplus against the United States) or indirectly (through countries that have a surplus with the United States). If the United States wants someone to revalue its currency in order to help reduce its deficits, it should ask every country that has a surplus.

The fact, however, is that if you want every country to revalue its currency, the real problem is not in others' currencies, but in yours. The question we should ask is not why China's RMB has not been revalued, but why, since the 1960s, the US dollar has had a tendency to devalue against everyone else? First we had the devaluation against the gold standard or against all other currencies in the 1970s (the Nixon shock), then the devaluation against the deutschmark and Japanese yen in the 1980s, and now the Chinese RMB.

'Currency asymmetry' and the persistent tendency of US dollar devaluation

Many commentators have said repeatedly in the past 40 years that under the present US-dollar standard in the global currency system, global financial stability depends on the good behaviour of the United States or the good monetary policy of the US Federal Reserve Bank.[3] Further analyses, however, show that the fundamental problem is not in US policies, but in the global currency system, which forces the United States to follow a certain pattern of behaviour. This has been an issue since the 1960s, but we still need to pay some attention to it otherwise we might fail to identify the real source of imbalance.

The breakdown of the Bretton Wood System and the de-linking of the US dollar from the gold standard in 1971 created a global currency system without a 'neutral standard' (such as gold) other than a national currency (that is, the US dollar).[4]

From then on, the world had major asymmetry, as it divided all nations into two categories: nations that issued their own currency, which serves at the same time as international currency (the United States), and nations that issue only their own currency and use the US dollar in international financial markets.

On the one hand, this arrangement of currency asymmetry has its positive effects. The United States is the largest and strongest economy with the most efficient financial markets in the world. The world financial system needs someone strong enough to play the role of anchor against the torrents of the global market. The unstable economies, such as developing countries, would like to hold some commonly trusted assets to increase their credibility in the international financial market. In one sense, Japan and China, which are the two largest foreign exchange reserve holders, do not finance US debts; to a certain extent they are paying the seigniorage of the United States by using the US dollar as their security against their own weakness in economic and financial systems, in the form of asset bubbles (Japan), or non-performing loans in the domestic banking sector (Japan and China), or massive underemployment of the rural labour force in the process of economic transformation (China).

It is also seen as convenient to have a national currency (the US dollar) to serve these purposes since it might be much cheaper than if international public goods, such as an international currency, were provided by an expensive international bureaucracy, provided that the United States was a good anchor.

On the other hand, such a currency asymmetry has negative consequences. The government of any country has the right to print money to stimulate domestic demand when growth is weak. But it has to bear the negative consequences, such as inflation and internal financial instability. Financial crises occur because of irresponsible domestic policies leading to high fiscal and current account deficits (or 'twin deficits'). However, the country that prints international money might face less penalties: along with the roughly 50 per cent of total printed papers and 50 per cent of US dollar-denominated financial assets used or held by all other economies,[5] the financial risks are spread over or externalised to other corners of the world. As a result, it seems that no matter how large the US fiscal deficits are, no matter how loose monetary policies and how much the excessive liquidity provided are, the United States is not likely to run into financial crisis that other countries have faced.

This might delude, if not corrupt, people and policymakers in the anchor country, as they might not see it as their problem that they run high deficits and print more money when the bad consequences become the problem of 'others'. Therefore, such a system would naturally result in the persistent fiscal deficits and/or over-provision of liquidity that we have seen in the United States since the 1960s.

From this perspective, the US twin deficits problem is not even a policy issue—it is an institutional issue—not of the US domestic institutions, but of international financial institutional arrangements. In one sense, the United States is subject to a kind of soft-budget constraint, and this external condition softens domestic policy discipline and results in excessive liquidity in the domestic market and the world.

Meanwhile, other countries might face greater financial risks. The huge stock of (oversupplied) financial assets denominated in US dollars moves around, knocking down the doors of developing countries, which still have fragile domestic systems and are incapable of handling the risks that the liberalised financial market and free capital flows might bring to them.

Many countries have, however, been seduced into welcoming more capital flows because those loans or portfolio investments were so attractive to the capital-scarce economies and they looked so cheap. When the trade deficits were financed by the provision of more cheap dollars (the present magnitude of capital flows is related to the previous printing of money), the other economies might overheat and have to face the consequences of overcapacity of production and oversupply. The so-called global imbalance today seems much more dangerous for other countries than it is for the United States.

Currency asymmetry is reflected most clearly in the following fact: when the US dollar devalues, US foreign assets appreciate and US domestic assets do not depreciate; meanwhile, for all other countries using the dollar as a denominating currency, if you devalue your currency, your assets depreciate. That is, while everyone else might lose by devaluation, the United States only gains from it. No wonder devaluation for the United States is such a temptation (Table 6.2).

The problems created by the US-dollar standard currency system have been debated by many people for a long time. History is repeating itself today in the new circumstances between the United States and China, in a similar manner to what happened between the United States and Europe in the 1960s and between the United States and Japan in the 1970s and 1980s. This history shows that it is not a problem of policy, but of institutions.

Effective exchange rate and real exchange rate: what are the possible responsibilities of developing countries for global imbalance?

As economics shows, two factors play a role in determining changes of real effective exchange rates and therefore the trends of exchange rates—the differences of inflation rates between two countries, and the differences of wage changes related to labour productivity changes between two countries.

Table 6.2 **Asymmetry in asset value changes by devaluation**

	United States	Any other country
Foreign assets	Up	Up
Domestic assets	Unchanged	Down

If country A's inflation is higher than B's, A's currency has to depreciate or be overvalued. Productivity changes might vary from country to country during different periods, however, as long as their wages can be adjusted fully to the extent of the productivity changes, the real exchange rate will remain unchanged. Otherwise, the country whose wage increase is less than productivity change should appreciate its currency; if not, its currency is undervalued.

In the previous section, we were dealing with the factors that might cause changes in effective exchange rates, that is, the factors of inflation. The existing currency arrangement, which makes the United States run high fiscal deficits and provide excessive liquidity to the world, has resulted in higher inflation rates in the United States than in some other countries, such as China, in past years. As a result, the US dollar tends to devalue against the RMB (Figure 6.6).

The main conclusions we can draw from the above arguments are that

- if we consider the financial factors only, the current problem is not RMB revaluation, but US dollar devaluation. This is the major cause of the current imbalance.
- this means that RMB revaluation will not solve the problem of United States deficits, not only because China's surplus is not equivalent to United States deficits, as we have seen in previous sections, but because the real root of the problem does not lie in China. United States inflation continues due to the loose monetary policies of the United States.
- if China can do something in this regard, it would only be to race against the United States in creating inflation or printing money. China might not want to do this because China does not print international money so it has to bear all the negative consequences of inflation within its own boundaries.

If, however, we consider productivity/real wage factors and think of the real exchange changes, the picture becomes more complicated and China is not completely innocent of causing the current problems. The issue is that, while in the United States wages increase basically up to the level of productivity changes (about 3 per cent per annum), China's wages seem more sticky. Since the early 1990s, China's labour productivity has improved at the annual average rate of

Figure 6.6   **Inflation: China and United States differential, 1997–2005**

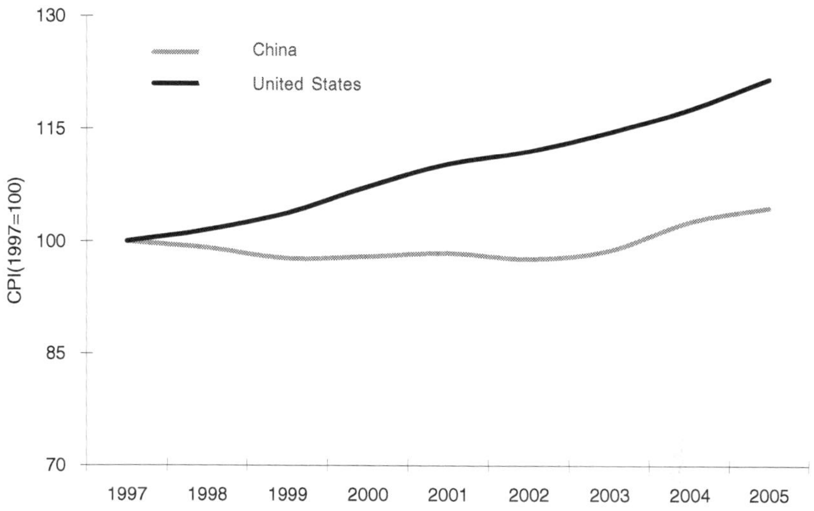

Sources: National Bureau of Statistics of China, various years. *China Statistical Yearbook*, China Statistics Press, Beijing.

10.41 per cent (Figure 6.7; McKinnon 2005[6]), thanks to reforms and technological progress. Wages, however, seem to have increased more slowly than that they increased at an annual average rate of 9.8 per cent in the manufacturing sector. This is indeed a factor that might make the RMB undervalued, although only by less than 1 percentage point annually.

Why are wages in China more sticky than in the United States? Is this because of Chinese government control? These days the Chinese government seems to be too worried about the slow increase of blue-collar wages as income disparities widen and social stability is threatened. The real reason behind the wage stickiness in China is market forces in the labour market.

Although about 200 million rural labourers have been reallocated from agricultural to the industrial and service sectors, earning about US$1,000 a year, there are another 200 million or more people still in the countryside earning about US$400 a year and eager to move to urban areas to look for better-paid jobs. Job competition and still unlimited labour supply sees Chinese wages changing more slowly than labour productivity gains (this also explains the higher capital gains for foreign investment and domestic savings, and increasing income disparities during this stage of

Figure 6.7   **China's real wage and labour productivity changes, 1994–2004**

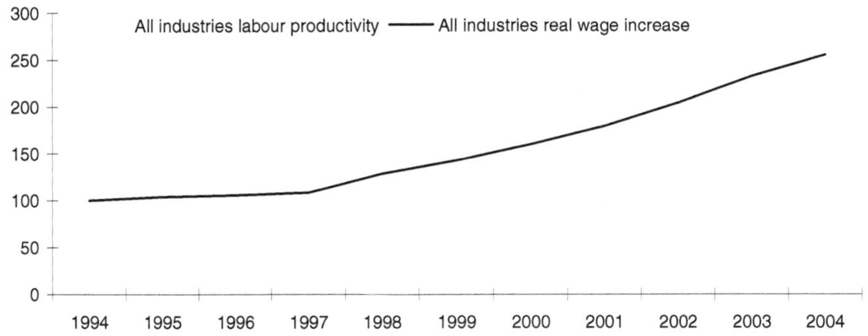

[Chart showing two lines, "All industries labour productivity" and "All industries real wage increase", rising from about 100 in 1994 to about 255 in 2004, with the steepest increase after 1997.]

Sources: National Bureau of Statistics of China, various years. *China Statistical Yearbook*, China Statistics Press, Beijing.

industrialisation and development, just as most countries have experienced in history).

So what are we doing at this point? We are blaming poor rural Chinese labourers for the global imbalance! This sounds ridiculous, but it reveals that there is another global issue—that is, the need for poverty reduction and economic development in poor countries. We know that these issues are related to currency problems, but they are even more important.

Of course, the analysis in this chapter shows that China has some responsibility for the imbalance and it calls for a revaluation of the RMB. It also shows that a reasonable revaluation of the RMB should not be more than the difference between the changes in wages and the increase of Chinese productivity. In a normal year, it might count for less than 1 per cent, not enough to solve the US deficit problem. The main cause of the global imbalance lies in currency asymmetry, which is out of China's control.

Concluding remarks

China's role in the global imbalance

Within the current global monetary system, characterised by a currency asymmetry that sees the United States providing excessive liquidity to the world, global imbalance will persist, and the global market will continue to face high volatility. China cannot be said to be the cause of this imbalance.

China might well have contributed to global imbalance through slow wages rising growth when compared with productivity growth, via the effective exchange rate mechanism. The renminbi, in this context, could be undervalued at about 1 per cent a year. China certainly has to face up to its responsibility in addressing global imbalance, but it must do so with due consideration to the task of poverty reduction and raising the living standard of its rural poor.

From this point of view a 'managed float' is a correct exchange rate regime for a country such as China. In today's global monetary system of currency asymmetry, a fully floating exchange regime for many developing countries means that they bear the major consequences of the liquidity glut created in the United States, or unilaterally bear the burden of adjustment for reducing global imbalance if the United States refuses to do anything.

Time to think again about alternatives to the currency asymmetry

From a policy point of view, the policy implication of the currency asymmetry is simple: if this asymmetry is not removed, the situation could continue to worsen. The US dollar is no longer a stable anchor in the global financial system, nor is it likely to become one, therefore, it is time to look for alternatives.

Ideally, there should be an international currency standard that is truly independent of the self-interests of participating countries, but providing common benefits to all. It should not be the currency of any particular country no matter how strong or dominant it is in the world market.

Here the 'gold standard' readily comes to mind again. Gold is not something that a government can print at will. A gold standard is totally impartial as well as unsparing when it comes to punishing those who are fiscally irresponsible and the profligate. And at least with a gold standard the global imbalance caused mainly by the US dollar's tendency to depreciate would not be interpreted or misunderstood as another currency's failure to appreciate. Critics of the gold standard have repeatedly (and correctly) pointed out that it is a rigid system, which leaves no room for policy action, however prudent and sensible.

A second alternative that has often been suggested is some form of 'international currency', governed by a truly disinterested body tasked with the job of maintaining global financial stability.[7] This could be started using the International Monetary Fund's special drawing rights as the reserve currency unit. One recent effort to think about alternatives is the World Currency Unit (WCU), which would be based on the inflation-adjusted real GDP of major economies (Ho 2006). It is suggested that governments and private firms issue bonds denominated with the WCU against market risks and hold these bonds as part of their reserve assets, as the first step towards a true global currency.

The gold standard and an international currency represent two ends of the spectrum. Both ends are extreme: the gold standard is extremely rigid, whereas a genuine international currency might prove to be unrealistically utopian. A practical answer might lie somewhere in between.

This highlights the core problem of our age: the lack of accountable global governance and insufficient provision of global public goods in a rapidly globalising world.

As stopgap measures, there are some regional efforts being made to deal with the problem. For example, encouraged partially by the success of the euro, Asians are trying to take collective action. In early May 2006, the Asian Development Bank held its annual general meeting in the Indian city of Hyderabad. At the meeting, the finance ministers of China, Japan and South Korea met with their counterparts from ASEAN and announced that they would sponsor a research project 'Towards greater financial stability in the Asian region: exploring steps to create regional monetary units'.

An Asian currency unit (ACU) would be an index that seeks to capture the value of a hypothetical Asian currency by taking a weighted average of several key regional currencies. The weight of a particular currency in the index could be determined by the size of the economy and the volume of its total trade. The reason why progress is likely to be quite fast in this development is an unusual consensus between China and Japan. While Japan has championed this idea since the 1997–98 financial crisis, China has been reluctant to be involved in a scheme that could potentially be dominated by the Japanese yen. More recently, the weight of China's GDP and total trade volume has made itself felt and there is now no fear of dominance by the yen. While the research for this project will be undertaken in Japan, the final determination of the composition of the ACU will be led by ASEAN, which has come increasingly under China's influence in recent years.

What is intriguing is that the ACU is not meant to be a real currency to replace regional currencies, as is the case of the euro. It is meant to be a guide for Asian countries to coordinate and manage their exchange rates. In other words, the ACU could become a new benchmark independent of the US dollar. Thus, the potential is for the ACU to become a viable currency for Asian countries to denominate their export prices, cross-border loans and cross-border bond issues, thus weaning themselves off their reliance on the US dollar.

The question remains as to whether it will replace currency asymmetry and thereby reduce global imbalance. An ACU might well reflect the monetary relationships among Asian economies, but it could lead to a collective revaluation against the US dollar under the pressure of market speculation and force Asian economies to bear all the burdens of currency asymmetry, leaving the United States doing nothing. Remember, without the United States doing something against its own short-term interests in the present global monetary system, nothing can really solve the problem of global imbalance in the long term.

Acknowledgments

This chapter draws on material in a paper 'Currency asymmetry, global imbalance, and rethinking the reform of the international monetary system', in a forthcoming volume published by the Forum on Debt and Development (FONDAD) in the Hague, The Netherlands.

Notes

1 Bergsten 2006.
2 It increased by almost 300 per cent in one year compared with the previous year's $30 billion trade surplus. This extraordinary change could be misleading: it could mean that there were some speculative capital movements under the trade pricing mechanism, as exported goods might be priced higher and imported goods might be priced lower when capital control was in place but people wanted to speculate on the revaluation of the RMB. See a recent report in *Business Week* (Green) 'China's trade surplus may be an illusion'. The article claimed that '[o]ur numbers show that China's trade surplus could have been as small as $35 billion in 2005. Trade could have disguised some $67 billion of non-trade capital inflows. We made a long list of assumptions to get to this number, and we are not claiming that it is absolutely accurate. But it does give a hint as to the potential scale of these foreign currency inflows.' I might not agree with the level of this problem, but even if the number was cut in half, it would be a serious problem. In the first half of 2006, this factor of disguised capital inflow became a 'must' in explaining the statistics, otherwise we would be not able to put things together: during these six months, investment growth accelerated to 31 per cent, consumption growth accelerated to 13.6 per cent in real terms; meanwhile, on the other side of the national income account identity, the current account surplus accelerated to almost 7 per cent of GDP (annualised) from the previous year's 6.7 per cent. Only capital inflow through trade channels (for example, by over-invoicing exports, under-invoicing imports, or making advanced financial transactions for imports) can make the accounting equation hold true.
3 As pointed out most recently by Clyde Prestowitz, 'When President Nixon announced the end of the dollar's link to gold and created today's dollar standard, he effectively made the global financial system *dependent* on America's good behaviour' (Prestowitz 2005:169).
4 The world has never faced such a situation before. Even when the British sterling was the de facto global currency, it was pegged to gold.
5 See US Department of Treasury 2003.
6 McKinnon writes: 'China's money wages had to grow in line with its rapid productivity growth. From 1994 through 2004, money wages in manufacturing increased 11.7 per cent in China per year and by just 3 per cent in the United States...This wage growth differential approximately reflected the differential growth of labor productivity: about 9.5 to 12 per cent in China versus 2.7 per cent in the United States over the decade' (2005:7).
7 Keynes was thinking about some kind of international currency, named 'bancor', when he was preparing for the Breton Woods Conference in 1944 (see Rothbard 1995).

7

Who foots China's bank restructuring bill?

Guonan Ma

International experience suggests that bank restructuring, including resolution of non-performing loans (NPLs) and the associated recapitalisation of banks, is often costly—but it is crucial for the stability and functioning of banking systems.[1] While effectively stemming the flow of new non-performing loans is necessary for a sustained improvement in the banking system, the importance of dealing with the legacy of such loans on the books of banks or within the system should not be understated: in no small measure, it reveals the political willingness of authorities to confront banking problems. Moreover, non-performing loan resolution is often linked with bank recapitalisation. Therefore, the questions of how bank restructuring should be financed and how the associated potential loss should be allocated among parties involved must not be swept under the carpet.

China's bank restructuring bill might eventually approach 30 per cent of GDP. Losses of this magnitude should not be surprising, given that non-performing loans are believed to have accounted for as much as 40 to 50 per cent of loans outstanding at their peak in the late 1990s (Lardy 1998; Bank for International Settlements 1999). Since then, the Chinese government has taken several major steps to recapitalise its banks and reduce non-performing loans. First and foremost, it has focused on repairing banks' balance sheets, but has also recognised the importance of other reforms.[2] The question of how such large-scale restructuring will be funded is of great interest.

This chapter aims to shed light on the potential cost of bank restructuring in China, how it will be funded and who will foot the bill. There has been limited research to understand these issues systematically. This chapter attempts to fill this gap and is organised as follows. The second section sets out a framework to suggest that there are three possible groups of players who might foot the bill: bank shareholders, bank customers and taxpayers. I also discuss relevant experiences from elsewhere in the world, and argue that predetermined and transparent institutional arrangements for apportioning the cost of financial restructuring work best in the long term. The third section reviews some of the measures taken by the Chinese government since 1998 to repair bank balance sheets, including how they were funded and the probable amounts involved. The fourth section discusses some of the short and long-term implications of how Chinese authorities have apportioned losses among the parties involved. Finally, the fifth section concludes the paper with a few brief remarks.

I have reached three main conclusions in this chapter. First, since the late 1990s, the Chinese government has made substantial efforts to face up to the costly and politically difficult challenges of cleaning up bank balance sheets—which, in my view, has enhanced the credibility of the overall economic restructuring process in China.

Second, the financing arrangements for China's bank restructuring so far have been elaborate. Taxpayers, shareholders and bank customers have all paid for the restructuring bill, with the Ministry of Finance and the People's Bank of China splitting some 85 per cent between them. Foreign banks and other foreign investors also have helped foot the bill—and in so doing have become an emerging force in the Chinese banking sector.

Third, the ways in which the restructuring task has been funded and losses apportioned could have implications for the prospects of the Chinese banking sector. I believe that, as the restructuring process deepens, a more transparent and rule-based framework for assigning financing responsibilities will be necessary in order to contain moral hazard, improve corporate governance, strengthen central bank credibility and further develop domestic capital markets.

Sharing the bank restructuring bill

How will the expected large financial cost and the associated losses in the Chinese banking system ultimately have to be recognised and paid for? Experiences from elsewhere in the world suggest that, in general, three possible groups of players can end up paying the bill for bank restructuring: existing and new bank shareholders, bank customers and taxpayers.

First and foremost, existing bank shareholders should normally absorb the first loss. In China, the largest banks are state-owned, so that the government might end up absorbing a portion of the losses. Sometimes, outside investors or new shareholders are willing to pay for a portion of restructuring costs because of a troubled bank's franchise value. Bank customers—meaning borrowers and depositors—also share the costs through a relatively wide net interest margin. The government, and ultimately the taxpayer, contribute their share when public funds are injected into the banking sector. This can take a number of forms: direct budget outlays funded by government debt as well as bank operating earnings and tax credits; debt issued by public agencies with full state backing (contingent liabilities); and financing by quasi-public agencies without explicit government guarantees.

Depending on the specific purposes, there could be a number of alternative approaches to gauging the potential costs of restructuring bank balance sheets. On one hand, a broad approach is to include all the resources needed to restore the balance sheets to a reasonably healthy state. On the other, a narrower measure would involve only the realised losses. In between, there could be various ways of defining the costs of bank restructuring. In this chapter, I define the 'bank restructuring bill' as the costs that have been incurred to clean up the bank balance sheets, whether the involved resources have been recovered or not. It includes but is not limited to realised losses.

Bank shareholders: old and new

It is often useful to distinguish between existing and new bank shareholders. Ideally, existing shareholders' capital should be extinguished first to cover losses. In principle, existing equity shareholders should absorb the loss until their capital is fully written off, before any funding from deposit insurance schemes or the treasury is deployed. If bank losses exceed shareholders' equity, but shareholders are allowed to retain a non-trivial claim on the insolvent bank, moral hazard might become an issue.

Sometimes, investors or new shareholders might pay part of a troubled bank's recapitalisation bill. They are willing to invest in an insolvent bank, through a merger or acquisition or simply by taking an equity stake, at a price above the undercapitalised bank's net asset value. These parties are willing to invest in a troubled bank because they recognise its potential franchise value or because regulatory and other costs associated with market entry are prohibitively high. New shareholders can be domestic or foreign banks, non-bank investors or government agencies (Hawkins and Turner 1999). These investors might help increase ownership diversification and strengthen corporate governance of the banks under restructuring; however, when the government itself becomes the only shareholder of a rescued non-state-owned bank (say, through nationalisation), the issues of future exit and (re-)privatisation must be addressed.

International experience varies, and the outcomes have been mixed on this score. Equity of existing shareholders was fully wiped out in troubled institutions in the early 1990s during the banking crises in the United States and Norway, and in the late 1990s in Indonesia in the wake of the East Asian financial crisis. In the United States, the Federal Deposit Insurance Corporation adopted the purchase-and-assumption approach, whereby the purchasing bank took over the assets and liabilities of the failed bank through a bidding process, after shareholder equity was eliminated. In Japan, Korea and Sweden, however, the equity of existing shareholders of insolvent banks was, in some cases, partially written down but not eliminated, even as public capital was injected into the failed banks. In Korea and Thailand, foreign and local banks or non-bank investors were allowed to buy equity in some troubled domestic financial institutions, as in the aftermath of the East Asian financial crisis.

Bank customers

The second group of agents who might, directly or indirectly, help pay the bill are bank customers, meaning borrowers and depositors.[3] Bank customers usually bear a portion of bank restructuring costs through interest margins earned by banks: specifically, by paying interest spreads above competitively determined market levels, borrowers and depositors contribute to bank operating profits that, over time, help rebuild bank balance sheets. In addition, captive or underdeveloped capital markets hamper competition among banks by limiting disintermediation, in which borrowers can bypass banks and directly tap the capital and money markets for financing. This is a flow approach to recapitalising troubled banks and often requires regulatory forbearance and accompanying tax incentives.

If, however, the initial capital deficiency is large, it might take many years before banks can be nursed back to health via a flow approach. After the East Asian financial crisis of 1997, Thai authorities granted regulatory forbearance to qualified Thai banks so they could continue operating and generate net cash flows. In China, undercapitalised banks have been earning a spread between the official one-year deposit rate and one-year working capital loan rate of 300 basis points, above the levels likely to be seen in a more deregulated environment. Alternatively, the Chinese government was concerned about possible 'adverse-selection' risk, opting to regulate deposit and loan rates before banks returned to reasonable health. If, however, a bank's negative equity is equal to 20 per cent of its assets, it could take many years to fill the hole in its balance sheet through the accumulation of net earnings—even assuming a wide interest margin, no new non-performing loans and no dividends paid.

More worryingly, moral hazard can emerge because of forbearance. For example, the Federal Savings and Loan Bank Board in the United States allowed many undercapitalised savings and loans to continue operating for some time, while excessive risk-taking by some weak thrifts aggravated their problems further (White 1991). Also, the US Federal Reserve was thought to have pursued an expansionary monetary policy in the early 1990s in order to steepen the yield curve, thereby widening net interest margins for banks. Some observers felt that this policy sent a signal that big banks making common lending errors, such as excessively risky loan booking, would be made whole by macroeconomic policy.

Taxpayers

Three general arguments have been put forward to support the use of public funds to bail out troubled banks. First, if the troubled banks are state-owned, the government has an obligation to repair their balance sheets or at least fund their exit from the market. In China, the big four commercial banks were solely state-owned until the recent foreign equity participation in them and their subsequent listing on stock markets.[4] Note that these four account for more than half of the total assets of the Chinese banking sector (Table 7.1).

Second, if bank losses are related substantially to past policy lending, the government is implicated directly and needs to take responsibility for cleaning up the banking sector. The government's role in this regard has been cited as a key contributor to China's high level of non-performing loans in the 1990s (Zhou 2004).

Third, with or without an explicit deposit insurance scheme, imposing big losses on a large number of small depositors can lead to even more costly systemic risks and even political crises. Given that bank deposits represent some 80 per cent of

Table 7.1 **The big four Chinese banks in the Chinese banking system, 2002–2005** (per cent)

	2002	2003	2004	2005
Their share in the total assets in the Chinese banking system	60.1	58.0	53.6	52.5
Average non-performing loan ratio	26.2	20.4	15.6	10.5

Note: end of period. The big four banks are the China Construction Bank, Bank of China, Industrial and Commercial Bank of China and Agricultural Bank of China.
Sources: China Banking Regulatory Commission; Moody's Investors' Service, 2005a. *Bank System Outlook for China: reform on track, but more needed*, June 2005, Hong Kong; Moody's Investors' Service, 2005b. *Reform of China's State Banks: moving beyond IPOs; positive rating actions likely*, November 2005, Hong Kong.

Chinese households' financial wealth, it is understandable that the government would be willing to intervene by injecting public money into the banking system.

Indeed, on all three of these cited grounds, the Chinese government might find it necessary and desirable to use taxpayers' money to fund bank restructuring. These considerations might have outweighed the legitimate concerns of Chinese policymakers about moral hazard, which can be dealt with through complementary reforms and a more transparent process of loss allocation.

Typically, there are three general modes of public funding to restore the health of the banking system. Their relative merits depend on the underlying condition of the banking system, as well as the initial endowments of local institutional arrangements and the market environment.

One is a direct budgetary outlay financed by taxes or government debt. This mode tends to enhance transparency and accountability and is consistent with best practice in corporate governance and capital-market development. Approval for these outlays, however, usually has to take place through a formal and sometimes drawn out legislative process, often with the result that the restructuring process is delayed substantially—especially when political consensus cannot be reached.

Another mode of public funding is non-performing loan resolution and bank recapitalisation through debt issued by quasi-government agencies but with full-faith government guarantees. Such guarantees are explicit contingent liabilities of the government. This approach is transparent and flexible, but it keeps the true costs of cleaning up the banking sector off the government's balance sheet for a time. It might impede bond-market development by splitting the domestic government debt market (McCauley 2003).

Finally, the financing of bank restructuring can be provided by the central bank or other quasi-government agencies without an explicit government guarantee. This approach is fast and expedient but does not always lend itself to accountability or contribute to capital-market development. It sometimes facilitates a desired early start of bank restructuring but might risk creating moral hazard, thus delaying a clear-cut loss allocation. At its limit, in a central bank's case, it can constrain monetary policy in undesirable ways.

Experiences elsewhere in Asia illustrate the various ways taxpayers' money can be used in bank restructuring. In Japan, the Bank of Japan provided liquidity support, secured lending to the stretched deposit insurance scheme and even injected risk capital into failed banks in the late 1990s (Nakaso 2001). However, except for some unresolved minor losses associated with the Bank of Japan's risk capital provision, Japanese government bonds and guarantees financed mainly the injection of public funds into the banking system. During the East Asian financial crisis, the Bank of Korea provided significant liquidity support to the financial system, as well as some limited financing to the Korea Asset Management Corporation (Fung et al. 2004). Such exposure by the Bank of Korea, however, was covered with full-faith government guarantees. Also, the Korean government injected much of the public resources directly into the financial system through funds raised by treasury bonds or officially guaranteed debt issued by other quasi-public agencies.

In the same crisis, Bank Indonesia suffered heavy losses because of its massive liquidity support to many local banks, most of which subsequently failed. The bank underwent prolonged negotiations with the finance ministry over partial settlement of such losses. The Bank of Thailand also incurred significant losses in the East Asian financial crisis from guaranteeing creditors and protecting depositors of failed financial institutions through its wholly owned subsidiary, Financial Institutions Development Fund (Fung et al. 2004). Eight years later, protracted and complicated discussions between the Bank of Thailand and Thai fiscal authorities—and partial funding by the government—still have not fully resolved the central bank's loss.

Towards an institutional framework

A policy question therefore arises as to how the costs of financial restructuring should be apportioned. The major challenge here is striking the delicate balance between safeguarding systemic financial stability, expediting the much-needed restructuring process and preventing or containing future moral hazard (Hawkins and Turner 1999; White 2004). In my view, a well-defined institutional framework for the cost-sharing process tends to work best for strengthening the banking system in the longer term, for at least the following three reasons (Crockett 1998).

Transparency. A well-defined institutional framework for cost sharing enhances transparency and disclosure, and promotes good corporate governance. In particular, transparency ensures the accountability of all players in the banking system, including regulatory authorities, bank shareholders, customers and the banks themselves. Moreover, sufficient and upfront financial commitments can help to minimise the costs of bank restructuring by instilling confidence in the process.

Accountability. Predetermined rules define the obligations of all parties involved and discourage shirking of responsibility, thereby reducing the potential for moral hazard, such as the expectation of bailouts in the future. Indeed, ambiguity of rules regarding apportionment of losses often gives rise to moral hazard and encourages accumulation of past bad debts, leading to even more new non-performing loans (Tang 2005).

Efficiency. Clear and *ex ante* loss-sharing frameworks are more efficient, since they reduce the need for repeated and often protracted ad hoc negotiations, avoid inefficient case-by-case legislative processes and enhance cooperation among different agencies and players in the banking system. Moreover, rule-based financing arrangements tend to be more compatible with and conducive to the development of capital markets.[5]

Recent bank restructuring steps in China

In practice, how the costs associated with China's financial restructuring are to be apportioned among bank shareholders, customers and taxpayers depends in part on the country's institutional realities, and the underlying condition of its financial system. Since the late 1990s, the Chinese government has taken a number of significant measures to repair bank balance sheets, with a cumulative headline restructuring cost possibly as high as 22 per cent of the newly revised 2005 GDP.[6] Its restructuring efforts were concentrated initially on the big four banks, which account for more than half of China's banking sector (Table 7.1), but now extend to the rest of the sector and even the troubled securities firms industry. This section summarises the principle measures taken by Chinese authorities since 1998 to strengthen bank balance sheets.

Issuance of RMB270 billion in special government bonds in 1998

In August 1998, the government issued bonds to recapitalise the big four banks. The People's Bank of China first lowered the statutory reserve requirement ratio for the banking sector as a whole from 13 per cent to 9 per cent; the Ministry of Finance then issued RMB270 billion (US$33 billion)[7] in special government bonds. The big four state-owned banks used the liquidity freed up by the lowering of the reserve ratio to purchase the bonds. The government then injected all the bond proceeds as equity into the big four banks (Mo 1999), with the consequence that the capital base of the big four banks more than doubled. As the initial sole owner of the big four banks, the Ministry of Finance thus met the capital call from these banks and explicitly burdened future taxpayers to fund a capital injection.

The first round of non-performing loan transfers

In 1999, the government carved out RMB1.4 trillion (US$173 billion, or 20 per cent of the total loan balance at the time) in non-performing loans from the big four banks at par value and transferred them to four state-owned asset-management companies. In return, these companies issued bonds to the four banks and assumed some of their liabilities to the People's Bank of China. Effectively, this batch of non-performing loan acquisition was 55 per cent financed by asset-management company bonds and 45 per cent by People's Bank of China credit. This move was a double act of non-performing loan removal and bank recapitalisation (Ma and Fung 2002).

However, because of the 'constructive ambiguity' of the Ministry of Finance towards its backing of these bonds, the value of the bonds issued by the asset-management companies was initially uncertain. Indeed, there might still be a risk that the big four banks swapped their non-performing loans for asset-management company bonds with uncertain prospects for timely debt service. Disclosure is such that it is not clear if the asset-management companies have made regular interest payments to the big four banks on their bonds, or to the People's Bank of China on the liabilities assumed by the purchasing companies. So far, the four asset-management companies have resolved about half of the acquired non-performing loans, with a 20 per cent cash recovery rate. This would not suffice, on a collective basis, to cover the interest payments on their bonds issued and the People's Bank of China loans assumed so far.

Therefore, at least for a period, the effective recapitalisation of the big four banks might not be as large as the headline non-performing loan removal would suggest, while the balance sheet of the People's Bank of China has clearly suffered. This is a case of recapitalising banks via injections by the central bank and other public agencies (asset-management companies) without an explicit government guarantee.[8]

US$60 billion in capital injections from foreign reserves since 2003

In exchange for equity, the People's Bank of China has hitherto injected US$60 billion of capital from its foreign reserves into three of the big four banks since late 2003. To bypass the Chinese central bank law that prohibits the People's Bank from owning any commercial banks, a state-owned investment vehicle called the Central Huijin Investment Corporation Limited (Huijin) was set up in 2003 to receive funding from the People's Bank, and to invest the money into the three commercial banks' equity. So far, Huijin has injected US$22.5 billion each into the China Construction Bank and the Bank of China and US$15 billion into the Industrial and Commercial Bank of China. Presumably, such equity investments form the risk capital of the restructured banks—which means that Huijin has become the largest financial holding company in China. Since funding at the margin can be taken to be interest-bearing People's Bank of China bills, this is a case of financing through debts issued by public agencies without full-faith state backing.[9]

Loss recognition by existing bank shareholders

Until recently, most Chinese banks were wholly state-owned. As the initial sole owner of the four big banks, the Ministry if Finance opted to recognise the loss of all of its equity in the China Construction Bank and the Bank of China (some RMB320 billion) as the counterpart of the loan loss write-offs and increases in provisions. Thus, through Huijin, the People's Bank of China took over these two recapitalised banks and became their controlling shareholder. In this case, the original bank shareholders—that is, China's taxpayers—absorbed the loss.

In contrast, in the case of the Industrial and Commercial Bank of China, the Ministry of Finance wrote down only one-third of its original RMB170 billion equity stake, and retained the rest of its equity claims in order to share equal control of the restructured Industrial and Commercial Bank of China with Huijin. However, a massive RMB246 billion of the Industrial and Commercial Bank of China's remaining loan losses has been parked in a special-purpose receivable account at the bank that yields interest to the bank and is reportedly funded by future dividends (supposedly accruing to the Ministry of Finance as a 50 per cent equity owner) and possibly additional tax credits.[10] Therefore, this is a real mixed bag: shareholders and therefore taxpayers recognise some of the loss instantly and some in instalments. Moreover, the latter arrangement smacks of regulatory forbearance granted by authorities to themselves. Whether the restructuring bill takes the form of receivables or outright write-off and provision of risk capital, taxpayers will eventually have to pick up the tab.

Additional non-performing loan transfers

Since 2004, the People's Bank of China's balance sheet has been tapped twice to fund transfers of doubtful loans at the recapitalised China Construction Bank, the Bank of China and the Industrial and Commercial Bank of China onto the books of the asset-management companies. The total book value of loans transferred has amounted to some RMB780 billion (US$96 billion). In 2004, the People's Bank of China bought the first batch of RMB320 billion in doubtful loans from the China Construction Bank and the Bank of China (as well as from the Bank of Communications: see below) for half their book value and then auctioned them to the asset-management companies for 30 to 40 cents on the dollar.[11] Presumably, the ministry wrote off its equity in the China Construction Bank and the Bank of China as well as giving up the 2003–04 net profits of the two banks to help fund the 50 per cent loss of the RMB320 billion non-performing loan transfer as well as to raise provisions. In 2005, the People's Bank of China bought another RMB460 billion in doubtful loans from the Industrial and Commercial Bank of China at par value and auctioned them to the asset-management companies for an average of 26 cents on the dollar.

In these two non-performing loan transactions, the People's Bank of China appeared to have made an outright loss, from the differences between the acquisition and auction prices of the doubtful loans involved, of nearly RMB400 billion (US$50 billion)—or some 20 times the bank's own reported capital. Furthermore, the People's Bank of China's balance sheet has additional exposure to the asset-management companies because it again provided the credit to finance their two non-performing loan acquisitions, as in the 1999 transactions.[13] In essence, the People's Bank of China has been decapitalised to finance bank recapitalisation, all without a government guarantee, at least on the public record.

Other domestic recapitalisation moves

In June 2004, the Bank of Communications, the fifth largest bank in China, was recapitalised to the tune of RMB35 billion (US$4 billion), after a large portion of its non-performing loans were purchased by the People's Bank of China at 50 per cent of the book value (see the above discussion). The Ministry of Finance and other existing bank shareholders wrote down some of their equity and contributed new capital of RMB7 billion; Huijin invested RMB3 billion (reportedly funded by interest-bearing People's Bank of China bills); the National Social Security Fund chipped in RMB10 billion in return for an equity stake; and HSBC Holdings paid RMB15 billion for a 19.9 per cent stake, a premium of some 40 per cent of the valuation for the Ministry of Finance and Huijin equity investment (see Table 7.2). This recapitalisation exercise was a hybrid one financed by funds from the government and public agencies and existing shareholders, as well as domestic and foreign investors.

There have been several other cases since the late 1990s of new shareholders putting equity capital into the Chinese banking sector. Two more recent examples are listed here. In May 2004, three large non-financial state-owned companies, as founding shareholders of the China Construction Bank, invested RMB8 billion in the newly restructured bank to become its founding shareholders. In addition to its aforementioned equity investment in the Bank of Communications, the National Social Security Fund made an equity investment of RMB10 billion in the newly restructured Bank of China at 1.17 times its 2004 book price and RMB18 billion in the newly restructured Industrial and Commercial Bank of China at about 1.2 times the 2005 book value.

Table 7.2 **Announced direct foreign investment in Chinese banks, 2002–2006**

	Target name	Acquirer name	Equity investment US$ million (per cent)
2002	Bank of Shanghai	IFC/HSBC/HK Shanghai Commercial Bank	133 (13)
2002	China Everbright Bank	IFC	19 (4.9)
2002	Nanjing City Commercial Bank	IFC	27 (15)
2002	Shanghai Pudong Development Bank	Citigroup	73 (5)
2004	Industrial Bank	Hang Seng Bank/IFC/GIC	326 (24.9)
2004	Minsheng Bank	IFC/Temasek	458 (6.2)
2004	Shenzhen Development Bank	Newbridge Capital	150 (17.9)
2004	Xian City Commercial Bank	IFC/Bank of Nova Scotia	6 (5)
2004	Bank of Jinan	Commonwealth Bank of Australia	17 (11)
2005	Bank of Beijing	ING/IFC	270 (24.9)
2005	Hangzhou City Bank	Commonwealth Bank of Australia	78 (19.9)
2005	Huaxia Joint Stock Bank	Deutsche Bank/Pangaea	454 (20.9)
2005	Bohai Bank	Standard Chartered Bank	123 (19.9)
2005	Bank of Communications	HSBC	1,750 (19.9)
2005	China Construction Bank	Bank of America/Temasek	3,966 (14.1)
2005	Bank of China	Royal Bank of Scotland/Temasek/UBS/Asian Development Bank	5,1373 (16.2)
2005	Tianjin City Commercial Bank	ANZ Bank	110 (20)
2005	Industrial and Commercial Bank of China	Goldman Sachs, Allianz, AE	3,780 (8.89)
2006	Ningbo City Commercial Bank	Overseas-Chinese Banking Corporation	70.6 (12.2)
Total			US$17 billion (approx.)

Note: The year is the announcement date of the investment. Some announced deals are still pending regulatory approval. The size of investment in the Bank of Communications, the China Construction Bank and the Bank of China are those before the Bank of China's recent initial public offerings (IPOs). The Bohai Bank is a new bank with Standard Chartered as one of its founding shareholders. IFC is the International Finance Corporation, GIC is the Singapore Government Investment Corporation.

Sources: *Caijing Magazine*, 2004. No. 123; *Caijing Magazine*, 2005. No. 136; *The Asian Wall Street Journal*, 2005. 20 June 2005; *The Asian Wall Street Journal*, 2006. 27 January 2006; *The 21st Century Economic Report*, 2005. 24 August 2005; *Financial News*, 2005. 7 September 2005; *Financial News*, 2005. 9 September 2005; Bank for International Settlements, 1999. *Strengthening the banking system in China: issues and experiences*, BIS Policy Papers, No. 7, October, Basel; China Construction Bank, 2005. *Global Offering Prospectus*, October, Hong Kong; Bank of China, 2006. *Global Offering Prospectus*, May, Hong Kong.

Foreign equity participation

Foreign investors are footing China's bank restructuring bill to the extent that they are paying a premium for equity stakes in Chinese banks. The official policy has been to encourage foreign strategic investors to become shareholders of Chinese banks and subsequently to list those banks on stock markets. The purpose of this strategy is not just to attract capital, but to diversify ownership, improve corporate governance, promote a credit culture, enhance disclosure and facilitate transfers of knowledge.[13] Moreover, private or public foreign equity participation provides an exit strategy for the State to recoup its equity investment in recapitalised banks—through sales of equity stakes to foreign investors.

Foreign capital committed to the Chinese banking sector, in the form of either direct or portfolio investment, has been considerable, and the inflow has accelerated since 2002 (Table 7.2 and Appendix 7.2). By early 2006, the total declared foreign direct investment in Chinese banks had reached US$17 billion, representing some 15 per cent of the banking sector's core capital, according to some estimates.[14] Since June 2005, the Bank of Communications, the China Construction Bank and the Bank of China have been listed on the Hong Kong Stock Exchange, raising a combined total of more than US$20 billion globally through new share placements.[15]

Cleaning up the rural credit cooperatives and city commercial banks

Since 2001, Chinese policymakers have turned their attention to the other two segments of the banking sector: the second-tier city commercial banks and 34,000 rural credit cooperatives (RCCs). In both segments, local taxpayers, the People's Bank of China and shareholders (existing and new) have footed the bill. The total bill for restructuring the balance sheets of these two sectors could well have exceeded RMB500 billion by late 2005.

To date, the People's Bank of China has issued at least RMB168 billion of its special interest-bearing bills to the RCCs to cover half of their negative equity arising from the recognition of their loan losses—apparently without receiving equity stakes in return. The remainder of the clean-up bill has been met by local governments (through their budgetary accounts or their investment arms) as well as by existing and new shareholders. Financing from the People's Bank of China puts the total estimated restructuring cost of the RCCs at a minimum of RMB336 billion (US$42 billion)—and that is just to keep the RCC sector's net worth positive. In addition, to lift the capital adequacy of the RCC sector towards international standards, existing and new RCC shareholders had reportedly injected capital of RMB104 billion for the sector as a whole by mid 2005.[16]

The clean-up of the city commercial bank sector has been funded mainly by a mixture of equity dilutions of existing shareholdings and contributions from local fiscal authorities or their investment arms, who have coughed up at least RMB36 billion (US$5 billion) so far.[17] Foreign investors might have also shared the bill by paying a premium to acquire equity stakes in a number of Chinese city commercial banks (Table 7.2).

The changing role of Chinese bank customers

Bank customers have in effect been contributing to the restructuring bill as well. While liberalisation has led to greater interest-rate flexibility in China, the authorities have continued setting benchmark deposit rate ceilings and minimum lending rates to maintain interest spreads of some 300 basis points. While such spreads might not be the widest in the world, they could shrink considerably if market forces played a more prominent role. In addition, the underdevelopment of China's money and capital markets means that larger depositors cannot seek higher returns on other instruments such as mutual funds, and that sound enterprises cannot lower funding costs by directly tapping the bond markets. In short, disintermediation has taken place on a much smaller scale than otherwise. Until 2004, corporate debt securities represented no more than 2 per cent of the total outside funding of China's non-financial firms (Table 7.3).[18]

If Chinese banks have been able to charge their customers a conservatively estimated 50 basis point excess interest margin in the past five years, I estimate that bank customers would have paid RMB270 billion (US$33 billion) towards the bank restructuring bill. Related to this issue is the use of pre-provision net earnings and tax credits to strengthen a bank's capital base. The annual reports of the four big banks suggest that in 2003 and 2004 alone, roughly RMB150 billion (US$18.5 billion) was injected into these banks in the form of pre-provision net earnings and tax credits.[19]

Inter-bank swaps of subordinated debt

Finally, since 2004, subordinated bonds have been issued by Chinese banks as tier-two capital to strengthen their balance sheets. As of late 2005, 12 banks issued at least RMB186 billion of subordinated debt, most of which was taken up by other banks and insurance companies.[20] Banks have been allowed to buy each other's bonds, with holdings of up to 20 per cent of their own stated core capital permitted. Of course, inter-bank swaps of two-tier capital do not strengthen the banking system as a whole against common adverse shocks. In addition, purchases of such bonds by insurers, as in Japan, pose a risk of contagion

Table 7.3   **Outside fund sources of the non-financial corporate sector, 1998–2004** (RMB billion)

	1998	2000	2002	2003	2004
Total sources of outside funding	1,354	1,524	2,065	3,120	2,794
Bank loans	1,015	932	1,449	2,374	1,771
Domestic corporate bonds	4	10	24	37	33

Source: The People's Bank of China *Quarterly Statistical Bulletin*, various issues.

across the financial system. The yields on the subordinated bonds issued by some Chinese state banks were reportedly on a par with or even below those on Ministry of Finance bonds of similar maturities, with little transparency about the pricing mechanism for the subordinated bonds placed publicly or privately, or the distribution of holdings. Taxpayers get little protection from such window dressing (Fukao 2002).

Implications

In order to gauge the total cost of bank restructuring in China, I have taken into account the financial resources incurred in recognising the past losses as well as those used to beef up the banking sector's capital base to the required levels. Adding up these restructuring exercises in a rather crude manner, the estimated payments towards China's bank restructuring bill to date have approached nearly RMB4 trillion (US$500 billion)—or 22 per cent of the revised 2005 GDP (Table A7.1). This figure is likely to be an underestimate. Indeed, the headline cost could eventually exceed RMB5 trillion (US$620 billion), or more than 28 per cent of GDP, given that the most troubled of the four big state banks has yet to be restructured, the three policy banks will have to be recapitalised and more RCCs and city commercial banks still need to be cleaned up.[21]

The financing arrangements for China's bank restructuring have been complex and wide-ranging. They have included outright Ministry of Finance bonds; tapping the People's Bank of China balance sheet; recent and promised future flows of tax credits and operating earnings; excessive interest margins shouldered by bank customers; capital write-down and calls on existing shareholders; and premiums associated with equity investment by domestic and foreign investors. Thus, taxpayers, shareholders and bank customers have all shared the restructuring bill. The Ministry of Finance and the People's Bank of China together have taken care of 85 per cent of the bill, with the rest of the tab being picked up by bank shareholders, investors and customers. Therefore, the consolidated public sector (ultimately taxpayers) is bearing the lion's share of the bill.

While one might debate the relative merits of various ways of funding and apportioning bank losses and the probable size of the restructuring bill, there is little doubt that the Chinese authorities have moved expeditiously in meeting the challenges to the banking system. Nevertheless, the Chinese experience raises a number of important questions. First, what is the likely effect of such restructuring efforts on bank balance sheets? Second, how should one interpret the estimated headline costs of bank restructuring in China? Third, how have the Chinese authorities managed the potential impacts of such large-scale funding exercises on monetary and exchange-rate policies? Finally, what are the long-term implications of these funding approaches? These questions are discussed below.

Balance sheet impact

The short-term impact of these restructuring exercises on the balance sheet of the Chinese banking sector has been marked (Table 7.1). After injections of public and private funds, the balance sheets of most Chinese banks are now in far better shape, with lower non-performing loan levels, enhanced provisions and a stronger capital base across the sector (Moody 2005a, 2005b; Garcia-Herrero et al. 2005). For instance, the recorded aggregate equity capital of China's RCC sector reportedly swung from a sickly –10 per cent at the end of 2002 to almost 6 per cent by June 2005. Similarly, the city commercial bank sector saw its average capital adequacy ratio jump to 5 per cent at the end of 2005 from less than 1.5 per cent just one year earlier.[22] The recent credit rating upgrades by several international rating agencies of several Chinese banks and the success of their recent IPOs have been an endorsement of such restructuring efforts.

Nevertheless, it is far from clear to what degree recapitalisation measures have strengthened the banking system. Particularly troubling was the ambiguous status of the asset-management company bonds until recently and the incestuous interbank swaps of subordinated debt. Moreover, some in the media claim that public capital taken from the foreign reserves should be principal-guaranteed. Such media opinions would raise doubts about whether such equity should be treated as core risk capital absorbing real shocks, or simply as a vase borrowed for decoration only. If such equity capital investments by the State are counted as forming genuine core risk capital at all, they should, by definition, be subject to downside as well as upside risks.

There have also been some concerns that, without other complementary reforms, such injections of public financial resources into the banking sector might give rise to moral hazard, which, in turn, would lead to new non-performing loans in the system and repeated state bailouts. While the risk of moral hazard clearly exists and needs to be taken seriously, my view is that the best approach is not to play down but to face up to the potential size of the bank restructuring bill. In fact, by not fully recognising past loan losses and recapitalisation needs, the risk of moral hazard is likely to be accentuated, not mitigated. [23]

Headline restructuring costs

The final bank restructuring bill might differ from the simple headline number, in part because of two factors: the continuing capital injection, non-performing loan transfers and use of tax credits and bank earnings flows to strengthen bank balance sheets; and possible gains/losses on new equity investment by the government in the restructured banks. Therefore, the size of the eventual total bill could remain uncertain for an extended period.

The first factor is straightforward, mainly because all segments of China's banking sector have not been fully restructured and it is no easy task to discount various timed flows to a common point in time. For example, in the case of future financial flows to fund bank restructuring, the State reportedly has promised the Industrial and Commercial Bank of China and city commercial banks additional tax credits and the use of future retained earnings to rebuild their balance sheets.

The realised gains or losses from Huijin's equity investment and the premium paid by new shareholders might influence not only the headline bill, but how it is apportioned. It is therefore interesting to consider the valuation effects of subsequent private and public equity transactions. For instance, the Bank of America and the Royal Bank of Scotland bought 14 per cent and 16 per cent, respectively, of Huijin's stakes in the China Construction Bank and the Bank of China. I estimate that relative to the original valuation of the initial investment in 2003, Huijin realised a capital gain of nearly RMB10 billion (US$1.2 billion) from selling down its China Construction Bank and Bank of China stakes in these two private equity deals (Table 7.2).

However, this headline realised capital gain for Huijin could be offset partially by the appreciation of the renminbi since the July 2005 policy change. Moreover, one needs to take into account the rest of the packages, including options, lock-ups or promises of net asset values above the acquisition prices (China Construction Bank 2005; Bank of China 2006). In the case of the China Construction

Bank private equity deal, the Bank of America received a call option to increase its stake up to 19.9 per cent, with an expiration date in 2011 and an elaborate strike price structure. The value of such a call option could be significant. By contrast, in the Bank of China private equity transaction, the Royal Bank of Scotland did not receive call options, but secured some downside protection for a limited period. Thus, the realised gains or losses related to Huijin's equity investment might not be known until these options expire or are eliminated and exercised.

Impact on monetary and exchange-rate policy

Chinese policymakers have tried hard to contain possible undesired interference and spillage between these large-scale bank-restructuring exercises, on the one hand, and monetary and exchange-rate policy objectives on the other. Using the central bank balance sheet to fund a big part of bank restructuring has indeed posed some challenges to monetary policy. To avoid injecting excessive liquidity into the banking system within a relatively short period, for example, the People's Bank of China has imposed requirements that its special bills issued to the RCCs and to fund the non-performing loan transactions during 2004–05 will not be transferable or used as collateral for a minimum period of two to three years. The RMB270 billion special government bonds issued in 1998 were also not transferable. Moreover, to cope with the intensified appreciation pressure on the renminbi since 2003, the three recapitalised banks are not allowed to convert their received foreign currency-denominated capital into renminbi for a vesting period of about three years. Therefore, the new bank capital might fluctuate in renminbi terms along with a more flexible exchange rate.

Two questions arise in relation to exchange-rate risks. First, what might the currency composition of bank capital look like? It differs from one bank to another. Whereas the core equity capital of the Industrial and Commercial Bank of China is likely to be denominated half in local currency and half in US dollars, almost the entire tier-one capital of the Bank of China and the China Construction Bank might be denominated in a currency other than renminbi. Indeed, while the Bank of China's core capital was a mix of US dollars and gold (Bank of China 2006), the China Construction Bank's would be mostly US dollar-denominated. This in turns raises the question of the optimal relationship between the currency compositions of a bank's equity and its assets (Fukao 1991).

Second, with a three-year vesting period preventing conversion of US dollars into renminbi, how might these recapitalised banks hedge their exchange-rate risks? In early 2005, Huijin issued currency options to the three recapitalised big banks to hedge, fully or partially, the US dollar portions of their capital. The banks paid premiums to acquire the options to sell US dollars against renminbi at strike prices around the prevailing exchange rate of RMB8.277 per US$ before the July 2005 policy change for a period of up to three years.[24] Effectively, Huijin and the three recapitalised banks share the foreign-exchange risks through these option arrangements.

Nevertheless, bank restructuring might still have some unintended repercussions, complicating monetary and exchange-rate policymaking. For instance, with an improved capital base, some of the newly listed Chinese banks have been increasingly motivated to lend. But if, in response, the People's Bank of China raised interest rates, capital inflows might pick up further, putting additional appreciation pressure on the renminbi. Another way to tighten monetary conditions, in light of strong external surpluses, could be currency appreciation. Nevertheless, with a big portion of the bank equity denominated in foreign currency, as well as the big net dollar exposures for many Chinese banks, the scope for Chinese policymakers to manoeuvre in the short term, especially at a time of dressing up the balance sheets of banks for their initial overseas listings, could be limited. Thus, without effective foreign-exchange regulations and capital controls, Chinese policymakers might find it quite challenging to juggle the three difficult tasks of bank restructuring, monetary stability and orderly policy shift towards greater currency flexibility.[25]

Longer-term implications

Four longer-term issues arise from the recent funding practices of China's bank restructuring. First, until the well-defined rules governing loss apportionment emerge and Huijin becomes more transparent, Chinese taxpayers might consider the funding arrangements murky. Lack of *ex ante* and *ex post* transparency about the financing of bank restructuring is not conducive to good corporate governance and could lead to moral hazard. To address the stock and flow issues facing the Chinese banking sector, accountability is key—and that needs to start with a set of well-defined rules stipulating financing responsibilities. Also, accountability would influence the level of loss given default in the Chinese banking sector.

Second, some of the ways to fund bank restructuring in China might not be conducive to debt-market development. Keeping bank interest margins high could have been one reason for the underdevelopment of China's bond and money markets. More developed debt markets, while possibly compressing bank interest margins for a while, would benefit the banking sector and economy in the long term. This is because a deeper and broader capital market would encourage banks to rely less on balance-sheet expansion and more on fee income-producing activities and enhance the resilience of the financial system (Gyntelberg et al. 2005). In addition, fragmented and often non-tradable debt issued by multiple agencies in financing the bank restructuring process tends to depress debt-market liquidity generally (McCauley 2003). Instead, unifying different issues by various agencies would help improve secondary-market liquidity and promote bond-market development.

Third, specific concerns have also arisen about the heavy use of the central bank balance sheet to fund bank restructuring in China (Ma and Fung 2002). Although taxpayers have footed some 85 per cent of China's restructuring bill, many conventional measures of government debt levels in China have not risen as much. This is possible, in my view, mainly because of the unusual expansion of the central bank balance sheet as well as other quasi-public agency debts not explicitly backed by the government. Between the end of 2001 and the end of 2005, the size of the People's Bank of China's balance sheet more than doubled—with the estimated central bank financing of the country's bank restructuring now representing at least 15 per cent of the entire balance sheet.

In essence, the People's Bank of China is being de-capitalised to the benefit of the banks. Excessive use of the central bank to fund such quasi-fiscal burdens could damage its balance sheet. This could be the result of either a mismatch between liquid liabilities and illiquid assets or the loss of budgetary autonomy (in the event that the central bank's cash flows become negative), or both. And such problems could hinder the long-term institutional development of the central bank in several respects.

- Given the potential conflict of interest between financing needs and monetary objectives, the credibility of a central bank's monetary policy could be compromised.
- Market confidence in the capacity of a central bank to act as a lender of last resort could be eroded over time.
- A large overhang of illiquid and often non-negotiable assets on the balance sheet of the central bank might retard the development of money and bond markets, limit the choices of monetary policy instruments and weaken transmission of monetary policy.

Fourth and finally, the recent pick-up in foreign equity participation in Chinese banks raises the question of how open China's domestic banking market is and how this will affect the sector's outlook. By some measures, such as the scale of foreign banks' local renminbi banking business, the Chinese domestic banking market remains arguably one of the most closed major emerging banking markets in the world.

On the other hand, despite the official ceilings on foreign ownership, substantial foreign direct investment and portfolio investment in domestic banks suggest that the Chinese banking sector is opening up. While the prevailing official ceilings on foreign ownership in a Chinese bank are 20 per cent for a single foreign investor and 25 per cent for all foreign investors combined, these restrictions appear to apply only to non-listed banks. For instance, according to my estimates, after their recent IPOs, the effective foreign ownership of the Bank of Communications might have approached 30 per cent, while those of the China Construction Bank and the Bank of China could have already exceeded 25 per cent. This trend of increased foreign equity participation might have an important bearing on the landscape of China's banking market in the long term. In a way, the Chinese banking sector might not be as closed as other measures suggest.

Concluding remarks

Since 1998, the Chinese government has stepped up the pace of cleaning up the balance sheets of the banking sector, confronting the sizeable restructuring task that might have cost as much as 22 per cent of GDP to date. Funding arrangements have been elaborate, with bank shareholders, bank customers and taxpayers all having shared China's overall financial restructuring cost. Taxpayers have footed most of it, often with little explicit recognition of this fact in official government debt totals. A significant portion of the funding burden could have fallen on the People's Bank of China, as seigniorage has been capitalised through the rising amounts of interest-bearing People's Bank bills and other liabilities.

While efforts to rebuild banks' balance sheets are not a panacea for all the challenges faced by the Chinese banking sector, lingering concerns about moral hazard are no excuse to shun these important measures. I argue, therefore, for a more transparent framework to apportion financing responsibilities among the parties concerned, since well-defined rules of loss allocation restrain moral hazard and promote accountability and market development. The recent increased foreign direct investment in the Chinese banking sector has not only helped fund the restructuring task, but might alter the sector's landscape in the long term—if the experience of the Chinese manufacturing sector in the past three decades is anything to go by.

Acknowledgments

I am grateful to my Bank for International Settlements (BIS) colleagues and to participants in the CEPII seminar 'China's financial system: the links between openness and banking crisis' in September 2005 in Paris and the Asian Economic Panel Meeting in May 2006 in Seoul. I am particularly indebted to Robert McCauley, Wing Thye Woo and Rikuichi Nikawa. Any remaining errors are mine. The views expressed in this paper are those of the author and are not necessarily the views of the BIS.

Notes

1   See, among others, Sheng 1996; Dziobek and Pazarbasioglu 1997; and Hawkins and Turner 1999.
2   Such reforms might include strengthening corporate governance, improving risk management, building up regulatory capacities, fostering a credit culture, liberalising markets and imposing more binding financial disciplines on state-owned companies.
3   Depending on seniority, bank customers could include other bank creditors generally. In a broader sense, fellow banks can also be bank customers contributing to the bill, say, via some deposit insurance scheme that shares the cost of deposit insurance across the banking industry.
4   After the recent foreign equity participation and stock market listings, the big four banks might no longer be appropriately called 'state-owned banks'. Perhaps a more precise name for them would be 'state-controlled banks'. This paper uses 'state-owned banks' and 'state-controlled banks' interchangeably.
5   *Ex ante* and rule-based frameworks for loss allocation are not necessarily inconsistent with flexible practical strategies to bank restructuring.
6   The latest census indicates that the size of the Chinese economy might have been underestimated by 17 per cent in 2004 GDP figures. This paper uses the census-based 2005 GDP throughout. Also, the discussion will be limited to balance sheet restructuring exercises during 1998–2006, without discounting them back to the same point in time.
7   In this paper, the exchange rate of the Chinese renminbi is RMB8.1/US$1, unless otherwise specified.
8   Lately, the Ministry of Finance has become more forthcoming about its willingness to support the bonds issued by two asset-management companies (Cinda and Orient), in the wake of the initial public offerings of the China Construction Bank and Bank of China on the Hong Kong Stock Exchange in November 2005 and June 2006. It says, '[I]n the event that Cinda is unable to pay any interest on the bond in full, the [ministry] will provide financial support...when necessary, the [ministry] will provide support with respect to Cinda's repayment of the principal of the bond' (China Construction Bank 2005; similarly, Bank of China 2006). Even here, there was no mention of the status of the bonds issued by the other two asset-management companies.
9   There have been reports in the press that Huijin has also made equity investments in some undercapitalised local securities houses. It is not apparent how such investment has been funded. One possibility is that the financial resources came from paid-out dividends accruing

Who foots China's bank restructuring bill?

to Huijin's equity stakes in the three big state banks. Another possibility is that the investment was financed by capital gains realised by the sale of part of Huijin's equity stake in the China Construction Bank to foreign investors. A third possibility is additional equity or debt financing from the People's Bank of China.

10 The main motive for the Ministry of Finance to give up future earnings rather than extinguish all of its equity could be to retain a say in the bank restructuring process.

11 Of the RMB320 billion worth of non-performing loans purchased, it is estimated that RMB166 billion were from the Bank of China, RMB129 from the China Construction Bank and the remaining RMB25 billion from the Bank of Communications. Of the RMB166 billion in the Bank of China non-performing loan transaction, RMB18 billion might have been purchased directly by the People's Bank of China at par value (Bank of China 2006).

12 The credit risk to the People's Bank of China loans in this case would be marginally smaller than in the 1999 case, given that this time, the asset-management companies purchased the non-performing loans at auctioned prices rather than at book value. Nevertheless, the People's Bank of China balance sheet remains exposed to the same debtors (asset-management companies), who might find it a huge challenge to service their 1999 loans without special state support.

13 Listing on overseas stock markets was also intended as one way for the Chinese government to push through bank restructuring without being held hostage to the vagaries of local stock markets, which have been undergoing an overhaul lately.

14 *Securities Times*, 17 December 2005.

15 I assume that foreign investors foot the bill only to the extent that they pay a premium for their equity stakes in Chinese banks. For instance, HSBC paid a 40 per cent premium to take a 19.9 per cent stake in the Bank of Communications, which was listed at an IPO price of 1.54 times the book value. The Bank of America paid 1.15 times book value for its investment in the China Construction Bank, which was later listed at an IPO price of 1.96 times book value. The Royal Bank of Scotland paid 1.17 times book value to take 9.6 per cent of the Bank of China, which was listed at an IPO price of more than two times book value, while a Goldman Sacks-led consortium paid 1.22 times book price for a minority stake in the Industrial and Commercial bank of China. Newbridge Capital paid 2.38 times book price to be the largest shareholder in Shenzhen Development Bank.

16 The *Financial News*, 20 October 2005.

17 *The 21st Century Economic Report*, 11 August 2005.

18 The situation has, however, been changing since May 2005 when the short-term corporate commercial paper was first introduced in the inter-bank market. It has been priced at less than 3 per cent, compared with the prevailing official one-year best lending rate of more than 5 per cent. To partially compensate the commercial banks, the regulators have limited the principal commercial paper underwriters mainly to these banks so that they can earn as much as 40 basis points of the commercial paper underwriting fees and charge primary rates at 60 basis points above the prevailing yields in the secondary market.

19 However, the operating profits taken to clean up the bank balance sheet might include the extra bank earnings due from captive bank customers.

20 *Caijing Magazine*, 3 October 2005.

21 Reportedly, the Agriculture Bank of China might require RMB700 billion to restore its balance sheet to health, while the tab for Guangdong Development Bank could run as high as RMB50 billion. I estimate that the city commercial bank sector might need additional injections of some RMB150 billion to clean up the balance sheets or fund their exit, while the restructuring bill for

the three state policy banks might reach RMB250 billion.
22 *China Securities News*, 7 September 2005 and 6 June 2006; China Banking Regulatory Commission.
23 See also Tang 2005. Concerns about moral hazard are real, as evidenced in a number of recent large-scale scandals and fraud at some of the newly restructured banks. Complementary reforms comprise not only those within the banking sector but others in the general economy, such as creditor rights, legal enforcement and the broader reforms of state-owned companies (Xiao 2005).
24 The China Construction Bank bought options to sell dollars to fully cover the US$22.5 billion foreign exchange capital injection from Huijin. The Bank of China bought options to cover only US$18 billion of the US$22.5 billion capital injection received from Huijin. The Industrial and Commercial Bank of China's option agreement with Huijin covers US$12 billion of the US$15 billion capital injection received from Huijin. The *Southern Weekend Magazine*, 19 April 2005; *China Money*, August 2005, No. 46.
25 Ma and McCauley 2006 discuss the question of whether China's capital controls still bind in the context of monetary independence and onshore/offshore renminbi yield gaps.

Appendix Table A7.1 **Estimating the cost of China's bank restructuring, by early 2006**

No.	Estimation	RMB billion
1	The RMB270 billion of special government bonds is straightforward.	270
2	A 20 per cent net cash recovery ratio of the RMB1.4 trillion non-performing loan transfer in 1999 should result in a loss of 80 per cent, or RMB1.12 trillion.	1,120
3	US$60 billion foreign exchange capital injection is worth RMB496 billion at the strike price of RMB8.27/US$1.	496
4	The Ministry of Finance wrote off its equity of RMB320 billion in the China Construction Bank and the Bank of China, and RMB50 billion in the Industrial and Commercial Bank of China. A loan loss of RMB246 is shelved under an Industrial and Commercial Bank of China receivable account to be funded by the ministry in instalments.	616
5	The People's Bank of China bore the RMB400 billion loss related to the carving out of the doubtful loans at the China Construction Bank, the Bank of China and the Industrial and Commercial Bank of China in 2004 and 2005.	400
6	RMB35 billion recapitalisation of the Bank of Communications in 2004 (net of HSBC investment of RMB14.6 billion). Three big state companies invested another RMB8 billion in the bank as its founding shareholders. SSF invested RMB18 billion in the Bank of China and the Industrial and Commercial Bank of China.	46
7	Foreign investors took equity stakes or purchased new shares at a premium through private equity (strategic investment) and public equity (stock listing) investment transactions. The combined premium is conservatively estimated at RMB60 billion.	60
8	RMB440 billion for recapitalisation and non-performing loan resolution related to the RCCs and RMB36 billion for city commercial banks.	476
9	RMB270 billion spent by bank customers in the past five years, and RMB150 billion in pre-provision net earnings based on forbearance in 2003 and 2004. It is assumed that there is an overlap of RMB70 billion between these two items.	350
10	Low-yielding bank subordinated debt (assuming free lunch).	0
Total		3,843

Note: This table serves to provide only a rough estimate of the bank-restructuring bill during 1998–2006. Often, the disclosed information is such that the reported numbers do not lend themselves to easy addition. Simple addition of the listed items in this table might suffer from potential problems of incompleteness, inconsistency, overlapping, double counting and discounting. For instance, there could be some overlapping and related double counting between (1) and (4). Inconsistency could arise between (6) and (7). Item (8) could understate while proper discounting of the earlier financing exercises to 2005 could lift my estimate considerably.
Source: author's own estimates.

8

Keeping fiscal policy sustainable in China: challenges and solutions

Jinzhi Tong and Wing Thye Woo

Among doomsayers of all stripes, a favourite mechanism for the forthcoming collapse of the economy is the inevitable fiscal crisis of the State. The Marxist economist James O'Connor (1973) predicted that the dynamics of capitalist America would precipitate a fiscal crisis that would completely destabilise the economy. In turn, the capitalist lawyer Gordon Chang (2001) predicted that a fiscal crisis could be the triggering event for the unavoidable disintegration of socialist China.

This fixation by the doomsayers on a large negative fiscal shock as a destructive systemic shock is understandable because fiscal imbalance is the proximate cause in most crises. The reason is that the state budget is often faced with the task of defusing the cumulative tensions unleashed by deeper, more fundamental social processes. To a first approximation, fiscal capacity is a fundamental determinant of system stability because economic sustainability depends on the ability to cover production costs, and political viability depends on the ability to reward one's supporters and to pay off one's enemies.

The reality in many cases is that fiscal sustainability is the prerequisite for economic sustainability and political viability, which are intricately linked and mutually reinforcing. To see the mutual interdependence of the two, one has only to recall the many times that near-bankrupt governments have been driven out of power after raising the prices of a subsidised item such as food, petrol or foreign exchange.[1] One could go so far as to say that the degree of economic and political resilience of a state can be measured by the State's ability to cover an unexpected, prolonged increase in expenditure or an unanticipated, protracted shortfall in revenue.²

A recent OECD report raised grave concerns about China's fiscal management. Specifically,

> China's officially reported spending figures reflect only about three-quarters of total government spending. Extra-budgetary spending, social security outlays and central government bond financing of local projects are not part of the official budget. Notwithstanding recent reforms, the government remains overly exposed to extra-budget and off-budget activities, which make public expenditures difficult to plan and control and which impair their accountability and transparency. Contingent liabilities have been a major source of unplanned spending and pose perhaps the greatest risk to the controllability of future expenditure (OECD 2006:10).

We share the concerns expressed in this report. We want to add that there are other equally important concerns about China's fiscal situation (for example, there are fundamental improvements that should be made to the public revenue side), and there is the even more important issue of fiscal sustainability. In our opinion, fiscal sustainability is more important than fiscal efficiency because the former determines the survival of the system, while the latter influences only the output growth rate.

In this chapter, we report the results from two different approaches to analyse the issue of fiscal sustainability

- the standard stock-flow analysis that focuses on the amount of public debt outstanding and the path of annual budget deficits
- the newer generational accounts approach that focuses on the difference between the tax burdens of the current generation and future generations of taxpayers.

We use both approaches because, as will become clear, they emphasise different aspects of the sustainability issue in fiscal management.³ In the stock-flow approach, the level of fiscal sustainability is indicated by the level of the steady-state debt–GDP ratio. In the extreme case of an explosive path for the debt–GDP ratio, the fiscal regime is definitely unsustainable. In the case of a very high steady-state debt–GDP ratio, especially when the value is beyond the international experience, this fiscal regime is deemed vulnerable to fiscal crises, for example, the cause could be an unexpected jump in emergency expenditure.

In this chapter, we give to the generational accounting approach an interpretation of sustainability that we have not seen discussed in the literature.⁴ Our interpretation is that the degree of intergenerational inequity is a measure of fiscal sustainability. If the tax burden of future generations is found to be much larger than the tax burden of the generation born today, present interest rates will be higher if financial markets perceive the possibility of high future taxes leading to a future tax revolt and/or future debt repudiation through inflation. In the extreme case, where debt repudiation is seen as certain, markets would refuse to finance the deficit, making the fiscal regime immediately unsustainable.

To get ahead of the analysis, our conclusions are that

- the present fiscal regime is sustainable, but China's low revenue–GDP ratio and its repeated recapitalisation of the state banks have made China vulnerable to a fiscal crisis
- the vulnerability to a fiscal crisis could be reduced easily with some straightforward reforms in the management of state assets, and in the regulatory regime of the financial sector
- the existing fiscal regime is highly inequitable towards future generations
- the intergenerational inequity could be reduced easily by reasonable reform of the pension system.

The stock-flow approach to fiscal sustainability

The fact that fiscal sustainability is central to economic management can be seen in the two fiscal targets that the original Growth and Stability Pact of the countries in the Euro-Zone specified for its members to meet

- the consolidated government budget deficit should not exceed 3 per cent of GDP except in the case of an unusually severe downturn
- the debt–GDP ratio should be brought down to 60 per cent or lower.

Table 8.1 gives an international perspective on the fiscal situation in China by comparing it with those of the OECD countries. We chose the year 2001 for China because we wanted to postpone until later discussion the fiscal consequences of the continuing recapitalisation of the state-owned banks. We use the year 2003 for OECD countries because the cross-country data for that year were conveniently available.[5] Table 8.1 reports that China's official debt–GDP ratio was 16.4 per cent, and compared favourably with the OECD average of 75.3 per cent. If we treat the tiny state of Luxembourg as an exception and exclude it from the comparison, the lower half of the OECD distribution of debt–GDP ratios ranges from 18.6 per cent (South Korea) to 55.5 per cent (Denmark); and the upper half of the distribution ranges from 58.1 per cent (Hungary) to 154 per cent (Japan).

As China's debt–GDP ratio of 16.4 per cent is below the 18.6 per cent of South Korea, and as China's annual budget deficit has nearly always been below 3 per cent of GDP, it would seem that China has a sounder fiscal situation than all the OECD countries.[6] Such an impression, however, needs to be qualified. Many

Table 8.1   Comparative perspectives on the size of the national debt, 1995 and 2003 (as a per cent of GDP)

(I)OECD's fiscal situation

	General government gross financial liabilities		Total tax revenue	
	1995	2003	1995	2003
Luxembourg	6.7	6.7	42.3	41.3
Korea	5.5	18.6	19.4	25.3
Australia	43.4	18.9	29.8	31.6
Ireland	81.2	31.1	32.8	29.7
New Zealand	51.7	32.0	36.9	34.9
Iceland	59.4	41.4	32.1	39.8
United Kingdom	52.7	41.9	35.1	35.6
Czech Republic	19.3	46.8	37.5	37.7
Slovakia	n.a.	49.7	n.a.	31.1
Norway	40.5	50.4	41.1	43.4
Finland	65.1	52.0	46.0	44.8
Poland	n.a.	52.1	37.0	34.2
Spain	68.8	54.8	31.8	34.9
Denmark	77.6	55.5	49.5	48.3
Hungary	n.a.	58.1	42.4	38.5
Sweden	82.2	59.8	48.5	50.6
Netherlands	87.0	61.9	41.9	38.8
United States	74.2	63.4	27.9	25.6
Germany	55.8	64.6	37.2	35.5
Portugal	69.9	66.6	33.6	37.1
Austria	69.6	69.4	41.1	43.1
France	62.6	71.7	42.9	43.4
Canada	100.8	75.7	35.6	33.8
Belgium	135.2	103.2	44.8	45.4
Greece	108.7	108.8	32.4	35.7
Italy	125.5	121.4	41.2	43.1
Japan	87.0	154.0	26.7	25.3
OECD total	72.8	75.3	35.7	36.3

(II)China's fiscal situation

	Debt–GDP (per cent)		Revenue–GDP (per cent)		
	2001		1995	2001	2007 estimate
Official data	16.4		10.7	16.8	21.6
Revised debt–GDP ratio in 2001 after taking into account					
	(a) 2nd recapitalisation costs		(b) all contigent liabilities		
Citigroup (2002)	65.9		114.9		
Fan (2003)	57.4		74.7		

Sources: OECD data available from http://stats.oecd.org/wbos/viewhtml.aspx?QueryName=2&QueryType=View&Lang=en. China revenue data for 1995 and 2001 from National Bureau of Statistics of China, 2005a. *China Statistical Yearbook 2005*, China Statistics Press, Beijing. Revenue estimate for 2007 is from Deutsche Bank (2006).

analysts have noted that China's official debt–GDP ratio understates the extent of the country's fiscal burden because it does not include the non-performing loans in the state-owned banks that the State would have to take over during recapitalisation, and it does not include many contingent liabilities (for example, pension schemes of state enterprises) that the State would have to assume responsibility for in order to preserve economic and social stability. Citigroup (2002), for example, estimated that the cost for state-owned bank recapitalisation was 46.9 per cent of GDP, social security obligations were 26.1 per cent and external debts were 15.6 per cent.

Part two of Table 8.1 uses estimates from Citigroup (2002) and Fan (2003) to revise China's official debt–GDP ratio. The outcomes are that China's debt–GDP ratio is 57.4 to 65.9 per cent when only state-owned bank recapitalisation is undertaken and 74.7 to 114.9 per cent when all contingent liabilities are recognised.

This change in China's debt–GDP ratio

- moves China from the bottom of the OECD distribution to the top half of the distribution
- in the worst-case scenario, puts China in the group of the five OECD countries with the highest ratios: 74.7–114.9 per cent for China versus 75.7 per cent for Canada, 103.2 per cent for Belgium, 108.8 per cent for Greece, 121.4 per cent for Italy and 154 per cent for Japan.

Should the much higher revised debt–GDP ratio raise concern about China's fiscal sustainability? Our cautious reading of the evidence is that a fiscal crisis in China is not imminent. China's ratio not only falls within the OECD experience, its worst-case ratio of 114.9 per cent is still lower than Italy, which has had a satisfactory overall economic performance. Most importantly, China's ratio is still substantially lower than the highest OECD ratio of 154 per cent (Japan).

While we believe that China's fiscal regime is sustainable, we do think that there are two fiscal features that have rendered the fiscal system vulnerable to a crisis. The first is that China has a lower capacity to service its public debt than all the OECD countries. While China's revenue–GDP ratio has been increasing rapidly, from 10.7 per cent in 1995 to 16.8 per cent in 2001, and to an expected 21.6 per cent in 2007, the 2007 level is still low by OECD standards.

The average revenue–GDP ratio in the OECD in 2003 was 36.3 per cent, with the three lowest ratios (25.3 per cent for Japan and South Korea, and 25.6 per cent for the United States) higher than China's. While China's best-case debt–GDP ratio of 57.4–65.9 per cent puts it in the same group as Denmark (55.5 per cent), Hungary (58.1 per cent), Sweden (59.8 per cent) and the Netherlands (61.9

per cent), China's revenue–GDP ratio is only 21.6 per cent compared with Denmark's 48.3 per cent, Hungary's 38.5 per cent, Sweden's 50.6 per cent and the Netherlands' 38.8 per cent. For the OECD countries with debt–GDP ratios similar to China's worst-case ratio of 74.7–114.9 per cent, all also have higher revenue–GDP ratios: 21.6 per cent for China versus 33.8 per cent for Canada, 45.4 per cent for Belgium, 35.7 per cent for Greece and 43.1 per cent for Italy.

The important point about this first fiscal feature is that as China's public debt rises from 16.4 per cent of GDP to 74.7 per cent with the incremental assumption of the contingent liabilities, the State will have to reduce expenditure steadily to accommodate the additional debt service unless there is an increase in state revenue.

The second feature that renders China vulnerable to a fiscal crisis is the constant need to recapitalise the state-owned banks. In 1998, state-owned banks were recapitalised to bring the average capital adequacy ratios (CAR) of the four biggest state-owned banks (the 'big four') to more than 8 per cent at the end of that year, but subsequent losses reduced the average CAR of the big four to 5 per cent at the beginning of 2002, making another recapitalisation necessary (see details in Tong and Woo 2006).

It needs to be emphasised that the incremental recapitalisation of state-owned banks that has been going on since 2003 is the second such recapitalisation. The serious implication is that if a third recapitalisation were to occur in the future, China's debt–GDP ratio would rise to the 154 per cent level of Japan, a country that suffered an economic stagnation that lasted more than 10 years.

The important point from this second fiscal feature is that the government cannot afford to continue recapitalising the state-owned banks; indeed, this is possibly the last time it can do so without upsetting confidence in the financial markets about the soundness of China's fiscal regime.

This point about the present recapitalisation being the last is confirmed by the dynamic analysis of the debt–GDP ratio in Tong and Woo (2006), who show that constant recapitalisation of the state-owned banks would make fiscal management very difficult. China can afford constant recapitalisation of the state-owned banks only if its long-term annual growth rate (say, for the next 80 years) is 9.5 per cent or higher. In the Tong and Woo (2006) analysis, the usual scenario of a long-term growth rate of 8 per cent would still produce a debt–GDP ratio that was too high.

How difficult is it to raise China's revenue–GDP ratio and to stop losses in the state-owned banks in order to ensure fiscal sustainability? With regard to raising state revenue, we make two interrelated observations.

The first is that since the State has the right to raise taxes, it is a mystery that fiscal crises have happened so often and in many parts of the world. In theory, a government faced with a repayment of principal could impose a new tax on bondholders and then use this new revenue to redeem the bonds. In practice, however, such an act would be perceived correctly as a confiscation of wealth by a profligate (possibly also incompetent) government, and could lead to political unrest that toppled the government. In short, even though governments can introduce new taxes at any time, this is an option many are cautious about exercising for political reasons. The worry is that raising taxes might be interpreted by the populace in the same way that a currency devaluation is usually interpreted—as a failure of governance.

The second observation about tax-raising ability is that the G-7 countries with the highest revenue–GDP ratios are in western Europe: for example, France (43.4 per cent), Germany (35.5 per cent), Italy (43.1 per cent) and the United Kingdom (35.6 per cent), versus the United States (25.6 per cent) and Japan (25.3 per cent). In these western European countries, citizens voted in politicians who then raised taxes to finance social democratic programs (for example, subsidised universal health care, subsidised higher education and public pension schemes).

The reasons why the United States has low taxes and fewer social programs than western Europe are many and complex, but two are that the United States was founded on the basis of a tax revolt against England and it has a stronger cultural emphasis on individualism. In short, a government could raise taxes and survive politically only if the citizens liked these state-provided services and were willing to pay for them. This explains why the highest tax burdens are found in democracies and not in authoritarian societies: the taxes could be collected in the former only because the people had agreed to their imposition and to their intended use.

On the issue of how to raise China's revenue–GDP ratio to make the fiscal regime sustainable, our opinion is that the ratio is unlikely to continue growing at the speed of the 1995–2001 period because the value-added tax (VAT) and the company income tax are becoming the main sources of state revenue—and these are flat not progressive taxes. Therefore, China's revenue–GDP ratio is unlikely to increase much more unless new taxes or higher tax rates are introduced. Because we doubt that it would be popular for the Chinese government to raise taxes in the name of covering the losses of the banks and of taking over the pension schemes of state enterprises, we think that it might be more astute politically to generate the needed revenue by selling state assets.

The solution for stopping the losses in the state-owned bank sector (the second requirement for fiscal sustainability) lies in imposing a hard budgetary constraint on the banks. State-owned bank managers have to be convinced that the present recapitalisation will be the last free supper (which the 1998 recapitalisation was announced as), and that their compensation and promotion will depend solely on the profitability of their banks relative to private banks.

At the same time, the prudential supervision and monitoring of bank operations will have to be strengthened to prevent asset stripping and to discourage reckless investments fostered by the asymmetrical reward system under the soft budget constraint.[7] The operations of state-owned banks could be improved further by bringing in foreign strategic investors who would be part of the management team, and by removing the influence of local governments on bank operations.

One additional way to harden the budgetary constraint faced by the state-owned banks is to privatise some of their branches and use the performance of the new private banks to gauge the performance of the remaining state-owned banks. The privatisation of some branches will also help convince the state-owned bank managers that the government is serious when it says the present recapitalisation will be the last free supper.

The generational accounting approach to fiscal sustainability

The generational accounting approach to evaluating fiscal policy pioneered by Auerbach et al. (1991) represents a clever reframing of the question about fiscal sustainability by operationalising the principle of 'there is no such thing as a free lunch'. The question of sustainability is not answered with 'yes', 'no', 'maybe' or 'it depends', it is answered by estimating the tax burden that future generations would have to bear in order for the present fiscal regime to be sustained.[8] What permits the estimation of this future tax burden is the imposition of the inter-temporal budget constraint on government finances. Whatever budget deficits a government runs today and has incurred in the past will have to be repaid by future budget surpluses.

The government, in short, cannot keep rolling over its debt and borrowing additional amounts to make interest payments and cover new deficits. This restriction thus rules out the existence a non-zero steady-state debt–GDP ratio because it regards a 30 per cent ratio as being just as unsustainable as a 3,000 per cent ratio. This implication is obvious once we recognise that the non-technical translation of the term 'inter-temporal budget constraint' is that no one (including the government) can create a free lunch for itself by employing a Ponzi game. The proponents of generational accounting do not identify explicitly (at least in the readings we have undertaken so far) what mechanism exists to prevent such a Ponzi game. The answer presumably is that the financial markets would step in by refusing to fund the bonds, giving them a zero price.

Generational accounting is based on the government's inter-temporal budget constraint, written as equation (1), which implies that the future net tax payments of current and future generations should be sufficient, in present value, to cover the present value of the government's future purchases plus its initial net debt. The term 'net payments' refers to the difference between government tax receipts of all types and government transfer payments of all types.

$$\sum_{s=0}^{D} N_{t,t-s} + \sum_{s=1}^{\infty} N_{t,t+s} = \sum_{s=t}^{\infty} G_s (1+r)^{t-s} - W_t^g \tag{1}$$

All terms in (1) are real values, that is, they are measured at constant prices. The first summation on the left-hand side of (1) adds together the generational accounts of existing generations. The term $N_{t,k}$ stands for the generational account of generation k and it equals the present value of the average remaining lifetime net tax payment at time t of the generation born in year k. The index k in this summation runs from $t-D$ (where D = the maximum length of life) to t in order to sum up the sum of the existing generations.

The second summation on the left side of (1) adds together the present values of the generational accounts of future generations, with k again representing the year of birth. The first term on the right-hand side of (1) expresses the present value of government purchases. The values of government purchases in year s, given by G_s, are also discounted to year t. The term r is the government's real before-tax discount rate. The remaining term on the right-hand side denotes the government's net wealth—its financial assets minus the sum of its financial liabilities and the market value of its public enterprises.

Generational accounts are defined specifically as the present value of net taxes (taxes paid minus transfer payments received) that individuals of different age cohorts are expected, under current policy, to pay over their remaining lifetimes. The generational account $N_{t,k}$ is defined by

$$N_{t,k} = \sum_{s=\max(t,k)}^{K+D} T_{s,k} P_{s,k} (1+r)^{t-s} \tag{2}$$

In equation (2), $T_{s,k}$ stands for the projected average net tax payment to the government made in year s by a member of the generation born in year k. The term $P_{s,k}$ stands for the number of surviving members of the cohort in year s who were born in year *k*. In the case of generations who are born before year *t*, the summation begins in year *t* and is discounted to year *t*. For generations born in year *k>t*, the summation begins in year *k* and is discounted to year *t*.

Given the right-hand side of equation (1) and the first term on the left-hand side of equation (1), we determine, as a residual, the value of the second term on the left-hand side of equation (1): the collective payment required of future generations. Based on this amount, the average present-value lifetime net tax payment of each future generation can be determined under the assumption that these payments rise for members of each successive future cohort at the economy's rate of labour productivity growth, *g*—that is, the net tax amount will increase by 10 per cent when income increases by 10 per cent.

So the growth-adjusted net tax of future generations is directly comparable with the per capita net tax payment of current newborns, which is equal to $N_{t,t}$ divided by $P_{t,t}$, because the generational accounts of newborns and future generations take into account net tax payments over these generations' entire lifetimes. The use of growth-adjusted net tax for the future generations means that if it is higher (lower) than the net tax of the zero-age generation then the future generation is paying a higher (lower) tax rate than the zero-age generation.

If the net tax payments (after adjustment of income growth) of each member of the future generations equals $\frac{N_{t,t}}{P_{t,t}}$, then generational policy is balanced; and if it exceeds (is smaller than) $\frac{N_{t,t}}{P_{t,t}}$, then a member of the future generations faces a larger (smaller) growth-adjusted lifetime net tax burden than do current newborns.

It should be noted that the generational accounts reflect only taxes and social insurance contributions paid less transfers received (including education, health and social security expenditures). The generational accounts do not show the net benefit or net burden that any generation receives from all government policies; they can show the change in a generation's net benefit (or net burden) from a particular policy change only if the impact of this change falls exclusively on taxes and transfers. Thus, generational accounting can tell us only which generations will pay for government spending; it does not tell us which generations will benefit from that spending. Furthermore, generational accounting does not incorporate induced behavioural effects to policy changes.

Applying the generational accounts approach to China

A recent paper by Jiang et al. (2006), henceforth referred to as JRW, applied the generational accounts framework to study China's fiscal situation.[9] The standard generational accounting approach separates the members of each generation into males and females. JRW has another fundamental dichotomy: urban residents versus rural residents, because most state institutions, including the tax social security systems, treat these two types of residents very differently.

Because China is a developing transitional economy that is changing very rapidly, the JRW analysis projected significant changes to the present patterns in population location, demographic distribution, output growth and institutional arrangements. For example, JRW built into the generational accounts the rural-to-urban migration process and the expansion of the social security system. Also because of the paucity of data that are required to draw reasonable assumptions on the incidence of taxes to members of each generation, JRW settled on the heuristic practice of producing two estimates (Net Payment 1 and Net Payment 2) for the distribution of the taxes and transfers.

JRW constructed Net Payment 1 in two steps
(a) distributed the aggregate amount in each category in the base year by age, sex and status based on relative age–sex–status tax profiles and age–sex–status transfer profiles that were derived from cross-section micro data sets; and
(b) assumed that these two profiles in the future would be the same as in the base year, with an adjustment for growth.

JRW constructed Net Payment 2 by distributing all taxes by an age–sex–status consumption profile.

The burden on future generations—the base case

Table 8.2 reports the JRW estimates of per capita net tax payments for urban males and females and rural males and females under the base case for the two different assumptions on the incidence of taxes and transfers. It shows positive values for the accounts of young and middle-aged urban cohorts alive in 2002, indicating that each member of these generations will, on average, pay more in present value than they receive.

For the urban males aged 46 and older, the generational accounts are negative—that is, the present value of the transfers they will receive exceed the present value of the taxes they will pay. The generational accounts are negative for urban females aged 40 and older. The younger age at which this switch occurs for urban females is attributable to their lower labour force participation rates and earlier retirement age.

For rural cohorts, the generational accounts are positive throughout their life span. This reflects the small amount of transfers that aged rural residents receive from the State.

Table 8.2 **Per capita net tax payments for different cohorts in JRW's base case simulation**

Age in 2002	Urban male		Urban female		Rural male		Rural female	
	Net Tax (1)	Net Tax (2)	Net Tax (1)	Net Tax (2)	Net Tax (1)	Net Tax (2)	Net Tax (1)	Net Tax (2)
0	55,439	52,924	30,292	28,086	16,964	21,431	11,995	18,218
10	71,749	66,499	40,198	34,606	24,395	27,131	16,839	22,040
20	92,334	82,916	54,443	44,524	34,096	33,536	21,988	24,955
30	82,597	75,044	42,728	35,973	32,328	33,424	19,725	24,423
40	37,410	34,731	−5,027	−6,151	25,649	29,757	15,389	22,068
50	−24,446	−21,471	−51,094	−47,173	16,472	23,980	9,809	18,207
60	−43,350	−40,287	−49,744	−45,440	7,708	13,733	6,036	12,876
70	−81,314	−78,100	−29,118	−25,066	3,836	8,108	3,587	8,634
80	−64,941	−63,262	−17,081	−14,801	2,151	4,525	2,144	5,074
90	−43,208	−42,430	−10,526	−9,400	1,269	2,589	1,199	2,748
Future	79,633	74,379	43,511	39,472	24,367	30,119	17,230	25,604
Ratio	1.4364	1.4054	1.4364	1.4054	1.4364	1.4054	1.4364	1.4054

Note: Net Payment 1 (Net Tax 1) assumes that the taxes are borne by those paying them; and Net Payment 2 (Net Tax 2) assumes that all taxes are distributed by age–sex–status consumption profiles.
Source: Reproduced from Jiang, Y., Ruoen, R. and Woo, W.T., 2006. A generational accounts analysis of China's fiscal fituation: que sera sera, the future's not ours to see?, manuscript, University of California.

The row in Table 8.2 labelled 'future' shows the present value of the amounts that each member of the generations born after 2002 will pay, on average (assuming that the tax bill of each person in the future generations will rise at the rate of productivity growth, PGR). In the case of Net Tax Payment 1, each member of the urban male generations born after 2002 will get a bill from the central and local governments for RMB79,633, which is 43.6 per cent larger than the bill paid by the urban males in 2002 (the zero-age males). Since the reported net tax of the future generations is income-adjusted,[10] the ratio (net tax of future generations/ net tax of zero-age generation) is a proxy for the ratio of the two tax rates paid by the future generations and the zero-age generation: that is, the tax rate of the future generations is about 44 per cent higher than the tax rate paid by the zero-age generation.

In the case of Net Tax Payment 2, the bill amounts to RMB74,379 for urban males, which is 40.54 per cent larger than the bill facing zero-age males in 2002.

Table 8.3   **The ratio of per capita net tax payments of future generations to the zero-age generation in 2002 under different retirement age assumptions**[a]

Scenarios	Base case male: 60; female: 50-55	All: 60	All: 63	Male: 65; female: 60
Net Tax (1)	1.4364	1.1826	1.0031	0.9822
Net Tax (2)	1.4054	1.1598	0.9858	0.9655

Note: [a] Ratio is a proxy for the ratio of the tax rates paid by the future generations and the zero-age generation.
Source: Reproduced from Jiang, Y., Ruoen, R. and Woo, W.T., 2006. A generational accounts analysis of China's fiscal fituation: que sera sera, the future's not ours to see?, manuscript, University of California.

The impact of retirement age on intergenerational inequity

In China, the present retirement age is 60 for urban males, 55 for urban female cadres and 50 for urban female workers. As the life expectancy in China is 74 for urban males and 78 for urban females, compared with the average life expectancy of 76 for people in industrial countries, the retirement age is much younger in China than in industrial countries.

Table 8.3 reports JRW's results of how intergenerational equity changed with different retirement-age assumptions for urban residents. The scenario labelled 'All: 60' means that the retirement age is 60 from 2003 onwards. The scenario labelled 'All: 63' means that the retirement age is 63 from 2003 onwards. The scenario labelled 'male: 65; female: 60' means that the retirement age from 2003 onwards is 65 for males and 60 for females. JRW found that the generational balance was essentially achieved in the 'All: 63' scenario and the 'male: 65; female: 60' scenario.

Concluding remarks

The state budget is often called on to change spending flows to stabilise price levels, to apply the grease of infrastructure investments to crash through production bottlenecks that are hindering economic growth, and to supply the financial glue to hold the polity together. It is therefore hard to overemphasise the importance of fiscal soundness in economic management.

We have used the standard stock-flow approach and the newer generational accounts approach to examine China's fiscal regime. The strong conclusion from the stock-flow analysis is that frequent bank recapitalisation is the biggest threat to China's fiscal solvency, and that the recapitalisation of the state-owned banks that has been happening since 1996 is the last such recapitalisation that China can afford.

Because fiscal solvency is ensured when the State keeps interest rates low through regulation to contain the cost of debt service, China faces a difficult trade-off between easy debt management and the promotion of financial market development via bank recapitalisation and interest rate deregulation.

The strong conclusion of the generational accounting approach is that the present fiscal regime produces severe intergenerational inequity in tax burdens. A member of a future generation will pay a tax rate that is about 40 per cent higher than the tax rate paid by a member of today's generation.

Our analysis arrives at three main policy suggestions to reduce China's vulnerability to possible future fiscal difficulties.

1. Increase the extractive capacity of the State so that the revenue–GDP ratio increases to 25 per cent in the medium term. This extra revenue will be the fiscal cushion that allows the State to accommodate unexpected expenditure demands or revenue shortfalls. As noted earlier, the collection of revenue might first require overcoming the challenge of forging the political consensus for a tax increase.
2. Reform the management of state assets and the regulation of the financial sector to eliminate the phenomenon of repeated recapitalisation of state-owned banks. The privatisation of some units of the state-owned banks, and the emergence of large domestic private banks, will help strengthen the budget constraints perceived by the managers of state-owned banks.
3. Raise the retirement age of the urban population to remove pressures on the pension system. This move would also accommodate the new demands of a population that is experiencing an increase in life expectancy and an improvement in physical health.

Notes

1   See Bates (2005) for examples of African governments falling after removing food subsidies, and see Cooper (1971) for examples of government changes after currency devaluations. President Suharto of Indonesia was pushed out of office in May 1998, one month after raising fuel prices.
2   Of course, a strong fiscal position cannot overcome all challenges: for example, when a challenger thinks that he can assume political power and hence take control of the fiscal mechanism, it will be very difficult to bribe him to go away.
3   See Auerbach et al. 1994; Kotlikoff 1993; and Jiang et al. 2006 for discussions of the differences between these two approaches.

4   I might, in short, be applying the generational accounts approach to a concept (sustainability) that was not intended by its founders, Auerbach et al. (1991).
5   Available from http://stats.oecd.org/wbos/viewhtml.aspx?QueryName=2&QueryType=View&Lang=en
6   Except for Luxembourg, which was excluded because of its atypical nature.
7   The asymmetry is from the absence of financial punishment when a loss occurs.
8   As the generational accounting approach assumes that the per capita tax burden of future generations increases at the rate of productivity growth and compares the tax burden of future generations with the tax burden of the generation born this year (labelled generation zero), this comparison of the two amounts paid is also a comparison of the tax rate paid by future generations and the tax rate paid by generation zero.
9   JRW is not the first application of the generational accounting approach to Chinese data. The first was by Ren et al. 2004. The generational accounts approach to analysing fiscal regimes has of course already been applied to many countries, for example, in Auerbach and Chun 2005; Banks et al. 1999; and Hagemann and Christoph 1997.
10 In JRW's computation, the amount of the net tax of the future generations rises in proportion with the rise in income: that is, net tax will automatically go up 10 per cent when incomes rise by 10 per cent. What is meant here? I think a word/s is missing or has been repeated.

9

Employment growth, labour scarcity and the nature of China's trade expansion

Cai Fang and Dewen Wang

Since the mid 1990s, China has deepened its reforms of state-owned enterprises, urban employment and social welfare systems in order to improve the efficiency of state-owned enterprises and enhance their survival capabilities in the face of fierce international competition. The reforms have released millions of rendundant urban workers and the issue of unemployment has become a top priority in Chinese social and economic policies.

China finally joined the World Trade Organization (WTO) late in 2001. Some commentators predicted that accession to the WTO might worsen urban unemployment. Rapid trade expansion has, however, not only fuelled Chinese economic growth, it has created more job opportunities by expanding non-agricultural sectors, mitigating the severe pressure of urban unemployment.

The emergence of a shortage of rural migrant workers signals, to a certain extent, the transition in the rural labour force supply from an unlimited to a limited surplus (Cai and Wang 2005, Wang et al. 2006). The wages of rural migrant workers have grown at an average annual rate of more than 10 per cent in recent years. If this trend continues, and unless labour productivity grows rapidly, increases in labour costs will be unavoidable, threatening the competitiveness of Chinese manufacturing industry.

This chapter has four parts. Part one examines employment growth and changing situations of urban employment. Part two describes the trade expansion and its impact on employment growth. Part three discusses labour scarcities and their impact on the international competitiveness of Chinese manufacturing. The chapter concludes with a discussion of some policy implications.

Employment growth and changing situations of urban employment

Economic and employment growth

Economic growth is a precondition for employment growth. Okun's Law states that there is a negative relationship between economic growth and unemployment. Empirical experiences from the United States indicate that a 1 per cent addition to GDP growth will lower the unemployment rate by 2 per cent (Mankiw 2003). Economic booming (or recession) often causes the acceleration (or slowdown) of employment growth. The Chinese economy experienced a boom in the first half of the 1990s, with an average 12 per cent annual growth rate, and a slowdown in the second half of the 1990s, with an average 8.3 per cent annual growth rate. Since 2001, Chinese growth has accelerated, with an average annual growth rate of 8.9 per cent (Table 9.1).

According to Okun's Law, employment growth should have been faster in the period between 1991 and 1995 than in the other two five-year periods. But the growth of total employment seems to contradict Okun's Law; it grew faster between 1996 and 2000 than in the other two five-year periods.

The growth of total employment was 1 per cent in the first half of the 1990s, 1.2 per cent in the second half of the 1990s and 1 per cent per annum in the first five years of the new century (Table 9.1). The inclusion of agricultural employment is the main reason for this paradox. In a traditional dual economy, the agricultural sector plays a role as a supplier of surplus labour to the modern economy in the process of economic expansion (or contraction). If we exclude agricultural employment, the growth of non-agricultural employment in the industrial and service sectors is consistent with the predicted direction in terms of Okun's Law.

GDP growth in the first half of the 1990s was 3–4 percentage points higher than in the second half of the 1990s and in the first five years of this century, so the growth of non-agricultural employment in the first half of the 1990s was also higher. From 1991 to 2005, employment growth had cyclical characteristics. Employment growth in secondary and tertiary industries in the first half of the 1990s was fastest, with average annual rates of 2.5 per cent and 7.1 per cent, respectively, while they dropped to 0.7 per cent and 3.3 per cent in the second half of the 1990s, and rose to 2.3 per cent and 3.7 per cent in the first five years of this century.

Economic growth is not a sufficient condition for fast employment growth because it can be driven by huge investment or the expansion of capital-intensive sectors. In an economy with abundant labour resources, cheap labour is the source of its

Table 9.1   GDP and employment growth in China, 1991–2005

	1991–95	1996–2000	2001–05
GDP growth (per cent)			
Total	12.0	8.3	8.9
Agriculture	4.2	3.5	3.9
Secondary industries	17.5	9.8	10.7
Tertiary industries	10.0	8.2	8.6
Employment growth (per cent)			
Total	1.0	1.2	1.0
Agriculture	–1.8	0.3	–1.2
Secondary industries	2.5	0.7	2.3
Tertiary industries	7.1	3.3	3.7
Employment elasticity			
Total	0.08	0.14	0.11
Agriculture	–0.43	0.09	–0.29
Secondary industries	0.14	0.07	0.21
Tertiary industries	0.71	0.40	0.43

Sources: National Bureau of Statistics of China, 2005a. *China Statistical Yearbook 2005*, China Statistics Press, Beijing. National Bureau of Statistics of China, 2006d. *The Statistical Communiqué on the 2005 National Economic and Social Development*, 28 February.

comparative advantage. If the development strategy follows the principle of comparative advantage to maximise the utilisation of its abundant labour resources, rapid economic growth can involve fast employment growth.

Employment elasticity measures the ratio of employment growth to output growth. If rapid economic growth leads to fast employment growth, its employment elasticity is high; otherwise, its employment elasticity is low. In Table 9.1, total employment elasticities do not change much over time due to the buffering effect of agricultural employment; that is, agricultural employment declines when an economic boom drives the expansion of non-agricultural sectors to absorb the transfer of the rural labour force, but it increases when economic recession releases labourers from non-agricultural sectors.

The employment elasticities in the secondary and tertiary sectors were higher in the first half of the 1990s, when Deng Xiaoping ushered in an economic boom, but they declined in the second half of the 1990s, when the central government started to deepen reforms of state-owned enterprises and urban social security systems.

Since 2001, accession to the WTO has supported the acceleration of economic growth and employment through unprecedented trade expansion. The employment elasticities in secondary and tertiary sectors rose above the levels of the late

1990s. The big jump in employment elasticity in the secondary sector was due mainly to the acceleration of export growth, which stimulated the expansion of the manufacturing sectors.

Employment growth differs between urban and rural areas and across different types of enterprises (Table 9.2). Urban employment has maintained fast growth since 1990 and reached 264.8 million in 2004. Between 1991 and 2004, average urban employment growth was 3.2 per cent annually. In contrast, average rural employment growth was 0.1 per cent in the same period. The decomposition of employment by types of enterprise ownership reveals the dramatic adjustment of employment structure.

In urban areas, the downsizing of state-owned and collective enterprises released millions of redundant workers. Employment growth in state-owned and collective units was at the average rate of –3 per cent and –9.2 per cent annually between 1991 and 2004, respectively, causing the sum of their shares in total urban employment to decline from 79 per cent to 32.5 per cent in the same period. Meanwhile, employment growth in the newly emerged non state-owned enterprise units, such as limited-liability corporations, shareholding corporations, private enterprises, enterprises with funds from Hong Kong, Macao and Taiwan, foreign-funded enterprises and self-employed businesses, increased rapidly, accounting for an average of 19.8 per cent of total urban employment between 2001 and 2004.

The dramatic expansion of self-employment in the 1990s and employment in undefined units (urban employment residuals) in the second half of the 1990s illustrates the increasing diversification and informalisation of urban employment. Statistically, the substantial increase of unit employment in such newly emerged non state-owned enterprise sectors does not sufficiently offset the decline in state and collective employment, causing a residual between classified and total employment. This residual accounted for 11.3 per cent in the first half of the 1990s, and increased to 38.4 per cent of total urban employment between 2001 and 2004.

The expansion of the missing employment not only emphasises the incapacity of the traditional labour statistics to reflect the actual labour market situation under the diversified and complicated economic structure. It also reflects increasingly severe unemployment and urban employment protection. In order to protect local employment, local governments often implement short-term policies that obstruct the expansion of the labour market, intervene in labour adjustment in enterprises and sometimes ask enterprises not to hire outside labourers (Cai et al. 2001). Entry barriers to formal sectors and social exclusion have left migrants and low-skilled workers being employed mainly in informal sectors with poor working

Table 9.2 **Employment growth in urban and rural areas, 1991–2004** (per cent)

	Growth (per cent)			Composition (per cent)		
	1991–95	1996–2000	2001–04	1991–95	1996–2000	2001–04
Urban employment						
Total	2.2	4.0	3.4	100.0	100.0	100.0
State-owned units	1.7	–6.2	–4.6	60.2	44.9	28.2
Collectively owned units	–2.3	–13.1	–12.0	18.8	10.4	4.3
Non-state-owned enterprise units	45.9	19.5	18.1	4.1	11.2	19.8
Self-employed individuals	20.9	7.0	4.3	5.6	9.7	9.2
Residuals	–5.5	38.6	5.4	11.3	23.8	38.4
Rural employment						
Total	0.5	0.0	–0.1	100.0	100.0	100.0
Township and village enterprises	7.0	0.0	2.0	23.7	26.4	27.5
Private enterprises	35.2	19.5	15.7	0.5	1.6	3.3
Self-employed individuals	15.7	0.0	–8.4	4.5	7.1	4.8
Agriculture	–2.4	–0.4	–1.0	71.3	64.9	64.4

Note: Non-state-owned enterprise units include shareholding cooperative units, joint-ownership units, limited-liability corporations, shareholding corporations, private enterprises, units with funds from Hong Kong, Macao and Taiwan, and foreign-funded units. Urban residuals equal urban total employment minus state-owned units, collectively owned units, non-state-owned enterprise units and self-employed individuals.
Source: National Bureau of Statistics of China, 2005a. *China Statistical Yearbook 2005*, China Statistics Press, Beijing.

conditions, low pay and a lack of social protection. This causes a reduction in security and safety in the labour market (Solinger 2001).

In rural areas, non-agricultural employment comes from township and village enterprises (TVEs), private enterprises and self-employment. The rapid output growth of TVEs in the first half of the 1990s drove their employment growth at an average annual rate of 7 per cent, but their employment growth dropped to zero in the second half of the 1990s because the East Asian financial crisis dramatically lowered the export demands of TVEs. In order to compete with other enterprises, the development of TVEs has been capital-intensive to improve labour productivity, which further constrained the employment expansion.

Since 2001, employment growth in TVEs has kept an average annual rate of 2 per cent, which is lower than the growth of total urban employment. In 2004, there were 138.7 million rural workers employed in TVEs, accounting for 27.5 per cent of total rural employment. Employment in rural private enterprises grew faster, but its contribution to rural non-agricultural employment was still small because it accounted for only 3.3 per cent of total rural employment in 2004.

A new round of economic growth since 2001, driven by investment and exports, has created vast non-agricultural employment opportunities that accelerate the transfer of the rural labour force into non-agricultural sectors against the background of increasing rural-urban income disparity. This has generated a declining trend in self-employment and agricultural employment.

The changing situation of urban employment

The economic transition was carried out in an incremental way until the mid 1990s. Under the pressure of the WTO accession, the massive restructuring of state-owned enterprises, intended to touch on the stock of state-owned enterprises, signalled a more radical reform, having caused dramatic changes in labour markets (Meng et al. 2004). Since the mid 1990s, economic reform in China has entered a stage of stock adjustment with no guarantee of benefit of compensation for everybody. There have been more and more layoffs and unemployment rates have increased.

Assuming rural unemployment is trivial, we can use the aggregate statistics to calculate the urban unemployment rate at the aggregate level. From published data on components of population, we first estimate the economically active population in urban areas by subtracting rural employment from the whole country's economically active population, then we take the difference between the economically active population and the employed population as unemployed population in urban areas. By definition, the ratio of urban unemployment to the urban economic population is the unemployment rate.

Figure 9.1 illustrates the trend in the urban unemployment rate from 1990 to 2004. The aggregate unemployment rate increased sharply in the late 1990s, from 4 per cent in 1995 to 7.6 per cent in 2000, but then declined and was 5.8 per cent in 2004.

In urban China, there are official statistics for registered unemployment. According to the official definition, the statistics cover only those job-losers who 1) are aged 16–50 for males and 16–45 for females,[1] 2) are not entitled to receive *xiagang* benefits, and 3) are locally registered as urban *hukou* ('waiting for employment'). Obviously, registered unemployment is not an effective indication of the real situation because it does not count workers who are unemployed but not registered, and then understates the real unemployment situation.

Figure 9.1   **Urban unemployment rate in China, 1990–2004** (per cent)

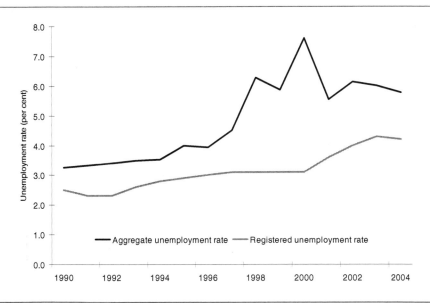

Source: National Bureau of Statistics of China, 2005a. *China Statistical Yearbook 2005*, China Statistics Press, Beijing.

In Figure 9.1, the registered unemployment rate is lower than the aggregate unemployment rate, and there is a large gap in the period when unemployment became more severe. Since 2000, the registered unemployment rate has kept an upward trend, which does not mean urban unemployment worsened. Rather, it represents only the provision of social protection for urban unemployed workers.

Combining the numbers of those laid off and registered unemployment also indicates a changing situation in the urban labour market from a tight to a loose status. The number of state-owned enterprise workers laid off increased from 5.9 million in 1998 to 6.6 million in 2000, but dropped afterwards (Table 9.3). In 2005, there were only 620,000 laid-off state-owned enterprise workers. The total number of laid-off workers follows a similar trend: it peaked at 9.1 million in 2000 and declined to 2.7 million in 2004. Even if we add up the total number of laid-off workers and the registered unemployed, their aggregate rose to 15.06 million in 2000 from 14.5 million, and declined to 10.9 million in 2004.

In 2000, the fifth population census asked respondents two questions about whether they were engaged in more than one hour of income-earning activities within the previous week or were looking for jobs. Based on the census data, the

Table 9.3   **Numbers of workers laid off and registered unemployment, 1998–2005** (million)

	State-owned enterprise workers laid off	Total laid off	Registered unemployment
1998	5.95	8.77	5.71
1999	6.53	9.37	5.75
2000	6.57	9.11	5.95
2001	5.15	7.42	6.81
2002	4.10	6.18	7.70
2003	2.60	4.21	8.00
2004	1.53	2.72	8.27
2005	0.62	..	8.39

Sources: National Bureau of Statistics of China, 2005a. *China Statistical Yearbook 2005*, China Statistics Press, Beijing. And NBS and MOLSS, *Statistical Bulletin on Labour and Social Security Development, 2005.*

national average urban unemployment rate was 8.3 per cent in 2000, and the figures were larger in large cites than in small cities or towns.

The Institute of Population and Labour Economics, Chinese Academy of Social Sciences, launched a two-wave *China Urban Labour Survey* (CULS) in five Chinese cities (Shenyang, Wuhan, Shanghai, Fuzhou and Xian) in 2001, 2002 and 2005. Although we cannot use the average of the unemployment rates in the above five cities to infer the national average, changes in unemployment rates in those cities do help us better understand the transformation of urban employment. Unemployment rates in the five cities all went up from 1996 to 2001, but declined from 2001 to 2005, except in Xian (Table 9.4).

Changes in the ratio of job vacancies to job seekers in the urban labour market further verify that more and more job opportunities have been created since 2001. In order to monitor the situation of labour supply and demand in the urban labour market, the Ministry of Labor and Social Security established a national monitoring network in chosen cities in 2000. At the beginning of 2001, 59 cities were chosen in which to establish a centre and collect information on labour supply and demand. By the end of 2005, 116 cities had established a monitoring centre to collect data.

Using the quarterly data, we can calculate the ratio of job vacancies to job seekers to observe changes in the employment situation in the urban labour market. If the ratio is greater than one, it indicates that the urban labour market is loose, with more job vacancies; if the ratio is less than one, it indicates that the urban

Table 9.4   **Urban unemployment rates in large cities, 1996–2005**

	January 1996	November 2001	August 2005	Changes in 1996–2001	Changes in 2001-05
Full sample	7.2	12.7	8.5	5.5	–4.2
By city					
Shanghai	4.9	10.4	6.1	5.5	–4.3
Wuhan	9.0	17.0	12.8	8.1	-4.2
Shenyang	10.8	14.5	7.2	3.7	–7.3
Fuzhou	5.7	9.8	5.4	4.1	–4.4
Xian	7.5	11.2	11.3	3.6	0.1

Sources: Institute of Population and Labour Economics, 2001, 2002 and 2005. *China Urban Labour Survey*, Chinese Academy of Social Sciences.

labour market is tight, with more applicants. The average ratio of job vacancies to job seekers has been increasing, from 0.65 in the first quarter of 2001 to 0.96 in the fourth quarter of 2005, indicating that the severe pressure of urban unemployment has been largely mitigated (Figure 9.2).

It is interesting that changes in the ratios for urban workers with middle school and lower education and for those with university education are different. Since the second quarter of 2002, the ratio for urban workers with middle school and lower education was higher than the average ratio and the ratio for urban workers with a university degree, implying a rapidly increasing demand for ordinary workers. The timing coincides with the emergence of a shortage of rural workers in southern coastal regions.

Trade expansion and employment growth

Increasing openness and trade expansion

Since the reform and opening-up started in 1978, China has fundamentally transformed the basis of its development strategy from priority for heavy industry to the principle of comparative advantage. Correspondingly, the traditional regime of import substitution was gradually replaced by an export-oriented policy. In the early 1980s, China set up Special Economic Zones (SEZs) to attract and encourage foreign investment. Since the mid 1980s, China has been taking an active role in the international division of labour. China first applied for a reinstatement of its original signatory-country status in the General Agreement on Tariffs and Trade (GATT) in 1986, but its initial request was turned down.

Figure 9.2   **Ratio of job vacancies to job seekers, first quarter of 2001 to fourth quarter 2005**

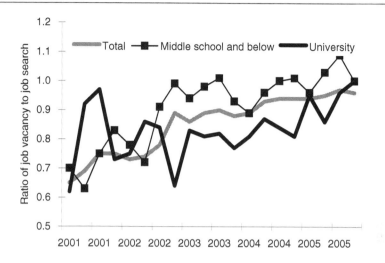

Source: Monitoring Center for China Labour Market Information, China Labour Market Network.

In order to accelerate its openness, in 1991, China decreased import tariff rates for 225 commodities and abolished import adjustment taxes. In 1992 and 1993, China continued to reduce tariff rates for 6,269 import commodities. The arithmetic average of import tariff rates in China dropped to 36.4 per cent in 1995 after five years of continuous reduction. In the meantime, China started to reform export subsidy policies and preferential credit policies for exporters, and let them take charge of their own profits and losses. In January 1994, China replaced the old fixed exchange rate regime with a single, market-based, managed floating exchange rate regime. In the same year, China started to reform the import quota system by auctioning the quota for some commodities.

In 1995, China immediately applied for membership of the WTO when it replaced GATT. In order to join the WTO, China took further measures to reduce custom tariffs and non-tariff barriers. The arithmetic average of import tariff rates was reduced to 23 per cent by the end of 1996 and further cut to 14 per cent in 2001, when China finally became a WTO member. At present, the arithmetic average of custom tariffs is 10.1 per cent for all commodities, 9.3 per cent for industrial commodities and 15.5 per cent for agricultural products.

Figure 9.3   **Share of trade in GDP in China, 1978–2004** (per cent)

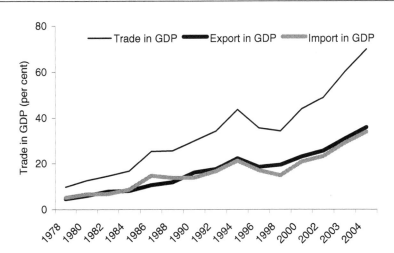

Sources: National Bureau of Statistics of China, 2003a. *China Statistical Yearbook 2003*, China Statistics Press, Beijing. National Bureau of Statistics of China, 2005a. *China Statistical Yearbook 2005*, China Statistics Press, Beijing.

As well as reducing custom tariffs, China relaxed control on import and export business rights. In 2003, the Ministry of Commerce issued a *Notice on Adjusting the Standards and Approval Procedures for the Qualifications to Engage in the Import and Export Business*, lowered the threshold for entrance and simplified the procedure for domestic enterprises to engage in foreign trade. In 2005, China abolished the import quota and licence system and revised the *Foreign Trade Law* to facilitate the expansion of foreign trade in services.

Figure 9.3 shows the increasing trend in China's trade in GDP since the reforms began. From 1978 to 1985, the share of trade in GDP rose from 9.8 per cent to 23.1 per cent. It rose to 30 per cent from 1985 to 1990, and continued this upward trend from 1990 to 40.2 per cent in 1995. From 1995 to 2000, it first dropped and then went up to a level a little higher than that in 1995, but close to the value in 1994.

Since 2000, Chinese foreign trade has entered an era of unprecedented rapid growth. Accession to the WTO stimulated the growth of trade and exports at an annual average rate of more than 30 per cent. The share of trade in GDP rose to 69.8 per cent in 2004, with an increase of 26.5 percentage points in two years, being the fastest increase since reforms began.

The growth of exports and imports kept almost the same pace, but export growth was slightly faster than that of imports after the 1990s (Figure 9.3). In the 1980s, the total value of imports was greater than that of exports in most years. In the 1990s, the total value of exports became greater than that of imports in most years. The growth of trade fluctuated over the years. In the mid 1990s, the growth of imports and exports declined sharply due to the shock of the East Asian financial crisis, but soon returned to the track of rapid growth due to the recovery of the world economy and the effect of accession to the WTO.

With rapid trade expansion, China has been quickly transformed from a major producer and consumer of agricultural and industrial products to a major player in international trade. In 1980, China accounted for only 0.9 per cent of global trade volume, ranking 26th among all countries in the world. In 2003, China's share in global trade volume rose to 5.1 per cent, ranking it fourth in the world, after the United States, Germany and Japan. Continued growth since then has lifted it into third position, behind Germany and the United States.

Trade expansion in China comes mainly from the dramatic growth in exports and imports of manufactured goods. Economic reform has gradually rectified the distortion of the traditional industrial and production structures, causing them to shift towards patterns suggested by the principle of comparative advantage.

China has comparative advantages in producing and exporting labour-intensive manufactured goods because of its cheap labour costs. It has comparative disadvantages in producing and exporting primary goods, because these are mostly natural resource-intensive (or land-intensive), and there is a shortage of natural resources (or land) per capita in China.

Changes in Chinese export structure have indeed begun to follow the principle of comparative advantage (Figure 9.4). The share of primary goods exported dropped from 50.3 per cent in 1980 to 6.8 per cent in 2004, while the share of manufactured goods exported increased to 93.2 per cent in 2004. As for the import structure, the share of primary goods imported dropped from 34.8 per cent in 1980 to 20.9 per cent in 2004, while the share of manufactured goods imported increased to 79.1 per cent in 2004.

With China becoming more open to the outside world, changes in trade structure are an outcome of international market competition. The revealed comparative advantage index can be used to reflect the competitive position of various Chinese commodities in the international market. It equals the total export volume of a specific commodity minus its total import volume, divided by the sum of its total export and import volumes. A positive value means that the commodity has strong competitive advantages in the international market and vice versa. The

Figure 9.4 **Changing components of China's trade, 1980–2004** (per cent)

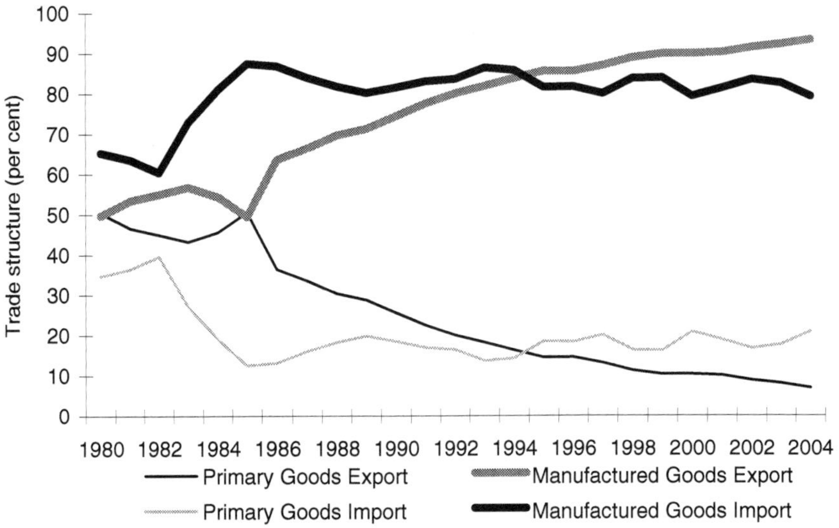

```
                              [Line chart showing trade structure (per cent) from 1980 to 2004
                              with four series: Primary Goods Export, Manufactured Goods Export,
                              Primary Goods Import, Manufactured Goods Import]
```

Source: National Bureau of Statistics of China, 2005a. *China Statistical Yearbook 2005*, China Statistics Press, Beijing.

dynamic change of the trade-competitive index indicates the intrinsic relationship between the adjustments of trade and industrial structure.

Using two-digit customs statistics, we calculated the revealed comparative indexes of 19 categories of commodities and report the results in Table 9.5. In 2004, commodities with a positive trade-competitive index included live animals and animal products; food, beverages, liquor and vinegar, tobacco and tobacco substitutes; raw hides, leather, furs and related products, saddles, travel articles, handbags and similar containers; wood and wood products, charcoal, cork and related products, straws, plaited products, baskets and wickerwork; textiles and products; footwear, headgear, umbrellas, canes, whips, processed feathers, artificial flowers, wigs; gypsum, cement, asbestos, mica, ceramic glass; natural or cultivated pearls, precious or semi-precious stones, precious metal or rolled precious metal jewellery, artificial jewellery, coins; machinery, electrical equipment and accessories, recorders, video recorders and accessories; locomotives, vehicles, aircraft, ships and related transportation equipment.

In 2004, commodities with a negative revealed comparative advantage index included vegetables, fruit and cereals; animal and vegetable oils, fats and wax,

Table 9.5 Revealed comparative advantage indices of export and import commodities, 1994–2004 (per cent)

Category	Items	1992	1994	1996	1998	2000	2002	2004
1	Live animals and animal products	69.1	63.2	62.9	56.9	31.3	27.2	25.6
2	Vegetables, fruit and cereals	37.0	54.4	9.1	32.6	9.3	18.1	−25.1
3	Animal and vegetable oils, fats and wax, refined edible oils and fats	−58.8	−57.0	−63.2	−63.9	−77.6	−87.2	−92.7
4	Food, beverages, liquor and vinegar, tobacco and tobacco substitutes	50.2	57.4	35.6	37.5	48.1	54.4	54.0
5	Minerals	8.0	−4.9	−11.2	−17.9	−45.4	−42.7	−60.4
6	Chemicals and related products	−27.0	−9.4	−10.5	−6.7	−21.7	−24.9	−26.8
7	Plastics and related products, rubber and related products	−48.8	−37.9	−39.7	−30.4	−34.6	−32.9	−32.0
8	Raw hides, leather, furs and related products, saddles, travel articles, handbags and similar containers	35.3	36.3	35.5	41.8	40.4	45.0	45.5
9	Wood and wood products, charcoal, cork and related products, straws, plaited products, baskets and wickerwork	−9.5	0.1	13.3	−4.0	−16.5	−7.8	7.3
10	Paper pulp and cellulose pulp, paper and waste paper, paperboard and related products	−61.2	−56.3	−61.0	−57.7	−58.0	−51.8	−46.1
11	Textiles and related products	41.7	45.4	35.4	47.5	49.8	54.6	58.8
12	Footwear, headgear, umbrellas, canes, whips, processed feathers, artificial flowers, wigs	82.1	88.4	89.9	92.9	93.4	94.2	93.6
13	Gypsum, cement, asbestos, mica, ceramic glass	48.0	46.2	44.6	47.0	38.9	44.8	48.4
14	Natural or cultivated pearls, precious or semi-precious stones, precious metal or rolled precious metal jewellery, artificial jewellery, coins	11.0	18.5	9.8	25.8	2.3	36.2	25.4
15	Base metals and related products	−26.6	−32.0	−9.8	0.6	−10.8	−16.3	−5.2
16	Machinery, electrical equipment and accessories, recorders, video recorders and accessories	−35.9	−35.7	−22.4	−7.8	−7.8	−3.9	2.9
17	Locomotives, vehicles, aircraft, ships and related transportation equipment	−47.3	−54.9	−12.3	6.7	18.8	−4.4	3.8
18	Optical, photographic, film, measuring and checking and medical instruments and equipment, precision instruments and equipment, clocks, musical instruments, related parts and accessories	−12.4	−1.4	5.5	14.2	2.1	−20.5	−36.8
19	Others	75.0	79.5	79.1	89.6	87.1	79.7	82.6

refined edible oils and fats; minerals; chemicals and related products; plastics and related products, rubber and related products; paper pulp and cellulose pulp, paper and waste paper, paperboard and related products; base metals and related products; optical, photographic, film, measuring and checking and medical instruments and equipment, precision instruments and equipment, clocks, musical instruments, related parts and accessories.

Most commodities with a positive revealed comparative advantage index were from labour-intensive industries and most commodities with a negative revealed comparative advantage index were from resource-intensive, capital-intensive or technology-intensive industries (Table 9.5).

China's exports of labour-intensive commodities have become more competitive over time. From 1992 to 2004, the revealed comparative advantage index for raw hides, leather, furs and related products rose from 35.3 per cent to 45.5 per cent. Similar increases were registered for textiles and related products, and for footwear, headgear, umbrellas, canes, whips, processed feathers, artificial flowers and wigs, with indices for the two categories soaring from 41.7 per cent to 58.8 per cent and from 82.1 per cent to 93.6 per cent, respectively.

China has, however, shown further weaknesses in exports of land-intensive and resource-intensive commodities. The revealed comparative advantage index for vegetables, fruit and cereals fell from 37.3 per cent to −25.1 per cent from 1992 to 2004. Similar declines were registered for animal and vegetable oils, fats and wax, refined edible oils and fats as well as minerals, with the indices for the two categories moving down from −58.8 per cent to −92.7 per cent and from 8 per cent to −60.4 per cent, respectively.

With the enlargement of production capacity and improvement of production structure, China's manufacturing industry has gained competitiveness in exports of machinery, vehicles and base metals. The revealed comparative advantage indices for these three categories rose from −35.9 per cent, −47.3 per cent and −26.6 per cent in 1992 to 2.9 per cent, 3.8 per cent and −5.2 per cent in 2004, respectively.

Impact of trade on employment growth and structure

According to the Heckscher Ohlin theory of comparative advantage based on factor endowments, two countries with different production-factor endowments can benefit from the production and exchange of products. The participation in international trade not only improves specialisation, it increases the number and types of consumable goods. This process allows trade to divert the accumulative pattern of physical and human capital, and reshape the steady-state condition of economic growth in both countries, giving rise to higher growth rates for both countries than in a closed economy. Therefore, the fundamental transformation of resource allocation from an import-substitution strategy towards an export-oriented strategy is vital for long-term economic growth (Krueger 1998). Empirical studies demonstrate that trade has significantly positive impacts on economic growth (Edwards 1993, 1998; Frankel and Romer 1999).

In the national income account, aggregate output can be decomposed into three components of consumption, investment and net exports. Change in any part can give rise to change in aggregate output and has an impact on economic growth. Because aggregate output is a function of labour input, change in any part of aggregate output will affect demand for labour, and then impact on employment.

Net exports equal export value minus import value. Using the annual change of net exports, we can calculate the contribution of trade to economic growth. Linking economic growth with employment growth, we can observe the impact of trade on employment. Table 9.6 shows that the share of net exports in GDP accounted for less than 5 per cent in absolute value, and its contribution to GDP growth fluctuated sharply from −34.6 per cent to 103.1 per cent.

This macroeconomic approach underestimates the contribution of trade to output and employment growth. There are also important effects in raising productivity through improved techniques, and more efficient allocation of resources across industries for a relatively labour-abundant economy like China at this stage of its development, it also increases the amount of employment expansion associated with a given amount of GDP growth. Some analysts suggest using trade growth or export growth to estimate the contribution of trade to economic growth. The cross-country studies shows that 1 per cent of trade growth will lead to 0.2 per cent of GDP growth (Berloffa and Segnana 2004). Lin and Li (2002) found that 1 per cent of export growth led to 0.1 per cent of China's GDP growth.

The impact of trade on employment growth also depends on the elasticity of employment. Trade expansion in China comes mainly from the export and import of manufacturing goods, so it is reasonable to employ the elasticity of non-agricultural employment to calculate the aggregate impacts of trade on employment. Compared with the first half the 1990s, employment growth and employment elasticity in the second half of the decade were lower, but they rose in the first five years of the new century (Table 9.7).

Taking 0.1 per cent as the lower boundary and 0.2 per cent as the upper boundary of the contribution of trade growth to economic growth, Table 9.7 estimates the contribution of Chinese foreign trade to employment growth in different periods. As shown in the table, trade growth in the first half of the 1990s caused an annual

Table 9.6   **Macroeconomic contribution of net exports to economic growth, 1978–2004**

	Net export values (100 million yuan)	Share in GDP (per cent)	Contribution to GDP growth		Net export values (100 million yuan)	Share in GDP (per cent)	Contribution to GDP growth
1979	–19.6	–0.5	–2.7	1992	275.6	1.0	–11.8
1980	–14.8	–0.3	1.7	1993	–679.4	–2.0	–24.2
1981	11.3	0.2	10.9	1994	634.1	1.4	27.6
1982	91.1	1.7	18.2	1995	998.5	1.7	5.1
1983	50.8	0.8	–7.1	1996	1,459.3	2.1	6.8
1984	1.3	0.0	–5.5	1997	2,857.2	3.8	22.9
1985	–366.9	–4.2	–34.6	1998	3,051.5	3.9	4.6
1986	–255.2	–2.5	15.5	1999	2,248.8	2.7	–13.4
1987	11.5	0.1	22.5	2000	2,240.2	2.5	–0.5
1988	–151.1	–1.0	–10.8	2001	2,204.7	2.3	–0.9
1989	–185.5	–1.1	–3.2	2002	2,794.2	2.7	7.4
1990	510.3	2.8	103.1	2003	2,682.1	2.3	–1.6
1991	617.5	2.9	4.0	2004	4,079.2	3.0	10.3

Note: The contribution of net exports to GDP growth is affected by GDP deflators.
Source: National Bureau of Statistics of China, 2005a. *China Statistical Yearbook 2005*, China Statistics Press, Beijing.

increment of employment of 2.5–5 million due to the large elasticity of employment. Because of the slowdown of trade growth and the decline of the elasticity of employment, the annual increment of employment dropped to 0.7–1.4 million in the second half of the 1990s. The acceleration of trade growth since 2001 has also produced a positive effect on employment growth, and promoted an annual increment of employment of 2.3–4.6 million in the first five years of this century.

Trade expansion has not only increased aggregate employment through economic growth, it sped up the adjustment of employment structure through a substitution effect. Trade liberalisation stimulates the development and export growth of domestic sectors that have a comparative advantage, and thus enlarges employment in those sectors, but it depresses the production of domestic sectors that have a comparative disadvantage.

The substitution of employment in comparative disadvantage sectors and the promotion of employment in comparative advantage sectors cause the reallocation of aggregate employment through the mechanism of employment creation and employment destruction. Meanwhile, changes in investment structure, especially the structure of foreign direct investment (FDI), also accelerate the pace of industrial

Table 9.7   **Employment increments driven by trade growth, 1991–2005**

	Real growth of trade (per cent)	Employment elasticity	Increments of employment (I) (million)	Increments of employment (II) (million)
1991–95	19.9	0.43	2.5	5.0
1996–2000	10.8	0.19	0.7	1.4
2001–05	22.5	0.26	2.3	4.6

Note: 1) The growth of trade was deflated by using the GDP deflator; 2) increments of employment (I) was based on the calculation of 0.1 per cent contribution of trade to GDP growth; increments of employment (II) was based on the calculation of 0.2 per cent contribution of trade to GDP growth.
Source: Author's calculations.

restructuring and induce employment reallocation. With the decline or collapse of some industries, employees in those industries will be laid off and released for reallocation. In the meantime, the expansion or emergence of some industries will create new opportunities for employment.

Since Chinese foreign trade and FDI are concentrated mainly in coastal regions, fast trade growth here also affects spatial employment distribution. We can take the spatial distribution of manufacturing employment as an example. According to the geographic location and similarity in industrial structure, we divided the mainland into six regions (Table 9.8). Total manufacturing employment in the early 1990s had an upward trend, with an annual average growth of 2.6 per cent from 1990 to 1995, but a decline afterwards, with an annual average growth of –3.9 per cent from 1995 to 2000. The number of manufacturing jobs in 2001 and 2002 increased, with an annual growth of 0.5 per cent and 2.8 per cent, respectively (Table 9.8).

Regional changes in employment, however, demonstrate a different picture. From 1993 to 2002, the numbers employed in manufacturing in the coastal region rose from 36.8 million to 39.7 million—an increase of 2.9 million; while manufacturing employment in the other five regions had a downward trend, with decreases of 2.1 million in the metropolis region, 4.7 million in the northeast region, 1.5 million in the central region, 1.4 in the southwest region and 1.3 million in the northwest region—a total reduction of 8 million.

Table 9.8 also shows that most manufacturing employment concentrates on the coastal and central regions, and their shares have kept an upward trend. From 1993 to 2002, the share of manufacturing employment in the coastal region rose

Table 9.8   Distribution of manufacturing employment by region, 1993–2002

	1993	1994	1995	1996	1997	1998	1999	2000	2001	2002
Manufacturing employment (million)										
Metropolis	7.6	7.6	7.4	7.0	6.7	5.4	5.4	5.1	5.1	5.4
Northeast	10.6	10.9	10.7	10.6	10.2	7.1	6.7	6.3	6.0	5.9
Coastal	36.8	39.0	40.3	40.3	40.1	37.1	36.6	37.2	38.5	39.7
Central	20.7	22.3	23.1	23.2	23.0	19.8	19.1	18.8	18.6	19.2
Southwest	10.0	10.5	10.6	10.6	10.4	9.0	8.7	8.5	8.4	8.6
Northwest	5.6	5.9	5.9	5.9	5.7	4.8	4.7	4.4	4.3	4.3
Total	91.3	96.1	98.0	97.6	96.1	83.2	81.1	80.4	80.8	83.1
Distribution of manufacturing employment (per cent)										
Metropolis	8.3	7.9	7.5	7.2	6.9	6.5	6.6	6.4	6.3	6.5
Northeast	11.6	11.3	10.9	10.8	10.6	8.5	8.3	7.8	7.5	7.0
Coastal	40.4	40.6	41.1	41.3	41.8	44.6	45.1	46.3	47.6	47.8
Central	22.6	23.2	23.6	23.8	24.0	23.8	23.6	23.4	23.0	23.1
Southwest	11.0	10.9	10.8	10.8	10.8	10.8	10.7	10.6	10.3	10.3
Northwest	6.2	6.1	6.1	6.1	5.9	5.8	5.7	5.5	5.3	5.2
Total	100.0	100.0	100.0	100.0	100.0	100.0	100.0	100.0	100.0	100.0

Note: Metropolis region includes Beijing, Shanghai, Tianjin; Northeast region includes Liaoning, Jilin, Heilongjiang; Coastal region includes Hebei, Jiangsu, Zhejiang, Shangdong, Gungdong, Hainan; Central region includes Shanxi, Anhui, Jiangxi, Henan, Hubei, Hunan; Southwest region includes Guangxi, Chongqing, Sichun, Tibet, Yunnan, Guizhou; Northwest region includes Inner Mongolia, Shaanxi, Gansu, Ningxia, Qinghai, Xinjiang.
Sources: National Bureau of Statistics of China, 1994–2005. *China Statistical Yearbook*, China Statistics Press, Beijing.

from 40.4 per cent to 47.8 per cent. The share of manufacturing employment in the central region rose from 22.6 per cent to 23.1 per cent, in the same period. Shares of manufacturing employment in the metropolis, northeast, southwest and northwest regions were all declining. Among them, the northeast region dropped from 11.6 per cent to 7 per cent in the same period, with the largest magnitude drop, of 4.6 percentage points.

Before 1998, the ratio of manufacturing goods imported and exported to Chinese manufacturing output was relatively low. The shocks of trade growth on the spatial distribution of manufacturing employment were therefore relatively small. At that time, the large decline in Chinese manufacturing employment was due mainly to industrial restructuring driven by changes in domestic demand. With the rapid growth of exports and imports of manufactured goods, however, trade played an increasingly important role in the spatial redistribution of manufacturing employment.

Thanks to earlier opening-up and integration into the global economy, labour-intensive manufacturing industries in the coastal region had a greater comparative advantage and their rapid growth promoted the growth of manufacturing employment in this region. In contrast, traditional manufacturing in the central and western regions was in capital-intensive heavy industries, and they had a comparative disadvantage under the shock of trade liberalisation; their shrinkage caused the decrease in manufacturing employment in those regions.

The coexistence of the above two factors led to rapid growth in the export of manufactured goods accompanied by a decline in manufacturing employment in the late 1990s. This situation has changed since China's accession into the WTO in 2001. The growth in exports of manufactured goods and the relative labour intensity of that production has promoted the growth of manufacturing employment.

Changes in the industrial distribution of FDI further stimulate the relocation of employment across sectors. Since China joined the WTO, FDI has concentrated increasingly in manufacturing sectors to take advantage of cheap labour. The manufacturing industry accounted for only 57.2 per cent of total Chinese FDI in 1998, but it leaped to 71 per cent in 2004. FDI moved increasingly in line with Chinese comparative advantage.

Because of the comparative disadvantage in agricultural and mining industries, their FDI shares are relatively low. Industries such as transportation, communication, storage and post, and so on, also have a low FDI share, because they are traditionally viewed as industries that have a natural monopoly, or are relevant to national security, so that institutional and policy obstacles to constrain FDI have remained in place. Although the government has encouraged foreign investment in infrastructure such as energy, transportation and ports, imperfect management systems have hindered the inflow of FDI to these industries.

Foreign-funded enterprises are mainly export-oriented, and account for more than half of Chinese exports. The expansion of foreign-funded enterprises has promoted employment growth in non state-owned enterprise sectors. Before 1978, China had no foreign investment. From 1979 to 1983, the accumulated amount of FDI in China was only US$1.8 billion. There was a large influx of FDI after 1985.

In 1985, the number of urban workers in FDI-funded sectors was 60,000, and the share of total urban workers was trivial. In 2004, however, the number of urban workers in FDI-funded sectors reached 10.3 million, and accounted for 3.9 per cent of total urban workers. In 1985, there were no FDI-funded enterprises in rural areas. In 2003, however, the number of rural workers in FDI-funded sectors was 7.3 million, and accounted for 5.4 per cent of total employment in township and village enterprises.

Employment in urban and rural FDI-funded enterprises amounted to 15.9 million people in 2003, accounting for 4.1 per cent of non-agricultural employment.

Changing patterns in labour supply and demand

Demographic predictions of labour supply and demand

Population age structure changes over time in response to long-run economic and social forces. By collecting data from 129 countries, the LOWESS estimation method depicts a non-parametric relationship between per capita income and age structure (Figure 9.5). The graphs on the left and right describe, respectively, the relationships between per capita gross national income (GNI), adjusted by purchasing power parity, and the proportion of the working-age population (aged 15–64 years) in the total population and the proportion of elderly (65 years and older) in the total population.

In the early phase of development, as per capita income increases, the proportion of the working-age population and the old-age population increase in line with each other, as indicated by the positive slope of the fitted lines in the two graphs Figure 9.5). When per capita income reaches certain levels, the proportion of the working-age population begins to increase more slowly, whereas the proportion of the old-age population increases more quickly. The slopes of the fitted lines, after the turning points are reached, become flatter in the former case (on the left) and steeper in the latter case (on the right).

In both graphs, China stands above the fitted lines, indicating that compared with countries with similar levels of per capita income, China has a larger proportion of working-age and old-age populations. That is, China is not only in its golden population structure, it has been confronted sooner than other countries with an ageing population, as its family planning policies have caused a significant drop in fertility, resulting in a rapid decline in the proportion of youth and a quick increase in the proportion of the elderly.

When the pace of the decline in the proportion of youth exceeded that of the increase in the proportion of the elderly, China began to enjoy a sufficient labour supply, a result of productive population structure. As the demographic transition process moves forward, the growth of the working-age population will slow, while population ageing speeds up. China is now at the turning points from which the fitted line for the proportion of the working-age population becomes flatter and the fitted line of the proportion of the old-age population becomes steeper (Figure 9.5).

The United Nations predicts that the ratio of the working-age population to the total population will continue to increase until 2010, and the absolute number of

Figure 9.5   **Per capita income versus population age structure**

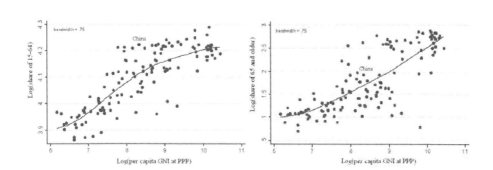

Notes: Purchasing power parity (PPP) adjusted per capita gross national income (GNI) is for 2001; the proportion of population age is for 2000.
Sources: World Bank, 2003. *World Development Indicators*, World Bank, Washington. United Nations, 2003. *World Population Prospects: the 2002 revision*, United Nations Population Division, Department of Economic and Social Affairs, Washington. Available from www.un.org/esa/population/publications/wpp2002

the working population will reach its peak of approximately one billion people in 2015, before beginning to shrink (United Nations 2003). The China Center for Population and Development predicts a similar pattern of population structure changes: the proportion of the working population will reach its peak of 72.1 per cent in 2013 and the total working-age population will reach its highest number, 997 million, in 2016 (Wang 2006). The entire process characterises China as becoming an ageing but not an affluent society.

Examining the working-age population by dividing it into four groups—15–24, 25–39, 40–54 and 55–64 years—we find that between 2000 and 2030, the proportions of the 15–24 and the 25–39 year-old groups in the total population will decline steadily, whereas the proportion of the 55–64 year-old group will increase and the proportion of the 40–54 year-old group will increase first and then decline after a certain point (United Nations 2003). This trend indicates that not only will the Chinese population age over time, the working-age population itself will tend to age 25 years from now. Furthermore, if a larger part of the 15–24 year-old group continues its schooling as higher education expands and a larger part of the 55–64 year-old group quits the labour market as a result of the discouraged-worker effect or the income effect (both tend to reduce labour-force participation), the labour supply will fall off further.

Observing the already diminishing net growth of the working-age population and the constantly increasing demand for workers in non-agricultural sectors during the eleventh Five-Year Plan (2006–10), we can expect a possible gap between supply and demand for labour in the near future (Figure 9.3). We assume that agriculture will have no further demand for workers; therefore, the incremental amount of the working-age population is a reasonable labour supply base for non-agricultural sectors.

Providing three scenarios for a non-agricultural growth rate (high growth of 10 per cent, medium growth of 9 per cent and low growth of 8 per cent) and two employment elasticities for non-agricultural growth (1 percentage point in growth creates a 0.297 percentage rise in employment — the average level from 1991 to 2003), as high elasticity and a 1 percentage point in growth create a 0.230 percentage point rise in employment (a half-standard deviation lower than the former) as low elasticity, we plot the six combinations of predicted labour demand of non-agricultural growth against the labour supply (incremental working-age population).

From 2004 on, the net increase of new entrants to the labour market tends to lag behind the various scenarios of an increase in labour demand and the gap widens over time (Figure 9.6). Although agriculture will continue to release its surplus labour as a result of enhanced labour productivity in the sector, structural labour shortages in terms of region, sector and specific skills are likely to occur from time to time.

Demographic transition provided an opportunity for China to take advantage of its demographic dividend in the mid 1960s,[2] but only after the initiation of reform could the opportunity have been used to promote economic growth. During the reform period, the potential demographic dividend was capitalised through trade liberalisation, development of factor markets and fast economic growth. Taking the total-dependence ratio as a proxy of the advantageous population structure (Figure 9.7) between 1982 and 2000, each 1 per cent decrease in the dependence ratio led to a 0.115 per cent growth in per capita GDP; that is, the decline in the total-dependence rate contributed to one-quarter of the per capita GDP growth in the reform period (Cai and Wang 2005).

The demographic dividend is performing a typical pattern of 'easy come, easy go'. That is, as a consequence of fast demographic transition, the earlier the high proportion of working-age population comes, the sooner it is gone. The fact, on the one hand, that demographic transition in China happened in a short time and

Figure 9.6 **Predictions for labour supply and demand in non-agricultural sectors, 2004–10**

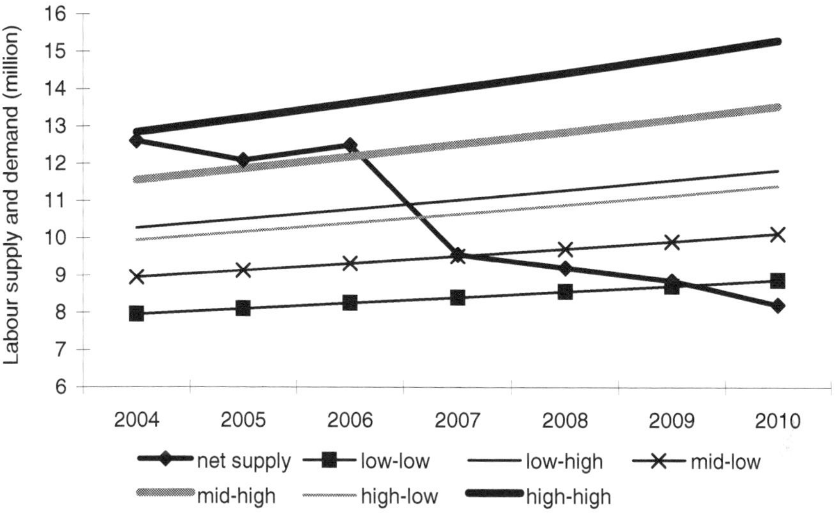

Source: Fang, C., Yang, D. and Meiyan, W. (eds), forthcoming. *An Overview on China's Labour Market, in National Development and Restructuring Commission.*

in a fast manner has no doubt provided China with an extra source of economic growth. On the other hand, it leaves a very short period for the Chinese economy to enjoy low population dependence. Population dependence will stay at a low level only for a short time in the second decade of this century and will increase rapidly afterwards (Figure 9.7). The lowest point of population dependence will be reached in 2013, when the ratio of the dependent population to the working-age population will be 38.8 per cent. After that, the population-dependence ratio will increase, mainly as a result of the increase in elderly dependence.

Population ageing is followed by a reduction in labour supply everywhere at any time in history. The impact of ageing on the sustainability of economic growth differs across stages of socioeconomic development. In most industrial countries that have already finished their demographic transition, population ageing is accompanied by high per capita income. The relative abundance of physical and human capital enables these countries to accomplish a necessary upgrading of industrial structure by substituting capital for labour, and generally leads to a

Figure 9.7   **Changes in population dependence, 1949–2048**

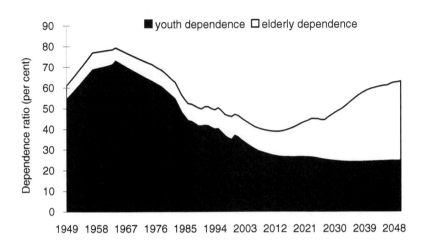

Sources: Figures on dependence are from National Bureau of Statistics of China, various years. *China Statistical Yearbook 2005*, China Statistics Press, Beijing, with estimations to fill in the years without data. Figures on savings rates are from ibid. and Wang, G., 2006, 'Population projection and analysis', in Cai Fang (ed.), *Green Book of Population and Labour — Demographic Transition and Its Social and Economic Consequences*, Social Sciences Academic Press, Beijing.

transformation from an economy dominated by labour-intensive industries to an economy dominated by capital-intensive industries.

A shortage of skilled workers in China would result in an increase in skilled workers' wages, and would hamper China's comparative advantage in labour-intensive industries without providing a gain in new comparative advantage in capital-intensive industries, because China's per capita income level is still low in terms of international ranking.

As early as 2003, a shortage of migrant workers occurred in the Pearl River Delta region. At that time, most observers considered the labour shortage to be a cyclical phenomenon caused by the upsurge of the regional export-driven economy under the circumstances of underpayment, abuse and a lack of security for migrant workers. Since then, the phenomenon of labour shortages has spread to the Yangtze River Delta region, and even to some central provinces, such as Jiangxi, Anhui and Henan, from which migrant labourers are generally sent.

The analysis of population age structure addressed in this chapter suggests that the causes of labour shortages have a demographic root and, therefore, tend to intensify over time. Since the 1990s, wage rates in China's manufacturing sector have increased rapidly in comparison with most parts of the world, which will soon put a a dent in international competitiveness in manufacturing (Banister 2005; Cai 2005).

Impact on Chinese manufacturing competitiveness

China's trade expansion benefits largely from its huge advantage of cheap labour. Given the production technology, there is a negative relationship between labour costs and corporate profit (capital returns). International commodity markets are generally perfectly competitive, and manufacturers are passive takers of market prices, therefore, labour costs have an important impact on returns to investment. Low labour costs will increase returns to investment, while high labour costs will decrease returns, so labour costs are important determinants of competitiveness.

Compared with industrial economies, China has an absolute advantage in labour costs in the manufacturing industry, but the gap has been narrowed dramatically. In 1995, China's annual average manufacturing wage was equivalent to 1/57–1/24 that of industrial economies, but increased to 1/26–1/13 that of industrial economies in 2002 (Table 9.9). The decline of China's absolute advantage in labour costs can be attributed to the rapid growth in wage rates. From 1995 to 2002, the annual growth rates of manufacturing wages were 11.6 per cent in China, –2.8 per cent in Japan, 3.1 per cent in the United States, 4.3 per cent in the United Kingdom, 2.5 per cent in South Korea, 2.2 per cent in Singapore and 3.3 per cent in Hong Kong. Even if the increasing speed is considered, China will maintain an advantage in manufacturing labour costs in the longer term owing to its significant absolute advantage over the industrial economies. This advantage will, however, face challenges from China's neighbouring countries, which have experienced fast economic growth, such as Malaysia, India, Thailand and Vietnam.

India's labour costs in the manufacturing industry in 1995 were about 70 per cent those of China, and this gap has been widening (Table 9.9). With increasing exports of manufacturing products from neighbouring countries, China's manufacturing exports will face a more competitive environment. If the labour costs of China's manufacturing products continue to increase, the competitive advantage of manufacturing product exports will be weakened.

Manufacturing wages can reflect one side of the international competitiveness of the manufacturing industry, but the productivity of the manufacturing industry represents another side of international competitiveness. The former measures labour input, while the latter measures labour output. Combining those two figures, we can compare the international competitiveness of the manufacturing industry with countries without adjusting exchange rates. If we define the competitive-advantage index as labour productivity divided by wage costs, this indicator reflects, to a certain extent, returns to investment and profitability.

In Table 9.9, the values of competitive-advantage indices for China's manufacturing industry were about 4–4.5, greater than all other countries in the table, and 1.5–3 times that in industrial countries. These figures show that China's manufacturing industry has a strong competitive advantage. The same trend of labour cost growth and productivity growth keep the competitive-advantage index almost unchanged. It has, however, had a slight decline since 1998 because labour cost growth is a little higher than productivity growth.

Table 9.9 **International comparison of manufacturing wage costs, 1995–2002**

	1995	1996	1997	1998	1999	2000	2001	2002
Annual average manufacturing wage (US$)								
China	619	679	716	853	941	1,057	1,181	1,329
Japan	35,569	31,296	28,485	26,547	30,667	32,638	29,376	28,366
United States	25,667	26,520	27,331	27,976	28,808	29,786	30,701	31,803
United Kingdom	25,997	26,902	29,319	31,588	32,139	31,345	31,530	34,412
South Korea	17,486	18,813	16,729	10,999	14,894	16,993	15,824	17,812
Singapore	18,264	19,740	20,097	19,474	19,844	21,132	20,876	21,137
Malaysia	4,801	5,318	5,161	..	..	4,383	4,835	..
India	434	402	367	345	429	336	..	..
Competitive index								
China	4.0	4.3	4.5	4.5	4.4	4.4	4.3	4.1
Japan	2.4	2.4	2.4	2.4	2.4	2.4	2.3	..
United States	2.5	2.4	2.4	2.5	2.6	2.6	2.4	..
United Kingdom	1.7	1.7	1.7	1.6	1.6	1.6	1.5	..
Korea	1.7	1.7	1.8	2.3	2.1	2.0	..	..
Singapore	2.6	2.6	2.6	2.4	2.4	2.7	2.5	3.0
Hong Kong	1.4	1.4	1.4	1.4	1.3	1.5	1.3	1.4
Malaysia	2.7	2.8	2.8	..	..	3.2	..	..

Note: 1) Figures in this table have been changed into US dollars according to the currency exchange rate of individual countries; 2) because of differences in wage statistics, hourly wages in the US and UK are multiplied by 40 hours a week and 52 weeks a year to get the annual wages; monthly wages in other countries are multiplied by 12 months to get the annual wages; 3) the competitive advantage index equals labour productivity divided by labour cost.
Source: International Labour Organisation, http://laboursta.ilo.org/.

Conclusion

GDP growth must be maintained at a high rate if China is to accomplish its goal of building a well-off society, with total GDP four times that of 2000 by 2020. The demand for labour, especially in the manufacturing and service sectors, will be strong in the coming decades of continued economic growth. The ageing population, however, is reducing the increase in the working-age population and, before an absolute labour shortage occurs, structural shortages will occur frequently. Furthermore, not only might the high savings rate in China drop because of its ageing population, international capital flows might become uncertain because of global ageing (Jackson 2005).

In order to sustain economic growth, a fundamental transformation of the growth pattern should be taken in China. In the economic development process of industrialised economies, the limitations of population growth and, therefore, labour scarcity have generated diminishing returns to capital, leading to a transformation of economic growth patterns from input-driven to productivity increase-driven growth.

The more rapidly completed demographic transition in East Asian economies, including in China, has offered them a demographic dividend (Bloom et al. 2002; Cai and Wang 2005), so as to defer the phenomenon of diminishing returns to capital. As the demographic transition continues, the characteristic of an unlimited labour supply will disappear and an era of labour shortages arrive, which requires an urgent transformation of growth patterns. The Chinese economy is now facing the transformation from input-driven to productivity-driven economic growth.

International experiences suggest that once labour shortages emerge, a host of institutional arrangements change accordingly. For example, state policies become more balanced in the provision of public services between rural and urban areas, government regulations tend to abolish institutional barriers deterring labour mobility and protection of labour rights, industrial relations shift from favouring employers to favouring employees, and trade unions play a greater role in coordinating interests between employers and employees.

The unique household registration (*hukou*) system established in the beginning of the planning system in the late 1950s still serves as an institutional obstacle preventing the rural labour force from permanently migrating to and working in cities. This is the best time for China to readjust institutional arrangements to acclimatise itself to a new era of labour market structure.

Studies show that the improvement of resource reallocation efficiency will not only be one source of China's sustained economic growth, it can help to maintain

China's manufacturing competitiveness through the development of a labour market system. A World Bank simulation suggests that moving 1, 5 and 10 per cent of the labour force out of agriculture and distributing them into other sectors will, respectively, add 0.7, 3.3 and 6.4 per cent to China's total GDP (World Bank 2005).

In their model, Whalley and Shuming (2004) testify that in removing migration restrictions, wage and income inequality disappears. Abolition of the various institutional obstacles that hinder the development of labour markets can build a solid bridge of labour transfer between sending and receiving areas, and enhances migration mobility between rural and urban areas and across regions to mitigate the pressure of wage rises and regional imbalance, so as to maintain Chinese manufacturing competitiveness.

In the long term, wage rises are an unavoidable trend with changes in labour supply and demand. In this situation, it is necessary for China to increase human capital investment in education, training, health and medical care to improve labour skills and to offset the negative effects of wage rises through the improvement of productivity.

Notes

[1] In 2003, the Ministry of Labor and Social Security broadened the range of ages for registering unemployment to 16–60 for males and 16–55 for females.

[2] As a result of demographic transition, population age structure can be more productive in a certain period than in other periods, and, therefore, it adds an extra source of economic growth. This source of growth caused by population structure is recognised as demographic dividend (Bloom et al. 2002).

10

The impact of the guest-worker system on poverty and the well-being of migrant workers in urban China

Yang Du, Robert Gregory and Xin Meng

Many countries adopt a guest-worker system to help meet labour shortages. Guest workers normally have a temporary visa to work in the host country but have no political rights or access to social welfare and other government-provided benefits. Under such a system, guest workers normally spend some part of their working life in the host country and return home when their work or family circumstances change. Their usual objective is to make and save as much money as they can before they return home.

China is, perhaps, the only country in the world that adopts a guest-worker system for its own rural citizens (Roberts 1997; Solinger 1999; Meng 2000). There are currently more than 120 million rural-to-urban migrants working in Chinese cities and they have contributed substantially to the country's recent unprecedented economic growth. Nevertheless, like all guest workers, they have temporary work visas and no access to the social benefits that are available to their urban counterparts. There are no safety nets, no adequate access to health facilities and their children do not have equal access to schooling.

Migrants often earn lower incomes than natives, especially in the initial stage of migration. This is due partly to lack of knowledge of local labour markets and partly to lack of local labour market-specific human capital (see, for example, Chiswick 1978 and Borjas 1985, 1995). Lower incomes are also due partly to employer (or government) discrimination. In China, discrimination against rural migrants is usually institutionalised, whereby city governments prevent rural migrants from obtaining higher-paying jobs, which are reserved for urban citizens

(Zhao 2003; Meng and Zhang 2001). Studies have continuously found that migrants often possess low-paying and 'three-D' jobs (disgraceful, dirty and dangerous) and that their earnings are much lower than their urban counterparts (Meng 2000; Meng and Zhang 2001; Zhao 2002; and Fang et al. 2003).

Under such circumstances, questions naturally arise as to the kind of lives migrants are living in cities and how their short-term objective of making and saving as much money as possible might affect their lives in the future.

The answers to these questions have important political and policy implications. First, migrant workers currently account for one-third of the Chinese urban labour force. In the next 10 to 20 years, this figure is predicted to double. If many migrant workers are living in poverty, and are concentrated in ghettos, conditions of crowding and poverty might lead to high crime rates and social and political instability.

Second, China's current urban social safety net is accessible only to urban residents. This situation, however, is not sustainable. As the Chinese economy grows and more and more rural migrants come to the cities, a coherent social safety net that covers urban residents and rural migrants will need to be established. Understanding the extent to which migrant workers currently live in poverty is a crucial piece of information to be used in designing an appropriate system and projecting its possible cost.

Third, even if migrant workers and their families are not currently living in poverty, the short-term objectives of making and saving as much money as they can by working exceptionally long hours might place them in an environment in which, in the near future, their health and hence their earning capacity might deteriorate. Any future health deterioration will not only adversely affect individual well-being, it will be of considerable social and political importance.

Using two recently available data sources, the *China Income Distribution Survey (CIDS)* (Chinese Academy of Social Sciences 2002) and the *China Urban Labour Survey (CULS)* (Chinese Academy of Social Sciences 2001), we examine three specific issues related to poverty and the well-being of rural migrants.

First, what proportion of migrant workers is currently living in poverty, as measured by the application of the usual income and expenditure poverty lines? Second, what is the relationship between these poverty levels and the long hours typically worked by migrants? And, finally, how might the long hours worked and current work and living conditions affect the future health of migrants?

The chapter is structured as follows. The next section provides background on rural-urban migration and describes the data. Section three assesses urban poverty using different poverty lines and examines how the urban poverty rate and poverty severity might change if we include a migrant sample. The fourth section discusses how extremely long hours worked by migrants enable them to live just above the poverty line and, had they worked 'normal hours', what proportion of them would have lived below the poverty line. Section five predicts the possible adverse impact of current long working hours on migrants' future health, while conclusions and policy implications are given in the final section.

Background and data

China's internal rural-urban migration takes place within a guest-worker system, whereby migrant workers are restricted in the type of job they can obtain and in terms of access to urban social services, such as education, health care, unemployment benefits and pensions. These restrictions prevent migrant workers from staying in cities for a long period and from bringing their families to the cities. Thus, migrants often work in the cities for a few months to a few years, depending on their personal and family circumstances, and then go back to their country home. Sometimes, they migrate back and forth.

When farmers migrate, their families are permitted to keep their land. In this way, land is a safety net for migrant workers. If they lose their jobs and are unable to find another job in a short time, they might return to the countryside to work on the farm. Similarly, if they become sick in the cities, they will have no choice but to go back to the countryside. In the countryside, there are relatives who can provide care, and the cost of living is much lower, although health care is much worse in the countryside and health expenditure is not cheap.

Under the guest-worker system, the effect of rural-urban migration on total urban poverty is unclear. On the one hand, as migrant workers can obtain only low-income jobs, it is possible that a larger proportion of migrants are living in poverty than their urban resident counterparts.

On the other hand, unsuccessful migrants are more likely to go back to the countryside. Those who stay in cities are usually employed and are a relatively successful group. In other words, the guest-worker system might act as a buffer that pushes unemployed and very poor migrants back to the countryside.[1]

In these circumstances, migrants might not contribute to an increase in total urban poverty.

There is another issue. Poverty, measured in terms of current income, might not capture current living conditions and the long-term poverty of migrant workers. This is because migrants do not see their future in the cities. They come to earn and save as much as possible and to take their savings home for their future prosperity. With such an objective in mind, they might sacrifice current living conditions for their own and their family's future. They might choose to work extremely hard and live in extremely poor conditions while working in the cities. Such short-term behaviour might damage their long-term health, and hence, hinder their long-term earnings capacity and future wealth.

To study these issues, we employ data from two recent surveys. The first survey is the *China Income Distribution Survey (CIDS)* 2002, conducted in 12 provinces[2] by the Institute of Economics at the Chinese Academy of Social Sciences, while the second is the *China Urban Labour Survey (CULS)* 2001, conducted in five large capital cities (Shanghai, Wuhan, Shenyang, Xian and Fuzhou) by the Institute of Population and Labour Economics at the Chinese Academy of Social Sciences.

Both surveys include samples of urban residents and rural-urban migrants in the same cities or provinces. The *CIDS* comprises 6,835 households and 20,632 individuals in the urban resident sample and 2,000 households and 5,327 individuals in the migrant sample, while the *CULS* consists of 3,499 households and 8,109 individuals in the urban resident sample and 2,400 individuals in the migrant sample.[3]

In each survey, the questionnaires were largely comparable for urban residents and rural migrants. Each survey has advantages and disadvantages relative to the other.

The *CIDS* has a larger sample than the *CULS* and includes large (37 per cent of the sample individuals), medium and small cities (63 per cent of the sample individuals). The survey has good records of individual income, including every person in the household for urban resident and migrant samples. In addition, there are detailed consumption expenditure data.

The *CULS* sample includes only five large cities.[4] The main advantage of the *CULS* is that it collects urban and migrant work histories and working hours at different stages of working life. One of its shortcomings is that the migrant survey asks questions only about the main respondent of each household. Although information is also gathered regarding age, education, working status, whether working in the same city and the type of job of the respondent's spouse, parents, children and siblings, no earnings information is available for these relatives. It is therefore impossible to derive household per capita income for migrants. Second, many household-level figures, especially expenditure, are not available for migrants due to the individual nature of the survey.

The *CULS* and *CIDS* have a large proportion of self-employed migrants (about 51–53 per cent in both samples). Whether this reflects the population occupational distribution is unknown as even the census did not ask questions as to whether a migrant was working as a wage or salary earner or was self-employed. Nevertheless, the common belief is that the proportion of self-employed from these surveys is too high. The main reason for this is that workers who live on construction sites and in factory dormitories do not normally register with the urban community authorities.[5]

To help offset any bias in the samples, the analyses below present results for total migrant samples and a sample of migrant wage and salary earners only. Table 10.1 presents summary statistics.[6] Many interesting facts are revealed from this table. First, on average, migrants are about 12–23 years younger and have about two to three years less education than their urban counterparts.

Second, the proportion of household members who are employed differs greatly between urban residents and migrants. About 70–86 per cent of migrants in cities are working, while this ratio for urban residents is between 40 and 50 per cent, suggesting that, as guest workers, migrants leave their non-working family members back in the rural villages.

Third, rural migrants earn less, spend less and save more than urban residents. On average, based on the *CIDS*, migrant earnings per worker are 9,142 yuan per annum and per capita income is 6,486 yuan, while these figures for urban residents are 12,162 yuan and 8,246 yuan, respectively. Urban residents earn 33 and 27 per cent more than their migrant counterparts.

Migrant savings, however, are higher than urban residents. On average, migrants save 2,214 yuan per capita per annum—34 per cent of their per capita income — while the average saving rate for urban residents is 24 per cent. The low income and high saving rates indicate that migrants live in much harsher conditions than their urban counterparts. This can be shown from their housing conditions. Per capita living area for migrants is about 11 square metres, while for urban residents it is 19–23 sq m. About 63 per cent of migrant households do not have a bathroom, while for urban residents it is 16 per cent.

Fourth, migrants have limited access to social benefits. For example, while 65 per cent of urban employed individuals are eligible for public health insurance, this ratio is 4 per cent for migrants. Despite this, migrants spend less on health. While per capita health expenditure is about 450 yuan annually for urban residents, the figure for migrant households is 243 yuan, almost half that for the urban residents. Obviously, saving motivations contribute to the low health expenditure of migrant workers. As medical expenditure is very high in many cities,[7] when health problems arise migrants often try to avoid seeing doctors.

As Xiang (2003) indicated, on falling ill, migrants would typically wait, hoping the illness would go away. If the situation got worse, they would go to small

Table 10.1 Summary statistics

Households	CIDS Urban	CIDS Migrants	CULS Urban	CULS Migrants
Age of the household head	48.00	36.00	53.00	30.00
Age of employed	41.00	35.00	41.00	31.00
Percentage of household heads are males	0.67	0.80	0.71	0.61
Years of schooling of household head	10.70	8.10	10.10	8.10
Years of schooling of spouse	10.20	7.20[a]	9.00	7.90
Household size	2.99	2.69	2.89	1.82
Percentage of household aged 0–5	0.02	0.06	0.00	0.03
Percentage of household aged above 65	0.07	0.01	0.16	0.00
Number of employed in household	1.49	1.72	1.16	1.41
Percentage of household members employed	0.50	0.70	0.39	0.86
Percentage of total employed who are self-employed	0.05	0.51	0.10	0.54
Employed annual earnings	12,162.00	9,142.00	13,900.00	11,158.00[b]
Employed monthly hours worked	191.00	291.00	195.00	306.00
Employed hourly earnings	5.74	3.01	..	..
Percentage employed who are eligible for health benefits	0.65	0.04	0.67	..
Percentage employed who are eligible for housing benefits	..	0.06	0.47	..
Percentage employed who are white-collar workers	0.52	0.06	..	..
Percentage employed who are unhealthy	0.04	0.02	0.06	0.01
Per capita income	8,246.00	6,486.00	8,690.00	..
Per capita total expenditure	6,294.00	4,272.00	6,224.00	..
Per capita savings	1,952.00	2,214.00	2,466.00	..
Saving rate	0.24	0.34	0.28	..
Annual remmitances	n.a.	1,072.00	n.a.	1,337
Per capita living area	18.82	1,1.25	23.24.00	11.58
Per capita expenditure on housing	643.00	1,178.00	..	..
Annual rent for those who are renting	560.00	2,624.00	..	3,431.00
Percentage of household living in housing without a bathroom	0.16	0.63	..	..
Percentage of expenditure on food	0.43	0.45	..	..
Per capita health expenditure	448.00	243.00	..	..
Per capita public health expenditure	408.00	n.a.	..	..
Number of observations (employed)	6,781.00	1,947.00	3,458.00	2,262.00
Number of observations (household)	10,135.00	3,357.00	4,010.00	3,394.00

Notes: [a] Only those whose spouse is present in the same city are counted. [b] Only the main respondents are asked this question, therefore, it is the mean of the main respondents.
Sources: Chinese Academy of Social Sciences, 2002. *China Income Distribution Survey (CIDS)*, Institute of Economics, Chinese Academy of Social Sciences. Chinese Academy of Social Sciences, 2001. *China Urban Labour Survey (CULS)*, Institute of Population and Labour Economics, Chinese Academy of Social Sciences.

pharmacies to buy medicines according to their own medical knowledge. Only when the illness became unendurable would they visit a doctor, by which time the disease might already have become very serious.[8]

Fifth, migrants, on average, work 52–56 per cent more hours per month than their urban counterparts and rarely have access to benefits that are commonly available to urban residents.

Finally, in both surveys, individuals were asked to rate their health condition against their age group. The ratings ranged from one for excellent to five for very ill. We group four (ill) and five (very ill) into a dummy variable indicating unhealthy and find that migrants, on average, are less likely than their urban counterparts to rate themselves as being unhealthy.

A simple poverty assessment

In China, there is no official poverty line for each province or city, however, governments in each region publish the income level at which a household can receive the Minimum Living Allowances (the Dibao Line). The Dibao Line reflects local minimum living standards and local government budgetary situations, as the Minimum Living Allowance is paid by local governments. The Dibao Line is, therefore, often lower than other poverty lines.

The more widely used poverty line is often defined as US$1 or US$2 a day. This line, however, relies heavily on the purchasing power parity exchange rate, which is not available across different regions within China. In this paper, we follow Ravallion (1994), China Urban Poverty Research Group (2003) and Meng et al. (2005) and use 'the cost of basic needs' (CBN) method.

This method defines the poverty line in four steps. The first step is to define the cost of acquiring 'the minimum nutrition requirement' (MNR). The MNR used in this study is 2,100 calories per person per day, which is used commonly in many poverty studies (Ravallion 1994; Prodhan et al. 2001) and is accepted as the MNR by the Chinese Academy of Preventive Medicine (2001).

The second step is to choose a reference group that purchases the MNR. Our reference group is the poorest 20 per cent of households. Third, we measure the cost of acquiring the MNR by the reference group. This is defined as the food poverty line. Finally, we calculate the non-food component of the cost of basic needs (CBN), as humans not only need food to survive, they need other things such as basic clothing and shelter.[9]

Earnings are not reported for non-respondents in the *CULS* migrant survey, and hence, it is impossible to obtain per capita income for migrant households. As a result, the simple poverty assessment presented in this section will not include the *CULS* sample.

To use the CBN method to calculate a local poverty line for different cities and provinces, we use the Urban Household Income and Expenditure Survey (UHIES) 2002. This survey samples households with urban household registration for every province in the nation (29 provinces before 1990 and 30 after 1990, due to the establishment of the province of Hainan in 1990).[10]

Households are expected to keep a diary of all expenditure (disaggregated for hundreds of product categories) for each day for a full year. Enumerators visit sample households once or twice each month to review the records, assist the household with their questions and collect the household records for data entry in the local Statistical Bureau office (Han et al. 1995; Fang et al. 2002; and Gibson et al. 2003).

The Dibao and poverty lines calculated using the CBN method for the 15 provinces included in the *CIDS* are presented in Appendix table 10.2. Although the Dibao line is always lower than the upper CBN poverty line, we use both in our poverty calculation and analyses below.

Table 10.2 presents poverty headcount indices, poverty gap and per capita income and expenditure for urban residents and migrants separately and for the total sample combined (including urban residents and migrants). Focusing on the total sample first, the poverty rate measured using the Dibao and CBN lines and measured in terms of income for urban residents is 3.5 and 6 per cent, respectively, while for migrants it is 10.1 and 15.7 per cent respectively. On average, the poverty rate for migrants is more than double that for urban residents. In addition, there is a larger proportion of poor migrant households with high levels of poverty than of urban residents. The average poverty gap for urban residents and migrants is 0.09 and 0.13, respectively, using the Dibao and CBN lines.

When the poverty rates are measured in terms of expenditure, they double for urban residents and migrants. The proportion of urban households living under the upper CBN poverty line increases to 12.5 per cent, and the proportion of migrant households increases to 32.4 per cent.

Note that including migrants in the sample increases the income-measured poverty rate by 1.4 to 2.1 percentage points, depending on the poverty line used. These results are largely consistent with the *Asian Development Report* (ADB 2002) estimates of poverty in urban China in 1998, which reported a 50 per cent higher poverty rate for migrants than for urban residents.

In the second and third columns of each panel in Table 10.2, we report the poverty rate for households without any self-employed and for households with at

Table 10.2 **Poverty rate, poverty gap and per capita income/expenditure, CIDS**

Headcount index Dibao Line	Income measure			Expenditure measure		
	Total	Wage/salary earners	Self-employed	Total	Wage/salary earners	Self-employed
Total	0.049	0.044	0.078	0.105	0.098	0.139
Urban residents	0.035	0.032	0.082	0.073	0.069	0.144
Migrants	0.101	0.130	0.076	0.215	0.306	0.137
Upper line						
Total	0.081	0.073	0.122	0.169	0.159	0.218
Urban residents	0.060	0.055	0.128	0.125	0.118	0.219
Migrants	0.157	0.200	0.120	0.324	0.447	0.218
Poverty gap						
Total	0.109	0.097	0.143	0.099	0.107	0.072
Urban residents	0.091	0.093	0.079	0.066	0.064	0.081
Migrants	0.131	0.103	0.172	0.139	0.175	0.067
Upper line						
Total	0.104	0.095	0.130	0.100	0.104	0.088
Urban residents	0.086	0.087	0.084	0.077	0.074	0.096
Migrants	0.127	0.110	0.151	0.132	0.159	0.084
Per capita income/expenditure						
Total	7,850	7,977	7,237	5,839	6,008	5,022
Urban residents	8,246	8,325	7,119	6,294	6,354	5,441
Migrants	6,486	5,558	7,287	4,272	3,607	4,847

Source: Chinese Academy of Social Sciences, 2002. *China Income Distribution Survey (CIDS)*, Institute of Economics, Chinese Academy of Social Sciences.

The impact of the guest-worker system

least one member self-employed. The main difference in poverty rates between urban residents and migrants occurs among wage and salary earners, where we observe 20 per cent of migrants with per capita income below the upper CBN poverty line, while the proportion for urban residents is 5.5 per cent.

For the self-employed, there is little difference in poverty rates between urban residents and migrants. If anything, self-employed urban residents are slightly more likely to be living below the poverty line. Note, though, there is only a very small proportion of urban residents who are self-employed (5 per cent in the *CIDS*; see Table 10.1).

Working your way above the poverty line

The key issue is why are migrants poor. Is it because they cannot find jobs or is it because hourly earnings are too low? In addition, for those whose incomes are above the poverty line, is this due to their extremely long hours of work?

We first investigate the labour force status of migrants and urban residents (see the first panel of Table 10.3). For individuals aged 16 to 65, about 86 per cent of migrants are working, while this ratio is 64 per cent for urban residents in the *CIDS*; the ratio is as high as 95 per cent for male migrants and 76 per cent for female migrants. For their urban counterparts, the ratio is 72 and 56 per cent for males and females, respectively. Similar results are found in the *CULS*. Thus, perhaps, additional migrant poverty is not the result of lower employment rates; it might be because hourly earnings for migrant workers are substantially lower than for their urban counterparts. In other words, they are working poor.

We also examine the average hours worked for workers and for household members aged 16–65 by migration status, gender (middle panel in Table 10.3) and poverty status (last panel in Table 10.3). We find that on average an employed migrant works about 52 per cent more hours than his/her urban counterpart. In addition, while households living below the poverty line work less hours, this situation is more so for urban residents than for migrants. Migrants who live below the poverty line work 218–274 hours a month, which is almost 51–69 hours a week, while urban residents living below the poverty line work only 13–25 hours a week.

Figures 10.1 and 10.2 present work hours per day, work days per month (per week in the case of the *CULS*) and hours worked per month for household members aged 16–65. As our migrant sample might include too many self-employed, who normally work longer hours, we present the figures for the total sample and the sample excluding self-employed.

The striking feature of these figures is that the majority of urban workers work a normal eight hours a day and five days a week, but most migrants work more than

Table 10.3 **Working status and working hours of migrants and urban residents**

	CIDS			CULS		
	Urban	Migrants	([M/U]-1)*100	Urban	Migrants	([M/U]-1)*100
Proportion of those aged 16–65 working						
Total	63.24	85.66	35.45	59.41	91.80	54.52
Males	71.46	95.16	33.17	70.29	95.83	36.34
emales	55.35	75.64	36.66	49.41	86.59	75.25
Monthly hours worked per employed individual						
Total	192.0	291.0	51.56	195.0	306.0	56.94
Males	194.0	288.0	48.45	197.0	301.0	52.45
Females	189.0	294.0	55.56	192.0	315.0	64.09
Age 16–65 per person monthly hours worked						
Above poverty line	125.0	256.0	104.80	104.0	294.0	182.69
Below poverty line	106.0	218.0	105.66	57.0	274.0	380.70
Total	124.0	250.0	101.61	100.0	293.0	193.00

Sources: Chinese Academy of Social Sciences, 2002. *China Income Distribution Survey* (*CIDS*), Institute of Economics, Chinese Academy of Social Sciences. Chinese Academy of Social Sciences, 2001. *China Urban Labour Survey* (*CULS*), Institute of Population and Labour Economics, Chinese Academy of Social Sciences.

eight hours a day and seven days a week. This is true even when we exclude self-employed individuals.

It appears that migrant workers spend most of their lives working while they are in the cities. An average of 9.7 hours a day and seven days a week suggests that apart from sleeping (eight hours) and eating (three hours), migrant workers have about only three hours a day left for themselves. Such extremely long hours, combined with high employment rates, should have pushed many above the poverty line.

The issue we are interested in is, if migrants worked similar hours to those worked by urban residents with similar characteristics, how many migrants would have had an income below the poverty line?

If migrants were urban residents, how many hours would they have worked per month?

To answer this question, we estimate the following hours equation

$$H_{iut} = W2_{iut}\beta + \delta Health_{iut} + \varepsilon_{iut} \tag{1}$$

The impact of the guest-worker system

Figure 10.1 **Hours worked per day and days worked per month/week**

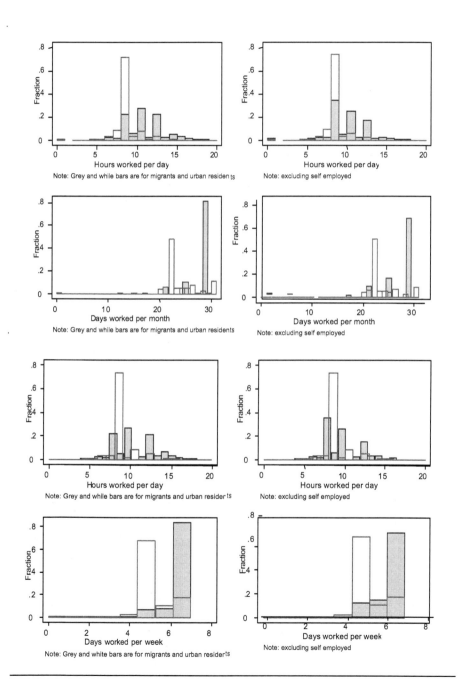

Figure 10.2 **Hours worked per month**

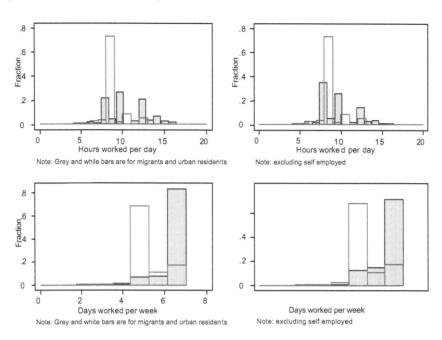

where H_{iu} indicates the hours worked for individual i with urban resident status u. W is a vector of control variables, including age, age squared, years of schooling, whether the individual is self-employed, the proportion of household members aged five and below, and provincial dummy variables controlling for regional variation in hours worked (related to weather, or culture).

Health is a dummy variable generated from a self-assessed health question. In the survey, each individual was asked to rate their health relative to individuals of their own age, ranging from one, indicating very healthy, to five, very ill. The dummy variable for unhealthy is set equal to one if an individual self-rated as ill (four) or very ill (five). Note that there might be a relationship between current health and past hours worked, but in Equation 1, we are interested in the relationship between current health and current hours worked, and our analysis should not suffer from the problem of reverse causality. Thus, we believe that *Health* in Equation 1 is an exogenous variable.

Equation (1) is estimated using a tobit model for urban residents aged 16–65 and for male and female samples separately. The results are presented in Table

10.4. Age has an inverse U-shape effect on hours worked: more-educated people work more, self-employed work extremely long hours, individuals with bad health work less, and people in large cities (Beijing in the case of the *CIDS* and Shanghai in the case of the *CULS*) work longer hours (the results on regional dummy variables are omitted from Table 10.4).

The presence of young children, however, does not seem to have a consistent effect over the two surveys. In the case of the *CIDS*, having young children increases male and female working hours, though the effect is marginally significant for females. In the case of the *CULS*, the effect is negative for males and females but not statistically significant for men. The reason for such a difference is not entirely clear. Perhaps, in large cities (*CULS*), where income levels are high, women can afford to quit jobs when they have young children. This might not be the case in medium and small cities (*CIDS*).

The results presented in Table 10.4 are then used to predict migrant hours worked

$$H_{imt} = W2_{imt}\beta_u + \delta_u Health_{imt} \quad (2)$$

Figure 10.3 shows the distribution of actual hours, H_{imt}, and predicted hours, H_{imt}.[11]

We find that had migrants behaved like urban residents, they would have worked about 50–100 per cent less hours on average than what they actually did (see also Table 10.5). The results are consistent across the two survey samples.[12]

What has been the impact of these long hours on migrant poverty?

This question is examined by first estimating the following household income per capita equation for the migrant sample

$$\ln Y_{jmt} = X2_{jmt}\beta + \delta H_{jmt} + e_{jmt} \quad (3)$$

where Y_{jm} is annual per capita income for migrant (m) household j, X is a vector of exogenous variables including age and age squared of the household head, years of schooling of the household head and his/her spouse, the gender of the household head, the proportion of the household members who are children (aged below 16), young adults (aged 16–20) and elderly (aged above 65), household size and regional dummy variables. H is hours worked per capita (total hours worked by all household

Table 10.4 Selected results from tobit estimation of hours worked for urban residents and real and predicted hours for migrants

	CIDS, 2002		CULS, 2001	
	Males	Females	Males	Females
Hours worked, urban residents				
Constant	-675.55***	-883.45***	-327.36***	-336.78***
	(15.17)	(22.73)	(30.26)	(41.18)
Age	41.63***	50.47***	23.11***	18.25***
	(0.71)	(1.11)	(1.39)	(1.90)
Age^2	-0.51***	-0.67***	-0.31***	-0.29***
	(0.01)	(0.01)	(0.02)	(0.02)
Years of schooling	2.39***	10.17***	5.86***	15.95***
	(0.41)	(0.58)	(0.74)	(1.10)
Proportion of household members aged 0–5	91.07***	36.55*	-36.05	-179.88***
	(15.17)	(19.93)	(30.82)	(38.814)
Dummy for self-employed	101.90***	154.32***	154.88***	262.07***
	(6.03)	(8.88)	(7.68)	(11.377)
Dummy for bad health	-57.74***	-36.08***	-68.66***	-60.98***
	(6.31)	(7.58)	(8.08)	(9.68)
Regional effect (province/city)	Yes	Yes		
Number of observations	7,836	8,144	3,181	3,459
Pseudo R^2	0.06	0.06	0.04	0.06

Table 10.5 Real and predicted work hours for rural migrants

	CIDS, 2002		CULS, 2001	
	Mean	Median	Mean	Median
Real hours worked	278	294	285	301
Predicted hours worked	186	188	171	152
(Real/Predicted)-1	49.46	56.38	66.67	98.03

Figure 10.3 **Real and predicted hours worked per month**

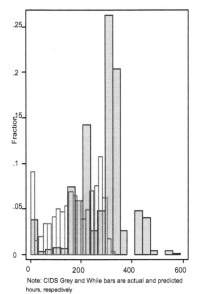

Note: CIDS Grey and White bars are actual and predicted hours, respectively

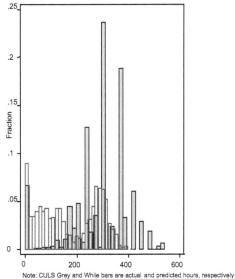

Note: CULS Grey and White bars are actual and predicted hours, respectively

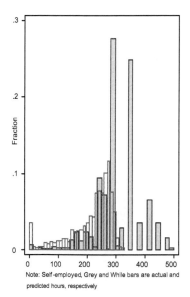

Note: Self-employed, Grey and White bars are actual and predicted hours, respectively

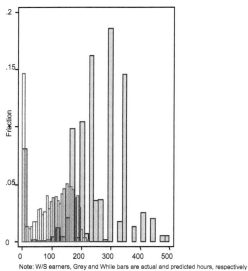

Note: W/S earners, Grey and White bars are actual and predicted hours, respectively

members divided by the total number of household members). Note that hours worked, H, might be endogenous in Equation 3 as household per capita income might affect per capita working hours.

We use the number of household members stated as being currently unhealthy as the instrument to handle this possible endogeneity problem. We argue that it is unlikely that an individual's current health should affect current income through channels other than hours worked. Thus, the exclusion restriction should be satisfied.

After fitting Equation 3, we calculate the predicted income level of migrant households as

$$\ln Y^{Himt}_{jmt} = X2_{jmt}\beta + \delta H_{jmt} + e_{jmt} \quad (4)$$

assuming that the household members had worked like urban residents, H_{jmt}.[13] Based on this predicted income level, we reassess the poverty rate of our migrant sample.

The results of estimated Equation 3 using OLS and IV-GMM for the *CIDS* total and wage and salary earner samples are reported in Table 10.6. They are largely consistent across the two estimations. In general, the age of the household head has an inverse U-shape relationship with per capita household income, although it is statistically significant only in the case of OLS estimation. The effect of years of schooling of the household head is strong and positive for both estimations, while spouse years of schooling is not statistically significant in the total sample for the IV estimate but is significant in any other cases.

Households headed by males seem to earn less in the case of the total sample, but this is not true for the sample of wage and salary earners, where the coefficients are positive, although only in the case of IV estimates is it statistically significant. The marital status of the household head does not seem to affect household per capita income, except for the IV estimate using the sample of wage and salary earners, where a negative and significant effect is found.

The proportion of household members who are children (aged 0–15) contributes negatively and significantly to household per capita income levels, so does household size, while the proportion of teenagers and old people have no statistically significant effect.

Turning to the most important variable of our estimation, household per capita monthly hours worked, we find that this has a positive and statistically significant effect on household per capita income. The effect is larger while using the IV-

Table 10.6 Selected results from per capita household income equation

	CIDS, total sample		CIDS, wage and salary earners	
	OLS	IV-GMM	OLS	IV-GMM
Constant	7.462	3.034	7.495	3.127
	(0.309)***	(2.310)	(0.381)***	(2.429)
Per capita hours worked	0.119	0.933	0.168	0.925
	(0.032)***	(0.424)**	(0.040)***	(0.419)**
Household head age	0.046	0.028	0.026	0.018
	(0.012)***	(0.016)*	(0.014)*	(0.017)
Household head age^2	-0.001	-0.000	-0.000	-0.000
	(0.000)***	(0.000)	(0.000)**	(0.000)
Household head gender, male=1	-0.07	0.015	0.091	0.217
	(0.037)*	(0.058)	(0.049)*	(0.083)***
Household head years of schooling	0.031	0.036	0.026	0.029
	(0.006)***	(0.007)***	(0.007)***	(0.009)***
Spouse years of schooling	0.007	0.006	0.015	0.023
	(0.005)	(0.005)	(0.006)**	(0.009)***
Household head married	0.032	-0.038	-0.099	-0.163
	(0.082)	(0.103)	(0.091)	(0.116)
Percentage of children aged 0–15	-0.51	0.453	-0.419	0.325
	(0.108)***	(0.522)	(0.136)***	(0.422)
Percentage of household aged 16–20	-0.171	-0.006	-0.083	-0.07
	(0.106)	(0.148)	(0.102)	(0.116)
Percentage of household aged above 65	-0.119	-0.292	-0.211	-0.338
	(0.248)	(0.353)	(0.236)	(0.290)
Household size	-0.135	-0.068	-0.186	-0.092
	(0.022)***	(0.042)	(0.028)***	(0.060)
Region	Yes	Yes	Yes	Yes
Number of observations		1,804	1,804	826	826
Adjusted R^2	0.23		0.33	
F tests for the strength of the instrument		19.49		22.78

Notes: Standard errors in parentheses. * significant at 10 per cent. ** significant at 5 per cent. *** significant at 1 per cent
Source: Chinese Academy of Social Sciences, 2002. *China Income Distribution Survey* (*CIDS*), Institute of Economics, Chinese Academy of Social Sciences.

Figure 10.4 **Real and predicted per capita income**

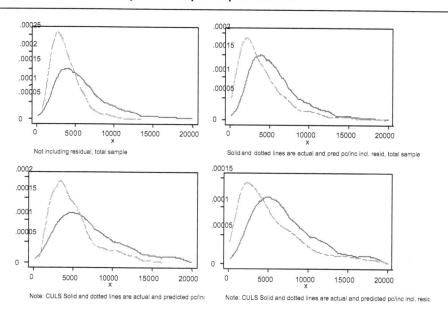

GMM estimate.[14] Using the IV estimate, the coefficient indicates that every additional household per capita hour worked per month increases household per capita annual income by 0.8 and 0.7 per cent for the total and wage/salary earner samples, respectively. Thus, if migrants work 100 hours less per month, which is about the difference in real and predicted hours worked for migrants (see Table 10.5), their per capita annual income would reduce by 50 per cent.

The distribution of the predicted and real incomes is presented in Figure 10.4. The top panel of this figure are graphs with and without including the residual term from the *CIDS* total sample, while the bottom panel presents the same graphs from the wage and salary earner sample. It is quite clear from these figures that the distribution of migrant per capita household income would have shifted to the left significantly. The mean and median income reduced by about 33–49 per cent (see Table 10.7).

Finally, in the bottom panel of Table 10.7, we present the real and predicted poverty headcount indices and poverty gaps. Not surprisingly, with predicted income, the poverty headcount index increased from 16 per cent to 41 per cent in the *CIDS* total sample, and from 20 per cent to 56 per cent in the sub-sample of

Table 10.7 Real and predicted per capita income and poverty rates

	CIDS, total sample		CIDS, wage and salary earners	
	Mean	Median	Mean	Median
Real per capita household income (R1)	6,486	5,200	5,495	4,863
Predicted per capita household income (no residual) (R2)	4,496	4,192	3,552	3,315
Predicted per capita household income (including residual) (R3)	5,747	4,131	4,253	3,295
(R1)/(R3)-1	12.86	25.88	29.20	47.59
	Poverty rate	Poverty gap	Poverty rate	Poverty gap
Real income	0.15	0.13	0.20	0.11
Predicted income (no residual)	0.16	0.07	0.35	0.1
Predicted income (including residual)	0.28	0.19	0.41	0.19

Source: Chinese Academy of Social Sciences, 2002. *China Income Distribution Survey (CIDS)*, Institute of Economics, Chinese Academy of Social Sciences.

wage and salary earners, an increase of 25–36 percentage points. Poverty severity also increased in both cases.

The above analyses suggest that below-average hourly income for migrants, relative to urban residents, is offset largely by above-average hours worked. In this way, migrant poverty as typically measured is considerably reduced. Once the difference in hours worked between migrants and urban residents is taken into account, we find that migrants would have suffered considerably more from poverty had they worked the same hours as their urban counterparts. Our findings raise many questions as to the relationships between poverty measures, hourly income and total work hours that have not received much attention in the poverty literature.

The health impact of long work hours

Guest workers come with very clear short-term objectives: earn and save as much money as possible in the limited time they have in the cities. As a result, they work extremely long hours. Such long working hours clearly have pushed many of them to earn an income that is above the poverty line—but at what cost? Perhaps the long working hours have long-term adverse impacts on their health. If we believe in

Goodman's (1972) model, where health is regarded as part of human capital, extremely long work hours might reduce healthy human capital and future earnings.

To analyse this issue, we need information on current health, $Health_{it}$ and previous hours worked, H_{t-n}, for rural migrants to eliminate the possible problem of hours worked being an endogenous variable. Fortunately, the CULS collected hours worked at the beginning of the current job, if the individual was working, and at the beginning of the last job, if the individual was not currently working. There is, however, a problem. Under the guest-worker system, migrants who are unhealthy are more likely to go back to their home villages because they have no access to health insurance,[15] unemployment benefits or a basic safety net in the cities. This is likely to generate a selection bias and make the observed relationship between hours worked previously and current health not meaningful.

To resolve this problem, we estimate the previous work-hours–health relationship for urban residents and assume that on average migrants: 1) have a similar level of inherited health; 2) have a similar level of nutrition intake; 3) have a similar level of access to a similar quality of health care; and 4) the type of jobs they take have similar effects on their health stock as their urban counterparts.

Under these assumptions, we can predict health conditions for rural residents as a result of their long working hours using estimated results for the urban sample. We acknowledge that these are strong assumptions, however, we believe that the direction of the violation of these assumptions is more likely to bias our predictions downwards. For example, migrants are more likely to have worse nutrition intake, and less access to good health care, and the type of jobs they take might have more adverse effects on health than jobs taken by urban residents.

The first assumption, however, is difficult to judge. Assuming urban and rural people have the same distribution of genetic health, it is not clear whether those with better or worse genes are more likely to migrate. If we assume the former, the violation of this assumption might bias our result upwards, but this upward bias might be offset by the violation of the other three assumptions.

The health equation might be written as follows

$$Health_{it} = W2_{it}\beta + \delta H_{it-n} + \hat{I}_{it} \qquad (5)$$

where $Health_{it}$ is individual i's self-assessed health measure. To estimate Equation 5, we use two health measures: one is from the question, 'Relative to last year, is your health worse?', and the second is from the question, 'Relative to your own age group, how do you rate your health?'.

As presented before, we create a dummy variable indicating ill or very ill. W is a vector of exogenous variables that might affect the individual's health, including age, years of schooling (knowledge of health care and proxy for income), height (proxy for genetic health), whether an individual has a disability, whether an individual is working and how long the individual has been working in the current/previous job. H_{t-n} is hours worked at the beginning of the current job if the individual is working and at the beginning of the last job if the individual is not working.

To estimate Equation 5, there are three issues that need particular attention. First, hours worked at the beginning of the current/last job might not adequately measure the hours worked since the beginning of the job. If this is the case, our main variable, H_{t-n}, might not capture our point of interest, which is the impact of continued long working hours on health.

To test whether hours worked in a job have continuity, we correlated the hours worked at the beginning and the end of the current/last job and the correlation coefficient was 0.95, suggesting a consistency in hours worked for the duration of a job. Second, the timing of the beginning of the current/last job differs significantly among different individuals. Some people started a job 20 years ago, and others started one year ago. To capture this variation, we include a variable 'How long has the individual been working in the current/last job?'. In addition, we restrict our sample to a certain starting year.[16] Third, age is a very important health factor. As the age distribution of urban residents differs considerably from that of migrants (see Figure 10.5)—migrants are much younger—we restrict our sample to those who were younger than 51 years of age at the time of the survey.

Equation (5) is estimated using a probit model and the results are presented in Table 10.8. The left and right panels present results for whether an individual's health is worse relative to the previous year, and whether an individual is unhealthy relative to individuals of their own age. For the first dependent variable, the only statistically significant independent variables are age and hours worked at the beginning of the current/last job. That is, older individuals are more likely to think that their health is deteriorating, and the more hours worked previously, the more likely that they think their health is worse.

Turning to whether individuals rate themselves as unhealthy relative to individuals of their own age, we find more statistically significant coefficients. Age has a strong positive impact on being worse off than the previous year and being unhealthy relative to an individual's own age group.[17]

There is no effect of gender, education or height on health, and is quite unusual. Perhaps this is due to the sample restrictions. We find that without our restrictions

Figure 10.5 **Age distribution of urban residents and migrants**

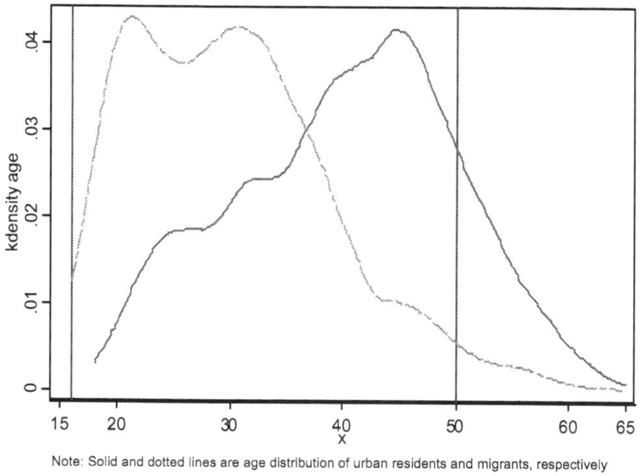

Note: Solid and dotted lines are age distribution of urban residents and migrants, respectively.

on age and hours worked, and excluding the hours worked variable (that is, including people who never worked), age has an inverse U-shape relationship with being unhealthy, and years of schooling and height contribute negatively to being unhealthy.

Whether an individual is currently working has no effect on whether he/she feels worse health-wise, relative to the previous year, but those who are working are significantly less likely to feel unhealthy. While the duration of current/last job has no effect on feeling worse or unhealthy, those who have a disability are more likely to state that they are unhealthy.

Our main variable of interest is 'hours worked at the beginning of the current/last job'. This variable has a consistent and significantly positive effect on an individual's self-rating as being unhealthy. Every additional hour worked per month increases the probability of feeling unhealthy by 0.02 per cent. The magnitude is smaller for estimations with less restrictions on the earliest starting year of a job, but they are still statistically significant at the 10 per cent level.

Using these estimated marginal effects, we then predict the effect of the extremely long hours worked by migrants on their health. The results are presented in Table 10.9. The first and second rows present the proportion of people who

Table 10.8 Marginal effects from probit estimation of Equation 5

	Is your health worse off compared with last year?			Are you unhealthy compared with your own age group?		
	(t-n)=earliest possible to 2000	(t-n)=1990–2000	(t-n)=1994–2000	(t-n)=earliest possible to 2000	(t-n)=1990–2001	(t-n)=1994 to 2001
Hours worked at the beginning of current/last job	0.0002* (0.000)	0.0002* (0.000)	0.0003*** (0.000)	0.0001*** (0.000)	0.0001* (0.000)	0.0002** (0.000)
Age	0.008*** (0.001)	0.007*** (0.001)	0.007*** (0.001)	0.004*** (0.001)	0.004*** (0.001)	0.005*** (0.001)
Years of schooling	0.000 (0.003)	0.000 (0.003)	0.002 (0.004)	-0.002 (0.002)	-0.000 (0.002)	0.000 (0.003)
Dummy for males	-0.018 (0.021)	-0.050* (0.028)	-0.046 (0.033)	-0.019 (0.013)	-0.023 (0.017)	-0.036 (0.022)
Dummy for those currently working	-0.023 (0.033)	0.021 (0.029)	0.026 (0.032)	-0.061*** (0.026)	-0.034* (0.023)	-0.039* (0.028)
Duration of current/last job	0.000 (0.001)	-0.001 (0.003)	-0.002 (0.006)	-0.001 (0.001)	-0.004** (0.002)	-0.001 (0.004)
Dummy for having deformity	0.031 (0.066)	0.008 (0.079)	-0.018 (0.089)	0.254*** (0.083)	0.309*** (0.124)	0.327** (0.161)
Height	-0.002* (0.001)	-0.001 (0.002)	-0.001 (0.002)	0.000 (0.001)	0.000 (0.001)	0.000 (0.001)
Number of observations	2497	1273	895	2497	1273	895
Pseudo R²	0.04	0.06	0.06	0.10	0.15	0.16

Source: Chinese Academy of Social Sciences, 2002. *China Income Distribution Survey (CIDS)*, Institute of Economics, Chinese Academy of Social Sciences.

Table 10.9 Real and predicted proportion of migrants who are unhealthy

	Is your health worse off compared with last year?			Are you unhealthy compared with your own age group?		
	(t-n)=earliest possible to 2000	(t-n)=1990–2000	(t-n)=1994–2000	(t-n)=earliest possible to 2000	(t-n)=1990–2001	(t-n)=1994 to 2001
Actual percentage unhealthy, urban residents (1)	14.78	12.80	13.08	6.26	6.00	7.05
Actual percentage unhealthy, migrants (2)	7.13	6.73	6.60	1.94	1.92	1.60
Predicted percentage unhealthy, migrants (3)	11.20	10.88	10.66	5.42	4.45	4.82
Migrants (3)-(2) (4)	4.07	4.15	4.06	3.49	2.53	3.23
([4]/[2])*100 (5)	56.99	61.57	61.49	180.13	131.26	202.18
([4]/[1])*100 (6)	27.52	32.38	31.03	55.73	42.10	45.72
Additional 103 hours worked monthly	2.06	2.06	3.09	1.03	1.03	2.06

Source: Chinese Academy of Social Sciences, 2002. *China Income Distribution Survey (CIDS)*, Institute of Economics, Chinese Academy of Social Sciences.

stated that their health was worse than the previous year or that they were unhealthy compared with their own age group, for urban residents and migrants, respectively.

The proportion of urban residents who stated that their health was worse than the previous year was more than double that of migrants, while for those who said they were unhealthy, the difference was more than three times. These differences, perhaps, are due to the selection effect on migrants, as discussed earlier. That is, those who are sick to start with do not come to the city and those who become sick leave.

If we assume that the distribution of genetic health between those who stay in the countryside and those who migrate to cities is similar, the major selection effect should be from those who have left for their rural home due to sickness developed in the city.

The third row uses the estimated coefficients from the urban equation to predict what would have been the proportion of migrants whose health was worse than the previous year, or who were unhealthy, had they had the same genetic health distribution, same nutrition intake, same health care and same occupation distribution as urban residents. The fourth row indicates the difference between the real and predicted proportions.

For the sample of migrants who started the current/last job no earlier than 1995 (third column of each panel in Table 10.9), the difference between the predicted and real proportions of those who stated that their health was worse than the previous year is 4.1 percentage points, and the difference between the predicted and real proportions of those who thought that they were unhealthy is 3.23 percentage points. These numbers are 61 and 202 per cent larger than the real occurrences for migrant workers, suggesting, perhaps, that the majority of those who are not healthy have gone home. This is the upper boundary of the proportion of people who are sick and have gone home. Relative to urban residents, these are 31 and 46 per cent of their urban resident real occurrences. This gives the lower boundary of the measure of the proportion of people who are sick and have gone home.[18]

Another way to predict the effect of long working hours on health is to use the average additional monthly hours worked by migrants times the marginal effect of the monthly hours worked on the probability of being worse off health-wise or being unhealthy. On average, migrants in the *CULS* sample worked 103 hours more per month than urban residents. This can translate to 3.1 percentage points more workers feeling worse off and 2.1 percentage points more workers feeling unhealthy, which is an increase of 50 and 130 per cent of the stated health for migrant workers.

Conclusions

In this chapter, we have examined poverty and the well-being of migrant workers in urban China. As guest workers, migrants have short-term objectives, which push them to work extremely hard in the cities. We have found that although a simple income assessment results in a low poverty rate, measured in terms of income for migrant workers relative to their urban resident counterparts, this is due mainly to their long working hours. Had they worked the same hours as urban workers, the poverty rate of the migrants would have increased from 15 per cent to 35 per cent.

Our finding that poverty among migrant workers in China is not related to unemployment in the cities is different from migrant poverty in other countries. Unlike migrant groups in other countries, Chinese rural migrants have very high employment rates—presumably because those who lose jobs are pushed back to the countryside by the guest-worker system and those who cannot find jobs are prevented from coming to the cities in the first place.

The extraordinarily long hours worked by guest workers are not usually factored into poverty analyses and focusing on weekly or annual income, as is usual in poverty studies, disguises how low hourly wages are. The large difference in hours worked between urban people and rural migrants raises a host of questions as to how to incorporate hours worked into a poverty analysis adequately. Obviously, a given income generated by 300 hours' work per month produces a lower level of well-being and a higher rate of 'poverty' than the same income produced by 160 hours' work per month.

In addition, in most poverty studies, a move from an income to an expenditure focus reduces the incidence of poverty, as in most countries the poor spend more than they earn. This is not true in China. Poor rural migrants have high saving rates and, indeed, save proportionately more than their city counterparts. If we examine poverty measured in terms of expenditure, the migrant poverty rate is as high as 32 per cent.

The tension between poverty as usually measured in income and a high savings rate by the 'poor' has a number of important implications. For example, the high savings rate suggests that some of the indicators of current poverty—poor housing in the city and low health expenditure—are partly the result of the decision to save as much as possible while in the city. The high savings rate also raises complex inter-temporal issues about enduring lower living standards now in order to enjoy higher living standards in the future.

Our study also raises important questions regarding the Chinese guest-worker system. It appears that the system acts as a buffer to reduce urban poverty and urban unemployment. Extreme poverty, which is often generated by urban unemployment and the associated development of urban slums, is largely avoided in China as unsuccessful workers are pushed back to villages if they lose their city jobs and those unable to find city jobs are usually prevented from coming to the cities in the first place.

The system can be thought of as one that minimises urban poverty and the social, economic and political tensions in cities. Pushing unsuccessful, unhealthy and poor people back to the villages, however, is not a long-term optimal solution to overall poverty reduction. The guest-worker system reduces the outflow of labour from the villages and thus keeps rural poverty higher than it would otherwise be. It restricts city employment opportunities and prevents migrants from investing in city skills and thus prevents them from building a long-term income base. In addition, one of our important findings is that the long work hours undertaken by guest workers, to increase their short-term income and savings, might damage their future health and hinder their long-term earning capacity.

Notes

1. We put aside any general equilibrium impact of migrants on the income levels of urban residents.
2. The provinces include Beijing, Shanxi, Liaoning, Jiangsu, Anhui, Henan, Hubei, Guangdong, Chongqing, Sichuan, Yunan and Gansu.
3. The *CULS* migrant survey does not include separate individual-level surveys for household members other than the respondent. Limited information on other family members is reported by the main respondent.
4. For detailed sampling procedures, see http://www.msu.edu/~gilesj/Protocol.pdf
5. The *CULS* claims that migrant workers who were registered by their work unit with local police stations were also included in the sample frame. This might be true to some extent but we still feel that the proportion of self-employed is too high.
6. Summary statistics for self-employed and wage and salary earners separately are presented in Appendix table 10.1.
7. According to Xiang 2003, one consultation for a minor health problem, such as a cold, in a big hospital in Beijing might cost RMB500, almost one month's salary for some migrants.
8. Many case studies and newspaper articles have presented facts with regard to migrants refusing to receive treatment for their health problems due to financial difficulties. For example, 14 migrant workers in a suitcase factory in Beijing were sent to a hospital by the local government when they were found to have severe benzene poisoning in 2002. More than 10, however, checked out soon afterwards due to a lack of money (Xiao 2002). Another example is that the department of external injuries in Guangdong Province People's Hospital receives about 200 migrant workers a year and more than one-third of them cannot pay the bill after treatment. Some hospitals now refuse to receive migrant patients (Cheng and Wen 2002).

9   The non-food component is obtained by the following procedure: first, we estimate the food share in total expenditure against the total expenditure deflated by the food poverty line and household size. Second, using the estimated coefficients for each province and each year, we calculate the non-food component of the poverty line for each province and each year. For detailed discussion of how the CBN poverty line is derived in this study, see Meng et al. 2005.
10 The sample is based on several stratifications at the regional, provincial, county, city, town and neighbourhood community levels. Households are selected randomly within each chosen neighbourhood community. The *UHIES* includes only households with urban household registration. Rural migrants to urban cities are not included in the survey. For a detailed description of the survey, see ibid.
11 Note that as the *CULS* surveyed only migrant household main respondents regarding their working hours, the real and predicted hours worked for migrants for the *CULS* are for the main respondents only.
12 The main real number of hours worked presented in Table 10.5 is slightly different from that presented in Table 10.1. This is because only those who do not have missing values on all the variables used in Equation 2 are included in Table 10.5.
13 Note that after predicting migrant household per capita income with H_{jmt}, we also give each household back its original error term, e_{jmt}, from Equation 3.
14 To test the strength of our instrument, the F-test for excluding the instrument from the first stage estimation is presented at the bottom of Table 10.6. We believe that our instrument is strong in both samples.
15 While about 53 per cent of urban residents have public health insurance, less than 2 per cent of migrants have such benefits.
16 Table 10.9 presents results for different restrictions. The first column for each of the two dependent variables shows the results for the sample of individuals who do not restrict the earliest starting year of the current/last job, but who restricted the latest starting year to 2000, so that everybody has to be in the job for at least one year as the survey was conducted at the end of 2001. The second column presents the results for individuals whose earliest starting year was 1990, while the third column is restricted to individuals whose earliest starting year was 1995. As a majority of our migrant sample (62 per cent) started the current/last job between 1995 and 2000, results from the third column might be more relevant (see Appendix figure 10.1 for the distribution of starting year).
17 The effect is linear due to the age restriction. Once the squared term is included, age and age squared become insignificant. Thus, the squared term is excluded.
18 Here we assume that nutrition intake, health care and occupational distribution are all the same for migrants and urban workers and that those rural workers who have bad genetic health did not come to the cities.

Appendix Table A10.1 **Summary statistics for wage/salary earners and self-employed (CIDS)**

Variables	Urban		Migrants	
	Wage/salary earner	Self-employed	Wage/salary earner	Self-employed
Age	41	40	34	35
Years of schooling	12	10	8	8
Individual annual income	12,213	11,168	7,643	10,562
Monthly hours worked	188	256	265	313
Hourly income	5.82	4.15	2.87	3.13
Number of observations	9,643	492	1,633	1,724

Source: Chinese Academy of Social Sciences, 2002. *China Income Distribution Survey (CIDS)*, Institute of Economics, Chinese Academy of Social Sciences.

Appendix Table A10.2 **Dibao and CBN poverty lines by province, 2002**

CIDS 2002	Dibao line (yuan)	Lower line (yuan)	Upper line (yuan)	(Up-DB)/Up
Beijing	3,480	3,286	4,433	0.21
Shanxi	1,872	1,620	2,345	0.20
Liaoning	2,460	1,861	2,523	0.02
Jiansu	2,640	2,233	2,874	0.08
Anhui	2,028	1,933	2,502	0.19
Henan	2,160	1,809	2,663	0.19
Hubei	2,520	2,039	2,742	0.08
Guangdong	3,600	2,925	3,790	0.05
Sichuan	2,136	1,836	2,318	0.08
Congqing	2,220	2,318	3,019	0.26
Yunnan	2,280	2,275	2,841	0.20
Gansu	2,064	2,095	3,012	0.31
Simple average	2,460	2,290	2,996	0.18

Note: Dibao Lines are for the capital city of each province apart from Beijing and Congqing.

Source: Chinese Academy of Social Sciences, 2002. *China Income Distribution Survey (CIDS)*, Institute of Economics, Chinese Academy of Social Sciences.

Appendix Figure A10.1 **Distribution of starting year for the current job**

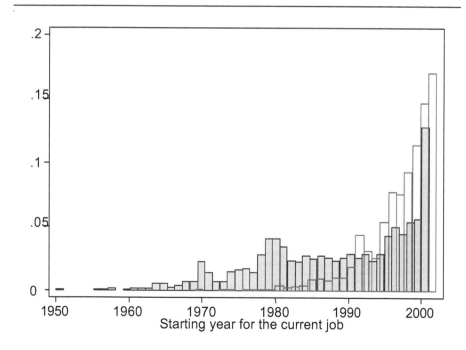

11

China's growth to 2030: demographic change and the labour supply constraint

Jane Golley and Rod Tyers

The world's most populous country has entered a period of rapid ageing, with the proportion of the population over the age of 60 projected to double in the next 25 years (United Nations 2005). This represents a significant turning point in China's economic development and one that places China in the unique position of being a transitional developing economy facing what is primarily an industrial-country phenomenon. As is so often the case for China, the appropriate policy responses are therefore likely to be unique as well. In particular, while many industrial countries are seeking ways to deal with ageing, such as pro-fertility policies, immigration and later retirement ages, developing countries are trying to ensure that their growing working-age populations can be absorbed into the workforce, through labour-market reforms and better education and training (International Monetary Fund 2004). As China's economic development and transition progress in the context of population ageing, Chinese policymakers will need to look both ways.

The demographic transition to slower population growth and the associated ageing of China's population have been profoundly affected by the one-child policy. Yet fertility rates would have declined anyway, affected as they have been in China's Asian neighbours by urbanisation, female education, higher labour-force participation rates, the improved life expectancy of new-born children and the high parental cost of preparing for and supporting children through increasingly competitive education systems. With a transition to a declining population in prospect, and with competing developing regions such as South Asia set to enjoy continued demographic dividends, there is now extensive discussion of whether the State should encourage higher fertility by relaxing its family planning policies.[1]

Indeed, unless there is a substantial change in population policy, the achievement of China's ambitious GDP growth objectives[2]—and, therefore, the retention of China's large share of global investment—will require further improvements in its investment environment, in its organisation of production and hence factor productivity and/or in its labour-force participation. Aged participation is low in China by Asian standards, but there are numerous reasons why we might expect an upward trend approaching the rates observed in neighbouring countries such as Japan. In this chapter, the linkages between demographic change, labour-force participation and economic growth are explored using a new global demographic sub-model, which is integrated with an adaptation of the GTAP-dynamic global economic model in which regional households are disaggregated by age and gender. In particular, the model is used to explore the growth implications of alternative fertility policies and increased aged participation.

The chapter proceeds as follows. The next section discusses recent trends in fertility, ageing and labour-force participation rates in China, along with related policy options. This is followed by a general description of the demographic sub-model, along with its integration within the GTAP-dynamic. Next, a baseline scenario is constructed for the global economy through to 2030, after which the results for alternative assumptions about fertility rates and aged labour-force participation are presented. Policy suggestions are offered in the conclusions.

Fertility, ageing and labour-force participation in China

While debates over the extent of China's fertility decline continue, it is widely accepted that by the turn of this century fertility rates had fallen to well below the replacement level of 2.1 births per woman. According to the National Bureau of Statistics (2002), the total fertility rate in 2000 was 1.22 children per woman, although even the Chinese government recognised that the figure was more like 1.8 because of under-reporting of births in surveys and censuses (Sharping 2003). Zhang and Zhao (2006) provide an extensive survey of the literature on fertility decline in China during the past two decades and conclude that the total fertility rate probably fell to about 1.6 by 2000. In a survey of rural women, Chu (2001) found many of them wanting fewer children, primarily because of new financial constraints associated with rapid increases in school fees and the cost of living. Retherford et al. (2005) concur that rapid fertility decline is highly plausible in light of China's rapid economic development and the socioeconomic forces unleashed by market reforms, combined with the one-child policy. While the causes are not the same, China's low and declining fertility rates place it alongside many industrial countries, including most Western European countries and Japan.

A declining fertility rate has been a major contributing factor to China's demographic transition.[3] The United Nations (2005) projects that the percentage of the population over 60 years of age will rise from 10 per cent in 2000 to 20 per cent by 2025 and 31 per cent by 2050,[4] while the percentage of the working-age population (aged 15–59 years) will fall by more than 10 percentage points during the same period. It is thereby suggested that some time between 2015 and 2020, the growth of the working-age population will become negative, in turn suggesting that GDP growth will suffer as a consequence.

To illustrate the striking slowdown in China's total population and labour force that is implied by the baseline projection in our model (discussed in detail below), both are contrasted with those of India (Figure 11.1). China's population is seen to begin declining during the next decade while its labour force declines earlier than that. Even though India is also ageing, its most populous age groups are very young

Figure 11.1 **China's and India's projected populations and labour forces, 1995–2035**[a]

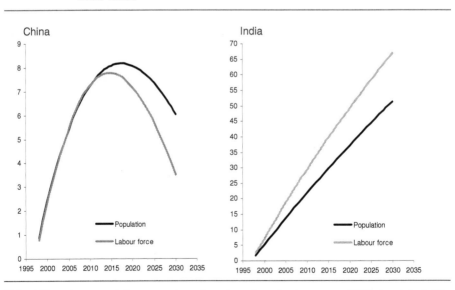

Note: [a] These are cumulative percentage departures from the base year, 1997, drawn from the baseline simulation in which China's fertility is projected to decline faster than India's and in which India begins with a much younger population.
Source: Baseline model simulation.

and, as these groups age, they raise the labour-force participation rate and the crude birth rate. Thus, in a period during which China's labour force shows little net growth, India's labour force rises by half. The same pattern is observed in other populous developing countries in South Asia and Africa. Compared with the rest of the developing world, then, the slow down in China's population must be expected to constrain its labour supply and hence to retard its overall economic expansion.

There are numerous policies that could potentially offset the negative consequences that China's pending demographic change will have for economic growth, including measures to increase fertility and labour-force participation rates.[5]

Fertility rates are key determinants of the rate of population growth and, in China, they have long been policy targets. Controlling for numerous other factors that affect population growth (including urbanisation, female education, increases in labour-force participation and improved life expectancy), Sharping (2003) estimates that, in the absence of the State's birth-control policies, China's population would have been 1.6 billion instead of the 1.27 billion reported at the end of the twentieth century. The question that remains is whether pro-fertility policies will impact significantly on fertility rates in the future. According to Demeny (2003:14), in the past the family planning programs that were most effective in reducing fertility rates in developing countries tended to work via 'heavy-handed methods of persuasion, and, in the especially important case of China, by coercion backed by legal sanctions'. The Chinese government is unlikely to utilise such methods to raise fertility rates in the future, and would instead need to resort to fiscal measures (such as tax breaks and family allowances) and policies to make motherhood and the women's labour force more compatible (through day-care services and more flexible working hours). Yet even if such policies were implemented—in itself a long shot—the impact on fertility rates is uncertain at best.[6] Moreover, there would clearly be a long lag before such policies, even if effective, would lead to an increase in the working-age proportion of the population and hence lower dependency rates.

An alternative policy approach would be to direct attention towards labour-force participation rates. Recent evidence suggests that labour-force participation by China's aged population is relatively low compared with other Asian economies. According to Jackson and Howe (2004), in 2000 the labour-force participation rates of men aged between 60 and 64 and over 65 were 60 per cent and 28 per cent respectively. For the same age groups, these percentages were 83 and 55 in the Philippines, 72 and 33 in Japan and 64 and 44 in Vietnam. Only Hong Kong and Singapore had lower participation rates in both age groups. Chan and Tyers (2006) provide a comparison of age and gender-specific labour-force participation rates in China and Japan in 1997 (the baseline year in the simulations conducted below), they find participation rates of 91 per cent and 43 per cent for 40–59-year-old Chinese males and females respectively, compared with 97 per cent and 67 per cent in Japan. Among those aged 60 and over, 24 per cent of Chinese men and just 4 per cent of Chinese women participated in the labour market, compared with 46 per cent of Japanese men and 23 per cent of Japanese women.

Labour-force participation rates were not only low at the turn of the century, but declining (Chan and Tyers 2006; Giles et al. 2006). Using data from the China Urban Labour Survey of five large cities conducted at the end of 2001, Giles et al. (2006) analysed the impact of economic restructuring on urban workers between 1996 and 2001, a period of widespread, large employment shocks in the labour market. During this period, unemployment reached double figures in all five cities, while labour-force participation declined by nine percentage points. The decline was most pronounced among workers approaching mandatory retirement: a 19 percentage point drop in participation rates of men aged 55–60 (down to 57 per cent in 2001) and an 11 percentage point drop for women aged 50–55 (down to just 34 per cent). These substantial declines are attributed to the replacement of implicit lifetime employment with massive lay-offs, widespread unemployment and forced early retirements.

Yet there are numerous reasons why China's labour-force participation rates could be higher in the future. Perhaps the most obvious of these would be an increase in the retirement age. In an influential World Bank (1997a) report on China's social security system, it was noted that current retirement ages of 60 for men and 55 for women were set at a time when life expectancy was only 50 years, compared with 71 years now. The report called for a gradual increase in the retirement age to 65 years, and even higher as longevity continues to increase.

It is obvious that the nature of any country's pension system will impact on retirement decisions and therefore on aged participation rates, although it is far from clear what the impact of continuing reforms on China's pension system will be. A multi-pillar system combining a pay-as-you-go component, a mandatory individual account and a voluntary supplementary scheme, first introduced in 1997, is being implemented in traditional Chinese fashion on an experimental and gradual basis.[7] Among other objectives, the introduction of individual accounts is intended to 'instil a spirit of self-help among workers who would look after their own retirement costs rather than depend on contributions from their children' (World Bank 1997a), thereby providing incentives to save more and retire later.

In 2000, 100 million workers were covered by the pension system in China, financing the pensions of 32 million retirees. This means that less than 10 per cent of the total population was covered (James 2001). The majority of this 10 per cent were employed by SOEs and urban collectives, with extremely low coverage in foreign-funded and private enterprises, and in rural areas. This low coverage implies that, in the foreseeable future, the majority of old people will not receive a pension and will have to rely on personal savings and a diminishing family system (James 2001). As the share of people employed in non-state sectors continues to rise, and as long as a majority in non-state enterprises continue to opt out of the pension system, it is likely that China's elderly will necessarily need to work longer in order to finance their retirement needs.

Of course, pension-related incentives for older generations to continue working are of little help if labour markets are inflexible or unable to absorb them. Despite significant improvements in the functioning of Chinese labour markets in the past three decades, there are still serious barriers preventing their efficient operation. Local protectionism and institutional barriers connected to the *hukou* system prevent potential gains from labour reallocation between rural and urban areas from being realised, while urban labour-market reforms are restricted by the fiscal burden of paying unemployment benefits and pensions (Fleisher and Yang 2003). Until the late 1990s at least, the lack of portability of the pension system impeded labour mobility, in turn reducing participation rates (World Bank 1997a). As solutions to these issues emerge, labour-force participation rates should rise, although there is clearly uncertainty as to when and how such solutions will materialise.

Bearing in mind the obvious uncertainties associated with identifying the extent to which various policies will impact on aged participation and fertility rates, in what follows we propose some plausible alternative scenarios and then demonstrate that the implications for GDP and real per capita income growth rates vary significantly depending on whether fertility or participation is targeted.

Modelling the economic implications of demographic change

The approach adopted follows Tyers (2005) and Tyers and Shi (forthcoming), in that it applies a complete demographic sub-model that is integrated within a dynamic numerical model of the global economy.[8] The economic model is a development of GTAP-dynamic, the standard version of which has single households in each region and therefore no demographic structure.[9] The version used has regional households with endogenous savings rates that are disaggregated by age group, gender and skill level.

Demography

The demographic sub-model tracks populations in four age groups and two genders: a total of eight population groups in each of 14 regions.[10] The four age groups are the dependent young, adults of fertile and working age, older working adults and the mostly retired over-60s. The resulting age–gender structure is displayed in Appendix Figure 11.1. The population is further divided between households that provide production labour and those providing professional labour.[11] Each age–gender–skill group is a homogeneous subpopulation with group-specific birth and death rates and rates of immigration and emigration.[12] If the group spans T years, the survival rate to the next age group is the fraction $1/_T$ of its population, after group-specific deaths have been removed and its population has been adjusted for net migration.

The final age group (60+) has duration equal to measured life expectancy at 60. It varies across genders and regions. The key demographic parameters, then, are birth rates, sex ratios at birth, age and gender-specific death, immigration and emigration rates and life expectancies at 60.[13] The migration rates are based on recent migration records and are held constant through time.[14] The birth rates, life expectancy at 60 and the age-specific mortality rates all trend through time asymptotically. For each age group, gender group and region, a target rate is identified.[15] The parameters then approach these target rates with initial growth rates determined by historical observation.

A further key parameter is the rate at which each region's education and social development structure transforms production-worker families into professional-worker families. Each year a particular proportion of the population in each production-worker age–gender group is transferred to professional (skilled) status. These proportions depend on the region's levels of development, the associated capacities of their education systems and the relative sizes of the production and professional labour groups. The skill transformation rates are based on changes during the decade prior to the base year, 1997, in the composition of aggregate regional labour forces as between production and professional workers. These are also held constant through time.[16]

Labour force projections. To evaluate the number of 'full-time equivalent' workers, we first construct labour-force participation rates by gender and age group for each region from International Labour Organization (ILO) statistics on the 'economically active population'. We then investigate the proportion of workers who are part-time and the hours they work relative to each regional standard for full-time work. The result is the number of full-time equivalents per worker.[17]

For each age group, gender group and region, a target country is identified whose participation rate is approached asymptotically. As with birth and death rates, the rate of this approach is determined by the initial rate of change. Target rates are chosen from countries considered to be advanced in terms of trends in participation rates. Where female participation rates are rising, therefore, Norway provides a commonly chosen target because its female labour-force participation rates are higher than for other countries.[18]

The aged dependency ratio. We define and calculate four dependency ratios: a youth dependency ratio is the number of children per full-time equivalent worker; an aged dependency ratio is the number of people over 60 per full-time equivalent worker; a non-working-aged dependency ratio is the number of non-working people over 60 per full-time equivalent worker; and a more general dependency ratio is defined that takes as its numerator the total non-working population, including children.[19]

The baseline population projection for China. The two key population parameters of interest—birth rates and labour-force participation rates—are listed in Tables 11.1 and 11.2, along with their assumed trends through to 2030. In these tables, the parameters are contrasted with those for Japan, towards whose development path China might be expected to trend in the coming decades. Most notable is the declining trend in Chinese fertility, extending the fall during the decade prior to the base year (1997) in an asymptotic approach towards the rates observed in Japan. The trends in participation rates assume that no significant policy changes take place, with slight declines in some of the age groups capturing the possibility that the downward trend observed through the 1990s could continue to some extent in the next 25 years as well. These figures are intended more for comparative purposes than to reflect accurately the expected changes in participation rates in the future.

Birth rates combine with age and gender-specific death rates and life expectancies to determine the baseline population structure, which indicates that the percentage of China's population over the age of 60 will increase from 9.7 per cent in 1997 to 21.5 per cent by 2030 (which is consistent with the UN's [2005] projections) (Table 11.3). The corresponding labour-force projection is summarised in Table 11.4.[20] Compared with the rest of the developing world, the slow down in China's population will constrain its labour supply and hence retard its economic growth. To assess the impact that this slow down will have, we have embedded the demographic behaviour introduced above in a global economic model.

The global economic model

GTAP-dynamic is a multi-region, multi-product dynamic simulation model of the world economy. It is a microeconomic model, in that assets and money are not represented and prices are set relative to a global numeraire. In the version used, the world is subdivided into 14 regions, one of which is China. Industries are aggregated into just three sectors: food (including processed foods), industry (mining and manufacturing) and services. To reflect composition differences between

Table 11.1 Baseline birth rates in China and Japan, 1997–2030[a]

	China		Japan	
Sex ratio at birth, males:females	1:10		1:06	
	Birth rate[b]	Fertility rate[c]	Birth rate[b]	Fertility rate[c]
Base year, 1997	76	1.90	59	1.48
2010	62	1.55	58	1.45
2020	59	1.48	57	1.43
2030	58	1.45	57	1.43

Notes: [a] Birth rates are based on UN estimates and projections as represented by the United States Bureau of the Census. The latter representation has annual changes in rates while the UN model has them stepped every five years. Initial birth rates are obtained from the UN model by dividing the number of births per annum by the number of women aged 15–39. These rates change through time according to annualised projections by the US Bureau of the Census. [b] Birth rates are here defined as the number of births per annum per thousand women of fertile age. They are modified to allow for the modelling simplification that the fertile age group spans 15–39. [c] Fertility rates are the average number of children borne by a woman throughout her life.
Source: Aggregated from United Nations, 2003. *World Population Prospects: the 2002 revision*, UN Population Division, February. Available online at <www.un.org/esa/population/publications/wpp2002>; US Department of Commerce–US Bureau of the Census, 'International data base', as compiled by Chan, M.M. and Tyers, R., 2006. *Global demographic change and labour force growth: projections to 2020*, Centre for Economic Policy Research Discussion Paper, Research School of Social Sciences, The Australian National University, December.

Table 11.2 Baseline age and gender-specific labour-force participation rates in China and Japan[a] (per cent)

	China		Japan	
	Males	Females	Males	Females
15–39 Initial (1997)	79	60	77	55
2030	77	61	76	58
40–59 Initial (1997)	91	43	97	67
2030	93	44	97	69
60+ Initial (1997)	24	4	46	23
2030	17	3	56	49

Notes: [a] Projections of these parameters to 2030 assume convergence on target rates observed in comparatively 'advanced' countries, as explained in the text. Only the end-point values are shown here, but the model uses values that change with time along the path to convergence.
Source: Values to 1997 are from Chan, M.M. and Tyers, R., 2006. *Global demographic change and labour force growth: projections to 2020*, Centre for Economic Policy Research Discussion Paper, Research School of Social Sciences, The Australian National University, December.

Table 11.3 **Baseline population structure in China, 1997–2030**

	Population (millions)	Female (per cent)	60+ (per cent)
Initial (1997)	1,252	48.5	9.7
2010	1,311	48.7	14.8
2020	1,321	48.8	18.4
2030	1,296	49.0	21.5

Source: Projection using the baseline simulation of the model described in the text.

Table 11.4 **Baseline labour-force structure in China, 1997–2030**[a]

	Labour force (millions)	Female (per cent)	40+ (per cent)
Initial (1997)	585	37.6	33.8
2010	628	37.1	41.1
2020	627	36.7	44.4
2030	606	36.5	46.6

Note: [a] Measured in full-time equivalent workers.
Source: Projection using the baseline simulation of the model described in the text.

regions, these products are differentiated by region of origin, meaning that the food produced in one region is not the same as that produced in others. Consumers substitute imperfectly between foods from different regions.

As in other dynamic models of the global economy, in GTAP-dynamic the endogenous component of simulated economic growth is physical capital accumulation. Technical change is introduced in the form of exogenous trends and skill (or human capital) acquisition is driven by the constant transformation rates introduced in the previous section. A consequence of this is that the model exhibits the property of all dynamic models of the Solow–Swan type that incorporate diminishing returns to factor use, namely that an increase in the growth rate of the population raises the growth rate of real GDP but reduces the level of real per capita income. What distinguishes the model from this simpler progenitor are its recursive multi-regional dynamics. Investors have adaptive expectations about the real net rates of return on installed capital in each region. These drive the distribution of investment across regions. In each, the level of investment is determined by a comparison of net rates of return with borrowing rates yielded by a global trust to which each region's saving contributes.

To capture the full effects of demographic change, including those of ageing, the standard model has been modified to include multiple age, gender and skill groups in line with the structure of the demographic sub-model. In the complete model, these 16 groups differ in their consumption preferences, saving rates and their labour supply behaviour. Unlike the standard GTAP models, in which regional incomes are split between private consumption, government consumption and total savings via an upper-level Cobb–Douglas utility function that implies fixed regional saving rates, this adaptation first divides regional incomes between government consumption and total private disposable income. The implicit assumption is that governments balance their budgets while private groups save or borrow.

In splitting each region's private disposable income between the eight age–gender groups, the approach is to construct a weighted subdivision that draws on empirical studies of the distribution of disposable income between age–gender groups for 'typical' advanced and developing countries.[21] Individuals in each age–gender group then split their disposable incomes between consumption and saving. For this, a reduced form of approach is taken to the intertemporal optimisation problem faced by each. It employs an exponential consumption equation that links a group's real per capita consumption expenditure to real per capita disposable income and the real interest rate. This equation is calibrated for each group and region based on a set of initial (1997) age-specific saving rates from per capita disposable income.[22] Importantly, these show transitions to negative saving with retirement in the older industrial regions. This gives rise to declines in average saving rates as populations age. The empirical studies on age-specific saving behaviour are less clear, however, when it comes to developing regions. In the case of China, only modest declines in saving rates are recorded when people retire. This is due partly to the complication that a comparatively large proportion of consumption spending by the Chinese elderly is probably financed from the income of younger family members. We have attempted to take this into account in selecting the age–gender income weights and initial saving rates for China.[23] If these rates represent Chinese behaviour accurately, they imply that ageing in China can be expected to have less impact on the average Chinese saving rate than it does in the older industrial economies.

Constructing the baseline scenario

The baseline scenario represents a business-as-usual projection of the global economy through to 2030. Although policy analysis can be sensitive to the content of this scenario, the focus of this chapter is on the extent of departures from it that would be caused by alternative trends in Chinese fertility on the one hand and aged participation rates on the other. Nonetheless, it is instructive to describe the baseline because all scenarios examined have in common a set of assumptions about future trends in productivity and because some exposition of the baseline makes the construction of departures from it clearer.

Exogenous factor productivity growth

Exogenous sources of growth enter the model as factor productivity growth shocks, applied separately for each of the model's five factors of production (land, physical capital, natural resources, production labour and professional labour). Simulated growth rates are sensitive to productivity growth rates since the larger these are for a particular region, the larger is that region's marginal product of capital. The region therefore enjoys higher levels of investment and hence a double boost to its per capita real income growth rate. The importance of productivity notwithstanding, the empirical literature is inconsistent as to whether productivity growth has been faster in agriculture or in manufacturing and whether the gains in any sector have enhanced all primary factors or merely production labour. The factor productivity growth rates assumed in all scenarios are drawn from a new survey of the relevant empirical literature (Tyers et al. 2005). Agricultural productivity grows more rapidly than that in the other sectors in China, along with Australia, Indonesia, other East Asian countries, India and other South Asian countries. This allows continued shedding of labour to the other sectors.[24] In the other industrialised regions, the process of labour relocation has slowed and labour productivity growth is slower in agriculture. In the other developing regions, the relocation of workers from agriculture has tended not to be so rapid.

Interest premiums. The standard GTAP-dynamic model takes no explicit account of financial market maturity or investment risk and so tends to allocate investment to regions that have high marginal products of physical capital. These tend to be labour-abundant developing countries whose labour forces are still expanding rapidly. Although the raw model finds these regions attractive prospects for this reason, we know that considerations of financial market segmentation, financial depth and risk limit the flow of foreign investment at present and that these are likely to remain important in the future. To account for this, we have constructed a 'pre-baseline' simulation in which we maintain the relative growth rates of investment across regions. In this simulation, global investment rises and falls but its allocation between regions is thus controlled.

To do this, the interest premium variable (GTAP-dynamic variable SDRORT) is made endogenous. This creates wedges between the international and regional borrowing rates. They show high-interest premiums for the populous developing regions of Indonesia, India, South America and sub-Saharan Africa. Premiums tend to fall over time in other regions, where labour forces are falling or growing more slowly. Most spectacular is a secular fall in the Chinese premium. This is because the pre-baseline simulation maintains investment growth in China despite an eventual decline in its labour force. This simulation is therefore overly optimistic with respect to China and so we reject the drastic declines in the investment premium that it implies. In constructing the final baseline scenario, we allow a fall in China's premium by 1.5 percentage points. Assuming all Chinese agents can borrow at the government's long-term bond rate, which exceeds the corresponding US rate by 40 per cent, this assumes that continuing financial reforms will wipe out about one-third of the initial Chinese premium, at the rates specified in the model.[25] The time paths of all interest premiums are set as exogenous and regional investment is freed up in all regions. Investment is then retained as endogenous in the model's closure in all subsequent simulations.

The baseline projection. Overall baseline economic performance is suggested by Table 11.5, which details the average GDP and real per capita income growth performance of each region from 1997 to 2030. In part because of its comparatively young population and hence its continuing rapid labour force growth, India attracts substantial new investment and is projected to take over from China as the world's most rapidly expanding region. Rapid population growth, however, detracts from India's real per capita income performance. By this criterion, China is the strongest performing region through the three decades. Indonesia and other East Asian countries are also strong performers, while the older industrial economies continue to grow more slowly. The African region enjoys good GDP growth performance but its high population growth rates limit its performance in per capita terms.

Higher fertility rates versus higher aged participation

Higher fertility rates

Following Sharping (2003) and the State Council of China (2000), two higher-fertility scenarios are constructed. These differ only in their fertility rates. Death rates and migration behaviour are assumed to remain as in the baseline projection. The first higher-fertility scenario offers a comparatively stable Chinese birth rate, with the fertility rate trending from 1.90 to 1.80 in the three decades to 2030. It is similar to the State Council's one-child policy, and to Sharping's 'tight rule, fraud as usual' scenario. The second scenario trends towards two children per couple throughout China, with a fertility rate of 2.3 achieved by 2030. It is similar to the State Council's 'two-child policy' and to Sharping's 'delayed two-child policy'. The implications for China's total population under these scenarios are indicated in Table 11.6.

The correspondence between these simulations and the State Council's projections is close. A transition to a two-child policy would raise the 2030 population by 11 per cent relative to the stable fertility case. Our low-fertility baseline, on the other hand, achieves a 2030 population 7 per cent below the stable fertility case. These implications are displayed graphically in Figure 11.2. Critically, the associated labour force changes are smaller in magnitude and transitions occur earlier than those in the populations. The Chinese population ages in all three scenarios, but more slowly the higher the fertility rate. This can be seen from the non-working-aged dependency ratio in Figure 11.3. While it rises substantially by 2030 in all three cases, there are discernable differences, with the two-child policy yielding a 2030 ratio that is lower by four percentage points than the low-fertility baseline.

The three main avenues through which higher fertility affects economic performance are via the labour force, which it expands; the savings share of income, which tends to rise with the share of the population of working age; and the product composition of consumption, which more strongly reflects the preferences of the young when population growth accelerates. The comparisons made by Tyers et al. (2005) suggest a general ranking that has the labour force avenue most commonly the strongest with the savings rate avenue next and with the influence of age-specific consumption preferences comparatively small. This is indeed borne out. The labour force effect can first be seen through its impact on the non-working-age dependency ratio. This ratio expands under all scenarios in China, as shown in Figure 11.3, but it grows least in the two-child policy case.[26]

Turning to the other avenues, age-specific consumption preferences can be expected to have little influence in the results presented here since product markets are aggregated into three broad sectors and the capturing of generational differences in preferences requires fine product detail. As to the savings rate, for reasons discussed previously, the effects of Chinese fertility changes on average savings rates can be expected to be smaller than they are in the older industrialised regions. Beyond the dependency ratio, the dominant economic theme might be changes in China's labour force that alter the productivity of its capital and therefore the return on Chinese investment. Greater population growth thereby attracts an increased share of the world's savings into Chinese investment and so China's capital stock grows more rapidly. China's GDP, therefore, might be expected to be boosted substantially by increased fertility, through its direct and indirect influence over the supply of the two main factors of production: labour and capital. In per capita terms, however, the Solow–Swan predisposition towards slower real wage growth, combined with the need to reward foreign capital owners, suggests that the average Chinese will not derive economic benefit from increased fertility.

Table 11.5 Baseline real GDP and per capita income projections to 2030

	Per cent change in 2030 over 1997		Implied average annual growth rate, per cent per annum	
	Real GDP	Real per capita income	Real GDP	Real per capita income
Australia	262	178	4.0	3.1
North America	253	171	3.9	3.1
Western Europe	159	178	2.9	3.1
Central Europe and former Soviet Union	205	210	3.4	3.5
Japan	166	217	3.0	3.6
China	340	378	4.6	5.0
Indonesia	490	376	5.5	4.9
Other East Asian countries	529	373	5.7	4.8
India	565	291	5.9	4.2
Other South Asian countries	430	127	5.2	2.5
South America	293	149	4.2	2.8
Middle East and North Africa	280	104	4.1	2.2
Sub-Saharan Africa	360	114	4.7	2.3
Rest of world	336	159	4.6	2.9

Source: The (low fertility) baseline projection described in the text.

Table 11.6 The Chinese population under alternative demographic scenarios, 2000–2030[a]

Millions	Baseline: low (declining) fertility 1.90 to 1.45	Stable fertility (one-child policy): 1.90 to 1.80		Transition to two-child policy: 1.90 to 2.30	
		State Council[b]	Our model	State Council	Our model
2000	1,252	1,270	1,253	1,270	1,257
2010	1,311	1,344	1,328	1,369	1,369
2020	1,321	1,393	1,369	1,466	1,462
2030	1,296	1,396	1,382	1,518	1,536

Notes: [a] The base year for our simulations is 1997, when China's fertility rate was approximately 1.91. [b] The comparable simulation for stable fertility by the State Council of China holds the one-child policy constant as at present; the corresponding projection by Sharping is entitled 'tight rule, fraud as usual'.
Source: Sharping, T., 2003. *Birth Control in China 1949–2000: population policy and demographic development*, RoutledgeCurzon, London; State Council of China, 2000. *China Development Studies: the selected research report of the Development Research Centre of the State Council*, Development Research Centre of the State Council of China, China Development Press; and simulations using the model described in the text.

Figure 11.2 **Growth scenarios for China's population and labour force, 1995–2035**[a]

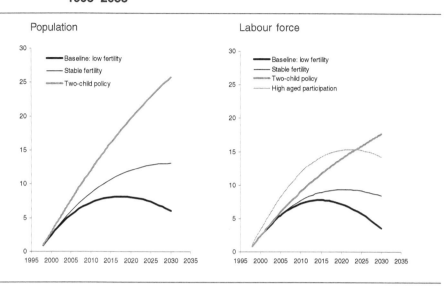

Notes: [a] These are cumulative percentage departures from the base year, 1997.
Source: Model simulations.

Figure 11.3 **Four scenarios for the Chinese non-working-aged (60+) dependency ratio, 1995–2035**[a] (per cent)

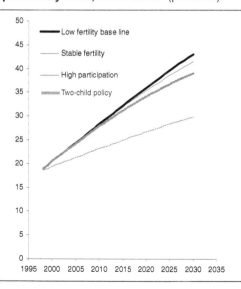

Source: Model simulations.

These expectations are indeed borne out in our simulations (Table 11.7). Higher fertility, relative to the baseline, does raise the rate of return on installed capital in China and hence the level of investment. In turn, China's GDP is higher (Figure 11.4). Yet higher fertility slows real wage growth, due to the increased relative abundance of labour and, in combination with the repatriation of an increased proportion of the income accruing to capital,[27] this causes real per capita income also to grow more slowly. A further negative complication is the large-country effect: as China's trade with the rest of the world expands, it turns its terms of trade against itself. This effect is small overall but of growing significance late in the period.[28] The corresponding dynamics of the real production wage and real per capital income are illustrated in Figure 11.5.

Higher aged labour-force participation

Here we ask how different the economic changes would be were fertility to remain low, as in the baseline, and were China's aged labour-force participation rates to approach those currently observed in Japan. Male 60+ participation is set to rise from 24 per cent in 1997 to 43 per cent in 2030, while female 60+ participation rises from 4 per cent to 21 per cent. The economic implications of these changes are summarised in Table 11.8.

A key bottom line is the effect of each policy scenario on real income per capita. The two-child policy slows real per capita income growth for reasons already discussed (Figure 11.5). The high participation simulation achieves almost the same GDP growth without this loss in per capita welfare relative to the low-fertility baseline. This happens because higher aged participation expands the workforce much faster than fertility does so there is an earlier growth dividend. Yet the additional output is achieved at the expense of the leisure that would otherwise be enjoyed by the aged. As long as continuing to work is net life-enriching, however, there are net gains at least as large as the per capita real income gains shown.

As already noted, the saving rates of China's elderly are assumed to be not all that different from those of working-aged people, due largely to estimation difficulties associated with intergenerational transfers. For example, initial saving rates (in 1997) among 40–59 year olds were set at 40 per cent of personal disposable income, compared with 31 per cent for 60+ year olds. These figures are similar to India's and close to other East Asian countries, but significantly different from Europe's and North America's, where retirees have negative savings rates (as large as -30 per cent in North America). If the savings rate of China's elderly in the future turns out to be much lower than assumed, the economic gains from higher labour-force participation will be even larger than we project here.

Table 11.7 **Economic effects of faster Chinese population growth to 2030**
(per cent departures of the two-child policy from the low-fertility baseline)

	Real investment	Real GDP	Real GNP per capita	Real production wage	Rate of return on installed capital	Terms of trade
2010 Stable fertility	0.7	0.3	−1.1	−0.2	0.1	-
Two-child policy	2.7	1.1	−3.6	−0.6	0.4	-
2020 Stable fertility	2.9	1.5	−2.7	−0.6	0.2	−0.1
Two-child policy	8.8	4.7	−7.3	−1.9	0.6	−0.5
2030 Stable fertility	5.3	3.6	−4.4	−1.4	0.3	−0.6
Two-child policy	14.7	10.3	−11.0	−3.8	0.6	−1.6

Source: The baseline, stable-fertility and two-child polity projections from the model described in the text.

Figure 11.4 **Chinese real GDP, departures from the baseline, 1995–2035**[a]
(per cent)

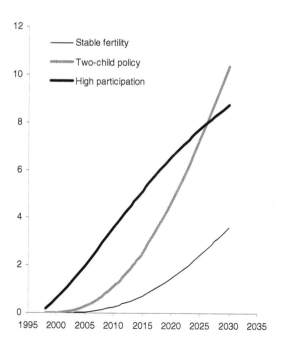

Source: Model simulations.

Figure 11.5 **Chinese real wage and per capita income, departures from the baseline, 1995–2035**[a] (per cent)

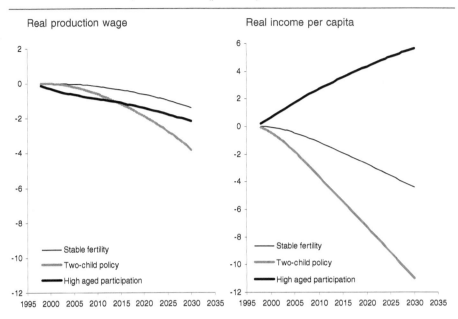

Note: [a] These are percentage departures from the baseline simulation for each year. Note that the baseline assumes declining fertility in China.
Source: Model simulations.

Table 11.8 **Economic effects of increased aged labour-force participation, 2010–2030**[a] (percentage departures of the high-participation simulation from the baseline)

	Real investment	Real GDP	Real GNP per capita	Real production wage	Rate of return on installed capital	Terms of trade
2010	7.5	3.6	2.7	−0.9	0.4	−0.3
2020	9.3	6.5	4.3	−1.4	0.02	−0.9
2030	9.7	8.7	5.6	−2.2	−0.8	−1.4

Note: [a] Here the low-fertility baseline is compared with a corresponding low-fertility simulation in which risk premium reductions are calculated to achieve the same GDP growth as would be achieved if the two-child policy was invoked.
Source: The baseline and high-participation projections from the model described in the text.

One caveat that is worth noting is that the labour-force participation rate for younger females, like all participation rates, is assumed to trend exogenously. In fact, we might expect it to be related to fertility because of child-care demands. For example, a relaxation of the one-child policy could result in higher fertility and hence lower participation rates, particularly in the absence of child-care centres and parent-friendly labour policies. Complicating this further is the possibility of young mothers going out to work while grandparents undertake child care. Higher participation rates among the aged population could result in reduced fertility or lower participation rates among younger women. This suggests that labour-force participation rates are likely to be endogenous and, in the scenarios depicted here, the benefits of higher aged participation rates could in fact be offset to some extent by lower participation rates in other age categories.

Conclusions

China's economic growth has hitherto depended on its relative abundance of production labour and its increasingly secure investment environment. Within the next decade, however, China's labour force is likely to begin contracting. This will set its economy apart from other developing Asian countries where relative labour abundance will increase, as will relative capital returns. This expectation is confirmed in this chapter using a new global demographic model that is integrated with an adaptation of the GTAP-dynamic global economic model in which regional households are disaggregated by age and gender. A transition to a two-child policy in China is shown to boost its GDP growth, enlarging the projected 2030 Chinese economy by about one-tenth. Yet this would slow the growth rate of real per capita income, reducing the level projected for 2030 by one-tenth.

Almost the same GDP growth performance might be achieved with continued low fertility, if China's aged participation rates rise gradually through 2030 to approximate the rates currently observed in Japan. Considering that China's current aged participation rates are very low by Asian standards, there is considerable scope for this expansion as the level of life expectancy at 60 and the proportion of workers in the private sector continue to grow. To the extent that increased employment of the aged might be considered sufficiently life-enriching to offset the decline in leisure time, the results suggest that this scenario offers superior per capita real income growth to what might be achieved via a policy-driven boost to fertility.

Not only do higher fertility rates offer less in terms of per capita income growth, there is much uncertainty regarding the efficacy of pro-fertility policies in low-fertility countries, with evidence from industrial countries now grappling with the same issue sketchy at best. With 'heavy-handed methods of persuasion' no longer a viable option, the Chinese government would need to consider market-based incentives, such as tax breaks and family allowances, and policies to ease the burden for working mothers. The low likelihood of identifying and implementing effective pro-fertility policies, combined with the long lag until those policies would alter the working-age proportion of the population, suggests that alternative policy approaches might be preferred.

The approach emphasised in this chapter focuses on aged labour-force participation rates, which were seen to be low and declining in China at the turn of this century. As longevity continues to rise, it seems reasonable to advocate later retirement as a way of expanding the proportion of workers and thereby reducing the burden placed on the fiscal system of a rapidly ageing population. Much more complicated is the impact that continuing reforms of the pension system will have on retirement decisions and therefore on aged participation rates, since different measures to deal with pension-related budgetary pressures will have profoundly different effects. As Greenspan (2004:782) points out, higher payroll taxes to finance ageing-related problems will exacerbate the slow-down in the growth of labour supply by diminishing the returns to work, while 'policies promoting longer working life could ameliorate some of the potential demographic stresses'. The interaction between pensions, savings and aged participation is clearly an area worthy of further research.

As China grapples with ways to cope with the burden of ageing—a problem primarily in the domain of the industrial world—it also faces challenges associated with its continuing transition and economic development. Successful industrial restructuring might well lead to higher labour-force participation rates, as people choose to work longer to take advantage of new opportunities offered by the rising non-state sector. On the other hand, it is possible that industrial restructuring might lead to even wider spread redundancies and rising unemployment. This risk will be reduced if labour markets can be made increasingly flexible, through the removal of institutional and other barriers to rural-urban and intersectoral migration. While not all that helpful for the current generation of retirees, whose average educational attainment is extremely low,[29] investment in education is likely to contribute to higher participation rates in the future, with evidence already showing an increasingly strong and positive correlation between education levels and participation (Zhang et al. 2002). Education and labour-market policies will be beneficial not only through their impact on labour-market participation, but will contribute to improvements in factor productivity, which will yield further income gains on those projected here.

Acknowledgments

Funding for the research described in this chapter is from Australian Research Council Discovery Grant No. DP0557889. Thanks are due to Heather Booth, Siew Ean Khoo and Ming Ming Chan for helpful discussions about the demography, Robert McDougall and Hom Pant for their constructive comments on the economic analysis and to Terrie Walmsley for technical assistance with the GTAP database as well as useful discussions on baseline simulations. Iain Bain provided research assistance.

Notes

1. See Bloom and Williamson 1997 for a discussion of the demographic dividend across developing countries; and Cai and Wang 2005 for a detailed examination of its implications for China. A recent news article, entitled 'Family planning becomes a controversial topic' (Xinhuanet, available online at <http://www.cpirc.org.cn/en/enews20051230htm> accessed 30 December 2005), reports that academics and government officials are showing increasing interest in the relaxation of the one-child policy.
2. The eleventh Five-Year Plan (2006–10) was delivered by Premier Wen Jiabao in March 2006 at the Fourth Session of the Tenth National People's Congress. In it, China's GDP is projected to grow by 7.5 per cent between 2005 and 2010, with per capita GDP increasing from 13,985 yuan to 19,270 yuan in the same period. These projections are in line with the central government's ambitions to raise the level of GDP in 2020 to four times the level in 2000, requiring an annual GDP growth rate of 7.2 per cent (Cai and Wang 2005).
3. See United Nations 2005; Peng 2005; Cai and Wang 2005; Heller and Symansky 1997; and Hussain 2002.
4. These figures are similar to the proportion of the United States' population over 65, which will rise from 12 per cent to perhaps 20 per cent in 2035 (Greenspan 2004).
5. See Tyers and Golley 2006 for an alternative response, which focuses on financial-sector reforms.
6. See the excellent discussion of population policy in low-fertility countries in Demeny 2003 for further details.
7. For example, a pilot program established in Liaoning in 2000 has recently been expanded to Jilin and Heilongjiang in 2004 (State Council 2005). See World Bank 1997a and Wang et al. 2004 for further details on the pension system.
8. See also Shi and Tyers 2004 and Tyers et al. 2005.
9. The GTAP-dynamic model is a development of its comparative static progenitor, GTAP (Hertel 1997). Its dynamics are described in Ianchovichina and McDougall 2000.
10. The demographic sub-model has been used in stand-alone mode for the analysis of trends in dependency ratios. For a more complete documentation of the sub-model, see Chan and Tyers 2006.
11. The subdivision between production and professional labour accords with the International Labour Organisation's occupation-based classification and is consistent with the labour division adopted in the GTAP database. See Liu et al. 1998.
12. Mothers in families providing production labour are assumed to produce children who will grow up to also provide production labour, while the children of mothers in professional families are correspondingly assumed to become professional workers.

13 Immigration and emigration are also age and gender specific. The model represents a full matrix of global migration flows for each age and gender group. Each of these flows is currently set at a constant proportion of the population of its destination group. See Tyers 2005 and Tyers et al. 2006 for further details.
14 The migration rates and the corresponding birth rates are listed in detail in Tyers et al. 2005 (Tables 2–5).
15 In this discussion, the skill index, s, is omitted because birth and death rates, and life expectancies at 60, do not vary by skill category in the version of the model used.
16 Note that, as regions become more advanced and populations in the production-worker families become comparatively small, the skill transformation rate has a diminishing effect on the professional population. These transformation rates are made endogenous to real per capita incomes and to the skilled wage premium in Tyers et al. 2006.
17 See Tyers et al. 2005 (Tables 11 and 12) for further details.
18 The resulting participation rates are listed by Chan and Tyers 2006 (Table 10).
19 All these dependency ratios are defined in detail by Chan and Tyers 2004.
20 These projections are low compared with those by the State Council of China (2000) and Sharping (2003), yet those make no attempt to allow Chinese fertility to follow the declining trends observed in neighbouring countries.
21 The analytics of income splitting are described in detail by Tyers et al. 2005.
22 For further details, see Tyers et al. 2005.
23 New research by Kinugasa and Mason (2005) and Feng and Mason (2005) offers useful results on the relationship between age and saving in China. For further details on the saving rates used in our model, see Tyers and Golley 2006.
24 Wang and Ding (2006) recently estimated that there were 40 million surplus workers in China's agricultural sector. While underemployment is not explicit in our model, the assumption of high labour productivity growth in agriculture implies that agriculture is capable of shedding labour more quickly than other sectors. This essentially mimics the surplus labour problem, which is thereby accounted for implicitly.
25 See Tyers and Golley 2006 for further details.
26 This result could have a number of economic implications that are not captured in our model, including that higher fertility would necessitate lower rates of distorting taxes to finance aged pensions and public health systems. Our scenarios maintain constant tax rates and fiscal deficits.
27 The more correct way to see the capital income effect is to recognise that China is—and these simulations suggest it will continue to be—a net saving region. The attraction of increased investment merely relocates the source of capital income but does little to raise its net value.
28 Empirical evidence for such terms-of-trade effects from growth is variable. In many cases, developing-country expansions have not caused adverse shifts in their terms of trade because their trade has embraced new products and quality ladders in ways not captured by our model. See the literature on the developing-country exports fallacy of composition argument, which includes Lewis 1952; Grilli and Yang 1988; Martin 1993; Singer 1998; and Mayer 2003.
29 In 2000, 29 per cent of China's 35–39 year olds had low educational attainment (primary school or less) compared with 83 per cent of 60–64 year olds and 91 per cent of 65–69 year olds.

Appendix Figure A11.1 The demographic sub-model

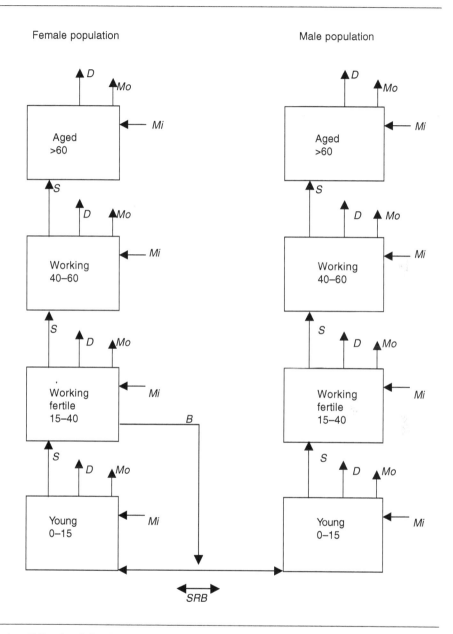

Notes: *D* Deaths, *S* Survival, *B* Births, *Mi* Immigration, *Mo* Emigration, *SRB* Sex ratio at birth.

12

Changing patterns in China's agricultural trade after WTO accession

Chunlai Chen

China's economy has been growing rapidly since the country's entry into the World Trade Organization (WTO) in 2001. The average annual growth rate of China's GDP was more than 9.8 per cent in 2002–05.[1] China's foreign trade has been expanding even more rapidly than its overall economic growth, with the total value of foreign trade increasing from US$457 billion in 2001 to US$1,263 billion in 2005, and an annual growth rate of 28.6 per cent compared with 9.4 per cent during the 1990s. Undoubtedly, China's economy has benefited from entry into the WTO, especially from a more open and liberalised international trade regime.[2]

After entry into the WTO, China's agricultural trade also increased dramatically. Agricultural imports, however, increased more rapidly than agricultural exports. From 2002 to 2005, the annual growth rate of agricultural imports was 31.5 per cent, while that of agricultural exports was 11.6 per cent. As a result, in 2004 and 2005 agricultural imports exceeded agricultural exports. It is expected that China's next agricultural imports will continue to increase.

The impact of China's entry into the WTO on its agricultural sector has been a major concern to the Chinese government and has been the hottest topic among policymakers and academics in and outside China (for example, Anderson 1997; Cheng 1997; Development Research Centre 1998; Huang 1998; Huang and Chen 1999; Wang 1997). Some experts have argued for some time that, based on China's resource endowments and comparative advantage, after entry into the WTO, China's land-intensive farming sector would shrink but the labour-intensive horticultural, animal husbandry and processed agricultural product sectors would expand. As a result, China would import more land-intensive agricultural products, such as grains and vegetable oils, and would export more labour-intensive agricultural products, such as vegetables and fruit, animal products and processed agricultural products.

What has really happened in China's agricultural trade since entry into the WTO in 2001? Have there been any changes in China's revealed comparative advantage in agriculture and, therefore, in the patterns of China's agricultural trade? What factors have driven these changes? This chapter intends to analyse and answer these questions.

The chapter is structured as follows. The following section will briefly review international trade theories and discuss the implications on China's agricultural trade. The third section introduces the classification of agricultural trade data. The fourth section examines the changes in China's revealed comparative advantage in agriculture. The fifth section analyses the patterns of China's agricultural trade and examines the changes since WTO accession. The sixth section discusses the factors driving the changes in China's revealed comparative advantage and in the patterns of China's agricultural trade. The final section summarises the chapter.

International trade and comparative advantage

A brief review of international trade theories

The theory of comparative advantage was first proposed by David Ricardo in 1817[3] and it remains the dominant explanation of why a country would specialise in exporting certain categories of goods and services and importing others. It can be seen as a cost-based explanation of international trade.

What underlying forces would create comparative advantage? Essentially, there are two explanations for why costs might differ between countries. First, one country might simply use the same resources more efficiently than another. Second, one country might be able to obtain key inputs more cheaply than another.

The Ricardian model is the first of the two explanations. According to Ricardian theory, comparative advantage is the result of international differences in the productivity of labour. A country has a comparative advantage in producing a good if it can produce that good in terms of other goods more efficiently than other countries. In the presence of international trade, countries would export goods that they produced relatively cheaply (more efficiently) compared with their trading partners and import goods that they produced relatively more expensively (less efficiently).

One of the most influential theories in international economics is the Heckscher-Ohlin model,[4] which is the second of the two explanations. In this model, resource differences are the only source of trade, and comparative advantage is determined by international differences in the supplies of factors of production. The model shows that comparative advantage is influenced by the interaction between the resource endowments of countries (the relative abundance of factors of production) and the technology of production (which influences the relative intensity with which different factors of production are used in the production of different goods). The model predicts that countries will tend to have a comparative advantage and, therefore, to export goods or services that make intensive use of those factors of production with which they are relatively well endowed. Conversely, countries will tend to have a comparative disadvantage and, therefore, to import goods or services that make intensive use of factors of production with which they are relatively poorly endowed.

The Heckscher-Ohlin theory of international trade has been tested empirically by many researchers. Among others, Leamer's (1984) work is the most comprehensive. Later, Song (1996) adopted Leamer's approach and updated the research. The studies have demonstrated that resource endowments are powerful sources of international comparative advantage. The Heckscher-Ohlin model has been the most powerful and influential theory in explaining international trade.

Implications of international trade theory on China's agricultural trade

The most prominent characteristics of China's resource endowments in terms of agricultural production are scarcity of land resources but abundance of labour supply. China's per capita arable land is 0.11 hectare, only 43 per cent of the world average, while its per capita pasture land is 0.3 hectare, only 33 per cent of the world average. China has, however, an abundant labour supply: a population of 1.3 billion, nearly 60 per cent of whom live in rural areas, and with half of the labour force working in the agricultural sector.

According to the Heckscher-Ohlin theory of international trade and based on China's resource endowments in terms of agricultural production, it is possible to draw some generalised predictions.

First, overall China should have no comparative advantage in agriculture as agricultural production in general is a land-intensive activity and land is relatively scarce in China. As a result, China should be a net importer of agricultural products.

Second, China should have a comparative advantage in labour-intensive agricultural production, such as processed agricultural products, animal and horticultural products, while it should have a comparative disadvantage in land-intensive agricultural production, such as grains, vegetable oil seeds and raw materials for textiles, such as cotton, wool and raw animal hides and skins. As a result, China should export more labour-intensive agricultural products and import more land-intensive agricultural products.

Third, entry into the WTO has increasingly integrated China's economy into the world economy. This will improve resource allocation in the Chinese economy as well as in its agricultural sector as it increasingly specialises in the production of goods in which it has a comparative advantage. As a result, it is expected that China's comparative advantage in agriculture and its pattern of agricultural trade will change gradually. China's overall comparative advantage in agriculture can be expected to decline in general, and its comparative advantage in land-intensive agricultural production to decline in particular. Consequently, China's exports of agricultural products can be expected to move towards concentrating more and more on labour-intensive agricultural products, such as processed agricultural products, while its imports of agricultural products will move increasingly towards concentration on land-intensive agricultural products, such as grains, vegetable oil seeds and raw materials for textiles.

Are these predictions valid? In other words, are China's patterns of agricultural trade consistent with its resource endowments and based on its comparative advantage? In the following sections, we will find the answers.

The classification of agricultural commodities and sources of data

To analyse patterns of agricultural trade, the first step is to identify the coverage of agricultural commodities in international trade. In this chapter, the classification of agricultural commodities in international trade is based on the Harmonised System (HS) of Trade Classification 1992. Table 12.1 presents the product coverage used in this chapter and the product coverage in the Uruguay Round Agreement on Agriculture (URAA). The product coverage in this chapter and in the URAA are very similar. The major difference is that the product coverage in this chapter includes fish and fish products. The main reason for this is that fish and fish products are very important agricultural products in China's international trade, and are produced mainly from aquaculture in China.

The agricultural trade data are from the United Nations Statistics Division's Commodity Trade Statistics Database, COMTRADE. All the values of agricultural trade data presented in this chapter are at 2000 constant US dollar prices.

For the purpose of analysing the pattern of China's agricultural trade, the agricultural trade data are grouped in two ways. First, the agricultural trade data are divided into five categories based on the nature of commodities

- the group of cereals, edible vegetable oil seeds and vegetable oils
- the group of horticultural products

Table 12.1 **Comparison of agricultural product coverage**

Product coverage in this chapter	Product coverage in the URAA
HS Chapters 1–24, plus	HS Chapters 1–24
HS Headings 41.01–3 (hides and skins)	(less fish and fish products, plus)
HS Heading 43.01 (raw furs)	HS Code 2905.43 (mannitol)
HS Headings 50.01–3 (raw silk and silk waste)	HS Code 2905.44 (sorbitol)
HS Headings 51.01–3 (wool and animal hair)	HS Heading 33.01 (essential oils)
HS Headings 52.01–3 (raw cotton, waste and carded or combed cotton)	HS Headings 35.01–5 (albuminoidalsubstances, modified starches,glues)
HS Heading 53.01 (raw flax)	HS Code 3809.10 (finishing agents)
HS Heading 53.02 (raw hemp)	HS Code 3823.60 (sorbitol n.e.p.)
	HS Headings 41.01–3 (hides and skins)
	HS Heading 43.01 (raw furs)
	HS Headings 50.01–3 (raw silk and silk waste)
	HS Headings 51.01–3 (wool and animal hair)
	HS Headings 52.01–3 (raw cotton, waste and carded or combed cotton)
	HS Heading 53.01 (raw flax)
	HS Heading 53.02 (raw hemp)

Sources: The Uruguay Round Agreement on Agriculture and author's own classification.

- the group of animal products (including fish)
- the group of processed agricultural products (including processed fish products)
- the group of raw materials for textiles.

Second, the agricultural trade data are grouped into two categories based on the factor intensity of production

- the group of land-intensive agricultural products, which includes cereals, vegetable oil seeds and vegetable oils, and raw materials (excluding silk) for textiles
- the group of labour-intensive agricultural products, which includes processed agricultural products, animal products, horticultural products and silk.

Agricultural trade data for the period 1995–2005 based on the above classifications are presented in Appendix Tables 12.1 and 12.2.

Revealed comparative advantage

It is difficult to measure comparative advantage directly; an alternative is to measure it indirectly. The most common approach is the principle of revealed comparative advantage (RCA) proposed by Balassa (1965). It argues that, since trade is generated by underlying comparative advantage, we can use data on exports and imports to infer this underlying pattern of comparative advantage. This principle has given rise to a number of indicators of revealed comparative advantage.

One of the measures is the net export ratio (NER_{ij}), which is defined as:
$$RCA\ (NER_{ij}) = (X_{ij} - M_{ij}) / (X_{ij} + M_{ij})$$
where X_{ij} are the exports of goods 'i' by country 'j' and M_{ij} are the imports of goods 'i' into country 'j'.

The rationale behind the index is that countries are revealed as having a comparative advantage in a particular good if they export more of it than they import. To simply consider net exports, however, might be misleading where, for example, we compare a large and a small country. For this reason, net exports are divided by total trade (exports plus imports). Net export ratios have a minimum value of −1 (the country only imports the good concerned) and a maximum value of +1 (the country only exports the good). Positive values are taken to reveal a comparative advantage and negative values are taken to reveal a comparative disadvantage.

RCA indices, however, have one major flaw. The principle of revealed comparative advantage presumes that observed trade flows are generated by underlying comparative advantage and disadvantage. It is this that allows us to use observed trade data to infer the underlying pattern of comparative advantage. Observed trade flows are, however, not created only by underlying economic forces, but are often affected significantly by government policies with respect to international trade. This problem has been potentially more serious for trade in agricultural products than in manufactured goods. With the establishment of the WTO and the implementation of the URAA, however, liberalisation of trade in agriculture has advanced somewhat. As a result, we might argue that the observed exports and imports of agricultural products in recent years have been affected less than previously by trade policies, although distortions from government interventions remain very important in this sector.

Revealed comparative advantage in China's agriculture

Appendix Table 12.3 presents China's revealed comparative advantage indices calculated by using the measure of net export ratio for agricultural products for the period from 1992 to 2005.

In terms of the commodity groups. China has a revealed comparative advantage in horticultural products, processed agricultural products and animal products, but a revealed comparative disadvantage in cereals, vegetable oil seeds and vegetable oils and in raw materials for textiles.

In terms of factor intensity of production. China has a revealed comparative advantage in labour-intensive agricultural products, but a revealed comparative disadvantage in land-intensive agricultural products.

In general, the above patterns are consistent with China's resource endowments.

Changes in revealed comparative advantage in China's agriculture

During the period from 1992 to 2005, China's revealed comparative advantage in agriculture changed gradually. As shown in Figure 12.1, China's revealed comparative

Figure 12.1 **China's revealed comparative advantage indices (NER) of the whole agricultural sector, 1992–2005**

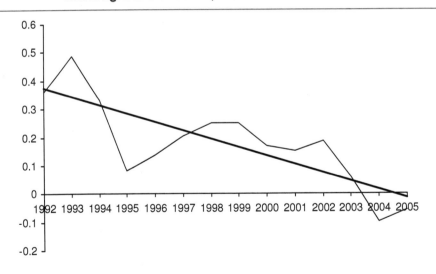

Sources: Author's calculations. Data are from the United Nations Statistics Division. Commodity Trade Statistics Database, COMTRADE. Available from http://unstats.un.org/unsd/comtrade/default.aspx

advantage in the whole agricultural sector presented a declining trend, especially after 2002. The values of China's revealed comparative advantage indices for the whole agricultural sector declined from about 0.4 in the early 1990s to about 0.2 in 2002, and declined further to −0.09 in 2004 before rising slightly to −0.06 in 2005.

In terms of agricultural commodity groups, as shown in Figure 12.2, during the period 1992–2005, the values of the revealed comparative advantage indices for processed agricultural products, horticultural products and animal products were positive. While the values of the revealed comparative advantage indices for processed agricultural products increased marginally, the values for horticultural and animal products declined especially quickly after the early 2000s. For horticultural products, the values of the revealed comparative advantage indices declined from more than 0.8 in the early 1990s to about 0.7 in the late 1990s, and to about 0.6 in the early 2000s. For animal products, the values declined from about 0.6 in the early and mid 1990s to about 0.4 in the late 1990s, and dropped further to about 0.2 in the early 2000s.

From 1992 to 2005, the values of the revealed comparative advantage indices for cereals, vegetable oil seeds and vegetable oils, and raw materials for textiles were negative and declined especially quickly after 2003. For cereals, vegetable oil seeds and vegetable oils, the values declined from about −0.2 in the early 1990s to about −0.3 in the late 1990s, and to about −0.5 in the early 2000s. For raw materials for textiles, the values declined from about −0.4 in the early 1990s to about −0.5 in the late 1990s, and dropped further to about −0.8 in the early 2000s.

In terms of factor intensity of production, as shown in Figure 12.3, although China has a revealed comparative advantage in labour-intensive agricultural products, the values of the revealed comparative advantage indices have declined continuously, especially since the late 1990s. The overall values of the revealed comparative advantage indices for labour-intensive agricultural products declined from more than 0.6 in the early 1990s to about 0.5 in the late 1990s, and to just more than 0.4 in the early 2000s.

The overall values of the revealed comparative advantage indices for land-intensive agricultural products declined from about −0.3 in the 1990s to about −0.4 in 2002, and further declined to −0.8 in 2004, with a slight increase to −0.7 in 2005.

The above analysis has revealed several important findings. First, China's agriculture as a whole has been losing comparative advantage at an accelerated rate since entry into the WTO. Second, although China still has a comparative advantage in labour-intensive agricultural products, apart from processed agricultural products, whose comparative advantage increased marginally, the levels of comparative advantage of horticultural and animal products have been declining

Figure 12.2 **China's revealed comparative advantage indices (NER) of agricultural products by commodity groups, 1992–2005**

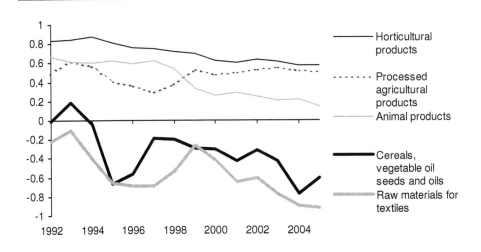

Sources: Author's calculations. Data are from the United Nations Statistics Division. Commodity Trade Statistics Database, COMTRADE. Available from http://unstats.un.org/unsd/comtrade/default.aspx

Figure 12.3 **China's revealed comparative advantage indices (NER) for agricultural products by factor intensity of production, 1992–2005**

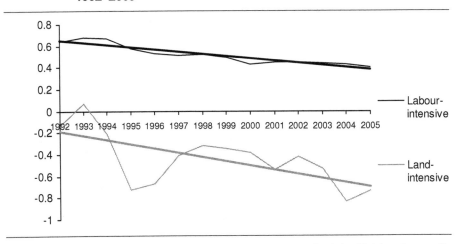

Sources: Author's calculations. Data are from the United Nations Statistics Division. Commodity Trade Statistics Database, COMTRADE. Available from http://unstats.un.org/unsd/comtrade/default.aspx

especially rapidly since entry into the WTO. Third, China has no comparative advantage in land-intensive agricultural products, and its comparative advantage has been declining quickly and dramatically, particularly since entry into the WTO.

These findings are consistent with the expectations introduced in the second section about China's comparative advantage in agriculture after entry into the WTO. If, however, China's agricultural trade is based on its comparative advantage, as revealed above, it could be expected that this would be reflected in the detailed patterns of China's agricultural trade.

Patterns of China's agricultural trade

As shown in Figure 12.4, before entry into the WTO, between 1992 and 2001, China's agricultural trade had stagnated, although with large fluctuations. After entry into the WTO in 2001, China's agricultural trade increased dramatically to US$50 billion in 2005, an increase of 90 per cent from 2001. Agricultural imports, however, increased more rapidly than agricultural exports. From 2002 to 2005, the annual growth rate of agricultural imports was 31.5 per cent, while that of agricultural exports was 11.6 per cent. In 2005, the value of agricultural imports surged to

Figure 12.4 **China's agricultural trade, 1992–2005** (at constant 2000 US$prices)

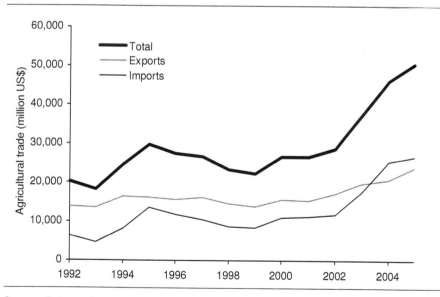

Source: Data are from the United Nations Statistics Division. Commodity Trade Statistics Database, COMTRADE. Available from http://unstats.un.org/unsd/comtrade/default.aspx

US$26 billion, increasing 136 per cent from 2001. The value of agricultural exports was US$23.81 billion, 55 per cent higher than in 2001. As a result, in 2004 and 2005, agricultural imports exceeded agricultural exports and China became a net importer of agricultural products. It is expected that the relatively higher growth of agricultural imports will continue.

In terms of the trade pattern of agricultural commodity groups, Figure 12.5 presents China's agricultural exports based on commodity groups for the period from 1992 to 2005. As the figure shows, China's agricultural exports were dominated by processed agricultural products, followed by animal and horticultural products. The export values of cereals, vegetable oil seeds and vegetable oils and, in particular, raw materials for textiles are small.

In terms of imports, as Figure 12.6 shows, China's imports of agricultural products were dominated overwhelmingly by cereals, vegetable oil seeds and vegetable oils, followed closely by raw materials for textiles. The imports of animal products, processed agricultural and horticultural products were relatively low but have been rising rapidly since 2003.

Figure 12.5 **China's agricultural exports by categories, 1992–2005** (at constant 2000 US prices)

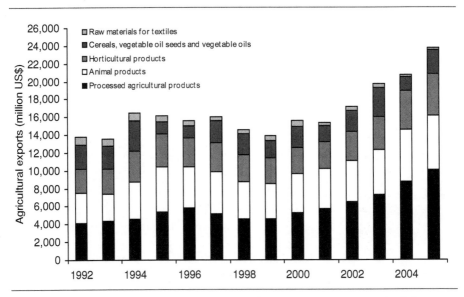

Source: Data are from the United Nations Statistics Division. Commodity Trade Statistics Database, COMTRADE. Available from http://unstats.un.org/unsd/comtrade/default.aspx

The above analyses have revealed three important points. First, China has become a net importer of agricultural products since 2004 and it will remain in that position in its international trade. Second, China's agricultural exports are dominated overwhelmingly by labour-intensive agricultural products, particularly processed agricultural products, which have accounted for about 40 per cent of China's total agricultural exports, followed by animal and horticultural products. Third, China's agricultural imports are dominated overwhelmingly by land-intensive agricultural products, in particular cereals, vegetable oil seeds and vegetable oils, followed by raw materials for textiles. These patterns in China's agricultural trade are consistent with China's comparative advantage, as revealed in the above section.

Figure 12.6 **China's agricultural imports by categories, 1992–2006**
(at constant 2000 US$ prices)

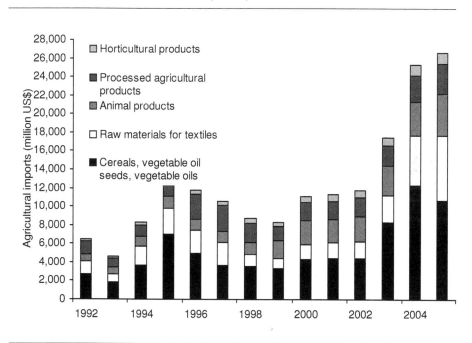

Source: Data are from the United Nations Statistics Division. Commodity Trade Statistics Database, COMTRADE. Available from http://unstats.un.org/unsd/comtrade/default.aspx

Changes in the patterns of China's agricultural trade by commodity groups

Have there been any changes in the patterns of China's agricultural trade since China's accession into the WTO? To answer this question, I compare China's agricultural trade patterns for the two periods of 1992–2001 and 2002–05 by commodity groups and by factor intensity of production.

Figure 12.7 shows the composition of China's agricultural exports by commodity groups for the two periods of 1992–2001 and 2002–05.

Figure 12.7 reveals several interesting points. First, China's agricultural exports are dominated by processed agricultural products, animal and horticultural products. Their combined share accounted for 81.2 per cent of China's total agricultural exports during 1992–01 and 86.1 per cent during 2002–05. Second, it is interesting to note that between the two periods of 1992–2001 and 2002–05, except for the group of processed agricultural products, whose export share increased by 7.3 percentage points, the export shares of all the other agricultural commodity groups declined. The export share of horticultural products declined by 0.7 percentage points, the share of animal products declined by 1.7 percentage points, while the export shares of the commodity groups of cereals, vegetable oil seeds and vegetable oils, and raw materials for textiles declined by 2.6 percentage points and 2.3 percentage points respectively. Third, these changes in the export shares of the commodity groups are consistent with the changes in their comparative advantage revealed in the above section. Fourth, China's agricultural exports are moving towards concentrating more and more on processed agricultural products.

Figure 12.8 shows the composition of China's agricultural imports by commodity groups for the two periods of 1992–2001 and 2002–05.

Figure 12.8 also reveals several interesting points. First, China's imports of agricultural products are dominated by the commodity groups of cereals, vegetable oil seeds and vegetable oils, and raw materials for textiles. Their combined share of China's total agricultural imports increased from 60.6 per cent in 1992–2001 to 65 per cent in 2002–05. Second, between the two periods of 1992–2001 and 2002–05, the import share of animal products increased by 2.6 percentage points, while the share of processed agricultural products declined by 7.4 percentage points. Third, China's agricultural imports are moving towards concentrating more and more on the commodity groups of cereals, vegetable oil seeds and vegetable oils, and raw materials for textiles.

Figure 12.7 **Shares of China's agricultural exports by commodity groups, 1992–2001 and 2002–05** (per cent)

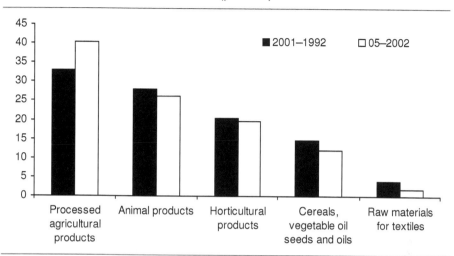

Source: Author's calculations. Data are from the United Nations Statistics Division. Commodity Trade Statistics Database, COMTRADE. Available from http://unstats.un.org/unsd/comtrade/default.aspx

Figure 12.8 **Shares of China's agricultural imports by commodity groups, 1992–2001 and 2002–05** (per cent)

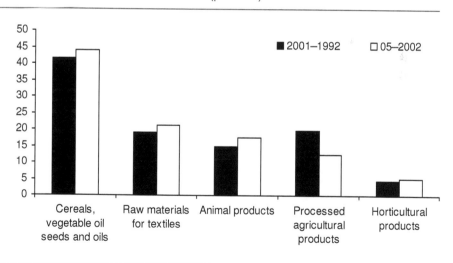

Sources: Author's calculations. Data are from the United Nations Statistics Division. Commodity Trade Statistics Database, COMTRADE. Available from http://unstats.un.org/unsd/comtrade/default.aspx

Changes in the patterns of China's agricultural trade by factor intensity of production

Figure 12.9 shows the composition of China's agricultural exports by factor intensity of production. China's agricultural exports were dominated overwhelmingly by labour-intensive agricultural products. For the period from 2002 to 2005, labour-intensive agricultural products accounted for 86.1 per cent of China's total agricultural exports, while land-intensive agricultural products accounted for only 13.9 per cent of China's total agricultural exports. Compared with the period from 1992 to 2001, in the period from 2002 to 2005, the share of labour-intensive agricultural products in China's total agricultural exports increased by 4.9 percentage points, while the share of land-intensive agricultural products declined by the same amount.

China's agricultural imports were dominated by land-intensive agricultural products, which accounted for 60.6 per cent and 65 per cent of China's total agricultural imports during the two periods of 1992–2001 and 2002–05 respectively

Figure 12.9 **Shares of China's agricultural exports by factor intensity of production, 1992–2001 and 2002–05** (per cent)

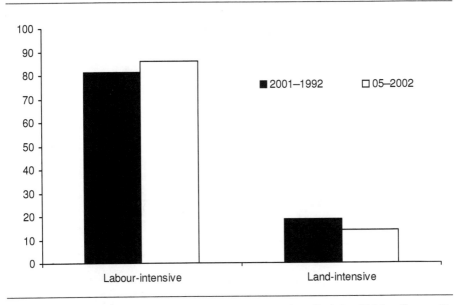

Sources: Author's calculations. Data are from the United Nations Statistics Division. Commodity Trade Statistics Database, COMTRADE. Available from http://unstats.un.org/unsd/comtrade/default.aspx

(Figure 12.10). Labour-intensive agricultural products accounted for 39.4 per cent and 35 per cent of China's total agricultural imports in the same two periods. The share of land-intensive agricultural products in China's total agricultural imports increased by 4.4 percentage points between 1991–2001 and 2002–05, while the share of labour-intensive agricultural products declined by the same amount.

It is clear that China has been exporting mainly labour-intensive agricultural products and importing mainly land-intensive agricultural products. This pattern of agricultural trade has been strengthened in the period from 2002 to 2005. The above findings reveal that since accession into the WTO the patterns of China's agricultural trade have been moving closer to its comparative advantage and are more consistent with its resource endowments of scarce land resources and abundant labour supply.

Figure 12.10 **Shares of China's agricultural imports by factor intensity of production, 1992–2001 and 2002–05** (per cent)

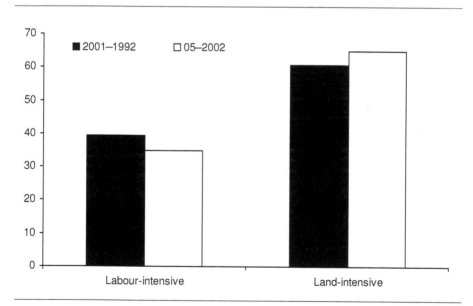

Sources: Author's calculations. Data are from the United Nations Statistics Division. Commodity Trade Statistics Database, COMTRADE. Available from http://unstats.un.org/unsd/comtrade/default.aspx

Factors driving the changes in revealed comparative advantage in China's agriculture

What are the reasons for the changes of China's revealed comparative advantage in agriculture? Empirical studies have shown that for many countries during the process of economic growth, the nation's comparative advantage in agriculture declines and, for those nations where arable land is scarce, the comparative advantage in agriculture tends to decline more rapidly (Anderson 1990). Undoubtedly, the changes of China's revealed comparative advantage in agriculture during the period from 1992 to 2005 have been the result mainly of the fast economic growth and dramatic structural changes happening in China, especially since entry into the WTO.

Economic factors

Since its entry into the WTO in 2001, China's economy has been growing very rapidly, with an average annual growth rate of more than 9.8 per cent. This has led to changes in the structure of China's economy. During the period from 2001 to 2004, the growth of the manufacturing and services sectors was much faster than the growth of the agricultural sector. Consequently, agricultural sector's share of China's economy has been declining. The share of agricultural GDP in China's total GDP declined from 15 per cent in 2001 to 13.8 per cent in 2004 (calculated from various issues of the *China Statistical Yearbook* [State Statistical Bureau]).

With the declining trend of the agricultural sector in China's economy, the structure of the agricultural economy has also changed. Within the agricultural economy, although the farming sector remained the most important sector, its share has been declining, from 55.2 per cent in 2001 to 50 per cent in 2004. Meanwhile, the animal husbandry and fishery sectors have been growing rapidly, with their share increasing from 41.2 per cent in 2001 to 46 per cent in 2004 (calculated from various issues of the *China Statistical Yearbook* [State Statistical Bureau]).

These changes demonstrate that, with China's rapid economic growth, especially since entry into the WTO, the comparative advantage of China's agricultural sector has been declining in general, and the comparative advantage of China's farming sector has been declining in particular. This changing pattern is consistent with China's resource endowments. It is also an indication of the improvement in resource allocation among China's economic sectors.

China's remarkable industrial growth played a large part in driving up agricultural imports. More than 30 per cent of the growth in China's agricultural imports in

2004 came from raw materials used in the production of non-food manufactured products: cotton, wool, animal hides and rubber, as well as other agricultural-derived products used in industrial production. In particular, growing textile production is generating demand for cotton and wool that is beyond China's production capacity. China's exports of apparel and footwear grew in double digits during 2004 and its domestic retail sales of apparel, shoes and textiles rose 18.7 per cent. Chinese yarn production grew 13.9 per cent and cloth production grew 18.8 per cent during 2004 (Gale 2005).

The continued increase in per capita income in China has led not only to a rise in food consumption, but to a change in the structure of that consumption. Since the late 1990s, China has dramatically increased imports of vegetable oil seeds (mainly soya beans) and vegetable oils (mainly soya bean and palm oils). Soya beans are crushed to produce vegetable oil for human consumption and animal feed to help the rapid growth in animal production. Driven by consumer and food industry demands, since the early 2000s, China has also increased imports of meat, fish, milk, cheese, wines and fruit.

Trade barriers

Apart from the economic factors discussed above, other factors could affect China's revealed comparative advantage in agriculture. As discussed above, revealed comparative advantage indices are not created only by underlying economic forces but are often affected significantly by government policies affecting international trade. This problem has been more serious for trade in agricultural products. There has been some liberalisation over the past decade, but egregious trade barriers in agricultural products remain. In particular, industrialised countries have increasingly resorted to sanitary and phyto-sanitary (SPS) measures for animal and plant health and technical barriers to trade (TBT) to block agricultural imports, especially from developing countries, seriously affecting developing countries' exports of the agricultural products in which they have a comparative advantage.

Chinese farmers and exporters had anticipated a large, positive impact on exports of agricultural products from accession to the WTO, especially for labour-intensive agricultural products such as vegetables, fruit, animal and aquatic products. In fact, these products have been hit hardest by the need to meet significant SPS standards and this has slowed growth in these agricultural exports.

According to official Chinese government sources, SPS measures and TBT have resulted in huge direct losses for China's agricultural exports. The indirect losses are even greater. In 2001, about US$7 billion worth of Chinese exports were affected by SPS measures and TBT. In early 2002, the European Union began to ban imports of Chinese animal-derived food, seafood and aquatic products, resulting in a 70 per cent slump in China's aquatic product exports during the second half of that year (Ministry of Commerce 2005). Also, according to an investigation by China's Ministry of Commerce, about 90 per cent of China's exporters of foodstuffs, domestic produce and animal by-products were affected by foreign TBT and suffered losses totalling US$9 billion in 2002 (China Daily 2003).

China's recent difficulties with SPS barriers have been mainly with the European Union, Japan and the United States.[5] These three economies accounted for 41 per cent, 30 per cent and 24 per cent respectively of China's trade losses attributed to SPS measures in 2002 (Zhu 2003). Because failure to pass SPS inspection often leads to closer inspection of future exports, China's agricultural products have confronted much stricter inspections in these markets after several SPS-related problems.

For example, in November 2001, 300 metric tonnes of shrimp shipped from Zhoushan in Zhejiang Province to the European Union were discovered to contain 0.2 parts per billion of chloramphenicol (Dong and Jensen 2004). As a result, the European Union suspended imports of Chinese products of animal origin intended for human consumption or for use in animal feeds. Affected products included rabbit and poultry meat and crustaceans such as shrimp and prawns. Later, other countries, including Hungary, Russia and Japan, implemented stricter inspections of poultry meat from China. As a consequence, exports of poultry meat from China declined by about 33 per cent in 2002 compared with the previous year.

In 2002, Japan strengthened the allowable maximum residual limit (MRL) of chlorpyrifos for spinach from 0.1 parts per million to 0.01 parts per million. As a result, in July 2002, Japan blocked imports of frozen spinach from China after finding the presence of pesticides. Before this ban, annual imports from China were worth about US$30–35 million, and accounted for 99 per cent of Japan's annual imports of 40,000–50,000 metric tonnes of spinach. Japan's restriction on Chinese frozen spinach lasted for about eight months (until February 2003). In May 2003, after detecting higher than permitted pesticide residue, Japan again advised importers not to import Chinese frozen spinach. This ban was not lifted until June 2004. As a result, (Figure 12.11), China's exports of spinach to Japan dropped dramatically, from the highest level of US$34 million in 2001, to US$14 million in 2002 and US$4 million in 2003. In 2004 and 2005, China's exports of spinach to Japan recovered slightly, but were still lower than the 1994 export level.

Figure 12.11 **China's exports of spinach and cabbage to Japan, 1992–2005**
(at constant 2000 US$ prices)

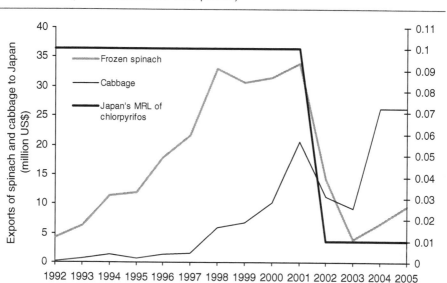

Source: United Nations Statistics Division. Commodity Trade Statistics Database, COMTRADE. Available from http://unstats.un.org/unsd/comtrade/default.aspx

The stricter standards for chlorpyrifos on spinach have effected China's exports of other vegetables to Japan. For example, China's exports of cabbage to Japan declined sharply from US$20.5 million in 2001 to US$11.2 million and US$9.2 million in 2002 and 2003 respectively. China's exports of lettuce to Japan declined from US$360,000 in 2001 to US$180,000 and US$60,000 in 2002 and 2003 respectively. In 2005, China's exports of lettuce to Japan amounted to US$280,000, still lower than in 2001.

In 2006, Japan introduced the 'Positive List System for Agricultural Chemical Residues in Foods' (Ministry of Health, Labour and Welfare of Japan 2006), which took effect on 29 May 2006. Under this system, agricultural chemicals include pesticides, feed additives and veterinary drugs in 797 categories. The system sets 53,862 standards for maximum residue limits. The uniform limit will be applied to agricultural chemicals for which MRLs are not established. The uniform limit is 0.01ppm, which means for 100 tonnes of agricultural products, the agricultural chemical residuals cannot exceed 1 gram.

Japan is the largest market for Chinese exports of agricultural products, accounting for 31 per cent of China's total agricultural exports in 2005. The introduction of the Positive List System will have a significant impact on China's agricultural exports to Japan. From January to April 2006, the growth rate of China's agricultural exports to Japan declined substantially, because many agricultural export companies were worried that their products would be refused entry due to the much stricter standards (Cai Jing 2006).

Currently, China's exports of seafood, vegetables and fruit, tea, honey, poultry and red meat are encountering the most severe SPS problems. United States' technical standards preclude imports of beef, pork and poultry meat into the United States in an effort to prevent the import of highly contagious animal diseases that are endemic in China, including foot-and-mouth disease. From August 2002 to July 2003, the United States Food and Drug Administration (FDA) refused entry to 1,285 shipments of Chinese foodstuffs. Agricultural and aquatic products accounted for 630 of these shipments, or nearly half of all refusals (Dong and Jensen 2004). Most recently, from June 2005 to May 2006, the FDA refused entry to 1,925 Chinese shipments, of which 945 shipments were agricultural products, accounting for 49 per cent of the total refusals (US FDA 2006). Most refusals resulted from violations of SPS measures. Excessive pesticide residues, low food hygiene, unsafe additives, contamination and misuse of veterinary drugs have been major issues.

Although the WTO's SPS agreement requires members to ensure that SPS measures are based on sufficient scientific evidence, there are some well-founded concerns that countries abuse SPS measures by using them as trade barriers. Because of very low production and labour costs, some agricultural products exported from China are very competitive in world markets. Consequently, importing countries might look to restrict imports from China by setting relatively high standards or strict inspections in order to protect domestic markets.

Conclusions

Entry into the WTO has boosted China's agricultural trade, especially its agricultural imports. The rapid growth of China's agricultural imports is mainly a result of the rapid increase in quantities of imports of land-intensive agricultural products, such as vegetable oil seeds, vegetable oils and grains (mainly wheat), and raw materials for textiles, such as cotton, wool and raw animal hides and skins. China has no comparative advantage in land-intensive agricultural production and, as found in this study, the values of the revealed comparative advantage indices of these agricultural products have been declining especially quickly since 2003.

China's agricultural export growth is being driven primarily by the rapid increase in exports of labour-intensive agricultural products, mainly processed agricultural products, followed by animal and horticultural products. China has a comparative advantage in some labour-intensive agricultural production. However, apart from processed agricultural products, whose revealed comparative advantage indices are increasing, the values of the revealed comparative advantage indices for animal and horticultural products have been declining especially quickly since entry into the WTO.

The pattern of China's agricultural trade is consistent with China's comparative advantage and resource endowments. After entry into the WTO, this pattern has been strengthened, indicating that China is moving closer to its comparative advantage in agricultural trade with the rest of the world.

Fast economic growth, structural change and increases in per capita incomes have all played a significant role in driving the changes in comparative advantage in China's agriculture. TBT and SPS measures, however, might also contribute to a rapid decline in China's comparative advantage in labour-intensive animal and horticultural products.

Some agricultural products exported from China are very competitive in world markets. Consequently, importing countries might look to restrict imports from China by setting relatively high SPS standards or by imposing strict inspections in order to protect domestic markets.

China should increase and strengthen SPS levels to meet international standards in order to increase exports of animal and horticultural products to international markets, especially to industrial-country markets. As China faces more SPS disputes, the government needs to initiate bilateral negotiations to counter unfair trade restrictions and discrimination and it could use the WTO to coordinate and resolve trade disputes. As a member of the WTO, China can now participate in the negotiation and establishment of international regulations and standards to obtain a more equal position for its agricultural exports.

Acknowledgments

I would like to thank Professor Christopher Findlay for his initial stimulus to write this chapter and for his valuable suggestions and comments. I also would like to thank Shiro Armstrong for helping to collect the trade data. In particular, I would like to thank Professor Ross Garnaut and Dr Ligang Song for their fundamental comments and suggestions in structuring and shaping the chapter.

This chapter is part of the research results of ADP/98-128 project extension funded by the Australian Centre for International Agricultural Research (ACIAR). I would like to thank ACIAR for funding the project.

Notes

[1] China revised its GDP growth rate for the period 1979–2004 in January 2006. The revised GDP growth rate was 9.1 per cent, for 2002, 10 per cent for 2003, 10.1 per cent for 2004 and 9.9 per cent for 2005.
[2] China's average tariff level dropped to 9.9 per cent in 2005 compared with 15.6 per cent in 2000. The average tariff on industrial products dropped to 9.3 per cent compared with 14.8 per cent in 2000, and that for agricultural products was 15.3 per cent compared with 23.2 per cent in 2000.
[3] The classic reference is Ricardo 1817.
[4] Ohlin 1933.
[5] These three economies on average accounted for 52 per cent of China's total agricultural exports in the period from 2002 to 2004, of which Japan accounted for 31 per cent, the European Union 11 per cent and the United States 10 per cent.

Appendix Table A12.1 China's agricultural exports by commodity groupings, 1995–2005 (US$ million at 2000 constant prices)

	1995	1996	1997	1998	1999	2000	2001	2002	2003	2004	2005
Total agricultural exports	16,095.57	15,530.50	16,054.78	14,528.82	13,904.08	15,524.50	15,405.71	17,108.66	19,715.37	20,777.77	23,808.82
Cereals, vegetable oil seeds and vegetable oils	1,413.01	1,368.27	2,477.60	2,382.56	1,873.40	2,345.10	1,746.44	2,327.66	3,299.59	1,595.50	2,664.70
Cereals (10)	85.88	205.30	1262.67	1,578.24	1,173.33	1,643.00	1,005.58	1,579.60	2,423.52	674.99	1,254.51
Vegetable oil seeds	830.58	776.96	556.24	512.77	585.73	605.70	646.72	671.38	793.70	830.61	1,228.59
Vegetable oils	496.54	386.01	658.69	291.56	144.33	96.40	94.14	76.68	82.38	89.89	181.60
Horticultural products	3,646.66	3,266.48	3,243.57	2,996.55	2,881.53	2,861.30	3,028.41	3,247.94	3,745.36	4,360.84	4,695.42
Live trees and other plants (06)	31.64	32.94	34.33	31.69	32.05	32.00	34.03	41.17	45.87	58.62	68.48
Edible vegetables (07)	1,935.77	1,692.91	1,623.13	1,566.62	1,570.26	1,545.00	1,698.01	1,802.66	2,040.66	2,313.16	2,710.94
Edible fruit (08)	542.42	506.12	497.77	459.53	439.35	417.00	423.04	531.32	703.93	835.45	947.84
Coffee, tea, mate and species (09)	525.47	540.15	593.25	549.32	505.51	506.00	527.10	528.45	584.11	788.22	823.77
Vegetable plaiting materials (14)	68.93	57.09	53.64	47.54	41.35	43.00	41.82	42.12	43.06	39.66	43.74
Other vegetable products (1210–14, 13)	542.42	437.28	441.45	341.84	292.97	318.30	304.40	302.23	327.72	325.74	100.65
Animal products	5,090.40	4,625.74	4,677.35	4,113.57	3,974.22	4,388.60	4,512.66	4,555.37	4,917.16	5,800.07	6,022.16
Live animals (01)	568.41	533.56	510.45	465.87	398.00	385.00	334.55	329.32	306.10	301.12	292.01
Meat/edible meat offal (02)	1,154.91	1,192.28	1,040.60	887.37	714.33	753.00	817.89	636.63	604.71	644.36	659.75
Fish/aquatic products (03)	2,358.40	1,908.09	2,126.26	1,833.89	2,012.75	2,270.00	2,519.79	2,750.41	3,121.83	3,697.33	3,863.76
Dairy products, eggs and natural honey (04)	183.07	214.08	177.01	184.87	169.54	188.00	186.72	185.72	207.81	213.51	237.51
Product of animal origin not elsewhere specified (05)	803.46	744.35	750.95	686.65	648.17	760.00	633.11	626.57	693.64	889.32	898.48
Animal fats (1501–6, 1516–18, 1520–1)	22.15	33.38	71.88	54.93	31.43	32.60	20.62	26.71	37.07	54.43	70.65

Changing patterns in China's agricultural trade after WTO accession

Category											
Processed agricultural products	5,342.85	5,811.00	5,194.43	4,638.60	4,555.82	5,259.00	5,735.41	6,527.09	7,311.73	8,735.53	10,122.25
Products of milling industry (11)	114.13	239.33	199.54	111.98	82.70	93.00	104.06	112.97	132.92	155.26	177.63
Preparations of meat, fish and aquatic products (16)	1,261.13	1,612.76	1,489.03	1,291.96	1,432.80	1,883.00	1,989.77	2,227.71	2,507.76	3,180.69	3,876.35
Sugar and confectionery (17)	264.43	333.75	208.12	193.32	144.73	173.00	151.71	217.31	183.47	229.92	371.61
Cocoa and cocoa preparations (18)	46.33	53.80	60.08	46.48	41.35	29.00	26.74	34.46	51.48	63.45	97.59
Preparations of cereals, flour (19)	238.44	258.00	290.73	276.77	299.79	360.00	401.65	434.63	493.32	595.13	674.77
Preparations of vegetables and fruit (20)	1,223.84	1,149.46	1,121.06	1,089.14	1,164.02	1,315.00	1,455.86	1,682.03	2,029.43	2350.35	2,748.85
Miscellaneous edible preparations (21)	244.09	275.56	326.13	347.55	348.38	359.00	388.03	441.33	509.23	559.03	635.42
Beverages, spirits and vinegar (22)	441.85	435.85	498.85	470.09	472.43	493.00	556.28	571.53	582.24	677.36	638.26
Residues from food industry and animal feeds (23)	379.70	380.96	295.02	200.71	222.26	252.00	285.92	390.59	360.39	456.10	424.60
Tobacco and manufactured tobacco substitutes (24)	1,128.92	1,071.52	705.89	610.59	347.35	302.00	375.39	414.52	461.49	468.23	477.17
Agricultural products as raw materials for textiles	602.65	459.02	461.83	397.52	619.12	670.50	382.78	450.62	387.54	285.84	304.29
Raw hides and skins, leather, furs and articles	57.29	35.35	45.38	26.73	12.72	11.30	10.60	11.87	8.61	8.15	7.94
Silk	400.04	343.63	335.78	265.15	291.21	331.70	273.76	256.18	223.63	215.24	237.19
Wool, fine or coarse animal hair	85.09	60.71	69.73	38.24	15.82	12.70	15.75	14.84	26.49	43.67	47.78
Cotton	55.15	15.37	5.26	62.33	294.83	307.90	79.65	165.43	126.46	15.77	8.45
Other vegetable textile fibres (5301–2)	5.09	3.95	5.69	5.07	4.55	6.90	3.01	2.30	2.34	3.01	2.93

Source: COMTRADE. Available from http://unstats.un.org/unsd/comtrade/default.aspx

Appendix Table A12.2 China's agricultural imports by commodity groupings, 1995–2005 (US$ million at 2000 constant prices)

	1995	1996	1997	1998	1999	2000	2001	2002	2003	2004	2005
Total agricultural imports	13,684.17	11,784.04	10,574.66	8,685.94	8,334.66	11,048.10	11,293.18	11,705.20	17,463.26	25,258.46	26,636.15
Cereals, vegetable oil seeds and vegetable oils	6,964.24	4,933.58	3,650.26	3,561.82	3,384.04	4,359.00	4,372.82	4,422.20	8,243.13	12,245.78	10,699.22
Cereals (10)	4,046.69	2,805.04	956.92	735.25	513.78	574.00	590.32	461.43	415.62	2,021.33	1,237.93
Vegetable oil seeds	165.44	404.78	1,006.38	1,364.96	1,649.38	3,029.80	3,207.45	2,609.88	5,266.68	6,677.36	7,248.27
Vegetable oils	2,752.11	1,723.76	1,686.96	1,461.62	1,220.88	755.20	575.05	1,350.89	2,560.84	3,547.09	2,213.02
Horticultural products	384.89	451.55	463.34	487.78	514.30	653.20	741.93	726.71	906.78	1,186.07	1,263.16
Live trees and other plants (06)	6.78	5.49	8.58	11.62	17.57	21.00	21.40	31.59	42.12	46.86	61.00
Edible vegetables (07)	88.14	84.55	79.39	75.00	85.80	82.00	204.23	185.72	226.53	369.04	465.13
Edible fruit (08)	94.92	216.28	252.10	255.65	266.71	368.00	356.91	361.87	464.30	564.23	583.96
Coffee, tea, mate and species (09)	16.95	30.74	10.73	21.13	19.64	23.00	20.42	22.02	26.21	29.54	37.00
Vegetable plaiting materials (14)	101.70	43.91	35.40	45.42	49.62	83.00	63.21	42.41	67.40	80.13	60.20
Other vegetable products (1210–14, 13)	76.39	70.59	77.13	75.95	74.95	76.20	75.76	83.10	80.22	96.27	55.87
Animal products	1,189.49	1,183.39	1,096.92	1,224.78	1,972.43	2,546.80	2,470.87	2,754.72	3,274.69	3,694.69	4,509.74
Live animals (01)	40.68	51.60	43.98	58.10	68.23	52.00	34.04	50.74	109.52	200.47	96.73
Meat/edible meat offal (02)	107.35	172.36	159.85	151.06	515.85	637.00	581.56	600.25	709.55	433.77	521.12
Fish/aquatic products (03)	676.90	655.42	583.60	703.55	912.82	1,212.00	1,294.42	1,498.22	1,745.79	2,133.19	2557.08
Dairy products, eggs and natural honey (04)	72.32	62.58	72.95	94.02	169.54	218.00	212.98	260.39	327.63	408.51	410.66
Product of animal origin not elsewhere specified (05)	80.23	104.30	123.37	107.75	121.98	160.00	168.25	183.42	205.00	229.10	196.67
Animal fats (1501–6, 1516–18, 1520–1)	212.00	137.12	113.18	110.29	184.01	267.80	179.62	161.69	177.20	289.63	727.50

Changing patterns in China's agricultural trade after WTO accession

Processed agricultural products	2,257.83	2,723.80	2,823.57	2,114.89	1,413.16	1,874.00	1,910.02	1,986.94	2,097.76	2,733.61	3,236.90
Products of milling industry (11)	81.36	77.95	72.95	58.10	81.67	64.00	78.77	90.95	127.31	172.03	164.96
Preparations of meat, fish and aquatic products (16)	13.56	8.78	8.58	7.39	12.41	12.00	13.62	18.67	25.27	23.89	25.53
Sugar/confectionery (17)	1,056.59	469.89	268.20	180.64	188.15	177.00	365.67	268.05	202.19	306.50	400.93
Cocoa and cocoa preparations (18)	66.67	64.77	76.17	67.61	55.82	71.00	77.80	76.59	108.59	123.71	157.65
Preparations of cereals, flour (19)	25.99	18.66	18.24	15.85	49.62	71.00	90.44	142.64	138.54	177.68	213.13
Preparations of vegetables and fruit (20)	16.95	17.57	19.31	25.35	44.45	60.00	82.66	105.31	125.43	129.46	139.06
Miscellaneous edible preparations (21)	74.58	93.32	93.33	87.68	123.02	147.00	177.00	171.36	292.06	433.22	271.23
Beverages, spirits and vinegar (22)	41.81	46.11	72.95	79.23	127.15	161.00	141.99	141.69	174.11	238.03	363.76
Residues from food industry and animal feeds (23)	474.62	1,425.03	1,921.36	1,481.06	639.90	907.00	621.44	739.06	616.88	862.89	1,159.76
Tobacco and manufactured tobacco substitutes (24)	405.69	501.72	272.49	111.98	90.97	204.00	260.63	232.63	287.38	266.20	340.89
Agricultural products as raw materials for textiles	2,887.72	2,491.71	2,540.57	1,299.67	1,050.72	1,615.10	1,797.54	1,814.62	2,940.89	5,398.31	6,927.13
Raw hides and skins, leather, furs and articles	444.22	396.77	429.33	418.75	412.27	627.80	819.54	739.25	929.34	1,268.85	2,755.22
Silk	18.42	7.58	21.24	13.20	13.13	14.20	9.82	6.80	9.08	14.22	13.86
Wool, fine or coarse animal hair	768.77	668.71	558.60	446.22	473.98	779.60	786.08	785.68	727.90	1,009.57	1,105.24
Cotton	1,607.15	1,388.25	1,497.61	379.24	85.80	86.10	81.40	183.23	1,111.32	2,913.48	2,865.61
Other vegetable textile fibres (5301–02)	49.16	30.41	33.79	42.26	65.54	107.40	100.69	99.66	163.25	192.19	187.24

Source: COMTRADE. Available from http://unstats.un.org/unsd/comtrade/default.aspx

Appendix Table A12.3   China's revealed comparative advantage indices (NER), 1995–2005

	1995	1996	1997	1998	1999	2000	2001	2002	2003	2004	2005
All agricultural products	0.08	0.14	0.21	0.25	0.25	0.17	0.15	0.19	0.06	−0.10	−0.06
By factor intensity of production											
Labour-intensive agricultural products	0.58	0.53	0.51	0.52	0.50	0.43	0.45	0.45	0.44	0.43	0.40
Land-intensive agricultural products	−0.72	−0.67	−0.41	−0.32	−0.34	−0.38	−0.54	−0.42	−0.53	−0.83	−0.73
By commodity groupings											
Cereals, vegetable oil seeds and vegetable oils	−0.66	−0.57	−0.19	−0.20	−0.29	−0.30	−0.43	−0.31	−0.43	−0.77	−0.60
Cereals (10)	−0.96	−0.86	0.14	0.36	0.39	0.48	0.26	0.55	0.71	−0.50	0.01
Vegetable oil seeds	0.67	0.31	−0.29	−0.45	−0.48	−0.67	−0.66	−0.59	−0.74	−0.78	−0.71
Vegetable oils	−0.69	−0.63	−0.44	−0.67	−0.83	−0.77	−0.72	−0.89	−0.94	−0.95	−0.85
Horticultural products	0.81	0.76	0.75	0.72	0.70	0.63	0.61	0.63	0.61	0.57	0.58
Live trees and other plants (06)	0.65	0.71	0.60	0.46	0.29	0.21	0.23	0.13	0.04	0.11	0.06
Edible vegetables (07)	0.91	0.90	0.91	0.91	0.90	0.90	0.79	0.81	0.80	0.72	0.71
Edible fruit (08)	0.70	0.40	0.33	0.29	0.24	0.06	0.08	0.19	0.21	0.19	0.24
Coffee, tea, mate and species (09)	0.94	0.89	0.96	0.93	0.93	0.91	0.93	0.92	0.91	0.93	0.91
Vegetable plaiting materials (14)	−0.19	0.13	0.20	0.02	−0.09	−0.32	−0.20	.000	−0.22	−0.34	−0.16
Other vegetable products (1210–14, 13)	0.75	0.72	0.70	0.64	0.59	0.61	0.60	0.57	0.61	0.54	0.29
Animal products	0.62	0.59	0.62	0.54	0.34	0.27	0.29	0.25	0.21	0.22	0.14
Live animals (01)	0.87	0.82	0.84	0.78	0.71	0.76	0.82	0.73	0.47	0.20	0.50
Meat/edible meat offal (02)	0.83	0.75	0.73	0.71	0.16	0.08	0.17	0.03	−0.08	0.20	0.12
Fish/aquatic products (03)	0.55	0.49	0.57	0.45	0.38	0.30	0.32	0.29	0.28	0.27	0.20
Dairy products, eggs and natural honey (04)	0.43	0.55	0.42	0.33	0.00	−0.07	−0.07	−0.17	−0.22	−0.31	−0.27
Product of animal origin not elsewhere specified (05)	0.82	0.75	0.72	0.73	0.68	0.65	0.58	0.55	0.54	0.59	0.64

Changing patterns in China's agricultural trade after WTO accession

Processed agricultural products	0.41	0.36	0.30	0.37	0.53	0.47	0.50	0.53	0.55	0.52	0.52
Products of milling industry (11)	0.17	0.51	0.46	0.32	0.01	0.18	0.14	0.11	0.02	-0.05	0.04
Preparations of meat, fish and aquatic products (16)	0.98	0.99	0.99	0.99	0.98	0.99	0.99	0.98	0.98	0.99	0.99
Sugar and confectionery (17)	-0.60	-0.17	-0.13	0.03	-0.13	-0.01	-0.41	-0.10	-0.05	-0.14	-0.04
Cocoa and cocoa preparations (18)	-0.18	-0.09	-0.12	-0.19	-0.15	-0.42	-0.49	-0.38	-0.36	-0.32	-0.24
Preparations of cereals, flour (19)	0.80	0.87	0.88	0.89	0.72	0.67	0.63	0.51	0.56	0.54	0.52
Preparations of vegetables and fruit (20)	0.97	0.97	0.97	0.95	0.93	0.91	0.89	0.88	0.88	0.90	0.90
Miscellaneous edible preparations (21)	0.53	0.49	0.55	0.60	0.48	0.42	0.37	0.44	0.27	0.13	0.40
Beverages, spirits and vinegar (22)	0.83	0.81	0.74	0.71	0.58	0.51	0.59	0.60	0.54	0.48	0.27
Residues from food industry and animal feeds (23)	-0.11	-0.58	-0.73	-0.76	-0.48	-0.57	-0.37	-0.31	-0.26	-0.31	-0.46
Tobacco and manufactured tobacco substitutes (24)	0.47	0.36	0.44	0.69	0.58	0.19	0.18	0.28	0.23	0.28	0.17
Agricultural products as raw materials for textiles	-0.65	-0.69	-0.69	-0.53	-0.26	-0.41	-0.65	-0.60	-0.77	-0.90	-0.92
Raw hides and skins, leather, furs and articles	-0.77	-0.84	-0.81	-0.88	-0.94	-0.96	-0.97	-0.97	-0.98	-0.99	-0.99
Silk	0.91	0.96	0.88	0.91	0.91	0.92	0.93	0.95	0.92	0.88	0.89
Wool, fine or coarse animal hair	-0.80	-0.83	-0.78	-0.84	-0.94	-0.97	-0.96	-0.96	-0.93	-0.92	-0.92
Cotton	-0.93	-0.98	-0.99	-0.72	0.55	0.56	-0.01	-0.05	-0.80	-0.99	-0.99
Other vegetable textile fibres (5301-2)	-0.81	-0.77	-0.71	-0.79	-0.87	-0.88	-0.94	-0.95	-0.97	-0.97	-0.97

Source: COMTRADE. Available from http://unstats.un.org/unsd/comtrade/default.aspx

13

Village elections, accountability and income distribution in rural China

Yang Yao

Village elections were first envisioned by the late chairman of the National People's Congress (NPC) Peng Zhen as a means to enhance village governance after the commune system was dissolved in China in the early 1980s. In 1987, the NPC passed a tentative version of the *Organic Law of the Village Committee* (OLVC), and started a 10-year experiment with village elections. In 1998, the NPC formally passed the law and elections quickly spread to the whole country. Since the inception of this system in the mid 1980s, however, controversies regarding the impact of elections on village life have been constant. The institutional environment for elections is by no means friendly. Within the village, the authority of the elected village committee is seriously constrained, if not superseded, by the Communist Party committee. Outside the village, the township and county governments still maintain a heavy hand in village affairs. As a result, even if the elected village committee is willing to advance the interests of the villagers, it might not be able to do so. On the other hand, the decentralised nature of the election might make it easier for local elites to capture local politics, so democracy does not necessarily lead to a fairer provision of public goods (Bardhan and Mookherjee 2005). There is evidence that business élites have begun to dominate elections in some villages (Liu et al. 2001). In addition, lineages are playing a significant role in aligning political interests in many village elections, and people worry that this will distort the results of an election.

Few empirical studies have been devoted to exploring the true performance of village elections. Using survey data from 48 villages for the period from 1986 to

2002, this chapter provides systematic evidence for the effects of elections in improving accountability and income distribution in the village.

In the literature, evidence suggests that local elections generally increase the responsiveness of local government to its constituency. Foster and Rosenzweg (2001) found that village elections in India led to more investment in road-building instead of irrigation facilities. They interpreted this finding as evidence for a pro-poor policy as road-building provides jobs for the landless whereas investment in irrigation facilities augments the capacity of landlords. Using data from a quasi-experiment in India in which a group of randomly selected villages was required to elect a woman village head, Chattopadhyay and Duflo (2004) found that the villages with a woman as village head tended to provide more women-friendly public services. Zhang et al. (2004) found in a sample of China's Jiangsu Province that village elections had increased the share of public investment and had no effect on the amount of taxes handed over to the township. Gan et al. (2005a, 2005b) further found that village elections helped to reduce the negative impacts of health shocks on farmers' incomes and strengthened farmers' consumption-smoothing capabilities. Last, Kennedy et al. (2004) found in a sample from Shaanxi Province that, compared with elections with government-appointed candidates, more competitive elections, in which candidates were nominated by villagers, produced village leaders who were more accountable to villagers in decisions regarding land reallocation.

As for the effects of village elections on income inequality, there are two possible ways for elections to play a positive role. One is that democracy leads the government to cater to the interests of the median voter, who generally favours redistribution of income (Alesina and Rodrik 1994; Benabou 1996). The other is that democracy presses the government to spend more to increase the incomes of the poorer portion of the population, on the basis that poverty exerts negative externalities on the richer portion (Gan et al. 2005a). However, existing studies using country-level data have not provided conclusive results.[1]

My data covers a critical period that witnessed a rapid increase in income inequality in rural China. Nationwide, the rural Gini coefficient increased from 0.29 in 1987 to 0.35 in 2000 (Riskin et al. 2002). In the meantime, government investment in the countryside decreased. Using the two-way fixed-effect panel method, we have found several important results. First, the introduction of village elections on average has increased the share of public expenditure in the village government's total expenditure by 4.2 percentage points, which is equivalent to 22.8 per cent of the average share in the sample. Second, it has reduced the share of administrative expenditure by 4 percentage points, equivalent to 18.2 per cent of the sample average. To the extent that public expenditure is used to advance the interests of the villagers and administrative expenditure is spent mostly to satisfy the needs of the village leaders, these two results suggest that elections have enhanced the accountability of the village committee.

Third, village elections have not led to more income redistribution; on the contrary, they have reduced the progressiveness of income redistribution. This means that the increased share of public expenditure has been devoted to productive investments since income transfer and investment are the only two components of public expenditure. Last, the introduction of elections, on average, reduces the Gini coefficient in a village by 0.016, which is equivalent to 5.7 per cent of the sample average and 32 per cent of the growth of the Gini coefficient in the period 1987–2002. Because income redistribution has not increased, this improvement has to be brought about by the village's pro-poor actions, such as increasing productive investments. These results have shown that village elections have worked despite all the constraints imposed on them.

The rest of the chapter is organised as follows. The second section reviews the experiment with village elections in the past 20 years and discusses the factors that might undermine the positive effects of elections. The third section describes the data and presents some descriptive evidence for elections, village expenditure, income redistribution and the Gini coefficient. The fourth section presents the results of the econometric analysis and the fifth section concludes the chapter.

An introduction to village elections in rural China

The Chinese commune system was dissolved in the early 1980s. As an administrative unit, the commune was replaced by the township, and the production brigade under the commune was replaced by the village committee. The 1982 Constitution defines the village committee as a self-governing body of villagers (Clause 111). Except in a few localities, committee members were appointed, rather than elected. In 1987, under the leadership of chairman Peng Zhen, the NPC passed a tentative version of the OLVC requiring that the village committee be elected, triggering elections in Chinese villages. By 1994, half of the Chinese villages had begun elections. By 1997, 25 of the 31 mainland provinces had adopted a local version of the OLVC, and 80 per cent of villages had introduced elections (Ministry of Civil Affairs 1998). In 1998, the formal version of the OLVC was passed by the NPC and elections have since spread quickly to almost all villages.

The village committee is comprised of three to seven members depending on the size of the village. The core members are the chairman, vice-chairman and accountant. Before 1998, candidates for the chairmanship were usually appointed by the township government, although popular nomination—a mixture of government appointment and popular nomination—and nomination by villager representatives also existed. The formal version of the OLVC requires that candidates be nominated by villagers, and the minimum number of villagers to propose a candidate is 10. A primer is held to reduce the number of candidates to two, and the formal contest is run between these two. This version of election is popularly called *hai-xuan*. Since 1998, *hai-xuan* has become increasingly popular. The term of the committee is three years, however, no limit is required.

Village elections in China operate in a weak institutional environment. In a typical village, the elected committee faces two major challenges that might hinder its ability to serve the will of the villagers. The first is its relationship with the Communist Party committee in the village. Despite the fact that the party committee is not popularly elected, the OLVC stipulates that the village committee work under the leadership of the party committee, reflecting the nature of China's one-party system. Since the party secretary is appointed by the higher authority, they often pursue an agenda different to that of the village committee. Backed by popular votes, however, the chairman of the village committee often defies the direction of the party secretary, although the result of the contest is not always in their favour (Oi and Rozelle 2000; Guo and Bernstein 2004). To reconcile conflict between the village committee and the party secretary, the central government has begun to encourage the latter to run for the village committee chairmanship in elections. While this will ease the tension inside the village (Guo and Bernstein 2004), the village committee still needs to face a second challenge, which comes from above.

Since village elections operate in an authoritarian institutional environment, where the upper-level governments—the township and county governments in particular—are not elected and often intrude in village elections and other village affairs, the effectiveness of such elections to serve the will of the villagers has been called into doubt. Evidence shows that informed local people tend not to trust elections. For example, in a survey conducted in Fujian Province, Zhong and Chen (2002) found that it was the villagers who had low levels of internal efficacy and democratic values who were more likely to participate in an election, and those with higher levels of internal efficacy and democratic orientation stayed away from elections due to their awareness of the institutional constraints placed on the process.

The above two challenges raise the question of whether elections enhance the village committee's accountability to the local population. This issue is compounded by the possibility of elite capture inside the village. Bardhan and Mookherjee (2005) found that in India, decentralisation could lead to elite capture at the local level if the financing of public goods provision was not designed properly. In the context of the Chinese village, rising business elites have been found frequently to dominate village elections (Liu et al. 2001). Although there are no *a priori* reasons to believe that business élites would necessarily steer the village committee towards adopting pro-rich policies, this belief lingers within Chinese academia and policy circles. In addition, lineages have regained their strength and frequently serve as vehicles for the expression of political interests in elections (see Liu et al. 2001 for a case study). There is concern that the revitalisation of lineages will distort the results of village elections.

Data and descriptive evidence

The data for this study comes from two sources. One is the Fixed-Point Survey (FPS) maintained by the Research Centre of Rural Economy, the Ministry of Agriculture, and the other is a retrospective survey conducted by the author in the spring of 2003. The FPS started in the early 1980s and has maintained a survey frame of about 340 villages and 30,000 households in all Chinese continental provinces. A strong feature of this is that it surveys a relatively large number of households (50–100) in a village, allowing, for the purposes of this study, a calculation of the Gini coefficient in a village with a fair degree of accuracy. Village-level data of 48 villages in eight provinces for the period 1986–2002 was obtained for this study.[2] These eight provinces were Guangdong, Zhejiang, Hunan, Henan, Sichuan, Gansu, Shanxi and Jilin. They cover diverse geographic settings and income levels. The 2003 retrospective survey provides information on village elections in the 48 villages. The household sample is smaller than the FPS sample. The FPS does not have a good record of the household codes, instead the study uses household characteristics to match households in order to establish the panel structure, resulting in a smaller sample, with 1,118 households left for household-level analysis. In addition, the starting year for household data is 1987 instead of 1986.

The village election

As the first election is likely to have more dramatic impact than subsequent elections, the focus is on studying the impact of the first election. Figure 13.1 presents the number of elections in villages and their accumulative percentage in each year. The year 1987 was the start of village elections in China and 12 of the sample villages had their first election in that year. By 1990, more than 50 per cent of the sample villages had at least one election and, by 2002, only one village had not had an election (it is a remote village in Gansu Province).

The introduction of elections had a clear regional pattern: villages in the same province tended to introduce elections in the same year that the province adopted

Figure 13.1   **Introduction of village elections in the sample villages, 1987–2002**

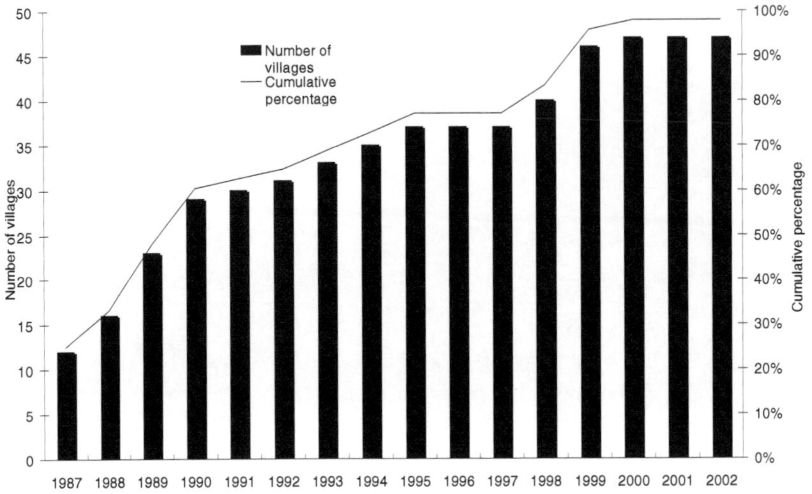

Source: Author's calculations.

the OLVC.[3] Table 13.1 shows the year each sample province adopted the OLVC, as well as the median and standard deviation of the year of the introduction of elections in its villages. Except Guangdong, all other provinces adopted the OLVC in the period 1988–92.[4] The median year of election was close to the year that the province adopted the OLVC, and the standard deviation was small in all provinces except Henan, Gansu and Shanxi, which had large standard deviations.[5] The median year and the adoption year were quite close in Henan and Shanxi, but were far apart in Gansu (the election lagged well behind the adoption of the OLVC). Overall, there were great regional and time variations in the introduction of the first election. One such variation is especially pertinent to this study—that is, high-income and low-income villages were mixed in terms of the timing of the first election. The introduction of elections is an irreversible process, so if the timing of the first election is associated closely with income levels, it will be hard to distinguish between the true effects of elections and the effects of incomes. The mixed nature of the data removes this possibility.

Table 13.1   **First election in the sample villages and adoption of the OLVC in the sample provinces**

	Guangdong	Hunan	Zhejiang	Henan	Sichuan	Gansu	Shanxi	Jilin
Year OLVC adopted	1998	1989	1988	1992	1991	1989	1991	1991
Median year of first election	1999	1988	1989	1991	1989	1995	1993	1989
Standard deviation of year of first election	0.5	1.7	3.9	4.6	1.7	6.8	4.6	2.7

Source: Author's calculations.

Village expenditure

Public goods provision in rural China is a joint effort between various levels of government and the villages. For major projects that involve several villages (such as road-building), it is usually the case that one or several levels of government provide part of the funds and the targeted villages provide the rest. For smaller projects within a village, the village budget is usually fully responsible, although governments also provide some funds (Song 2004). Villages obtain their revenue from fees, profits from collective firms and rents for village properties. Fees are surcharges (the so-called *san-ti-wu-tong* in Chinese documents) designated specifically for local public goods provision and should be shared with the township government to provide public goods within the township territory. Seven types of village spending are recorded in the FPS: investment in village businesses, public expenditure, office maintenance, salaries for village committee members, revenue handed to the township government, other spending, and surplus/deficit. To study the accountability of the village committee, the study is concerned with public expenditure, office maintenance and village committee salaries.[6] Public expenditure includes transfers to households and spending on public projects such as local roads, schools, irrigation systems and healthcare facilities, which are likely to benefit the majority of villagers. In contrast, office maintenance costs are spent on the village government's daily operations and can easily become the prey of village committee members. Together with village committee salaries, maintenance costs have the opposite implication of public expenditure for the village committee's accountability. Consequently, I will add them together and call them 'administrative costs'. In the econometric exercises to be presented in the next section, I will study the shares of public expenditure and administrative costs in total village spending.

Figure 13.2 presents the trends of the two shares for the period 1986–2002. The share of public expenditure in village spending was remarkably stable, remaining just below 20 per cent for the entire sample period. In contrast, the share of administrative costs increased dramatically after 1993. By 2002, 43 per cent of total village spending was used to operate the village government, whereas the share was less than 20 per cent before 1993. These two time trends have an important implication for our tests of the role of elections. If we find that elections increase the share of public expenditure but reduce the share of administrative costs, we will obtain strong evidence to support the proposition that elections enhance the village committee's accountability because the effects of elections run against the time trends.

Income redistribution

Before the central government announced the abolition of agricultural taxes and fees in 2005, households paid fees (*san-ti-wu-tong*) to the village to finance village public projects and affairs.[7] In villages with income from village-sponsored businesses (such as factories and land rentals), households also receive income transfer from the village. Figure 13.3 presents the trends of per capita fees, per capita income transfer and per capita net income transfer based on 1,118 households in the sample villages in the period 1987–2002. The amount of fees increased in the early 1990s but stabilised after 1995. The amount of income transfer was high in the early years but declined substantially over time. This might have a lot to do with the privatisation of collective enterprises in the 1990s. Net income transfer was kept positive in all the years.

Gini coefficients

The Gini coefficient is calculated on the per capita net income of the original FPS sample households (so each village has 50–100 households). Household net income is defined as household income net of operational costs and taxes but with transferred income from the government. We calculate the Gini coefficient for each village in each year. To take care of possible bias caused by household size, I weigh the calculation by household size, that is, I enter a household in the calculation by the number of its members. Figure 13.4 plots the average Gini coefficients of the 48 villages during 1987–2002. There was apparently an increasing trend of income inequality in the period, rising from 0.26 in 1987 to 0.28 in 1992, and then to 0.32 in 2001, decreasing slightly to 0.31 in 2002. This matches the

Figure 13.2 **Shares of public expenditure and administrative costs in village spending, 1986–2002**

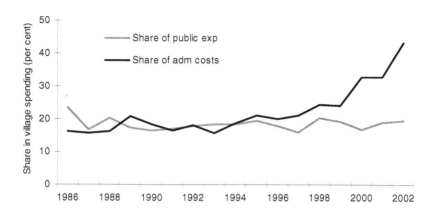

Source: Author's calculations.

Figure 13.3 **Fees and income transfer, 1987–2002** (yuan)

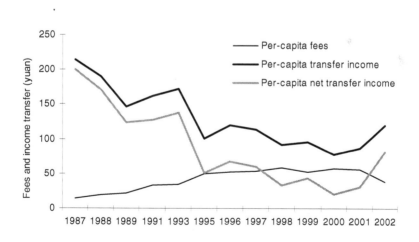

Note: Fees and income transfer are in 2002 yuan adjusted by the CPI published in *China Statistical Yearbook*. Data for 1990, 1992 and 1994 are missing.
Source: Author's calculations.

Figure 13.4 **Trend of the Gini coefficient in the sample villages, 1987–2002**

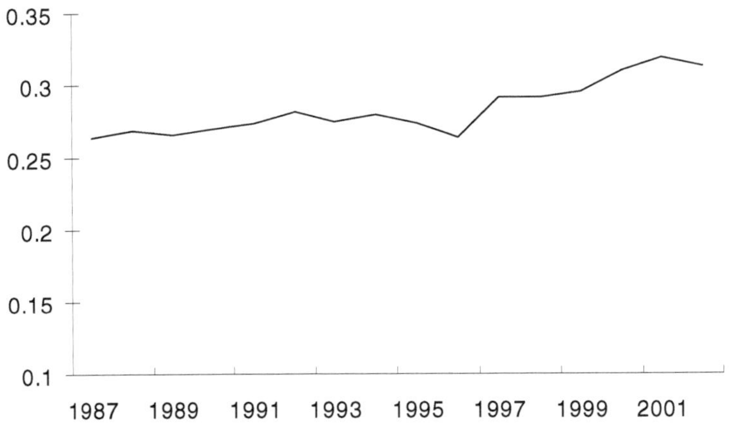

Source: Author's calculations.

national trend. The Gini coefficient in rural China increased from 0.29 in 1987 to 0.35 in 2000 (Riskin et al. 2002).[8]

Figure 13.5 provides the histograms of the Gini coefficients in 1987, 1999 and 2002. They largely agree with the histograms provided by Benjamin et al. (2005), who used a sample that contained my own. It is clear that income distribution was becoming more unequal. In particular, the distribution of 2002 dominates the distribution of 1987 by the first-order stochastic domination.

Econometric results

The study uses the two-way fixed-effect panel model for the estimations. This model allows us to control unobserved village or household characteristics and time events that might simultaneously determine the introduction of the election and the dependent variables. The main explanatory variable is a dummy variable indicating the introduction of elections. It is equal to zero if a village had not begun elections by a certain year, and equal to one if it had had at least one election. I will introduce the dependent and control variables when we study individual topics.

Elections and accountability

As indicated before, I study the share of public expenditure and the share of administrative costs in the total village budget for the effects of elections on the

Figure 13.5 Histograms of the Gini coefficients in 1987, 1999 and 2002

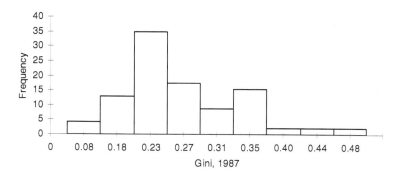

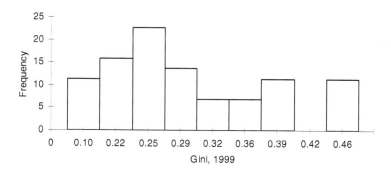

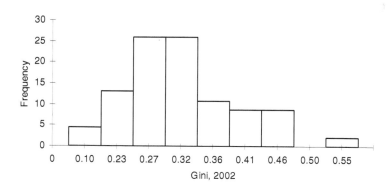

Note: The number for each bar in the figures is the average of the Gini coefficients represented by the bar.
Source: Author's calculations.

accountability of the village committee. The data coverage is from 1986 to 2002. The control variables include village population, per capita net income, the share of collective income in total village income, per capita land territory, the unemployment rate and the share of migrant workers who work outside the county. Village population (entering the regressions in logarithm terms) controls the village size. A larger population might make public decision-making more difficult so it would tend to have a negative effect on village governance. Per capita net income (converted into 2002 yuan and entering the regressions in logarithm terms) controls the level of economic development of a village, and the share of collective income in total village income controls the relative size of the collective economy. Studies frequently find that people in villages with higher incomes or a larger collective economy are more likely to participate in village elections, presumably because the stakes are higher in these villages (Hu 2005). Per capita land territory is introduced to represent the amount of resources that a village possesses. Land resources are particularly important in the coastal provinces, as fast growth of the local industry has significantly raised the demand for land. Recent literature suggests that natural resources can be a curse for a country, as they tend to lead to easier elite capture (Hoff and Stiglitz 2004). It is thus interesting to see whether a larger territory reduces a village government's accountability in our case.

Table 13.2 presents the results. Two regressions are run for each dependent variable, one with and one without any control variable. The first regression provides the estimate for the total effect of elections, and the second provides the estimate for a marginal effect. For the share of public expenditure, the total and marginal effects are statistically significant.[9] They are also meaningful economically as they are equivalent to 22.8 per cent and 26.4 per cent respectively of the average share of public expenditure in the sample. For the share of administrative costs, the total effect of elections remains statistically significant. The introduction of elections reduces administrative costs by about 4 percentage points, which is equivalent to 18.2 per cent of the sample mean. The marginal effect, however, turns only weakly significant (the p-value is 0.12). This shows that the positive effect of elections on administrative costs is through the impact on the control variables.

The above results are very strong in terms of the two time trends shown in Figure 13.2. The share of public expenditure was stable, so the result—that elections increase this share—is not an artefact of the time trend. In the case of the share of administrative costs, there was even a significant upward trend, so the result—that elections reduce the share—goes against the time trend.

Table 13.2 **The effects of elections on public and administrative expenditure**

	Share of public expenditure		Share of administrative costs	
Variables	R1	R2	R3	R4
Constant	15.67**" (1.52)	−11.79 (52.72)	24.75*** (1.31)	−14.76 (45.46)
Election dummy	4.21** (2.13)	4.87* (2.14)	−3.96** (1.83)	−2.80 (1.84)
Ln (population)		3.59 (7.44)		5.77 (6.42)
Ln (per capita income) ('000 yuan)		−1.65 (1.62)		2.14 (1.40)
Share of collective income in total income (per cent)		−0.14** (0.05)		−0.14*** (0.04)
Per capita land territory (mu)		0.55*** (0.15)		−0.43*** (0.13)
Unemployment rate (per cent)		−0.46 (0.98)		−0.38 (0.85)
Share of migrant workers (per cent)		0.03 (0.05)		−0.02 (0.05)
Adjusted R^2	0.26	0.28	0.44	0.45

Notes: * significant at the 10 per cent significance level ** significant at the 5 per cent significance level *** significant at the 1 per cent significance level
The regressions are based on data from 48 villages in the period 1986–2002, and the total number of cases is 806. All the regressions use the panel model with village and year fixed effects. Standard errors are in parentheses.
Source: Author's calculations.

Income redistribution

Data is used from 1,118 households in the period 1987–2002 to study the net and total income transfer. In the regressions, there are sets of control variables. One set is comprised of household variables including relative per capita earned income (RELINC), per capita land, per capita productive assets, average age, average education of family labour, male ratio, five dummies indicating whether a family has a member working in a government agency other than the village council, working in the village council, being a Communist Party member, with a regular wage job, and in the army, and a dummy indicating whether a family is a designated *wubaohu*, that is, a household receiving welfare from the village. Earned income is the income earned by the household in agricultural production, business and labour hiring. The study divides the per capita earned income by the village average income in each year to obtain the relative per capita earned income. This variable is included in the regressions to control for a household's relative position in the village. Its coefficient reflects the progressiveness (if it is negative) or regressiveness (if it is positive) of income redistribution. The other family attributes control for the factors that might affect the amount of fees paid by a household and the amount of income transfer received by it. The other set is comprised of the village variables that were used in Table 13.2. This set of variables controls for village characteristics.

The estimation results are presented in Table 13.3. Four regressions are performed. R1 and R2 study per capita net income transfer, and R3 and R4 study per capita total income transfer. R2 and R4 include the interaction term between RELINC and the election dummy, whereas R1 and R3 do not. The results are generally consistent with expectations. Income redistribution is progressive. A household that is richer, has more land or assets or has at least one regular wage earner, receives less net income transfer; on the other hand, a *wubaohu* and a household with a member in the army receives more net income transfer. The progressiveness of the total income transfer is, however, not as strong as the net income transfer. The somewhat surprising result is that households with a village cadre receive significantly less net and total income transfers. This shows that, on average, village cadres are not taking advantage of their position in receiving documented income from the village.[10]

R1 and R3 provide the estimates for the election dummy's average effects on the net and total income transfer. Neither is statistically significant, so village elections do not increase income redistribution. By adding the interaction term between RELINC and the election dummy, R2 and R4 tell us how village elections change the progressiveness of income redistribution. The coefficient of the interaction term is positive in both regressions, and, surprisingly, they are both positive. This means that elections have reduced the progressiveness of income redistribution. By the estimate provided in R2, in a village without elections, a household receives 114 yuan less of net income transfer for each of its members if its income is twice the village average. Elections close this gap by 86 yuan. The effect of elections is even stronger for the total income transfer, in which case the gap is reduced by 107 yuan. The commune system in Chinese villages had a long history, so villages' income redistribution had been quite progressive before any elections happened. To the extent that it empowers not just the poor, but the rich, the village election can lead to less progressive income redistribution.

Income inequality

To study the impact of elections on income inequality, I have run four regressions on the Gini coefficient that were obtained in the previous section. In the first

Table 13.3 Village elections and income distribution

Variable	R1 Estimate	R1 Statistical error	R2 Estimate	R2 Statistical error	R3 Estimate	R3 Statistical error	R4 Estimate	R4 Statistical error
Election dummy	–0.51	12.84	–56.34***	15.79	5.93	12.46	–63.94***	15.31
Household variables								
RELINC	–45.20***	6.86	–113.71***	14.13	–19.52***	6.66	–105.26***	12.81
RELINC × election dummy			85.65***	13.21			107.19***	13.70
Per capita landholding (mu)	–12.35***	3.60	–12.31***	3.59	–0.91	3.49	–0.87	3.48
Per capita productive assets (yuan)	–0.84***	0.18	–0.81***	0.18	–0.87***	0.18	–0.83***	0.18
Average age	–0.46	2.10	–0.52	2.10	–0.26	2.04	–0.34	2.03
Average education	–3.60	5.21	–3.13	5.21	–5.55	5.06	–4.97	5.04
Ratio of male members	–20.44	21.55	–21.47	21.52	–15.88	20.91	–17.16	20.88
Having a member in government	–8.69	14.94	–4.57	14.93	–4.31	14.49	0.84	14.47
Having a member as village cadre	–111.23***	17.91	–109.83***	17.88	–121.75***	17.37	–120.00***	17.33
Having a member as Communist Party member	1.17	12.20	3.01	12.18	6.10	11.82	8.40	11.80
Having a regular wage earner	–7.86***	1.42	–7.94***	1.42	0.05	1.38	–0.06	1.37
Being a *wubaohu*	84.83***	32.75	79.38***	32.72	69.40**	31.77	62.59**	31.71
Having a member in the army	46.52*	24.74	49.99*	24.71	40.48	24.00	44.82	23.95
Village variables								
Ln (village population)	5.89	49.13	13.03	49.07	–39.84	47.66	–30.91	47.56
Ln (village average income) (yuan)	41.41***	11.24	40.96***	11.23	41.31***	10.91	40.74***	10.89
Share of collective income (%)	6.39***	0.38	6.44***	0.38	6.32***	0.37	6.38***	0.37
Per capita land territory (mu)	–1.32	1.14	–1.29	1.14	–1.49	1.10	–1.45	1.10
Unemployment rate (%)	–1.90	6.21	–2.64	6.20	–0.99	6.02	–1.91	6.01
Share of migrants (%)	1.21***	0.34	1.19***	0.34	1.12***	0.33	1.09***	0.33
Constant	–249.33	382.71	–261.79	382.15	116.41	371.27	100.81	370.36
Adjusted R^2	0.38		0.38		0.38		0.3	

Notes: * significant at the 10 per cent significance level. ** significant at the 5 per cent significance level. *** significant at the 1 per cent significance level. Regressions are based on 13,366 cases of 1,118 households in the period 1987–2002. R1 and R2 are for per capita net income transfer (in 2002 yuan), and R3 and R4 are for per capita total income transfer (in 2002 yuan). All the regressions use the panel model with household and year fixed effects.

Source: Author's calculations.

regression, the results of which are presented in R1 of Table 13.4, I include only the election dummy and control the village and year fixed effects, so this regression provides us with the estimate for the election's total effect. It is shown that an election reduces the Gini coefficient by 0.016 and this effect is significant at the 1 per cent significance level. It is equivalent to 5.7 per cent of the sample average of 0.28, but is 32 per cent of the Gini coefficient's increase in the period 1987–2002. This is a large effect. In particular, it is obtained against the growth trend of the Gini coefficient.

In the other three regressions, I have included different sets of control variables to obtain different estimates for the marginal effect of the village election. R2 adds village per capita income, its square and the logarithm of village population. The two income variables are added to represent the Kuznets Curve that is frequently studied in the literature. The coefficient of the election dummy has remained essentially the same as in R1 and it is still significant at the 1 per cent significance level. The Kuznets Curve is verified. In addition, a larger village tends to have a larger Gini coefficient.

R3 then adds the other village variables that I used before—the share of collective income in total village income, per capita land territory, the unemployment rate and the share of migrants. Now the coefficient of the election dummy becomes barely significant (the p-value of the t-statistics is 0.12) and its magnitude becomes smaller. The three old control variables remain significant. Among the new control variables, only the share of collective income has a significant coefficient. An increase of 1 percentage point of the collective income would reduce the Gini coefficient by 0.008, which is a very strong effect. The average of the share of collective income is 6.8 per cent in the sample, and the standard deviation is 15.2 per cent, so there are wide variations in the data. If the share of collective income increases by one standard deviation, the Gini coefficient will decrease by 0.122.

R4 further adds four coefficients of variations (CVs) to the regression, which are those of household size, household average education of adult members, per capita household landholding and the number of regular household wage earners. These four CVs are meant to capture the variations that have impacts on the Gini coefficient and, in the meantime, are possibly correlated with the election. The previously significant control variables are still significant. Among the new control variables, the CVs of household size and household wage earners are significant and increase the Gini coefficient, which is an understandable result. The election dummy has, however, become highly insignificant.

The above results show that the village election has a significant effect to reduce income inequality, and this is channelled mainly by increasing village

Table 13.4 **Village elections and income distribution**

	R1	R2	R3	R4
Election dummy	−0.016***	−0.015**	−0.010	0.001
	(0.006)	(0.006)	(0.006)	(0.006)
Per capita net income ('000 yuan)		0.197E-2***	0.150E-2**	0.167E-2***
		(0.630E-3)	(0.631E-3)	(0.606E-3)
Per capita net income squared		−0.307E-4***	−0.248E-4***	−0.288E-4***
		(0.679E-5)	(0.681E-5)	(0.657E-5)
Log village population		0.058***	0.057***	0.050***
		(0.021)	(0.021)	(0.020)
Share of collective income (per cent)			−0.794E-3***	−0.768E-3***
			(0.151E-3)	(0.145E-3)
Per capita land territory (mu)			−0.385E-3	−0.115E-3
			(0.457E-3)	(0.446E-3)
Unemployment rate (per cent)			0.127E-4	−0.479E-3
			(0.269E-2)	(0.259E-2)
Share of migrants (per cent)			0.133E-4	−0.500E-4
			(0.168E-3)	(0.167E-3)
Coefficient of variation of household size				0.166***
				(0.032)
Coefficient of variation of average education of household adults				−0.006
				(0.035)
Coefficient of variation of per capita household landholding				−0.007
				(0.005)
Coefficient of variation of household wage earners				0.013***
				(0.002)
Constant	0.266***	−0.124	−0.111	−0.153
	(0.007)	(0.151)	(0.149)	(0.144)
Adjusted R^2	0.662	0.677	0.689	0.715

Notes: * significant at the 10 per cent significance level. ** significant at the 5 per cent significance level. *** significant at the 1 per cent significance level. The regressions use data from 48 villages in the period 1987–2002. The number of observations is 706. Both regressions use the panel model with village and year fixed effects. Standard errors are in parentheses.
Source: Author's calculations.

collective income, creating wage jobs or changing the distribution of land. With more collective income, the elected village committee can engage in more income redistribution and public investment. However, our early study of the net and total income transfer shows that the election has not increased income redistribution. Therefore, its positive effect to reduce income inequality must come from greater public investment. The creation of wage jobs in many cases is also tied to the growth of the collective income. In the past, village-run enterprises were the main source of village-generated jobs. In the past decade, most collective enterprises have been privatised and collective income now comes mainly from land and building rentals to outside investors who set up factories on village land. With more such investors coming in, the number of jobs in the village increases. Finally, the village committee can redistribute land to ensure it is held more equally among the households. According to the Constitution, land is owned collectively by villagers, so each villager has an entitlement to village land (Liu et al. 1998). This provides the legal basis for the village committee to undertake land redistribution.

Conclusions

The village election has been a significant step for China in a move towards full democracy. Using a unique panel data set, this study finds that elections have played a significantly positive role in enhancing the accountability of village committees and have reduced income inequality in villages. I have further found that elections have not led to more redistributive policies. Therefore, the positive impact of elections on income inequality is not brought about by more income redistribution, but by more public investment. These results have significant implications for the current debate in China and the developmental literature in general.

First, the results show that grassroots democracy can work even in a distorted institutional environment. It appears that village elections have only created numerous isolated democratic islands because above the village are the township and county governments—that do not draw their mandates from elections. These two upper-level governments still intervene in village affairs, either through direct orders or through the party secretary inside the village. In some cases, the upper-level governments intervene directly in a village election to make sure that the people who they favour are elected. These people then care more about their image in the eyes of the higher-level governments than they do about villagers' voices. The results of the study show, however, that on average, elections have made the elected village committee more accountable to villagers. Indeed, the elected village committee often uses the mandate created by an election to defy the directives of the party secretary and sometimes of the higher authorities (see Liu et al. 2001 for an example). Recent interest in the literature is to study how democracy works in a less institutionalised environment (Acemoglu 2005). The results provide one piece of evidence for this literature: as long as people are empowered, so that the threat of being voted out of office is real for village leaders, elections can work even in a distorted institutional environment.

Second, the results also show that villagers can quickly learn how to run a functioning democracy. At least at the introduction of village elections, many people had doubts about farmers' capabilities to run a successful democracy in China. These kinds of doubts have been diminishing recently, but there are still those who doubt whether the experience of the village election can be transplanted to higher-level governments. At the other extreme, there are people who believe that only the direct election of government officials can be accepted as true democracy. A compromise might be the direct election of delegates to the local and national People's Congress because this would not require a radical change of the Constitution, but, at the same time, it would enhance the accountability of local governments.

Third, the finding that village elections have not led to more income redistribution, but have improved equality defies the conventional wisdom that democracy leads to more distributive policies (Alesina and Rodrik 1994; Benabou 1996). This might be related to the small scale of the village election. Within the village setting of lineage and other intimate ties, it might be easier for villagers to reach more productive decisions than to fight for short-term redistributions. My finding might, however, still be indicative of larger-scale democracies.

Acknowledgments

I am grateful for financial support from the Chinese Medical Board and the National 211 Projects Fund and thank the excellent data collection efforts provided by the Research Centre of Rural Economy, the Ministry of Agriculture, People's Republic of China. Dwayne Benjamin, Loren Brandt and John Giles shared some of their data; Mengtao Gao, Ang Sun, Shuna Wang and Shenwei Zhang provided excellent research assistance; Yan Shen contributed to part of the research. I thank all of them for their help and generosity.

Notes

1 For a recent and comprehensive study, see Milanovic and Ying 2001 and the references therein.
2 The FPS did not conduct the survey in 1990, 1992 and 1994. We fill up the village-level data of these years by the average of the nearest two years, but leave the household data intact.
3 When the NPC passes a law that involves government action, each province enacts a local law that specifies the details of the implementation of the central law. It is noteworthy that most provinces adopted the OLVC even when it was in the experimental stage.
4 Guangdong adopted the OLVC in 1999. Before then, the province did not treat the village as a self-governing administrative unit, but rather as a delegated branch of the township government. This is why it had not adopted the law.
5 Notice that in Hunan, Henan, Sichuan and Jilin, the median year of the first election was earlier than the year of adopting the OLVC. It seems that these provinces waited for some experiments to provide the implementation details of the law.
6 The relationship between investment in village businesses and accountability is unclear. In many cases, village businesses are either pet projects or pork-barrels for village leaders. However, they can also benefit the villagers if the village committee is relatively clean.
7 After the abolition, villages had to get approval from the village conference to finance local public projects on a case-by-case basis.
8 It is understandable that the national Gini coefficients were larger than those in our sample villages because the latter are calculated within a much smaller
9 The fact that the marginal effect is larger than the total effect shows that there are correlations between elections and the control variables and these correlations reduce the impact of elections on the dependent variable.
10 My results do not tell us whether village cadres receive under-the-table income from the village.

14

China's resources demand at the turning point

Ross Garnaut and Ligang Song

China has contributed a majority of the increase in global demand for energy and metals over the early twenty-first century. In the first years of the century, with global economic growth subdued in the aftermath of the collapse of the technology boom, this moderated what would otherwise have been large falls in commodity prices. In more recent years, with recovery in the United States and Europe, and then the end of the long Japanese stagnation, it has been the driving force behind the lifting of energy and metals prices to levels that have only been seen before at high points of sustained global prosperity or, in the case of petroleum, major disruption to supplies entering world markets. This has transformed the immediate economic prospects of a wide range of countries with comparative advantage in the natural resource-based industries, including Australia, Papua New Guinea and Russia in China's Western Pacific neighbourhood, and beyond that in Central Asia, the Middle East, Africa and Latin America. At the same time, it has raised challenges for economies that are poorly endowed with natural resources, and questions about global environmental amenity.

How has the large recent lift in global energy and metals prices related to Chinese economic growth? Is it a temporary phenomenon, that will pass with some adjustment to Chinese or global demand or expansion of supply? Will scarcity and rising prices for resources, and the environmental management challenges with which they are associated, threaten the sustainability of rapid economic growth in China? In particular, how does it relate to the turning point in Chinese economic development?

An old story

No economically valuable resources are scarce in nature in an absolute, as distinct from an economic, sense. If demand rises for some source of energy or metal, the price tends to rise. This encourages substitution in demand. It causes the owners of existing mines to drive them harder to produce more through various modifications to production processes. It causes firms with relevant capacities to invest more in exploration for more potentially profitable mines, and to build new mines. Sometimes the development of new mines in new mining regions requires large investments in transport capacity and infrastructure, and even longer-term investments in the development of new economic institutions. Through some combination of adjustments to demand and supply, at some price and expectation of future prices, a balance will come to be struck.

It is usually possible for a mining firm to increase output modestly from established mines at relatively low cost. On the other hand, the establishment of new mines is usually highly expensive. It follows that if global demand grows at a moderate pace—say, at a couple of per cent per annum—relatively low prices will attract enough expansion of supply to keep the market in balance. But beyond some rate of growth in global demand for each commodity, prices will have to be high enough—or rather, expected future prices will need to be high enough—to cover not only the cost of producing minerals from established mines, but also to secure recovery of large capital expenditure in exploration and new mine development, together with a return on that investment that exceeds its supply price (Garnaut and Clunies Ross, 1983; Garnaut and Song, 2006; Garnaut, 2006).

It follows that world prices for energy and metals at any time tend to be on one of two tracks. If the growth in world demand is such that it can be met by incremental expansion from existing mines, average prices may be little higher than is necessary to cover the current costs of production in higher cost established mines. But if growth in world demand is expected to be so rapid that many new mines are required to meet it, prices will be on a much higher track, at levels that will justify large amounts of new investment.

The real world of minerals and energy prices is complicated by uncertainty about all of the factors that affect expectations of future demand, of costs of expanding future output, and therefore of price. Changes in expectations will generate large fluctuations in price around average levels of either the lower or higher track. The fluctuations in price are most extreme when fluctuations in either real conditions or expectations of them are so large that they cause switches from one of the average price tracks to the other. Fluctuations in energy and minerals prices are a management challenge both to economies with comparative disadvantage (importers of commodities) and advantage (exporters) in their production. In this chapter we focus on the longer term determinants of average prices rather than on their short-term fluctuations.

Over the history of modern economic development, there have been some long periods during which the rate of expansion of economic activity has been relatively strong in economies in the middle stages of industrialisation, and in which the intensity of energy and metals use has risen rapidly, and others when it has been tepid. To paint the historical picture with the broadest of brushes, the several decades before the First World War can be recognised as a period of strong economic expansion in newly industrialising economies (broken by a serious downturn in the early 1890s), with rapid industrialisation of Germany and the United States as they moved towards the global technological frontiers that were being advanced in the United Kingdom. The First World War ushered in several decades of relative stagnation—not everywhere or in every year, but generally and on average. Demand for energy and metals was temporarily boosted and then deflated by war and the associated destruction of economic capacity. The long stagnation was followed by a long boom, commencing with reconstruction in Japan and Europe through the 1950s. This was enhanced and extended by sustained rapid growth in Japan until that country, was approaching the global productivity frontiers in the early 1970s, with the extension ending sharply in 1974 with the oil crisis and recession. From then until the turn of the twenty-first century, rapid growth in newly industrialising economies in East Asia, including China from the beginnings of reform in the late 1970s, offered some leavening of a slowly growing global lump. But at first this was in relatively small economies and from a low base, so that the average contribution to global growth in demand for energy and metals was modest.

By the early twenty-first century, the Chinese economy had been growing rapidly for long enough to be a substantial component of the global economy. This was more obvious when purchasing power rather than national accounts at current exchange rates was used as a basis for comparison—and it is purchasing power that is relevant in assessing the impact of Chinese demand on global energy and metals markets (see the discussion in Wang (this volume, Chapter 3). Continued rapid growth in China from that time had a large impact on the balance between the world's supply and demand for a wide range of commodities.

The growth in Chinese demand derived to a considerable extent simply from growth in the economy. But it was enhanced by the stage of economic development that China had reached by the early twenty first century. The advancing state of urbanisation, the increase in economic activity and incomes to the point where comparative disadvantage in natural resource-based products was manifested in rapidly growing import propensities, the structural shift from comparative advantage in relatively labour-intensive to more capital-intensive production, and the increasing export orientation of the economy—features associated in some ways with the turning point in Chinese economic development—all magnified the effects of aggregate demand growth on pressures on global commodity markets.

Continued rapid growth in the Chinese economy from a much higher base and changes in economic structure interacted to increase China's import demand for a wide range of minerals rapidly. The effect was large enough to usher in a third period of exceptional growth in world demand for energy and minerals, tending to require relatively high prices to induce the necessary expansion of supply.

Why only tending to require high prices? Because the expected prices that are necessary to encourage an adequate level of investment depend on supply conditions in particular industries. Later we illustrate these generalisations with specific empirical examples, for copper and energy.

The turning point, structural change and demand for minerals in Northeast Asia

The 'turning point in economic development' derives from Lewis' (1954) celebrated article on economic development in a surplus labour economy (see also Chapters 1 and 2, this volume). The concept was elaborated and applied explicitly to the densely populated economies of East Asia, first of all Taiwan, by Fei and Ranis (1964), and tested for the Japanese case by Minami (1973).

The central idea is that in a densely populated and underdeveloped economy, with population concentrated in the rural sector, the average marginal product of labour in agriculture is very low, in the extreme zero. Marginal product in modern sector employment in urban areas is positive. Total economic output can proceed rapidly for a considerable time through the transfer of labour from low productivity employment in rural areas to more productive modern sector employment, without significantly increasing the cost of labour in either sector. During the potentially long period of extensive economic growth, the rapidly growing economy's comparative advantage remains concentrated in labour-intensive activities, which happen generally to require relatively low inputs of energy and minerals.

Rapid economic growth in the modern sector continues to absorb labour from the countryside, until labour is no longer in abundant supply. The removal of surplus labour from the countryside eventually raises per capita endowments of land and other economic resources to the point where marginal product as well as average output per worker rise significantly. Wages have to rise in modern sector employments if labour is to continue to be attracted from the countryside. By this stage, the scale of modern and urban employment is considerable, so that a given rate of increase is associated with large absolute increases in demand for labour. Real wages and urban purchasing power increase rapidly. Rising labour costs also force a shift in comparative advantage in international trade, from labour-intensive to more capital-intensive production using energy and metals much more intensively.

Something like this has happened in most of the countries that are now developed—excepting only those like Australia and New Zealand which were born into the modern economic world already rich from their abundant per capita natural resource endowment. The model fits most closely the Northeast Asian economies that have experienced rapid economic growth involving the absorption on a huge scale of surplus labour from rural areas into modern sector employment. It fits Northeast Asia most closely because Japan, the Republic of Korea and at least one coastal province of China with one third of the country's population are amongst the most densely populated on earth, with the poorest per capita endowments of natural resources; and because they each had great capacity for rapid economic growth once certain conditions had been met. Even Hong Kong through the decades of early industrialisation met the conditions of the surplus labour growth model, when the countryside from which it drew large amounts of unskilled labour was its mainland hinterland.

Much can be learned about the likely relationship between growth and demand for resources in China in the period ahead, from the experience of its Northeast Asian neighbours in their own periods of industrial transformation. Somewhere in the per capita income range of US$2,000–5,000 in today's values, the metals on and energy intensity of economic growth increased, and then stayed at high levels until, in Japan's case, at per capita incomes of about US$20,000, there was a marked reduction (Figure 14.1). Figure 14.3 shows that the general relationships observed in Northeast Asia between per capita incomes and metals' use has global analogues. Korea's intensity of metals and energy use has tended to be higher than Japan's at any given level of income. The metal intensity of production and growth has tended to be high by global standards in all Northeast Asian economies, and particularly high in Korea. China so far lies between the Japanese and Korean intensities, but closer to the higher Korean numbers. Low per capita resource endowments have made all Northeast Asian economies exceptionally dependent on imports. Energy intensity of production and growth has been lower than the global average in Japan, and higher in Korea. China's energy intensity so far has been even higher than Korea's, especially in the form of coal, in which China's domestic endowments are large.

Figure 14.1 **Total energy consumption intensity: China, Japan and Korea**

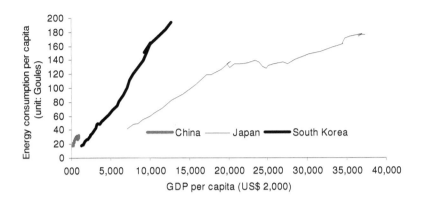

Note: Based on national accounts GDP at 2000 constant US dollar price.
Source: Authors' calculations with data from US Department of Energy and World Bank.

Figure 14.2 **China's coal consumption in comparison with East Asian economies**

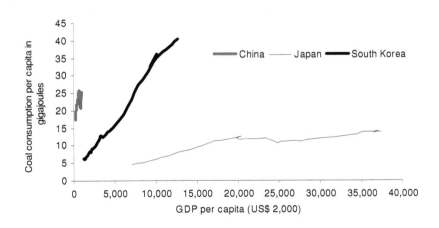

Note: Based on national accounts GDP at 2000 constant US dollar price.
Source: Authors' calculations with data from US Department of Energy and World Bank.

Figure 14.3 Steel demand and economic growth in Northeast Asia (using PPP exchange rates for China)

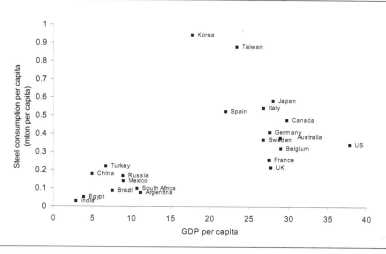

Source: Data from Westpac Economic Research.

What structural factors drive the differences in metals and energy intensities of growth at different stages of development and across countries? Three variables are especially powerful: the investment share of output; the export share of production; and the proportion of population living in urban areas.

Let us first examine the investment share of economic output. There is a general tendency for the energy and metals intensity of investment to be higher for investment than other components of national production (Table 14.1). This is a source of unusually high metals and energy intensity of production in Northeast Asian economies at their times of rapid growth as exceptionally high investment shares have been a characteristic of rapid growth in Northeast Asian.

China in recent years has been exceptional even in Northeast Asia for its high sustained investment shares of GDP (Figure 14.4). The exceptional Chinese investment share shows no sign of falling (Garnaut and Huang 2005), and can be expected to support unusually high metals and energy intensity of growth in China for the foreseeable future.

A second is the export orientation of production—beyond the point at which labour begins to become scarce, wages rise and comparative advantage and export specialisation shift from labour-intensive towards more capital-intensive products. China's export orientation is shaping up to be relatively high on a global scale.

Table 14.1 **China's shares of energy and metal products in investment, exports and outputs, 1997 and 2000** (per cent)

Sector	Investment		Export		Total output	
	1997	2000	1997	2000	1997	2000
Coal and petroleum	2.09	5.58	1.51	1.92	1.91	3.35
Metal product	11.29	13.56	6.94	7.81	6.25	6.28

Source: Calculated using the Input-Output Tables of China: 1997 and 2001

Within Northeast Asia, export orientation is much greater than Japan, but less than Korea. It is still rising strongly, and will continue to do so, through a period in which most of the growth in Chinese exports is outside the labour-intensive items that dominated in the early period of rapid internationally oriented growth.

A third is the level of urbanisation. Figure 14.5 shows the general tendency for per capita use of steel to rise with the proportion of people living in urban areas, until a ratio of around 60 per cent has been reached. China's early industrialisation was characterised by articificial constraints on rural-urban migration. As a consequence, the urban proportion of the Chinese population remains considerably lower than in other countries, historically and in the contemporary world, at similar levels of development. The absolute constraints on movement have now been removed for practical purposes, but disincentives to movement remain (Chapter 10 by Du, Greogory and Meng, this volume). The removal of the absolute constraints, the likely amelioration of the current disincentives, and the large and increasing differentials between rural and living standards are likely to lead to an increase in the rate of migration in the years ahead, and to an exceptional contribution from rapid urbanisation to growth in demand for metals and energy.

For all of these reasons, the strong growth in demand for metals and energy in China is likely to continue through the period of rapid industrial transformation that will be associated with strong economic growth over the next two decades. The increasing absolute and relative size of the Chinese economy will magnify the impact on world markets beyond the high levels experienced in the recent past (Figures 14.6 and 14.7). At the end of this period, on the assumption of no dislocation to the Chinese growth process, China is likely to account for greater consumption of energy and metals than all of the currently industrial economies today.

It may be useful to underline some of the points made in this chapter about growth in demand for resources in general, with a closer look at copper and energy.

Figure 14.4 **Long-run investment shares of GDP: China, Japan, Korea and India, 1965–2004**

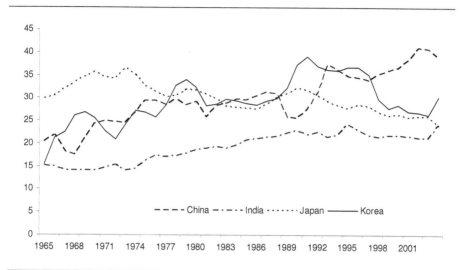

Source: Calculated using the data from Garnaut and Huang (2005) and the World Bank.

Figure 14.5 **Steel consumption per capita with urbanisation**

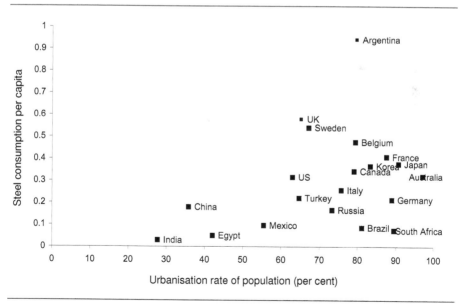

Note: Urbanisation is defined as the ratio of urban population in total population.
Source: Plotted using the data from Westpac Economic Research.

The case of copper

Per capita global copper consumption has been highly sensitive to average global incomes. It has fallen sharply in any setback to incomes in depression and recession, and risen with incomes growth (Figure 14.8). The periods of most rapid consumption growth have been those when large economies have been experiencing rapid industrialisation, at a time of relatively buoyant global economic conditions. The rapid growth in Japan in the 1960s to 1974 is the most recent completed episode of such accelerated demand growth. The world seems to have entered another such period with the rapid industrialisation of China in the early twenty first century.

Figure 14.9 makes the point that there is no long-term average copper price. The price in real terms can be well above or well below the long historical average according to whether the rate of increase in global demand is such as to require large additions of new capacity in mining. The periods up to and including the First World War and that from the late 1950s to 1974 stand out for the high average prices. The periods between the two World Wars and the last quarter of the twentieth century stand out for their relatively low average prices. Recent including current prices take us back into the range of the 1890s and early twentieth century, and beyond the experience of the Japan boom of the 1960s and early 1970s to the historical peaks.

The extent to which the recent strong growth in demand is a 'China boom' is illustrated in Figure 14.10. As a result, the China share of total world demand for major industrial metals has risen steeply—although not for several metals in 2004—when demand growth was checked temporarily by controls on investment expenditure (Figure 14.4). The increase in the Chinese share of global consumption over the past decade means that a given rate of growth in Chinese demand will have a larger impact on growth in world demand.

The case of energy

China is a substantial oil producer and by far the world's largest importer of coal. Unlike the case of metals, energy demand has therefore been met mainly from domestic resources. Indeed, China was a significant oil exporter in the early years of reform, and remained a coal exporter in the early twenty-first century. China became a large net importer of energy for the first time in 2005 (Figure 14.11).

China's energy demand has been growing more rapidly than economic output since 2002. This follows several years of relatively low energy intensity in economic growth, as distortions in the price system were removed with other parts of the

Figure 14.6 **Shares of petroleum consumption in the world: Japan, Korea, China and total Northeast Asia, 1960–2005** (per cent)

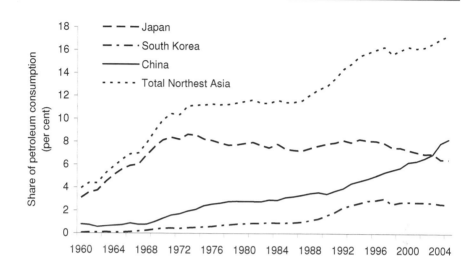

Source: Calculated using the data from US Department of Energy.

Figure 14.7 **China's shares of incremental world demand for four metals, 1995–2005** (per cent)

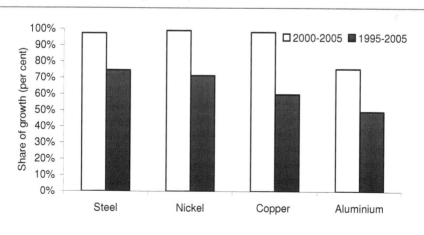

Source: Plotted using the data from Macquarie Research Metals and Mining 2004 and data for 2004 and 2005 are from Chinese Mining and Resource (http://www.ChinaMR.net).

Figure 14.8 **World copper consumption per capita, 1905–2005**

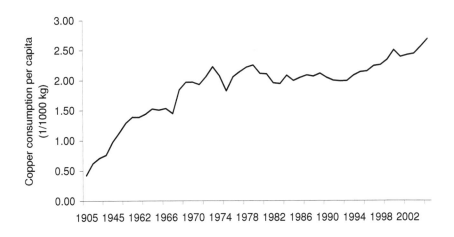

Source: Plotted using data from Macquarie Research Metals and Mining 2004.

Figure 14.9 **The copper price of the world in 2004 US dollars, 1895–August 2006** (US dollar/tonne)

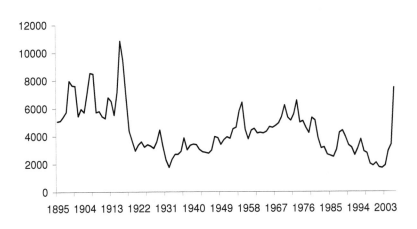

Source: Plotted using the data from Westpac Economic Research with authors' updating.

legacy of central planning. There is considerable scope for increased energy efficiency in future, including through the bringing of all prices to international levels, although considerably less than the gains that have already been achieved.

We have already noted that in Northeast Asia, high energy intensity in economic growth has been associated with rapid urbanisation, high investment shares of output, and high and increasing export orientation after the turning point in economic development. The high energy intensity of growth through the middle stages of industrialisation has been observed in other economies as well. For example, it was present in the United Kingdom through the middle decades of the nineteenth century (Humphrey and Stanislaw, 1979:41), with energy intensity of growth later falling to relatively low levels.

Over the past half century, the relationship between global petroleum demand in particular, and global prices, has been very different from the corresponding relationship for metals. For a long period, from the end of the Second World War until around the time of the oil crisis in 1973–74, global demand grew strongly, while prices in real terms were stable at low levels, or falling (Figures 14.12 and 14.13). The difference derives from the special circumstances of supply in the petroleum industry. The new political circumstances of the Middle East after the

Figure 14.10 **China's shares of demand growth for four metals, 1995–2005**

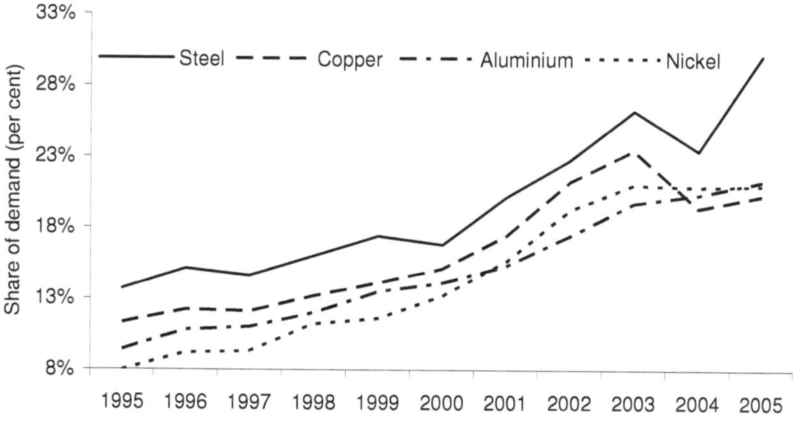

Source: Plotted using the data from Macquarie Research Metals and Mining 2004 and data for 2004 and 2005 are collected from websites of Chinese Mining and Resource (www.ChinaMR.net)

Figure 14.11 **Energy production and consumption in China, 1989–2005** (100 million metric tonnes oil equivalent)

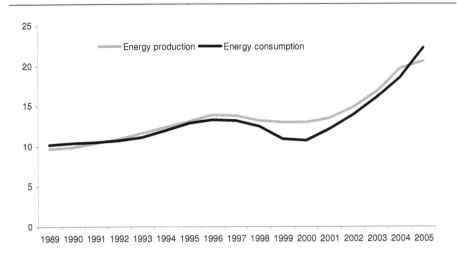

Source: China Industrial Maps (2005) and authors' own calculation using the data from BP energy statistics for 2005.

Figure 14.12 **Growth rates of demand for petroleum: Northeast Asia and the world, 1961–2005** (per cent)

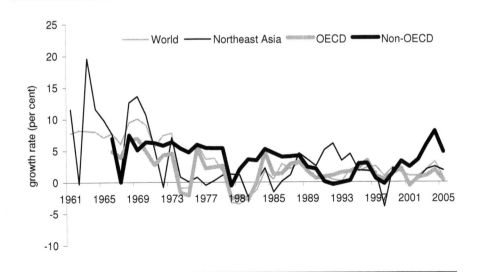

Source: Calculated using the data from US Department of Energy.

Second World War were conducive to rapid expansion of oil supply capacity. Uncertainty about the continuation of those conditions encouraged rapid rates of depletion of known reserves, even when prices were judged to be lower than average expectations of prices in later years.

The industrialisation of Japan and later Korea therefore occurred in an environment of abundant cheap oil. The Northeast Asian share of global oil consumption rose strongly, at first mainly through Japanese demand, and later through Korea.

The oil market began to tighten in advance of the OPEC-led restrictions on supply in the early 1970s—indeed, this tightening can be seen as establishing the conditions for effective action by the OPEC cartel. Constrained supply growth and higher prices were reflected quickly in lower rates of demand growth. Chinese demand growth became a major element in the global petroleum story from the mid 1990s, and especially from 2005 when China suddenly became a large net importer of energy, mainly in the form of petroleum. High growth and energy intensity of growth and the fact that almost all of the increment in demand will now be met from imports ensures that the Chinese influence on the world petroleum market will continue to grow. That influence is correctly credited for much of the price increases in 2005 and early 2006. The China influence will be greater in future, mainly for petroleum, but also for natural resources that are required in a wide range of alternative energy sources, notably uranium.

The Chinese impact on global markets

So long as the established path of rapid economic growth in China is not disrupted by internal or external political dislocation, the pressure of Chinese demand on global resources markets is in its early and moderate stages. Lin (Chapter 4, this volume) discusses the likelihood that Chinese output will quadruple over the next two decades, and the possibility that it will grow at a rate that will cause it to increase almost eight-fold over that same period. From one perspective that is not at all surprising or even novel—the greater of these prospects requires a rate of growth that was close to being achieved over two decades and longer by Japan, Korea, Taiwan and Hong Kong and Singapore, and by China itself in the first quarter century of reform continuing to today. The larger current gap between domestic productivity levels and the world frontiers, the unprecedentedly high investment rates (Garnaut and Huang 2005), and the extraordinarily rapid rate of integration into the international economy (at least in comparison with Japan and Korea) suggest the reasonableness of higher expectations.

For reasons explained in this chapter, China is now entering a stage of growth in which the relationship between incremental output and incremental demand for energy

Figure 14.13 **Crude oil price adjusted for inflation, 1946–July 2006** (constant 2005 US$)

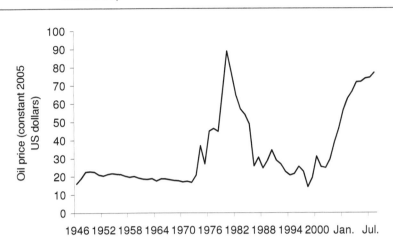

Source: Plotted using the data from http://www.iea.org/Textbase/stats/oilresult.asp and www.eia.doe.gov/.

and metals is exceptionally strong. As China's absolute and proportionate economic size increases over time, the same rate of growth, and the same intensity of resource use in economic output, generates absolutely and proportionately larger effects on total global demand. And with Chinese domestic production of almost all resource-based commodities rising at a substantially lower rate than domesticdemand as a proportion of global production, consumption and international trade.

The interaction of these realities will cause Chinese pressure on world markets for resources over the next two decades at least to be proportionately larger and maintained over a longer period than that exerted by industrialising Japan in the 1950s and 1960s. The increase in metals' demand over this period may be comparable to the total of the industrial world's demand today. The increment in Chinese energy demand may be proportionately a bit more modest, because of the exceptional conditions that support current North American demand, the supply constraints on energy in its most economically convenient form (liquid petroleum) and the global environmental conditions that may constrain the use of energy in its present form.

It is therefore likely that global prices will need to be sustained on the high track for the foreseeable future—at average levels that provide incentives for continued rapid growth in supply over a long period.

How will those prices compare with the exceptional levels of August 2006?

Metals' prices will not be as high on average as they are at present, because current prices provide ample incentives for new investment and adequate expansion of global production capacity. But they will remain on average much higher in real terms—for most metals, perhaps twice as high—as they did during the slow global growth in global metals' demand of the last quarter of the twentieth century.

The story for energy prices is complicated by the geological and economic constraints on petroleum supply, especially in liquid form. The balancing of global demand (augmented by rapid growth in China), would require continually rising liquid petroleum prices if there were no opportunities for substitution. However, at current prices, a wide range of capital-intensive substitutes for liquid petroleum are economically viable—conversion of gas to liquids, coal to liquids, oil from shale and tar sands, bio-fuels of various kinds and, for the generation of electricity, nuclear energy, so long as markets come to reflect the view that oil prices of at least forty to fifty dollars—two thirds of today's levels—are here to stay. Over time, it is likely that energy prices will head back towards those levels, although the uncertainty about future prices and commercially new technologies and the immense capital requirements could hold prices up above the average long-term levels for many years. In the meantime, with continued strong pressure on global oil supplies, the concentration of global production in locations that are vulnerable to political instability and disruption of supply will generate spikes of higher prices from time to time.

For China, the relatively rich per capita endowment of coal resources will, in the absence of an effective international regime to control 'greenhouse' emissions, support disproportionately large expansion of energy supply from that source. That would go some limited way to ameliorating Chinese demand pressures on global energy markets.

Resource limits to growth?

The most important constraint on metals and energy supplies being available to meet the 'natural' growth in Chinese demand is environmental (see Chapter 17 by McKibbin, this volume). Local environmental problems within China are likely to be solved over time through changes in preferences between environmental amenity and other forms of consumption, and associated reallocation of priorities, as incomes rise. The global environmental pressures, and especially global warming problems described as the 'greenhouse effect', are less tractable.

The costs through the greenhouse effect of one country's consumption of fossil fuels are mainly external to that country. It follows that in the absence of an effective international regime with the effect of internalising the external costs, economic rather than environmental considerations will limit their use. In these circumstances, China will meet a high proportion of its energy requirements from fossil fuels in relatively damaging forms, particularly coal, much of it with low ratios of energy generation to greenhouse emissions. It is likely that, within two decades, Chinese emissions would exceed those of all of the currently industrial countries together. The environmental damage would be immense, but for the world as a whole, and not particularly for China.

The likelihood that other large developing countries, first of all Brazil and India, would be generating rapidly increasing quanta of emissions, and over time becoming large sources of pressures for global change, would exacerbate the global problem. India is currently well behind China as a source of emissions. Continued rapid growth at the rate of the post reform era (that is, through the 1990s and early twentieth century) will mean that India in two decades time will potentially be as large a source of greenhouse emissions as China today, with the likelihood of continuing to expand at a rapid rate after the rate of increase has eased in China.

Such statement of the obvious facts argues its own case for an effective international greenhouse regime. So far in human history, however, necessity has not been the mother of invention in the field of international institutions. But if an effective international regime were established, it would greatly increase pressure to expand capacity to supply energy from sources other than fossil fuels, to a point that would require even higher prices for energy than those that are in contemplation as a result of Chinese and global economic developments.

Under any of the possible scenarios, China's imports of metals and energy from the rest of the world will rise to levels well beyond those of any other country at any time. This alone will give China a powerful interest in political stability throughout the world, including around the global transport networks through which its requirements would be supplied. China will have powerful incentives to innovate in the development of the political and economic institutions that would encourage production of minerals and their substitutes for world markets. It would be one more factor compelling China into a global political role, whatever the proclivities of its leadership from time to time.

15
Economic growth and environmental pollution: a panel data analysis

Bao Qun and Shuijun Peng

The relationship between economic growth and environmental quality has been debated widely for a long period; controversy goes back to the debates about the limits to growth at the end of the 1960s. At one extreme, environmentalists and the economists of the Club of Rome (Meadows et al. 1972) argued that the finiteness of environmental resources would prevent economic growth from continuing forever and argued for a steady-state economy with a zero growth rate to avoid dramatic ecological scenarios in the future. At the other extreme, some economists claimed that technological progress and the substitutability of natural with man-made capital would reduce dependence on natural resources and allow an everlasting growth path. As Beckerman (1992) concluded, 'there is clear evidence that, although economic growth usually leads to environmental degradation in the early stages of the process, in the end the best—and probably the only—way to attain a decent environment in most countries is to become rich.' Bhagawati (1993) wrote, 'economic growth may be a precondition for environmental improvement.' So, according to Panayotou (1993), 'growth could be a powerful way for improving environmental quality in developing countries'.

These theoretical debates induced a number of researchers to examine the systematic relationship between income change and the environment in the past decade. Substantial empirical evidence suggested that the relationships between many forms of pollution and national income followed an inverted-U curve relationship: environmental degradation gets worse in the early stages of growth, but eventually reaches a peak and starts declining as income exceeds a certain threshold level. This inverted-U shape has been defined as the Environmental Kuznets Curve (EKC) after the work of Simon Kuznets (1955), who first observed a similar relationship between inequality and economic development.[1] The logic of EKC relation is intuitively appealing. In the first stage of industrialisation, pollution grows rapidly because high priority is given to increasing material output, and people are more interested in jobs and income than clean air and water (Dasgupta et al. 2002). The rapid growth inevitably results in greater use of natural resources and emission of pollutants, which in turn put more pressure on the environment. People are too poor to pay for pollution abatement and/or disregard environmental consequences of growth. In later stages of industrialisation, as incomes rise, people value the environment more, regulatory institutions become more effective and pollution levels decline. Thus, the EKC hypothesis posits a well-defined relationship between the level of economic activity and environmental pressure (defined as including the level of concentration of pollution or flow of emissions and the depletion of resources).

Following Grossman and Krueger's (1991) groundbreaking study of the potential impact of the North American Free Trade Agreement (NAFTA) on environmental quality through three different channels (that is, scale effects, composition effects and technological effects), an extensive literature has developed reporting EKC estimates and discussing their implications. Earlier papers by Shafik and Bandyopadhyay (1992), Panayotou (1993), Selden and Song (1994) and Grossman and Krueger (1995) presented initial evidence that some pollutants followed an EKC pattern. These findings then led to a naive idea that economic growth is, by nature, the remedy to environmental problems. However, recent researchers have focused on the effects of different pollutant indicators on environmental degradation, the use of a wider range of explanatory variables than income alone and the estimation of different models (see survey in Stern 1998; Ekins 2000; de Bruyn 2000; Panayotou 2000; and Dinda 2004). Within this literature, the EKC results are not generally reproduced.

One important critique of the existing empirical EKC studies is that they are based on a single polynomial equation model in which there is no feedback effect from the environment to economic growth and therefore environmental damage is invariably viewed only as the outcome of economic growth.[2] Among all of the empirical EKC literature, the effect of economic growth on environmental quality is estimated directly. However, it is well known that, in addition to the effect of economic growth on environmental quality, environmental degradation might impact directly or indirectly on economic growth through multiple channels. First, environmental degradation might act as a negative externality, directly reducing production through the restraints of limited natural resource inputs and the productivity of man-made capital and workers (Barbier 1994; Lopez 1994; Smulder

1999; de Bruyn 2000). Examples are the loss of working days due to health problems, the corrosion of industrial equipment due to polluted air or water, and product voided because of being polluted. Second, since permitting greater levels of emissions might increase the availability of human and other capital for production, when firms abate pollution emissions, their production costs are raised and outputs are reduced. Generally, economic growth and environmental quality are determined jointly (Perrings 1987). Therefore, it is inappropriate to estimate a single equation model assuming unidirectional causality from economic development to environmental quality change. As Stern (1998) concluded, '[E]stimating single equation relationship by ordinary least squares where simultaneity exists produces biased and inconsistent estimates'. Hence, a simultaneous equations model might be more appropriate for understanding the environment–income relationship.

As de Bruyn (2000) pointed out, however, there have been few empirical studies that estimated the simultaneous relationship between income change and environmental quality. This has been due mainly to the difficulty of model specification and a lack of available environmental data. The first purpose of this chapter is to formulate a simultaneous equations model between per capita income and pollution emission and then to estimate the EKC in China. Based on theoretical implication, a simultaneous two-equation model is constructed. The first (pollution) equation is a polynomial equation used commonly in the EKC empirical literature. The second (income) equation manipulates the pollutant emission as an input in an extended Cobb-Douglas production function. After the simultaneous model is constructed, the second purpose of this study is to investigate the contribution of pollution to production activities and, consequently, to economic growth. In recently developed endogenous growth models, factors such as fertility choice, physical and human capital accumulation, research and development, and pollution have been proposed as the means of explaining output growth. While pollution has been considered important theoretically among these factors (the role of inputs, the adverse impacts on labour, man-made inputs and production) no studies have yet examined empirically the effects of pollution on production in China. The third purpose of our chapter is to investigate pollution control variables and use improved data for testing the EKC hypothesis in China. Recently, abundant provincial macro-data have become available in the *Chinese Statistical Yearbook* and the *Chinese Environmental Statistical Yearbook*. Thus, this study uses Chinese provincial data from 1996 to 2000 for our empirical analysis. Most of the previous EKC studies focus on using cross-country panel data to estimate the relationship between per capita income and various pollution indicators. In this study we move from a cross-country study to an individual country's cross-region study.

Two water pollutants (industrial water pollution emissions and chemical oxygen demand [COD] in industrial water pollution), three air pollutants (industrial dust emissions, industrial smoke emissions, and sulphur dioxide emissions) and one solid pollutant (industrial solid waste) are examined here. The relative abundance of a pollutant variety makes the income–pollution relationship caused by different pollutants comparable. Moreover, unlike other researchers, we study more pollution indicators and add additional important pollution control policy variables—such as the share of agriculture and manufacturing in the total output, the degree of openness, and government pollution abatement policies—into pollution equations to explain the impact of those variables on China's environmental quality change.

Model specification and data description

Based on the discussions in the previous section, we specify the simultaneous two-equation model of income and the environment as follows to estimate the relationship between pollution emissions and per capita income in China

$$\begin{cases} P_{it} = c_i + \gamma_1 Y_{it} + \gamma_2 Y_{it}^2 + \gamma_3 X_{it} + \mu_{it} & (1) \\ Y_{it} = \alpha_i + \beta_1 P_{it} + \beta_2 K_{it} + \beta_3 H_{it} + \beta_4 L_{it} + \varepsilon_{it} & (2) \end{cases}$$

Equation 1 represents the pollution equation, where P_{it} denotes pollutant emission in province i for year t; Y_{it} denotes per capita income in province i for year t; c_i is the specific effect on province i; and μ_{it} is a normally distributed error term. Here, income (Y_{it}) functions as a surrogate variable representing the aggregate effects of those direct and indirect driving forces on pollution. Of particular importance are the signs and magnitudes of g_1 and g_2 in Equation 1. Pollution emissions can be said to exhibit an inverted-U EKC relationship with per capita income if g_1 is greater than zero and g_2 is less than zero, and if the turning point, $-g_1/2g_2$, is a 'reasonably' low number. In addition to the income terms, we add other important variables into the pollution equation, such as trade, industrial structure, technological progress and environmental policy, to investigate the impact of various exogenous variables on the EKC relationship. Here, X_{it} represents this kind of control variable.

Equation 2 is an extended Cobb-Douglas production function. In this specification, output is a function of pollution emissions (P_{it}), physical capital (K_{it}), raw labour (L_{it}) and human capital (H_{it}). Here, a_i is the specific effect on province i; and e_{it} is a normally distributed error term. It is expected that all but the pollution variable should contribute positively to output growth. Here too, pollution (P_{it}) functions as a surrogate variable representing the aggregate effects of those direct and indirect driving forces on production.

Data description

We study the interactions between pollution emissions and per capita income using China's provincial data during 1996–2000. The form of panel data used provides us with a larger number of sample data than only time-series or cross-sectional data sets. We chose the sample period from 1996 to 2000 because average educational attainments in each province were available only since 1996. Thirty provinces are included in our sample, excluding Tibet, since the time-series data of some key indicators in Tibet Province were unavailable.

Pollution indicators are chosen in this study as follows: two water pollutants (industrial water pollution emissions and COD in industrial water pollution), three air pollutants (industrial dust emissions, industrial smoke emissions and sulphur dioxide emissions) and one solid pollutant (industrial solid waste), from 1996 to 2000 in 30 of China's provinces and metropolitan cities. Table 15.1 lists the description of all the pollutant variables and our data sources.

Income per capita is used as the independent variable instead of the total national income, since changes in income per capita can better capture the real impact of income levels on environmental quality. In this chapter, income per capita is measured as GDP per capita, which has been deflated, with 1996 as the base year price. The data sources of GDP per capita are the various issues of the *Chinese Statistical Yearbook*.

There are a number of pollution control variables. The first are government environmental regulation policies. It has been generally acknowledged that environmental regulation and monitoring by governments plays an important role in environmental pollution control. The cumulative number of environmental standards issued by local governments in each province (symbolised as *nums*) is used to measure the impact of environmental policies on pollution emissions, including water pollution and air pollution standards. The data sources are various issues of the *Chinese Environmental Statistical Yearbook*. The second variable is the regional degree of openness. Based on the theory of comparative advantage, international trade affects environmental quality differently in different countries since pollution-intensive industries generally shift from industrial countries to developing ones, or from those countries which conduct stronger environmental regulation to those whose environmental regulation is much weaker (Copeland and Taylor 1995). Therefore, the inverted-U shape of the EKC identifies the different international specialisation patterns among different countries. Industrial countries generally specialise in those industries with less pollution emissions, while developing countries specialise in resource-intensive or energy-intensive products

Table 15.1 Six indicators of environmental pollution

Pollutant	Unit	Sign
Industrial water pollution emissions	100 billion kilograms	*indwater*
Chemical oxygen demand in industrial water pollution	10 million kilograms	*indcod*
Industrial dust emissions	10 million kilograms	*inddust*
Industrial smoke emissions	10 million kilograms	*indsmoke*
Sulphur dioxide emissions	10 million kilograms	SO_2
Industrial solid waste	10 million kilograms	*indsolid*

Sources: Various issues of *Chinese Statistical Yearbook* and *Chinese Environmental Statistical Yearbook* during 1996–2000.

(Cole et al. 2000), which is usually concluded as the Pollution Haven Hypothesis. The degree of openness (*open*), which is the ratio of total trade volume to GDP in each province, is used to measure the effects of international trade on environmental pollution, and the data sources are the various issues of the *Chinese Statistical Yearbook*. The third variable is the technology progress effect, which means that with the enhancement of income levels and economic development, it is possible to spend more on research and development of cleaner technology and more environmental abatement technologies might be adopted; therefore, environmentally friendly technological progress and research and development expenditure might directly help to decrease pollution emissions. We use environment-related research and development expenditure to measure such technology effects, which are symbolised as *envrd*, and the data sources are various issues of the *Chinese Environmental Statistical Yearbook*. Finally, we also consider the effect of industrial structural change on pollution emissions since there is a close relationship between the two. In the initial take-off stage of industrialisation, rapid economic development usually occurs, with an increasing share of manufacturing among the total national output, leading to the excessive depletion of natural resources and the rapid increase of industrial pollution emissions (Dasgupta et al. 2002). With the adjustment and update of economic growth patterns and industrial structures, the share of manufacturing in the total output will remain constant or even decline, while the share of tertiary industries will rise. Therefore, since economic development depends less on energy and natural resource inputs, and technological advances and productivity improvement play key roles in economic growth, environmental protection pressures will be alleviated due to such changes in growth patterns. To capture the impact of industrial structural change on pollution emissions, we use the share of agriculture and manufacturing in the total output, symbolised as *shagri* and *shaind* respectively. The data sources are various issues of the *Chinese Statistical Yearbook*.

The effects of the following factor inputs as well as environmental pollutants on provincial economic growth are also investigated in our output equation. The first is physical capital stock (K_{it}), and we cite the estimation data of Zhang et al. (2004) on China's provincial physical capital stock from 1952 to 2000 to measure the effect of physical capital stock change on provincial economic growth. The role of human capital investment is also considered. As usual (Barro and Lee 2000), the average educational attainment is used to measure the growth effect of human capital accumulation, which is the ratio of total educational attainment to the total population. Following Wang (2000), the education attainment is specified as six years for primary school graduates, and nine, 12 and 16 years for junior middle school graduates, senior middle school graduates and university graduates respectively. Finally, we also consider the effects of labour inputs (L_{it}) on provincial economic growth, which are measured as the total employment in each province, and the data sources are various issues of the *Chinese Statistical Yearbook*.

Empirical estimation and results analysis

For our estimation method consideration, we chose a feasible GLS specification (FGLS) to consider the presence of cross-section heteroskedasticity, that is, cross-section weights are used to correct for the cross-section heteroskedasticity. First, we perform preliminary estimations to obtain cross-section specific residual vectors, and then we use these to form estimates of the cross-specific variances. The estimates of the variances are then used in a weighted least squares procedure to form the FGLS estimates. A two-stage least squares estimation method is also used since the output and pollution equations are estimated simultaneously. Meanwhile, considering the significant regional disparity between economic development and other economic indicators, cross-section specific effects are also included in our estimations to capture the specific regional disparity.

Simultaneous estimation results for six pollution indicators

Estimation results of the simultaneity model of economic growth and environmental quality changes are provided in Tables 15.2 and 15.3 respectively, with the upper set of regressions being the pollution equations. As shown in Tables 15.2 and 15.3, in the pollution equations various pollutants are functions of GDP per capita as well as a series of pollution control variables, including the degree of openness and changes in industrial structure. The lower set of regressions is the output equation, among which we regress output levels on three commonly used production factor variables, including physical capital, human capital and labour, as well as flows of pollutants.

Analysis of pollution equations estimations

As for the estimated results of six pollution indicators, we focus on two issues: whether there is a Kuznets inverted-U curve relationship between China's economic growth and environmental quality change; and, what is the effect of various pollution control variables on the emission of various pollutants?

We first analyse the effects of economic growth on the quality of China's environment. According to our simultaneous estimation results in Tables 15.2 and 15.3, among the six pollution indicators we have chosen, five fit into the inverted-U shape curve, except $indcod_{it}$, which has a U-shape relationship with economic growth. A further analysis of the turning points of the inverted-U curve demonstrates two interesting findings. Firstly, the turning point of GDP per capita can be calculated as 33,010 yuan per capita ($indwater_{it}$), 34,040 yuan per capita ($indsolid_{it}$), 32,200 yuan per capita ($indsmoke_{it}$), 32,690 yuan per capita ($inddust_{it}$) and 32,850 yuan per capita (SO_{2it}). It can be concluded that the threshold values of GDP per capita along China's Kuznets inverted-U curve generally are above 30,000 yuan per capita. Interestingly, during our sample period, the real GDP per capita for the 30 provinces was much lower than the threshold values we have estimated here. Comparing the GDP per capita for the top five provinces, (Table 15.4) with the calculated threshold values, we conclude that even though a Kuznets inverted-U curve exists for China's environmental quality and its economic growth, the real provincial GDP per capita hasn't reached the threshold value of the EKC yet. Specifically, the average GDP per capita in 2000 was only 8,490 yuan (1996 as the base year price), nowhere near the estimated turning point of the EKC. Even for Shanghai, which has the highest of our estimated inverted-U curve. Therefore, although our estimated results support China's EKC hypothesis, as far as China's real GDP per capita is concerned, the economy still lies on the left side of the inverted-U curve; that is, a further increase in GDP per capita will lead to an increase in the amount of pollution emissions, and the cost of rapid economic growth will be the degradation of the environment. The simultaneous-equation estimation method considers the feedback on environmental pollution on China's economic growth, identifying a more realistic relationship between economic growth and environmental quality than single-equation estimations. In addition, the turning points of China's EKC that we estimated could not be calculated using single-equation estimations.

We can also compare our estimated turning points for China's EKC with those of other authors. Table 15.5 lists some of them.[3] Interestingly, compared with

Table 15.2 **Simultaneous estimation results on water pollutants and solid pollutants**

Pollution equation estimation results

	Water pollutants		Solid pollutants
	$indwater_{it}$	$indcod_{it}$	$indsolid_{it}$
Y_{it}	1.393 (1.675)*	−4.804 (−8.038)***	107.87 (1.821)*
Y_{it}^2	−0.211 (−1.997)**	2.292 (7.192)***	−15.834 (2.179)**
$nums_{it}$	0.021 (1.256)	0.142 (0.591)	−3.251 (−0.635)
$open_{it}$	−0.122 (−1.986)**	−0.369 (−5.570)***	−1.901 (−1.134)
$envrd_{it}$	−0.028 (−2.382)**	−0.159 (−3.047)***	−0.638 (−3.053)***
$shagri_{it}$	0.142 (5.933)***	−0.209 (−2.371)**	0.861 (0.762)
$shaind_{it}$	0.166 (7.211)***	0.049 (0.347)	2.752 (1.985)**
$adjust - R^2$	0.578	0.395	0.441
Shape of the curve	Inverted-U curve	U-curve	Inverted-U curve
Turning point (10,000 yuan per capita)	3.301	3.229	3.404

Output equation estimation results

	Y_{it}	Y_{it}	Y_{it}
$indwater_{it}$	−0.0021 (−5.534)***	n.a.	n.a.
$indcod_{it}$	n.a.	−0.0012 (−2.583)***	n.a.
$indsolid_{it}$	n.a.	n.a.	−0.0041 (−0.153)
K_{it}	0.048 (18.037)***	0.046 (15.471)***	0.046 (15.104)***
H_{it}	0.0936 (6.158)***	0.0922 (5.183)***	0.0955 (5.498)***
L_{it}	0.00041 (1.513)	−0.00025 (−0.125)	−0.00035 (−0.176)
$Adjust - R^2$	0.764	0.791	0.618

Note: The values in the parentheses are t-statistic of the estimated coefficient, and ***, **, * indicate that a coefficient estimate is significantly greater than zero at 1 per cent, 5 per cent or 10 per cent respectively.

other estimations, it can be concluded that China's environmental Kuznets inverted-U curve has the turns at much lower levels of GDP per capita. China may surmount its EKC when it is still at a low stage of economic development, since the values of our estimated turning points are obviously lower than those reported in Table 15.5. In Table 15.5, the turning points of GDP per capita generally range from US$5,000 to US$20,000. For example, List and Gallet (1999) use state-level data in the United States and find that estimated turning points at US$22,675 GDP per capita. On one hand, such comparisons demonstrate that the EKC hypothesis depends strongly on the pollution indicators, sample data and estimation methods the authors have used. On the other hand, it reminds us that even for developing countries such as China, it is possible that the threshold value of GDP per capita

Table 15.3 Simultaneous estimation results on air pollutants

Pollution equation estimation results

	Air pollutants		
	$indsmoke_{it}$	$inddust_{it}$	SO_{2it}
Y_{it}	17.710	43.167	6.878
	(1.894)*	(1.979)**	(1.755)*
Y_{it}^2	−2.751	−6.595	−1.035
	(−1.998)**	(−1.986)**	(−1.748)*
$nums_{it}$	−0.604	−0.791	−0.141
	(−1.084)	(−0.705)	(−0.299)
$open_{it}$	−0.676	−1.152	0.092
	(−3.093)***	(−2.653)***	(0.601)
$envrd_{it}$	−0.549	−0.532	−0.548
	(−5.430)***	(−1.843)*	(−5.863)***
$shagri_{it}$	−1.192	−1.446	−0.439
	(−3.388)***	(−2.249)**	(−2.139)**
$shaind_{it}$	−0.362	0.113	0.153
	(−0.981)	(2.026)**	(1.978)**
$adjust - R^2$	0.416	0.517	0.499
Shape of the curve	Inverted-U curve	Inverted-U curve	Inverted-U curve
Turning point (10,000 yuan per capita)	3.22	3.269	3.285

Output equation estimation results

	Y_{it}	Y_{it}	Y_{it}
$indsmoke_{it}$	−0.00046	..	..
	(−0.153)		
$inddust_{it}$	..	−0.00096	..
		(4.988)***	
SO_{2it}	n.a.	n.a.	0.00019
			(0.473)
K_{it}	0.046	0.046	0.045
	(14.531)***	(14.279)***	(14.921)***
H_{it}	0.091	0.088	0.093
	(5.098)***	(4.787)***	(5.351)***
L_{it}	−0.00021	−0.00062	−0.00068
	(−0.115)	(−0.364)	(−0.314)
$adjust - R^2$	0.713	0.769	0.694

Note: The values in the parentheses are t-statistic of estimated coefficients, and ***, **, * indicate that a coefficient estimate is significantly greater than zero at 1 per cent, 5 per cent or 10 per cent respectively.

along the EKC can be reached in a relatively low stage of economic development.

Observing the effects of other pollution control variables on pollution emission, we can better understand the reason why China might reach the turning point of its EKC with a lower level of GDP per capita.

First consider the effect of government environmental policies, measured as the cumulative number of environmental regulations issued by local governments. It has been acknowledged that it is necessary for governments to regulate and monitor pollution emissions by individual firms. However, our estimations do not show strong support for the positive role of such government policies. Among the six pollutants we have chosen, the estimated coefficient of $nums_{it}$ is not statistically significant and the signs of $nums_{it}$ also vary. Two possible explanations for this are provided here. First, whether a government's environmental policies are effective essentially depends on the expectation and response of individual firms, especially those that produce pollution-intensive products. In addition, information asymmetry between governments and individual firms increases the cost of environmental monitoring. What is more, in order to implement stricter environmental regulations, governments usually have to make a decision based on a cost-benefit ratio. It has long been argued that, as with many other government policies, environmental policies, once implemented, usually fail to meet expectations. The second explanation concerns the problem of policy instrumentation when governments attempt to regulate and monitor pollution emissions. It is generally argued that if pollution permission rights can be defined clearly and traded freely in an efficient market, the negative externality of individual pollution activities can be internalised, and direct environmental regulation is not necessary. Therefore, a better outcome might be reached if governments make the effort to promote the establishment of a mature and efficient market for pollution permission rights.

Governments can also regulate environmental quality by increasing expenditure on environmental research and development. The effects of such expenditure have been estimated in Tables 15.2 and 15.3. It can be seen that the estimated

Table 15.4 **GDP per capita; the five highest cities in 2000** (10,000 yuan per capita)

City (rank)	Shanghai (1)	Beijing (2)	Tianjin (3)	Zhejiang (4)	Jiangsu (5)	Average
Real GDP per capita	2.799	1.847	1.686	1.329	1.174	0.849

Note: The real GDP per capita in Table 15.4 are measured with 1996 as the base year price.

coefficient of $envrd_{it}$ is significantly negative in all six of the pollution equations. While the estimated coefficient of $envrd_{it}$ in the two pollution equations $indwater_{it}$ and $inddust_{it}$ is significant (5 per cent and 10 per cent respectively), the other four pollutants all show a level of 1 per cent. In addition, the negative sign of the estimated coefficient means that the increase in environmental research and development expenditure helps to abate pollution emissions, which is also the positive technology effect highlighted by Grossman and Krueger (1995). If such a result is compared with the estimated result of $nums_{it}$, it can be concluded that when governments attempt to regulate environmental quality, increasing fiscal expenditure on research and development into clean technology might be more effective than direct environmental regulation.

Economic openness is another important pollution control variable, especially for developing countries such as China. According to the famous pollution haven hypothesis, the effects of international trade on environmental quality differ greatly between industrial and developing countries. If international trade or investment help industrial countries to shift their resource-intensive and even pollution-intensive industries to developing countries, which usually have lower environmental

Table 15.5 **Summary of some empirical results on EKC estimations**

Author(s)	Sample	Pollution indicator(s)	Turning point(s) (GDP per capita)
Grossman and Krueger (1995)	NAFTA countries, data source: GAMS	SO_2, smoke	4,000–5,000
Shafik and Bandyopadhyay (1992)	*World Development Report*, 1992	Ten indicators including air and water pollution	3,000–4,000
Panayotou (1993)	55 industrial and developing countries	SO_2	3,137
Selden and Song (1994)	Only industrial countries	SO_2, **SPM, CO**	7,114–13,383
Panayotou (1997)	Cities in 30 industrial and developing countries	SO_2	5,965
List and Gallet (1999)	US state-level data	SO_2	22,675
Stern and Common (2001)	73 industrial and developing countries	SO_2	101,166

Note: SPM is suspended particulate matter.

standards, then such international production specialisation patterns will inevitably worsen the problems of environmental degradation in developing countries. Considering China, however, it can be seen from Tables 15.2 and 15.3 that, except that the estimated coefficients of *open* for the two pollutants SO_{2it} and $indsolid_{it}$ are not statistically significant, the effects of *open* on the other four pollutants are significantly negative, and their values are –1.152 (*inddust*), –0.676 (*indsmoke*), –0.369 (*indcod*) and –0.122 (*indwater*). The negative signs of *open* demonstrate that, unlike in the pollution haven hypothesis, a higher degree of openness helps to abate pollution emissions in China. Two possible explanations are provided here. First, multilateral trade agreements, especially international agreements on environmental regulation, and cooperation indirectly encourage developing countries to update their production technology and adopt cleaner technology. What is more, if developing countries attempt to export to industrial countries, the higher environmental standards imposed on their export commodities usually propel the exporters to adopt more environmentally friendly production technology. Second, technological spillage due to international trade and foreign investment helps to enhance the productivity of local firms in developing countries, and has an indirect effect on the developing country's technological progress and the adjustment of local industrial structures. A large number of studies have confirmed such technology spillage from international trade and foreign investment,[4] though it is still being debated whether technology absorption depends on the host country's absorptive capability. Empirical studies of China's foreign trade have also justified the important role of international trade in promoting the technological progress of local firms (Lai et al. 2003). Therefore, unlike in the pollution haven hypothesis, international trade might have a positive effect on environmental quality due to this technological spillage. Certainly, since trade volume is the only such indicator used in our estimation, further studies should investigate the effects of trade structure and foreign direct investment on environmental quality in China.

Finally, let us consider the effects of regional industrial structural change on environmental quality. The shares of agricultural (*shagri*) and manufacturing (*shaind*) industries are used to measure regional industrial structure. It can be seen from Tables 15.2 and 15.3 that, as far as $shagri_{it}$ is concerned, except that the effects of $shagri_{it}$ on $inwater_{it}$ and $indsolid_{it}$ are significantly positive (0.142) and statistically insignificant, the estimated coefficient of $shagri_{it}$ in the other four pollution equations is significantly negative. On the other hand, a significant positive effect of $shaind_{it}$ on pollutant emission is estimated. Except for the two pollutants $indsolid_{it}$ and $indsmoke_{it}$, it has been found that a larger $shaind_{it}$ leads to greater emissions of the other four pollutants.

The general trend of China's regional industrial structural adjustment during our sample years was characterised by the obvious decline of the share of agriculture, while the share of manufacturing remained steady (Table 15.6). Therefore, although China's regional environment is not degraded by the change of manufacturing output, it is degraded by the decrease in the share of agriculture.

If, however, we compare the industrial structure of different regions, those provinces that have a relatively higher share of manufacturing industries are subject to higher pressure for environmental protection. For example, the share of manufacturing industries in Heilongjiang, Zhejiang, Shanxi, Jiangsu as well as Shanghai during 1996–2000 was 54.4 per cent, 53.7 per cent, 51.8 per cent, 51.1 per cent and 50.5 per cent respectively, significantly higher than the national average. Accordingly, those provinces have to make greater efforts to protect their environment from degradation. Generally, as pointed out by many other studies (for example, Dinda 2004), change of industrial structure has been a key variable determining the relationship between economic development and environmental quality, especially the so-called industrialisation process in many developing countries.

Analysis of output equation estimation results

For output equation estimations, we mainly consider two inputs. The first is fundamental factor inputs, including physical and human capital as well as labour, as emphasised in standard growth theories. The second is the pollutant indicator, which is used to measure feedback from environmental quality change on economic development.

Let us first consider the effects of factor inputs on output change. As the literature on growth theories (neoclassical growth theory and the endogenous growth theory) emphasizes, Tables 15.2 and 15.3 show that physical and human capital accumulation are key variables in determining China's economic growth, which is in line with most theoretical growth models. Among all six output equations, the coefficient of K_{it} and H_{it} is significant (1 per cent), especially the t-statistic of the estimated coefficient of K_{it}, which has a p-value of nearly zero, showing strong evidence that capital accumulation is the key source of China's economic growth. On the other hand, the coefficient of labour inputs, L_{it}, is not statistically significant, and its sign is negative, which doesn't support the role of the raw labour inputs in economic development.[5]

Note here that we use GDP per capita as the dependant variable rather than GDP, and it can be expected that only if labour productivity were obviously enhanced would labour inputs positively affect GDP per capita.

Table 15.6 **Average trends of China's regional industrial structural change, 1996–2000** (per cent)

	1996	1997	1998	1999	2000
The share of agriculture	22.9	21.6	20.6	19.2	17.8
The share of manufacturing	43.0	43.5	43.2	43.1	43.7

Source: The authors' calculations, based on relevant issues of the *Chinese Statistical Yearbook*.

As far as the output effect of pollution emissions is concerned, it can be seen from Tables 15.2 and 15.3 that our estimations can be classified as two types. The effects of *indsolid*$_{it}$, *indsmoke*$_{it}$ and SO_{2it} on output are estimated to be insignificant, which doesn't support the feedback from environmental quality change on economic growth. In the second type, the pollutants, including *indwater*$_{it}$, *indcod*$_{it}$ and *inddust*$_{it}$, have a significantly negative effect on Y_{it}, and their estimated coefficients are -0.0021 (*indwater*$_{it}$), -0.0012 (*indcod*$_{it}$) and -0.00096 (*inddust*$_{it}$), which implies that an increase in those pollutant emissions will cause a decrease in GDP per capita. One of the reasons why environmental pollution negatively affects GDP per capita is that environmental variables affect production via environmental policies that raise production costs and reduce outputs, as emphasised in many theoretical papers such as Selden and Song's (1994). Therefore, improving environmental quality reduces production. On the other hand, the multiple effects of air pollution on production may cancel one another out. For example, improving environmental quality might enhance the productivity of other factor inputs and therefore increase production. When these forces counteract one another, the aggregate effects of air pollutants on GDP per capita are small and the direction might be ambiguous. Additionally, polluters have to pay all of the environmental control and external costs. However, at present in China, external environmental costs of pollution are usually partially internalised because of pressure from economic interest groups and the growth considerations of local governments. For example, the pollution emission fee might not be set sufficiently high to offer enough economic incentives to local firms to adopt cleaner technology and reduce their emissions, especially those polluters that account for a large share of total local output.

Policy implications of the EKC in China

Combining the simultaneous estimation results of pollution and output equations, we can further investigate the impact of changes of exogenous variables on equilibrium pollution emissions and output levels by solving our simultaneity model.

Let us first examine the impacts of pollution control variables. For example, let us investigate how the changes in environmental research and development expenditure will affect pollution emissions and output levels, shown in Figure 15.1. In Figure 15.1, the inverted-U shaped curve is an environmental curve (EC), and the downward line is the output curve (OC), the slope of which is determined by our simultaneous estimation results since the coefficient of pollutants in output equation estimations is negative. The intersection point, A_0, of the curves EC_0 and OC at the initial state determines the initial level of equilibrium pollution emission, P_0, and equilibrium GDP per capita, Y_0. Let us consider how government expenditure on the research and development of green technology will affect the pollution emissions and GDP per capita, other things being equal. The estimated coefficient of *envrd* in our pollution equations is negative, implying that an increase in environmental research and development inputs will cause the environmental curve to shift vertically downward to the new curve, EC_1, while the output curve, OC, remains the same, since *envrd* does not directly affect output levels in the output equations. The new intersection point, A_1, determines the new level of pollution emissions, P_1, and GDP per capita, Y_1, in the new state of equilibrium. Thus, by comparing the initial P_0, Y_0 with the new P_1 and Y_1, respectively, we can study how *envrd* will affect environmental quality and economic development. First, it is easy to see that P_1 is greater than P_0, implying that the increase in environmental research and development helps to alleviate environmental pressure due to pollution emissions, the direct environmental effect of *envrd*. Second, changes in *envrd* also indirectly affect output levels, since they help decrease pollution emissions. More specifically, Y_1 is larger than Y_0, and means that *envrd* has a positive effect on GDP per capita. This happens because pollution emissions negatively affect output levels, and the decrease in pollutants due to more environmental research and development expenditure will result in a higher GDP per capita, the indirect output effect of *envrd*. What should be mentioned here is that since the estimated coefficient of pollutants in output equations is relatively small, it means that in Figure 15.1 the slope of the line OC is very steep. Thus, the direct pollution decrease of *envrd* is much larger than the indirect output increase.

In Figure 15.2, we also investigate the impact of the change of factor inputs on the equilibrium of pollution emissions and GDP per capita. Similarly, it can been seen in Figure 15.2 that the intersection point of EC and OC is the initial equilibrium state, B_0, and, accordingly, P_0, Y_0 are the initial equilibrium pollution emission and GDP per capita respectively. Let us consider the impact of physical capital accumulation, K.

Figure 15.1 **The impact of pollution control variables**

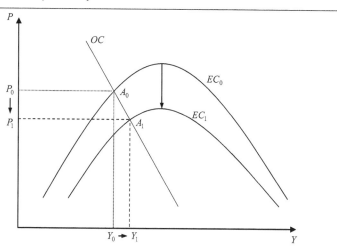

With the increase in physical capital, K, the output curve, OC, will shift to the right to the new position, OC_1, since the marginal output effects of physical capital accumulation are estimated to be positive, while the environmental curve, EC, remains unchanged. The new intersection point of OC_1 and EC, B_1, determines the new equilibrium level of pollution emission (P_1) and GDP per capita (Y_1).

The impact of physical capital accumulation on environmental quality and economic growth are shown in Figure 15.2. On one hand, since physical capital accumulation enhances output level, we have Y_1 being greater than Y_0. On the other hand, the increase in GDP per capita will affect pollution emissions. As we have estimated, the turning points of China's regional EKC lie with the GDP per capita being 30,000 yuan (1996 as the base year price), thus generally, at present, China's regional economic development has been the left part of the EKC. What is more, except in a few regions such as Shanghai and Beijing, most of China's provinces are still a long way from the turning points of our estimated EKC. As a result, physical capital accumulation will inevitably exert a negative effect on local environmental quality through the increase in GDP per capita. Thus, it can be concluded that there are both positive direct output effects and negative indirect environmental effects as a result of physical capital accumulation.

Finally, combining the analyses in Figures 15.1 and 15.2, we can see the policy implication of the EKC. Although the EKC might capture the general relationship between economic growth and environmental quality change, it might lead us to certain misleading policy suggestions. Since the environmental pressure due to rapid economic growth can be alleviated only after the economy has crossed the turning point along the EKC, it seems that the most effective way to protect the environment is to promote rapid economic growth further until it exceeds the threshold value along the EKC. Such policy implications, however, might be misleading. As estimated in this chapter, for most of China's provinces at present, their real GDP per capita are a long way from the threshold value in the EKC, and means that there is still a long way to go before those provinces reach the turning point of their estimated EKC. Before they get there, environmental degradation will continue to be a consequence of economic growth, since the income–environment relationship remains negative. As is shown in Figure 15.2, only when the economy arrives at the point B_2, that is, when the GDP per capita is as high as Y_2, will it be possible to return to the initial environmental quality, P_0. Also, since environmental abatement costs usually increase with pollution emissions, it is better for governments to regulate and monitor environmental pollution in the economic take-off stage rather than when environmental quality has greatly declined. Additionally, in certain cases, environmental damage cannot be remedied once it has occurred—for example, land erosion, deforestation, irradiation, the loss of species diversity and even the extinction of species. Finally, it should be mentioned that since pollution control variables essentially affect environmental quality, we can simultaneously adjust the levels of environmental pollution and output by combining certain policies. If we combine the analyses of Figures 15.1 and 15.2, for example, a policy combination of increasing environmental research and development expenditure and investment promotion is required. Economic growth can be enhanced by physical capital accumulation and environmental research and development helps to alleviate pressure on the environment due to the negative pollution effect of economic development. In the meantime, the positive output effect of environmental research and development also promotes rapid economic growth, which helps the economy to reach the turning point of EKC more quickly.

Conclusions

By using the panel data of China's 30 provinces during 1996–2000, this study has made a modest attempt to estimate the interaction between economic development and environmental quality simultaneously. Our empirical results confirm that the hypothesis of simultaneity exists in some pollutants, and our estimations and

Figure 15.2 **The impact of factor inputs**

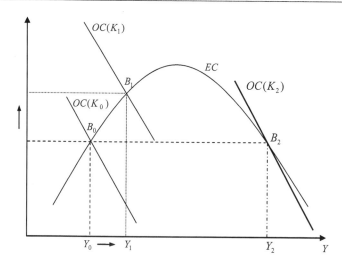

policy implications are explicitly different from those based on single pollution equation estimations.

First, among the six pollution indicators we have chosen, while $indcod_{it}$ has a U-shaped relationship between economic developments, the five other indicators show an inverted-U curve relationship with changes of GDP per capita. The further estimation demonstrates that the threshold value of GDP per capita along our estimated EKC is generally above 30,000 yuan. It reveals that although the EKC relationship for China has been estimated here, at present China's economic development has been on the left side of the inverted-U curve, implying a negative relationship between economic growth and environmental quality change. In addition, comparing the EKC's threshold value with real GDP per capita of China's 30 provinces, it is easy to see that for most provinces, real GDP per capita is a long way from the threshold values. This means that substantial environmental costs have to be paid before they reach the turning point along their EKC. As emphasised previously, however, promoting economic growth is not the only way to adjust environmental quality, and more attention should be paid to the role of pollution control variables such as environmental research and development, government regulation, industrial structural change and economic openness. Our estimations strongly support the role of these variables in environmental quality change. Specifically, increases in environmental research and development expenditure, as well as improved economic openness, help to abate pollution emissions. The role of activist government environmental policy, however, which is measured as the number of environmental regulations, is estimated to be statistically insignificant.

The results of our output equations also support feedback on the effects of environmental quality on economic growth. While three pollution indicators are found to have significantly negative effects on economic growth, the effects of the other three indicators are estimated to be insignificant. It is estimated that the accumulation of physical and human capital investment are key driving forces of economic growth, while the effect of labour inputs on GDP per capita change is insignificant.

Combining our simultaneous estimations of the pollution and output equations, it can be concluded that even though the EKC reflects the relationship between economic growth and environmental quality change in most countries, the view that promoting economic growth is the best way to protect the environment might be misleading. As shown in our analysis, accelerating economic growth by capital accumulation in order to reach the estimated turning point along the EKC is not the optimal policy. It has been estimated that the use of cleaner, environmentally friendly technology, the adjustment of industrial structures and economic openness all play important roles in alleviating the pressure of rapid economic growth on the environment. Therefore, developing countries such as China would be best served by a policy combination of acceleration of economic development and enhancement of environmental abatement capability.

Notes

1 The first set of empirical EKC studies appeared independently in three working papers: an NBER working paper as part of a study of the environmental impacts of NAFTA (Grossman and Krueger 1991), the World Bank's 1992 *World Development Report* (Shafik and Bandyopadhyay 1992) and a Development Discussion Paper as part of a study for the International Labor Organization (Panayotou 1993). Grossman and Krueger (1991), in an NBER working paper, which was published in 1993 (Grossman and Krueger, 1993), first pointed out an inverted-U relationship between pollutants (sulphur dioxide SO2 and smoke) and income per capita. Kuznets' name was attached to the inverted-U relationship between pollution and economic development later due to its resemblance to Kuznets' inverted-U relationship between income inequality and economic development. However, Panayotou (1993) first coined it as the Environmental Kuznets Curve or EKC.
2 Pearson (1994), Stern et al. (1996), Arrow et al. (1995), Stern (1998), Ekins (2000) and de Bruyn (2000) provide a series of critiques of the EKC studies.
3 For the literature review on empirical EKC research, see, for example, Stern (1998), Ekins (1997), de Bruyn and Heintz (1998), Stagl (1999) and Dinda (2004).
4 See Keller (2004) for a review of international technological spillage.
5 It is generally acknowledged that as the economy is transforming to a more service and technology oriented one, the role of human capital will become more important in production, while raw labour becomes correspondingly less important.

16

Harmonising the coal industry with the environment

Xunpeng Shi

Coal contributes greatly to social and economic development. It triggered the industrial revolution and has driven industrialisation in the past several centuries. At present, many developing countries are still heavily dependent on energy-intensive industries, such as metals and manufacturing. While the World Coal Institute (WCI 2001) says that the coalmining industry employs seven million workers globally, five million of whom are in China, it has elsewhere been estimated that China alone has about six million coalminers (China Coal 2002). Due to the abundance of town and village-owned coalmines in China, particularly illegal mines not registered in any statistics, such figures are far lower than the reality. The coal industry plays a special role in alleviating poverty. For example, most coalmines are in rural or remote areas where they are usually the largest employers, the largest providers of welfare for poor communities and the sole producers of affordable energy.

The coal industry is, however, also problematic. Occupational health and safety in mines are old but prominent issues; fatal accidents happen frequently, and mostly in developing countries. Occupational diseases also often cause slower, but larger numbers of deaths. World Combined Services (2003) observed that black lung, a lung disease caused by breathing coal dust, killed 55,000 miners between 1968 and 1990 and continues to kill 1,000 miners a year.

Environmental issues have been emerging to shift the focus from those traditional problems. Coal is one of the primary environmental polluters. Its production and consumption have local, regional and international negative impacts on the environment. Local environmental impacts are predominantly those caused by mining activities and can include land subsidence, water pollution and mine waste. Regional and international environmental impacts are derived from emissions from coal combustion, such as particulate pollution and the emission of nitrogen oxides, carbon dioxide and sulphur dioxide. Since the 1972 Stockholm Conference, environmental issues have become more prominent worldwide. The number of international conventions for protecting the environment has increased considerably (United Nations 2002). In general, environmental regulations affect the coal industry in terms of production, transportation and consumption.

Even though sulphur dioxide, nitrogen oxides, and particulate pollution have received attention, carbon dioxide emissions and climate change have gradually become primary concerns because of their global impacts. This chapter studies the regional and global issues raised regarding emissions from coal use. Environmental regulations are defined as international treaties, agreements, guidelines, directives and national laws that are related to regional and global issues (for example, air pollution and climate change), such as regulations on emissions of sulphur dioxide, nitrogen oxides, particulates and carbon dioxide. Among these, regulations governing carbon dioxide emissions are of the most concern because of the unpredictable and adverse impact on the global coal industry.

Due to the additional costs involved in making coal more environmentally acceptable, environmental regulations have negatively affected the coal industry. Arguably, these regulations will change the ability of coal to compete with other fuels; for example, higher carbon dioxide emission taxes give petroleum compounds an advantage against coal. Since environmental concerns have priority over the future of the coal industry, it is easy to conclude that the industry's future is bleak. In China, the view that the coal industry is *XiYang Gongye* (the Setting Sun, that is, hopeless) is widely held. But, on the contrary, many Chinese scholars have argued that there is a promising future for the coal industry (Shang 2001; Li 2003; China News 2001). However, these arguments are not convincing as they cannot answer the key questions: how can the coal industry overcome the adverse impact of environmental regulations? How should the decline of the coal industry in Western Europe be interpreted? Could alternatives replace coal? They also omit the beneficial effects of environmental regulations and thus fail to consider the possibility that protection of the environment could be harmonised with coal production and consumption.

This chapter argues that growth of the coal industry can be harmonised with environmental objectives. Through case studies and the comparative analyses of economic, technical and theoretical issues, it argues that in the long term, environmental regulations will probably not lead to the decline of the coal industry globally. On the contrary, the enforcement of the environmental regulations can help the coal industry to maximise its contribution to society, assisting the industry to achieve sustainable development. Historical experience has demonstrated that the coal industry was able to continue parallel development with stonger environmental regulations.

Environmental regulations and the coal industry: historical experiences

Despite many uncertainties surrounding the relationship between greenhouse gases and climate change, many global activities are being initiated to control greenhouse gas emissions. A key example is the controversial Kyoto Protocol, under which industrial countries agreed to reduce their greenhouse gas emissions by at least 5 per cent below 1990 levels in the committment period 2008–12. Although the United States—the world's largest emitter of carbon dioxide—has refused to ratify the Kyoto Protocol, it nonetheless became effective on 16 February 2005. Even though carbon dioxide is one of the most significant greenhouse gases by volume, its global effects vary compared with those of other greenhouse gases (Birnie and Boyle 2002:501). Regardless, the Kyoto protocol will place great pressure on countries to minimise carbon dioxide emissions.

The main international environmental regulations relating to coal are the 1979 United Nations' Convention on Long-Range Transboundary Air Pollution, the 1985 Sulphur Protocol, the 1992 UN Framework Convention on Climate Change (UNFCCC), the 1997 Kyoto Protocol to the UNFCCC (the Kyoto Protocol) and the 1998 Nitrogen Oxides Protocol. There are many other guidelines, including those from sources such as non-governmental organisations (for example, the World Bank Environmental Guidelines). Regulations on pollutants such as sulphur dioxide and nitrogen oxides affect the coal industry greatly because they directly restrict coal use, alter coal consumption and change the coal industry's structure or its markets. Since these kinds of controls have been in place in many parts of world for some time now, their effects are obvious. However, the control of carbon dioxide seems to have the most serious impact on the coal industry as coal combustion produces the largest amount of carbon dioxide per unit of energy. Since controls on carbon dioxide emissions have been introduced only recently and the targets have been contracted, the outcomes are unclear. Therefore, compared with other environmental regulations, the UNFCCC and the Kyoto Protocol will affect the coal industry in unpredictable ways.

With the emergence of more environmental regulations, many observers think that the future for the coal industry is unpromising (Keay 2003). This view can be traced back to the 1960s and 1970s in the United States, when the government was considering regulating coal pollution. The coal industry and its supporters in government worried that such regulation would limit coal's ability to compete with other fuels (McGinley 1992:261).

The reality, however, is that even with an increasing number of environmental regulations on coal in the past three decades, global demand for coal has increased by more than 60 per cent since 1970 (Figure 16.1). In 1999, world coal consumption was 4.7 billion short tonnes and was projected to increase in the United States, Japan and developing countries in Asia. It should be pointed out, however, that this forecast does not consider the effects of environmental regulations such as the Kyoto Protocol (EIA 2001).

BP (2005) demonstrates that, in the past decade, global production and consumption have increased despite environmental pressures, particularly in Asia and the Pacific. The decline of coal in Europe and Eurasia is probably due to the economic breakdown in the former Soviet states.

Clarification of the relationship between environmental regulations and the coal industry in Western Europe

The experience of Western Europe is an interesting case, the recent and dramatic decline of its coal industry is often cited as proof of a general global trend. This

Figure 16.1 **World coal consumption, 1990–2030** (billion short tonnes)

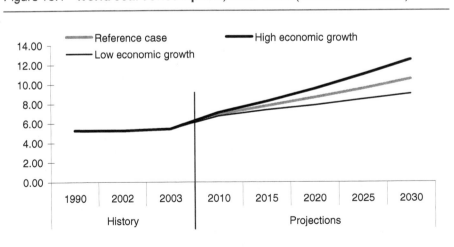

Source: Energy Information Agency, 2004. *International Energy Outlook 2004*:75.

view ascribes the decline to tightening environmental regulations and predicts that the coal industry in other parts of the world will also decline as more environmental regulations are implemented.

The European Community did not have an environmental policy until 1972, when the first Action Program on the Environment was formulated. More recently, more than 200 regulations have been agreed as part of the European Commission policy (Bell and McGillivray 2000:123). The first European Commission-wide air-quality standard was the 1980 Air Quality Directive (Smoke and Sulphur Dioxide). Further standards encompassing nitrogen oxides were established in 1985 (Haigh 1990:182, 195). Other environmental regulations that might affect the coal industry are the 1988 European Commission Large Combustion Directive, the European Union Climate Change Strategy and the UNFCCC. The European Union agreed to an 8 per cent reduction in emissions, of which the United Kingdom's share was 12.5 per cent (UNFCCC 2004). The European Commission (including the United Kingdom) signed the Kyoto Protocol on 29 April 1998 and ratified it on 31 May 2002 (UNFCCC 2006).

The European Union's 1992 proposal to tax carbon dioxide emissions and energy was supposed to raise the price of anthracite by 58 per cent, natural gas by 14 per cent and petrol by 6 per cent, if the entire tax were to be passed on to the consumer (Johnson and Corcelle 1997:176). At the end of 2001, eight member states had implemented this tax, although, to date, no such tax exists at the European Union level (further details are available in European Environment Agency 2000).

The annual coal output in Western Europe declined from approximately 600 million tonnes in the early 1960s to 86 million tonnes in 2000. In Western Europe, only Germany, the United Kingdom and Spain are still producing coal. Coal consumption in Western Europe decreased 36 per cent from 894 million tonnes in 1990 to 573 million tonnes in 2002 (EIA 2005a).

Germany, France, Spain and the UK granted substantial subsidies for coalmining, totalling 6.3 billion euro in 2001 (Commission of the European Communities 2002:24). In these countries, domestic production costs are much higher than the price of imported coal; for example, in Germany, Spain and France, domestic production costs are three to five times more than imported coal prices (Table 16.1). When these countries phase out subsidies and liberalise their coal trade, domestic coal production will inevitably decline because more coal will be imported. In 2004, Germany imported an estimated 39 million short tonnes of coal (EIA 2005b).

The decline of the coal industry in Western Europe has not resulted from changed environmental regulations. The huge gap between production costs and prices for imported coal implies that the decline of coal production is due to domestic producers losing competitiveness with cheaper imported coal. If environmental

Table 16.1 **Western European coal industry subsidies, production and import prices, 2000**

	Subsidies (US$ 2,000 million)	Hard coal production (million tonnes) (US$ 2,000)	Average subsidy per tonne of coal produced (US$ 2,000)	Average price per tonne of coal imported
Germany	4,245	40.4	105	32
Spain	1,035	16.4	63	32
France	933	4.9	192	36
United Kingdom	132	35.3	4	38

Source: Energy Information Agency, 2002. *International Energy Outlook 2002*:77.

regulations were the main reason for the decline, coal consumption should have decreased earlier and to a greater extent than production because environmental regulations would have affected coal use first. The reality is that production has decreased more than consumption. Those claiming that the Western European case indicates a trend assume a spurious relationship between changed environmental regulation and the decline of the coal industry.

As the largest coal producer in the European Union, the United Kingdom's case is compelling evidence that disproves this conclusion, because in the United Kingdom the decline of coal has not coincided with the introduction of environmental regulations. The environmental regulations that potentially affect the United Kingdom coal industry have been in place for a long time and include the *Clean Air Acts* of 1956 and 1968, the *Control of Pollution Act 1974* and the *Pollution Control and Local Government (Northern Ireland) Order 1978*. It was, however, not until the early 1980s that coal production fell sharply. Coal production in 2004 was less than one-fifth of that in 1980 and about one-quarter of the 1990 level. Imports grew steadily to reach 20 million tonnes a year in the 1990s, then expanded rapidly to overtake domestic production. Except for a slight decrease in 2002, imports exceeded domestic production in 2003 and 2004, reaching a new record of 36 million tonnes (Figure 16.2). This demonstrates that there is little logical relationship between the decline of the domestic coal industry and the implementation of new environmental regulations.

In fact, the decline in coal consumption in the United Kingdom resulted mainly from the privatisation of the electricity industry, which led to a rapid increase in natural gas-fired electricity generation at the expense of the use of coal (EIA 2002). Because of its plentiful reserves of natural gas, the British government has a long tradition of encouraging the use of natural gas as a substitute for coal and oil in industry and for power generation (EIA 2006a). Whatever role changed environmental regulations played in the general decline of the coal industry, they are not considered to be the main cause.

The decline in the United Kingdom's coal production was also due to high domestic production costs. Before 2000, consumers were compelled to buy subsidised domestic coal, enabling the domestic industry to survive. After the removal of such restrictions in 2004 and with the increased importation of cheaper coal from other countries, United Kingdom prices for coal purchased by major power producers decreased by 33 per cent when compared with the price in 1994 (Figure 16.3).

Notably, compared with oil and gas prices, the price of coal has remained stable (Figure 16.3). In the future, this will help coal to become more competitive. The International Energy Agency (IEA) forecasts that, although Europe's local output continues to fall, future consumption will be stable. In its latest *World Energy Outlook*, the IEA predicts that European coal consumption will fall by only 0.4 per cent in the next 30 years (cited in Keay 2003).

Figure 16.2 **Coal production and consumption in the United Kingdom, 1980–2004**

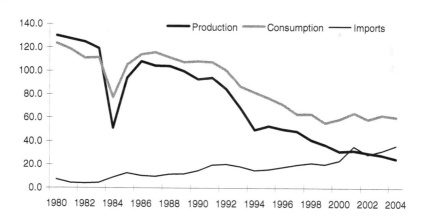

Source: Department of Trade and Industry (DTI), 2005. *Energy statistics: coal*, URN No. 05/87a10. Available from http://www.dti.gov.uk/energy/statistics/source/coal/page18529.html (accessed 21 June 2006).

The joint development of environmental regulations and the coal industry in the United States

United States has a unique combination of a large coal industry and strict environmental regulations, providing evidence of the real effects such regulations have on the coal industry.

In the United States, the first important coal-related regulation was the *Clean Air Act*, passed in 1963. In 1970, the United States Congress passed the first amendment to the act, setting in motion a nationwide effort to improve the country's air quality. Since then, additional laws and regulations have been added. In particular, the 1977 amendment to the *Clean Air Act* established for the first time 'ceilings' for different air pollutants, including particulate matter, carbon monoxide, sulphur dioxide and nitrogen oxides. The *Clean Air Act* also manages many standards at a federal and state level, forming the air pollution control system. Since environmental regulations began to affect the coal industry in 1977, this chapter will focus its analysis on the industry from this time until the present.

Figure 16.3 **Average prices of fuels purchased by major United Kingdom power producers, 1990–2006**

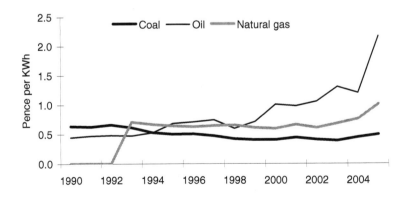

Source: Department of Trade and Industry (DTI), 2006. *Quarterly Energy Price Tables*, URN No. 6/276b/tab:Table 3.2.1. Available from http://www.dti.gov.uk/energy/statistics/publications/prices/ (accessed 28 June 2006).

To date, the United States has not ratified the protocol. However the government has accepted the intention of Kyoto and has expressed a commitment to controlling carbon dioxide emissions.

After the implementation of the 1977 *Clean Air Act* amendments, the coal industry did not lose competitiveness, defying the expectations of many observers. Conversely, coal production continued to increase, while its price continued to decline (see Figures 16.4 and 16.5).

The EIA forecasts that coal production in the United States will continue to grow in the next 25 years and the coal prices will continue to decline largely because of an increase in mining productivity. The average mine-mouth price of coal declined with the annual ratio of 4.9 per cent (EIA 2006a:99). The global reality is that the coal industry continues to grow despite the continual implementation of environmental regulations, and, such regulations were not the main cause of the decline of the coal industry in Western Europe. The case of Western Europe should not be used to suggest that the future of the coal industry is unpromising.

The United States' case clearly demonstrates that, in the long term, environmental regulations do not harm the coal industry; in fact, they can help the industry become more competitive. McFarland, Herzog and Jacoby (2004:6) studied the future of coal consumption under different scenarios of changing carbon prices, gas prices and clean coal technological costs and found that in the United States and among European Union countries, coal would continue to be viable. It is possible that the coal industry will not only overcome the adverse impact of environmental regulations, but will continue to grow. This can be demonstrated by the continuing growth of coal consumption, alongside a decline in prices. Technological advances play an important role in the case of harmonising the coal industry with environmental regulations.

The economic logic of environmental regulations

Coal is a non-renewable and therefore scare resource. This means that any one extra (marginal) unit of use will have higher costs and lower benefits than the former unit. That is, there is an increasing marginal social cost (MSC) and a decreasing marginal benefit. In Figure 16.6 at point Q_1, the marginal social benefit (MSB) equals the MSC, where coal is used most effectively. One additional unit will bring a net loss to society.

Unfortunately, without environmental regulation, more than the optimum quantity of coal will be used because some costs will be externalised and will not be paid by consumers. Therefore, the consumers' marginal private cost (MPC) curve would

Figure 16.4 **United States' coal real price, 1977–2003** (dollars per short tonne)

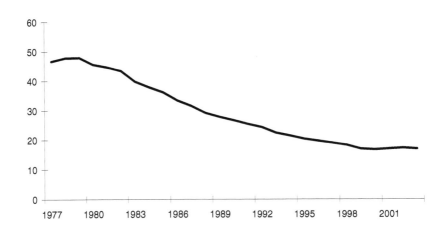

Note: The price is chained in US dollars (2000 as the base year price), calculated by using GDP implicit price deflators.
Source: Energy Information Agency, 1949–2004. *Coal Prices.* Available from http://www.eia.doe.gov/emeu/aer/txt/stb0708.xls (accessed 28 June 2006).

Figure 16.5 **United States' coal production, 1977–2003** (million short tonnes)

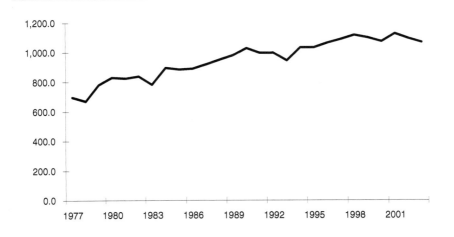

Source: Energy Information Agency, 1949–2004. *Coal Production.* Available from http://www.eia.doe.gov/emeu/aer/txt/ptb0702.html (accessed 28 June 2006).

lie below the MSC curve, except at the original point where they meet. Simultaneously, the MSB curve, whether it pertains to the whole society or individual average, would remain the same.

For the individual, the private optimum quantity will be at Q_r, which is higher than Q_1. At this point, the whole society will suffer a marginal net loss to $MSC_r - MSB_r$. The greater the externalities, the higher the Q_r, and, thus, the higher the marginal social net loss.

Environmental regulations will internalise costs of coal utilisation and thus drive MPC close to MSC. This will cause coal to be used in a socially efficient way, even based on individual decisions, which would make coal more attractive to society. Warhurst (1994:133) states that enforcing environmental regulations on mining operations does not always cause detriment to its economy. Rather, it might bring economic advantage. In this case, it is easy to see that some low-grade coal resources, quantity at $Q_r - Q_1$, are reserved. When new technologies (for example, sulphur emission controls) cut costs or when marginal society benefits rise (that is, when the MSB and the MSC move to MSB_1 and MSC_1 respectively), those previously saved marginal resources could be used without a negative contribution to society.

This mechanism is the economic basis for coal to harmonise with environmental regulations. This has been proved in the United States case. In 1997, the US Environmental Protection Agency studied the benefits resulting from the *Clean Air Act* between 1970 and 1990 and showed that the net present value (NPV), with a 5 per cent discount rate, was US$21.7 trillion.[1]

Technological improvement and the declining trend of unit coal emissions

Setting a ceiling for carbon dioxide emissions does not necessarily lead to a decline in coal production and consumption. Environmental regulations can encourage the use of clean-coal technologies, which separate and seize carbon dioxide instead of discharging it, reducing emissions per unit of coal. For example, an integrated gasification combined cycle (IGCC) technology (most likely to be in commercial use soon) could increase generating efficiencies by 20 to 30 per cent and reduce emission levels (especially of carbon dioxide and sulphur dioxide) more effectively than present pollution-control technologies (EIA 2001). Figure 16.7 displays the relationship between coal use and carbon dioxide emissions. If the relationship was line I, when environmental regulations demand reducing carbon dioxide emissions from P to P_1, a dramatic decline of coal consumption from Q to

Figure 16.6 **Economic logic of environmental regulations**

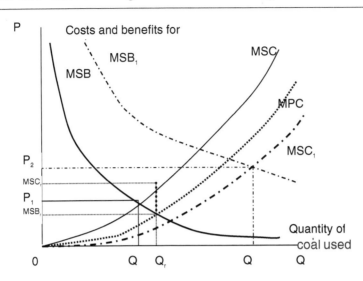

Q_1 will occur. However, if new technologies change the relationship between coal and carbon dioxide emissions to line F_I, the coal decline from the same reduction will not be as great as the former. If the relationship were line F_{II}, a small increase in coal consumption would occur.

A study in the United Kingdom shows that even a simple replacement of one or two coal-fired power stations with modern supercritical and ultra-supercritical plants can do more to reduce carbon dioxide emissions than the entire United Kingdom renewable programs have done thus far (Keay 2003). The study indicated that new technologies, such as IGCC, combined with carbon sequestration, could achieve a zero discharge.

The United States Department of Energy states that it is possible for a coal plant to emit no pollution. It points out that, besides IGCC, integration of gasification with a fuel cell (IGFC) has the potential to achieve near-zero emissions. The Bush Administration has launched a public–private partnership to develop a coal-fired electricity-generating facility with near-zero emissions (Shimkus 2005). If carbon sequestration can reach reasonable cost targets, carbon fuel might achieve a price comparable with or even cheaper than carbon alternatives (Keay 2003). Therefore, it cannot be concluded whether environmental regulations would dramatically change the energy consumption structure.

Figure 16.7 **Different emissions per unit of coal consumption**

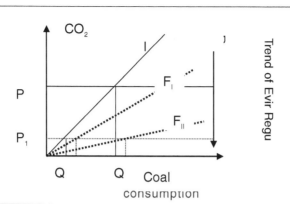

Benefits of environmental regulations to the coal industry

Care should be taken when talking about benefits, as this does not mean that the cost side is not important, however, there are some benefits to the coal industry from environmental regulations.

First, environmental regulations can promote the upgrading of enterprises and the optimisation of industry structures. Regulations can help to provide a level playing field for competition through the internalisation of costs. Warhurst (1994:133) shows that strict environmental regulations can make enterprises achieve better technological standards. That is, new technology with lower production costs and causing less environmental harm could, more or less, offset environmental costs. Those companies that are unable to upgrade in accordance with new environmental standards will be forced into bankruptcy. This will improve the coal industry as a whole.

Second, environmental regulations inspire companies to innovate. Porter and Linda (1995:98) believe firms can even benefit from properly designed environmental regulations because they could lead to unexpected technological innovation, which could reduce pollution and total costs. Examples of such innovative technologies include new combustion processes, such as fluidised bed combustion or low-nitrogen oxides burners, to remove pollutants or prevent their formation; new pollution-control devices, such as advanced scrubbers, which clean pollutants from flue gases before they escape from a plant's smokestack; coal-transfer technologies, which convert coal into fuel forms, such as gas and oil; and carbon capture and storage technologies, which will help achieve zero emissions.

Finally, environmental regulations can help the coal industry attract foreign investment by clearly identifying environmental liabilities. Research shows that states with inadequate environment regulations will have difficulty attracting foreign investment in the mining sector (Otto and Barberis 1994:12), because responsibility for environmental problems is uncertain. For example, in China, many of the old coalmines facing closure have serious environmental problems. At present, it is not clear who is responsible for solving these problems, as current stakeholders, such as governments, coal companies and mining communities, are not able to make the necessary changes. A new investor might be asked to solve these issues which pose a risk and therefore a deterrent to the investment. Regulations can reduce the uncertainty of environmental liability and thus facilitate investment decisions.

Coal's alternatives

Coal is the most abundant fossil fuel and, in the near future, it will retain its advantage over other fossil-fuel energy. At the end of 2004, the world's total recoverable coal reserves were approximately 909 billion tonnes, which, with current exploitation levels, could last for 164 years, while oil and gas could be depleted in 40.5 years and 66.7 years, respectively (BP 2005).

Currently, renewable resources have not matured enough to support world development significantly. The EIA (2001) points out that nuclear energy and hydroelectricity have an uncertain future. For example, some countries plan to restrict and even eliminate nuclear power, which is a frequent target of public protest and opposition. Large-scale hydroelectricity is also becoming increasingly unpopular because of its extensive ecological effects. Hydroelectricity is also problematic because of seasonal fluctuations in water flow. In some places, available resources have already been heavily exploited. Therefore, limited prospects for nuclear and/or hydroelectric capacity in some areas could increase the use of coal for power generation.

A strong supporting view is that distinctions in greenhouse gas emissions between coal and its substitutes are much less than traditional studies have shown. Contrary to popular belief, hydroelectricity can seriously damage the climate because it produces greenhouse gases (methane emitted from turbines and spillways; methane produced from the growth and decomposition of soft green vegetation when water levels fall and rise, and carbon dioxide emissions from above-water decay of standing trees) (Fearnside 2004). Fearnside (2004) also points out that 'any weighting of the emissions impacts for time preference will strongly favour fossil fuel alternatives over hydroelectric generation'.

On the contrary, clean-coal technologies can help coal compete with its alternatives. A new technology that could change the outlook for the coal industry is coal gasification and liquefaction, which will reduce pollutant emissions. There are many coal liquefaction plants in operation or being built in China and southern African.

China's coal industry and environmental performance: past evidence and future prospects

Environmental protection was established as one of China's basic national policies in the 1980s. By 2005, China had introduced nine environmental laws, 15 resource laws, more than 50 state and 200 ministry-level environmental regulations, and more than 2,000 state environmental standards and local environmental legislation (SEPA 2005). Such legislation places many pressures on the coal industry. Meanwhile, China has had double-digit rates of economic growth for much of the past two decades. This has had huge implications for energy consumption and environmental impact.

Although China began its reform in 1978, the transformation procedure for the coal industry began only in 1993, when the central government started to liberalise coal prices and reduced subsidies to the coal industry. Therefore, this chapter will focus on the past 13 years.

The recession period, 1998–2001

China is rich in coal while short of oil and gas reserves. Therefore, in the past few decades, coal has represented about 70 per cent of China's total primary energy consumption, and more than three-quarters of electricity is generated from coal-fired power plants. Before 1997, China's demand for coal exceeded supply; however, from the end of 1997, the Chinese coal industry suffered a surplus and entered a four-year recession. Prices gradually decreased, output shrank and payments for coal sales remained largely in arrears. China's statistical coal output fell from a peak of 1.397 billion tonnes in 1996 to a low of 998 million tonnes in 2000 (see Table 16.2). With the nominal fall in production, coal producers, especially state-owned mines, have fallen into deficit (Shi 1999:19).

During the recession, state-owned mines laid off a large number of employees, and the remaining workers were not paid on time; new mine construction was postponed; the government suspended matured debts from state-owned mines; and retired workers could not get a pension because the mines could not pay social insurance.

The sudden and large fall in coal production, the large deficits experienced by state-owned mines and the poor living conditions of coalminers during the recession period were the main causes of a pessimistic outlook for the future of the coal industry.[2] Many think the decline of the Chinese coal industry will continue because it inevitably exists in opposition to environmental protection. In 2001, an advertisement on China Central TV claimed that coal was a dirty energy and coal-fired power plants should be closed down. The advertisement triggered a nationwide debate about the future of the coal industry (cited in Feng and Guo 2001). Even today, Greenpeace's Chinese web site (http://www.greenpeace.org/china/zh/campaigns/stop-climate-change/our-work/asia-clean-energy-revolution-tour/dirty-energy) still declares that coal is a dirty industry.

However, the reality does not support such a pessimistic view. Table 16.2 demonstrates that from 2001, the production of coal increased dramatically. In 2005, the annual coal production was 2.11 billion tonnes (China Coal News 2006), nearly double that of 2001.

Indeed, the extremely low production levels from 1998 to 2001 are suspicious, and do not explain why GDP and coal consumption grew while coal production was falling. The average annual growth rate of GDP from 1990 to 2003 was 9.3 per cent and, from 1998 to 2003, 8 per cent (NBS 2004). Electricity, steel and cement industries continued to grow, and parallel the growth of GDP, while the figures indicate that coal production fell (Figure 16.8). What filled the big gap between consumption and production, especially in the three years from 1999 to 2001 (Table 16.2)?

The turning point of the coal market is possibly a result of the Asian financial crisis, however, this nominal decline in demand is enlarged by Chinese coal industry policy. To deal with excess supply, in November 1998, the Chinese State Council initiated a policy 'Closing Up Mines and Restricting the Total Yield', which prepared to cut production by 250 million tonnes by closing 25,800 of 51,200 illegal town and village owned coalmines (Shi 1999:19). Based on the assumption that the problems in the coal industry were caused by oversupply, the government moved to control total output by setting production quotas for each province and threatening punishment for those who exceeded their quota.

Under this regime, in order to meet the unrealistic output targets, provincial governments and coal companies reported less production. In April 2000, a senior officer of the coal industry bureau in Henan Province complained to the author that the production quota assigned for the province would not allow it to meet its own demand. Strictly obeying the policy would see his province change from

Table 16.2 **China's coal production and consumption, 1995–2004** (million tonnes)

	1995	1996	1997	1998	1999	2000	2001	2002	2003	2004
Production	1,361	1,397	1,373	1,250	1,045	998	1,161	1,380	1,667	1,956
Consumption	1,376	1,447	1,392	129	1,263	1,245	1,262	1,366	1,445	1,890

Source: National Bureau of Statistics (NBS), 2005. *China Statistics Year Book 1995–2005*, China Statistics Publishing House, Beijing.

Figure 16.8 **Outputs of coal, electricity, cement and steel, 1995–2004**

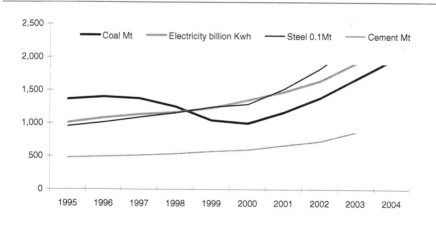

Source: National Bureau of Statistics (NBS), 2004. *China Statistics Year Book 1995–2004*, China Statistics Publishing House, Beijing.

being the second largest coal-exporting province to a importing province, which was ridiculous. The only choice for him was to cheat the central government and try to avoid punishment. Consequently, the statistics registered in the national targets. For example, in 2000, the total production set by the coal industry's state bureau was 980 million tonnes, which exactly matches the final number in the official statistics.

Another possibility is that production from illegal mines was not reported and therefore not included in the official statistics. Illegal town and village-owned mines that were established under previous conditions of strong demand and favourable government policies, and which were supposed to be closed down, continue to operate because their lower production costs make their prices lower than those of the state-owned mines. Since the illegal mines bring many benefits (taxes, fees and illegal income to local government officials, supporting local business), county and town governments have a strong interest in protecting them from closure. Therefore, production was underestimated from 1999 to 2001 when the mine closure policy was emphasised by the central government.

Many researchers believe that coal production in the period from 1997 to 2001 was higher than that registered in the official statistics (Logan 2001; Barlow Jonker 2002a, cited in Ball et al. 2003). They estimated that the unreported coal production amounted to 200 million tonnes. The International Energy Agency (IEA) believes that coal production in 2000 was 1.231 billion tonnes, which was 233 million tonnes more than the official Chinese statistics (IEA 2002, cited in Ball et al. 2003).

Environmental performance and the coal industry

The Chinese case shows the co-development of the coal industry with increased environmental protection. As shown in Figure 16.9, coal consumption has increased rapidly since 2000, but emissions of dust and smoke are declining. Even though there is a slight growth in sulphur dioxide emissions, the increase is far lower than the level of coal consumption. Coal consumption increased nearly 50 per cent between 2000 and 2004, yet the emission of sulphur dioxide in that period showed an increase of only 13 per cent (NBS 2004; SEPA 2004). This clearly shows that the coal industry and environmental protection can develop simultaneously.

The way forward

Improvements in technology provide ways for the coal industry to harmonise with the environment. With the expansion of Chinese coal production, more advanced environmental technologies have been designed and implemented. Besides traditional clean-coal technologies, coal liquefaction provides a cleaner way to

Figure 16.9 **Coal production and air pollution emissions, 1997–2004**

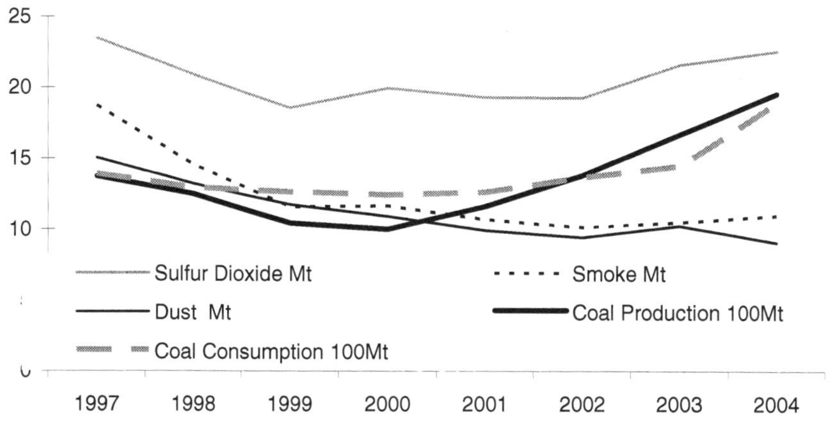

[Chart showing Sulfur Dioxide Mt, Smoke Mt, Dust Mt, Coal Production 100Mt, and Coal Consumption 100Mt from 1997 to 2004]

Source: NBS, 2004. China Statistics Year Book, 1997–2004, China Statistic Publishing House, Beijing.

use coal. Many Chinese companies are working to transform coal into oil, a procedure in which more pollution elements are separated and utilised, minimising emissions. The first direct coal-to-oil plant is being built by Shenhua Group, the largest and safest coal producer in China. The plant wants to discharge no pollution other than carbon dioxide and to research the technology of carbon dioxide seizure and storage. In his recent visit to the plant, Chinese Premier, Wen Jiabao, announced that coal liquefaction was a national strategic project for securing a supply of energy. By 2020 the Shenhua Group plans to transform 100 million tonnes of coal per annum. The Shenhua Group and Southern African Sasol Energy Company are also planning to build several indirect coal liquefaction plants in Shaanxi and Ningxia. Other liquefying technologies are also being tested. Furthermore, coal gasification will reduce a large amount of pollution created by coal combustion. The Shenhua Group has launched the world's first coal-to-olefin plant in Baotou City, Inner Mongolia Autonomous Administration Region.

New policy initiatives

The current Chinese government is working to change the nation's attitude towards energy development and use, and, if realised, this will provide more favourable conditions for the coordinated development of the coal industry and the economy.

Chinese President, Hu Jingtao, advocates a new Science Development Concept to build 'A Saving Society' and 'A Harmonious Society'. Reasonable utilisation of resources and environmental protection are at the top of his agenda, not only as slogans, but as action plans. A good example is the dramatic change in energy and environmental goals for the next five years. On 11 October 2005, the Central Commission of the Chinese Communist Party published a suggestion for the eleventh Five-Year Plan, stating that, in the next five years, energy intensity should be cut by 20 per cent, major pollutants should be reduced by 10 per cent, while the per capita GDP in 2010 should be double that of 2000 (Xinhua Net 2005). It also asks for the formation of a market mechanism for resource allocation and pricing. This suggestion has been incorporated in China's eleventh Five-Year Plan (2006–10) and thus becomes an official goal for the nation (People's Daily 2006).

At the same time, the pricing system is being liberalised and resource prices are increasing. Coal prices have historically been distorted due to explicit and implicit subsidies for coalmining, however, the transition from central planning towards a market economy will begin to alter this. Pricing reforms started in 1993. At the end of 2005, the Chinese central government announced that it would not intervene in the pricing of coal for electricity generation. That indicates that the coal price will be decided solely by the market. Meanwhile, the price is expected to become a tool to inspire saving resources. Therefore, the current government wants to gradually increase the price of non-renewable resources, including coal.

Additionally, in April 2006, the Chinese State Council began testing the sustainable development of the coal industry in Shanxi Province. A key aim of this trial is to internalise such externalities as environmental damage and resource waste (State Council 2006). This indicates that the Chinese government is working towards developing the coal industry in harmony with the environment.

Conclusion

The view that high costs brought about by environmental regulations will harm the coal industry might prove incorrect if the industry can find positive ways to meet regulatory challenges.

Historically, environmental regulations have not hurt the coal industry very much. A detailed study of the coal industry in Western Europe reveals that its decline was not caused directly by environmental regulations and therefore does not indicate a general trend of decline in the coal industry globally. The United States and Chinese cases demonstrate that the development of the coal industry can occur in conjunction with environmental protection.

Theoretical study demonstrates that coal alternatives are not as promising as once thought. In the long run, environmental regulations can assist the coal industry to practise sustainable development by compelling it to achieve a more harmonious relationship with nature and humankind. On one hand, these kinds of environmental pressures can serve as a positive motivation to promote the coal industry. The internalisation of costs will ensure that coal is used in a socially effective way, improving environmental standards will optimise the coal industry's structure, environmental regulation systems will facilitate investment decisions, and so on. On the other hand, coal has a potentially positive relationship with the environment and could keep developing in harmony with environmental regulations. Improvements in productivity, technology and other factors will make coal more competitive with other fuels in terms of clean use and price.

In practice, environmental regulations should be tightened to a point at which almost all externalities in the coal industry have been internalised. This will help humankind make rational economic decisions about utilising coal, and in turn will help coal to maximise its contribution to society.

Currently, China's government is dedicated to formulating a free and conservative coal market and trying to liberalise the coal-pricing system, as well as incorporating external and opportunity costs into the price of coal. Such efforts to create a sustainable and optimal use of coal will drive more socially and environmentally friendly development, favourable for the development of the coal industry and for the environment.

Acknowledgments

The author is the first scholarship holder under the Rio Tinto–ANU China Partnership.

Notes

1 Here, benefits mean improvement in human health, natural beauty and agricultural production, but it cannot include all the benefits. There are two kinds of costs: 1) the high prices generated, and 2) the cost to implement regulations (Tietenbery 2002:29).
2 In April 2000, I was part of a team required by Primer to investigate the situation of local state-owned coalmines. In Henan Province, I visited a mine whose operations had been suspended, where duty workers had only porridge to eat every day and retired workers received no pension for more than a year. Many families affiliated with such mines went into bankruptcy.

17

Growth, energy use and greenhouse gas emissions in China

Warwick J. McKibbin

Energy is a key issue for the Chinese economy, now and in future decades. The need for expanding sources of energy as an input into a rapidly growing economy and the environmental implications of rising energy use are well understood within China. Chinese energy use is also becoming an increasingly important issue for the global economy because of the scale of China's energy requirements and because of the implications for global climate change of quickly rising greenhouse emissions from China.

With roughly 20 per cent of the world's population and economic growth in the range of 10 per cent per annum, China is already having a significant impact on global energy demand. By 2002, China was the world's third largest energy producer and the second largest energy consumer.[1] Although China has large reserves of energy and rising capacity it shifted from being a net energy exporter to a net energy importer in 1998 (Figure 17.1). This massive increase in the use of energy has had important implications for local environmental problems such as air quality, public health problems and local climate change. Energy generation and its related emissions of sulphur dioxide from coal use, has caused local and regional problems with acid rain.[2] The large and growing emissions of greenhouse gases (particularly carbon dioxide emissions from burning coal) are a critical input into the global issue of climate change.[3]

In 1990 China accounted for 7.8 per cent of world energy use, which was roughly 1.5 times the energy use of Japan and seven times that of South Korea (Table 17.1). By 2002, China's share of global energy use had risen to 10.3 per cent. The

Figure 17.1   **China's total energy consumption and supply, 1980–2003**
(quadrillion Btu)

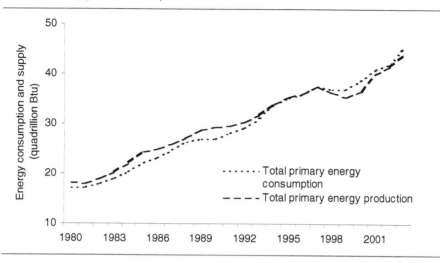

Source: Energy Information Agency, 2006b. *International Energy Outlook 2006*, Department of Energy, Washington, DC.

Table 17.1   **China's share of global energy consumption and carbon dioxide emissions, 1990–2030**

	1990	2002	2003	2010	2015	2020	2025	2030
Energy consumption								
China	7.8	10.3	10.8	15.1	16.3	17.4	18.3	19.3
India	2.3	3.4	3.3	3.8	4.0	4.2	4.4	4.5
Other non-OECD	33.1	29.9	30.2	30.8	31.8	32.5	33.1	33.4
South Korea	1.1	2.0	2.0	2.1	2.2	2.2	2.2	2.1
Japan	5.3	5.4	5.3	4.5	4.2	3.8	3.6	3.4
United States	24.4	23.9	23.3	21.2	20.3	19.7	19.1	18.6
Other OECD	26.1	25.2	25.0	22.5	21.3	20.2	19.4	18.7
World total	100.0	100.0	100.0	100.0	100.0	100.0	100.0	100.0
CO_2 emissions								
China	10.6	13.5	14.1	19.3	20.8	22.2	23.3	24.5
India	2.7	4.2	4.1	4.5	4.7	4.9	5.0	5.0
Other non-OECD	33.1	29.1	29.2	29.3	29.9	30.2	30.3	30.4
South Korea	1.1	1.9	1.9	2.0	2.0	2.0	2.0	1.9
Japan	4.8	4.9	4.8	4.0	3.6	3.3	3.0	2.8
United States	23.5	23.6	23.2	21.0	20.0	19.4	18.9	18.6
Other OECD	24.3	22.8	22.7	20.0	19.0	18.1	17.4	16.8
World total	100.0	100.0	100.0	100.0	100.0	100.0	100.0	100.0

Source: Energy Information Agency, 2006b. *International Energy Outlook 2006*, Department of Energy, Washington DC.

United States Energy Information Administration predicts that by 2030, China will account for more than 19 per cent of global energy use, or more than five times the energy use of Japan and nine times that of South Korea. China is already the world's largest coal producer, accounting for 28 per cent of world coal production and 27 per cent of world coal consumption by 2002 (Table 17.2). China's share of world coal consumption is projected to rise to a massive 44 per cent by 2030 (Table 17.2), and at the time will be more than 2.5 times the coal consumption of the United States. China's share of world oil consumption in 1990 was 3.5 per cent, but it is projected to rise to 12.7 per cent by 2030 (Table 17.2).

Until recently, the focus of policy in China has been on sustaining economic growth and energy needs rather than the environmental consequences of rapid industrialisation. This is beginning to change as rising income levels in China make the environment a more important issue and as environmental quality continues to deteriorate.

This chapter summarises the recent history of energy use in China and presents some estimates of future projections of energy use. Although there is a range of environmental issues associated with energy, this chapter focuses primarily on the emissions of carbon dioxide—a critical driver of global climate change.[4] Although economic growth is still a priority in China, environmental policy is emerging as an important issue.[5] Indeed, China has shown a commitment to tackle local environmental problems with encouraging outcomes.[6] For example, Jiang and McKibbin (2002) find that Chinese policy has been effective in reducing environmental problems in a number of areas, relative to what otherwise would be the case. However, many environmental problems continue to worsen despite policy intervention, due to other factors driven by strong economic growth.

The remainder of this chapter is structured as follows. The second section presents a brief overview of energy use and carbon dioxide emissions in China. It also summarises projections from the United States Energy Information Administration's *International Energy Outlook* (2006b) of energy use and carbon dioxide emissions in China until 2030. The third section summarises the current policy debate on climate change and the implications for future Chinese energy. The fourth section focuses on the sensitivity of projections of energy use and carbon dioxide emissions to assumptions about the sources of economic growth. This analysis is based on projections from the G-cubed multi-country model under different assumptions about the sources of economic growth in China. Finally, the sensitivity of projections to the price of carbon is assessed in the fifth section. A conclusion appears in the final section. Appendix Table A17.1 summarises the G-cubed multi-country model that forms the basis of some of the analysis in this paper.

Energy use and carbon dioxide emissions in China

History

The importance of China in world energy use and the projected increases in this importance are summarised in Table 17.1. In 2003, China accounted for 10.8 per cent of world energy use (compared with the United States at 23.3 per cent) and 14.1 per cent of global carbon dioxide emissions from fossil fuel use (compared with the United States at 23.3 per cent). Chinese GDP (in 2003) was estimated in PPP terms to be roughly 59 per cent of the size of that of the United States.[7] This implies that although carbon emissions per unit of energy use are higher in China than in the United States, energy use per unit of GDP (in PPP terms) is slightly lower in China than in the United States.

China has roughly 9.4 per cent of the world's installed electricity generation capacity (second only to the United States) and in the next three decades it is predicted to be responsible for up to 25 per cent of the increase in global energy generation. China's size and the composition of its energy use, with a large reliance on coal, are reflected in carbon dioxide emissions. China is estimated to have emitted 14.1 per cent of global carbon emissions from fossil fuels in 2003 (second only to the United States in terms of individual countries) and this share is projected to rise to 24.5 per cent by 2030 (Table 17.1). In an attempt to move away from reliance on fossil fuels, China has plans for another 30 nuclear power plants in the next two decades to supplement its nine existing nuclear reactors.[8] It is estimated that China has the largest hydroelectric capacity in the world (largely in the southwest of the country), currently generating 20 per cent of Chinese electricity. The Three Gorges hydroelectric dam on the Yangtze River will be the world's largest power plant when completed about 2009. The National Development and Reform Commission (NDRC) approved the largest wind farm in Asia in March 2005, to begin construction in 2006. There is projected to be a rapidly rising share of nuclear energy and renewable energy (particularly hydro) in Chinese energy production in coming years (Table 17.3). Despite the impressive scale of this expansion, the emergence of renewable energy will dent only slightly the overall dominance of coal in the foreseeable future in China, at least under current relative energy prices. The large rise in coal as a source of primary energy implies that China will need to respond to a range of environmental problems resulting from burning fossil fuels, including air quality (including black carbon emissions), acid rain (from emissions of sulphur dioxide and nitrogen oxides) and climate change (from carbon dioxide emissions).

Figure 17.1 gives another perspective on the recent history of energy production and consumption in China. Energy demand and supply in China has been rising quickly—more than doubling between 1980 and 1996. In 1998, Chinese energy consumption began to outstrip production, with China becoming a net energy importer.

Figure 17.2 shows that an abundance of low-cost coal has been the predominant source of Chinese energy supply (located mainly in the northern part of the country). Crude oil (petroleum) is the next largest source of energy supply, followed by hydroelectricity, natural gas and nuclear energy. The major source of demand for energy in China[9] is industry, which accounted for 68.9 per cent of the total in 2002.

Table 17.2 **China's shares of global consumption of fossil fuel energy components, 1990–2030** (per cent)

	1990	2002	2003	2010	2015	2020	2025	2030
Coal consumption								
China	21.3	26.9	28.1	36.4	39.1	40.8	42.3	44.0
India	4.9	8.2	7.9	8.4	8.8	9.0	8.8	8.4
Other non-OECD	25.4	18.4	18.4	16.6	16.5	16.2	15.7	15.1
South Korea	0.9	1.5	1.5	1.7	1.7	1.6	1.7	1.7
Japan	2.4	3.3	3.2	2.5	2.3	2.0	1.8	1.6
United States	17.2	20.3	20.1	17.7	16.4	16.1	16.7	16.9
Other OECD	28.0	21.4	20.7	16.5	15.2	14.2	13.1	12.4
World total	100.0	100.0	100.0	100.0	100.0	100.0	100.0	100.0
Oil consumption								
China	3.5	6.6	7.0	9.5	10.2	11.2	11.9	12.7
India	1.8	2.9	2.9	3.2	3.4	3.6	3.7	3.8
Other non-OECD	32.7	29.6	29.6	30.9	31.7	32.0	32.5	32.8
South Korea	1.5	2.7	2.7	2.8	3.0	2.9	2.9	3.0
Japan	7.8	7.0	7.0	5.9	5.6	5.2	5.0	4.6
United States	25.5	25.2	25.1	24.2	23.9	23.8	23.6	23.4
Other OECD	27.2	25.9	25.7	23.5	22.4	21.2	20.4	19.7
World total	100.0	100.0	100.0	100.0	100.0	100.0	100.0	100.0
Natural gas consumption								
China	0.7	1.2	1.3	2.6	2.9	3.4	3.7	3.8
India	0.5	1.0	1.0	1.3	1.3	1.5	1.9	2.5
Other non-OECD	48.5	44.2	45.1	48.0	49.3	50.6	51.7	52.9
South Korea	0.1	0.9	0.9	0.9	0.9	0.9	0.8	0.7
Japan	2.6	3.1	3.2	2.7	2.6	2.4	2.2	2.1
United States	26.2	24.9	23.4	20.1	19.3	17.9	16.3	14.8
Other OECD	21.3	24.8	25.0	24.5	23.8	23.3	23.3	23.2
World total	100.0	100.0	100.0	100.0	100.0	100.0	100.0	100.0

Source: Energy Information Agency, 2006b. *International Energy Outlook 2006*, Department of Energy, Washington DC.

Table 17.3 **Shares in global consumption of non-fossil fuel energy components, 1990–2030** (per cent)

	1990	2002	2003	2010	2015	2020	2025	2030
Nuclear energy consumption								
China	0.0	1.0	1.7	2.9	4.4	5.5	7.1	9.2
India	0.3	0.7	0.6	2.0	2.6	3.2	3.3	3.4
Other non-OECD	14.0	12.8	13.1	13.5	15.0	17.0	18.3	17.5
South Korea	2.6	4.4	4.9	5.2	6.0	6.4	6.7	7.2
Japan	10.1	11.0	9.4	10.0	9.8	10.2	10.8	11.2
United States	30.2	30.6	30.3	29.5	28.2	27.9	26.9	26.4
Other OECD	42.7	39.5	40.1	36.8	34.0	29.8	36.8	25.0
World total	100.0	100.0	100.0	100.0	100.0	100.0	100.0	100.0
Hydroelectricity and other renewable energy consumption								
China	4.9	8.7	8.9	13.5	13.8	13.4	12.6	12.2
India	2.7	2.2	2.1	2.9	2.6	2.8	3.1	3.5
Other non-OECD	31.6	34.5	35.5	35.8	38.1	39.5	41.5	43.1
South Korea	0.0	0.0	0.3	0.4	0.6	0.6	0.5	0.5
Japan	4.2	3.4	4.3	3.1	3.1	2.8	2.6	2.6
United States	23.2	18.3	17.4	15.9	15.3	15.3	15.1	14.6
Other OECD	33.1	32.9	31.2	28.5	26.5	25.6	24.6	23.6
World total	100.0	100.0	100.0	100.0	100.0	100.0	100.0	100.0

Source: Energy Information Agency, 2006b. *International Energy Outlook 2006*, Department of Energy, Washington DC.

This is followed by the household sector at 11.4 per cent and transportation at only 7.5 per cent.

Projections

Projecting future energy use in China, especially over horizons of more than a decade, is very difficult. It is tempting to base future projections on extrapolations of recent trends; however, as shown by Bagnoli et al. (1996) and McKibbin et al. (2004), overall economic growth need not be the key determinant of energy use. The sources of economic growth are critical. A number of projections are available publicly. The Energy Information Administration of the United States Department of Energy, in its annual *International Energy Outlook* (2006b), provides one source of projections. Projections for Chinese energy consumption in quadrillion BTU are shown in Figure 17.3 for three scenarios: high and low economic growth and a reference case.

Figure 17.4 shows the Energy Information Administration's projections for carbon dioxide emissions by energy source in China for the reference case scenario. It is

Figure 17.2 **Energy consumption by source in China, 1980–2003**
(quadrillion Btu)

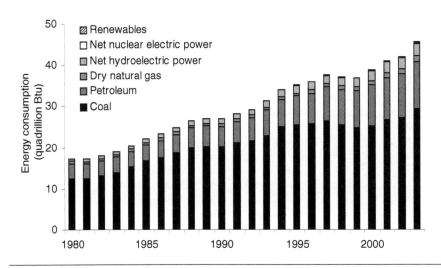

Source: Energy Information Agency, 2006b. *International Energy Outlook 2006*, Department of Energy, Washington, DC.

clear that coal burning is the overwhelming source of carbon dioxide emissions in China historically, and in these projections it is expected to be the major source of energy and therefore emissions in the foreseeable future. This is not surprising given the large quantity of low-cost coal available in China and the assumptions of unchanging relative energy prices in these projections. Over time, the share of emissions from petroleum is projected to rise as greater use of motor vehicles and other non-stationary energy uses rise. It will be shown in the next section that these types of projections are contingent on assumptions about the price of energy relative to other goods and the relative price of alternative energy sources.

Figure 17.5 shows the global sources of carbon dioxide from burning fossil fuels, by region, in 1990 and those projected for 2030 in the 2006 *International Energy Outlook*. Not only is China currently an important source of carbon dioxide emissions, its share is expected to grow quickly. Its absolute size (Figure 17.5) and its share of global emissions (Table 17.1), suggest that China is a critical country in the debate over policies to deal with potential climate change. These projections assume business as usual, and therefore incorporate global Kyoto Protocol commitments.

Figure 17.3 **Projections of energy consumption in China, 1990–2030** (quadrillion (10^{15}) Btu)

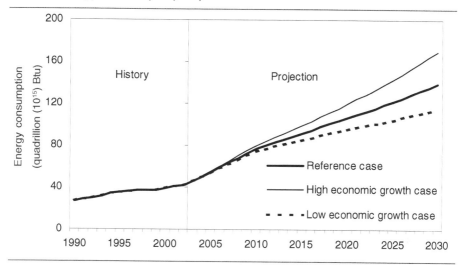

Source: Energy Information Agency, 2006b. *International Energy Outlook 2006*, Department of Energy, Washington, DC.

Figure 17.4 **Projections of carbon dioxide emissions by fuel type in China, 1990–2030** (million metric tonnes)

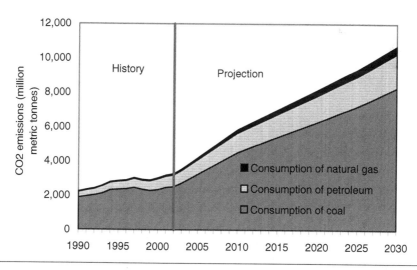

Source: Energy Information Agency, 2006b. *International Energy Outlook 2006*, Department of Energy, Washington, DC.

Carbon emissions and climate change

China has begun to take action to address local environmental problems. There has been direct action to substitute non-fossil fuel energy sources such as wind, hydro and thermonuclear energy for fossil fuels in energy generation. China has also attempted to reduce the emissions of sulphur dioxide from burning fossil fuels by implementing a range of policies, from closing high-sulphur coalmines to developing markets for trading sulphur dioxide emission rights. As argued in McKibbin (2006a), a greater focus is required to address the emissions of black carbon. From a global perspective, the discussion above on future carbon emissions suggests that a critical area where China will need to take greater action is in the emissions of carbon dioxide.

The most important cause of human-induced climate change is the accumulation of greenhouse gases in the atmosphere over many decades. The most important greenhouse gas is carbon dioxide. The global community has been struggling for several decades with how to respond effectively to the threat of climate change. The United Nations Earth Summit in Rio de Janeiro in 1992 produced a landmark treaty on climate change that undertook to stabilise greenhouse gas concentrations in the atmosphere. The agreement, signed and ratified by more than 186 countries, including the United States and China (the world's largest carbon dioxide emitters), spawned numerous subsequent rounds of climate negotiations aimed at rolling back emissions from industrialised countries to the levels that prevailed in 1990. Unfortunately, the negotiations have had little effect on greenhouse gas emissions and have not produced a detectable slowing in the rate of emissions growth.[10] The treaty's implementing protocol, the 1997 Kyoto agreement, was diluted heavily at subsequent negotiations in Bonn and Marrakech.[11] The Kyoto Protocol entered into force on 16 February 2005 after ratification by Russia, yet there are still many problems to be faced before it will be evident that Kyoto is reducing emissions. More than a decade of negotiations has produced a policy that is likely to be ineffective in practice.

The difficulty at the international level is worse than it appears from the troubled process of Kyoto ratification. The Kyoto Protocol places restrictions only on industrial economies, excluding the world's largest greenhouse emitter, the United States. Developing countries, including China, have ratified the agreement but have not taken on any responsibilities for reducing emissions except those that emerge from mechanisms such as the Clean Development Mechanism (CDM) and joint implementation. That developing countries are not taking on targets as commitments is one of the reasons given by the United States and Australia for

Figure 17.5 **Global carbon dioxide emissions from fossil fuels, 1990 and 2030** (million metric tonnes)

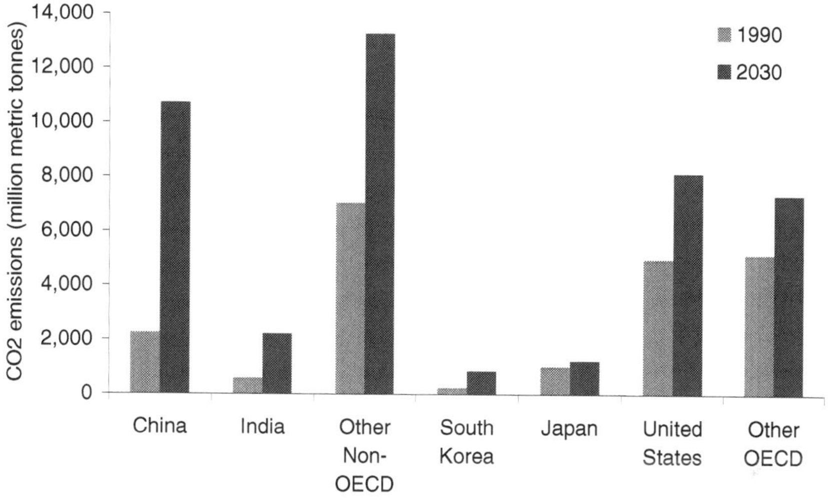

Source: Energy Information Agency, 2006b. 'Reference case', in *International Energy Outlook 2006*, Department of Energy, Washington, DC.

not ratifying the Kyoto Protocol. Because there have been no binding commitments by the key developing countries of China, India, Brazil and Indonesia (among others), effective action against possible climate change is still largely a hypothetical debate.

Developing countries have argued legitimately that while they are prepared to be part of a regime to tackle climate change, they should not be required to bear a disproportionate part of the costs of taking action. Current concentrations of greenhouse gases in the atmosphere are primarily the result of economic activities in the industrial economies since the Industrial Revolution. Because it is the stock of carbon in the atmosphere that matters for temperature changes, any climate change in the near future will be largely the result of the historical activities of industrial economies. One of the main dilemmas for developing countries is not just the reality that at some stage they will need to make some form of commitment to curbing greenhouse gas emissions, but the fact that most estimates of the damages from climate change are borne by developing countries.[12]

It is worth clarifying several important facts about the costs and benefits of climate policy and exploring whether there are approaches available to China and other developing countries that are being delayed by countries clinging to the Kyoto Protocol. Given the uncertainties of climate change and the decisions on energy systems being made in the rapidly growing regions of the developing world, this delay in providing clear incentives for moving away from fossil fuel-based systems might ultimately prove to be extremely costly.

Fossil fuel combustion is one of the largest sources of anthropogenic greenhouse gas emissions. Given the cost of changing existing energy systems substantially in the short term, one of the cheapest means of making the global energy system less reliant on fossil fuels is to remove these carbon emissions from future energy systems. As was shown in the second section, China is heavily reliant on coal for energy production and is likely to be so for many decades into the future. Technology will ultimately be the source of reductions in emissions, whether through the development of alternative sources of energy or through sequestration of carbon released from burning fossil fuels. Developing countries have a huge potential to avoid the pitfalls in terms of carbon intensities experienced by industrialised economies in their development process. The key issue is how to encourage the emergence of energy systems in developing countries that are less carbon-intensive over time. Ultimately, if climate change does emerge as a serious problem, developing countries will have to move towards a less carbon-intensive future. It is likely to be significantly cheaper to do this over time than to face a massive restructuring at some future period—the sort of problems being faced within industrialised economies today.

The current state of global climate policy is that the United States (the largest emitter of greenhouse gases) has rejected Kyoto and is arguing for policies that directly or indirectly reduce emissions through technological change; the European Union is committed to emission targets (assuming Russia provides a great deal of the reductions required through selling emission permits) and on 1 January 2005 it implemented a Europe-wide emissions trading scheme (which exempts key sectors such as aluminium, motor vehicles and chemicals), but with caps that appear to bind only by the end of 2008; Japan is considering what it can do given current emissions are 16 per cent above targets in an economy recovering from a decade of recession; and developing countries have refused to discuss taking on commitments officially.

Given this background, there are a number of ways a country such as China could begin to address carbon emissions and make a major contribution to a global response. One policy would be to move energy prices closer to world levels by removing energy subsidies. The second would be to raise the price of energy further to reflect the true economic and environmental cost of burning fossil fuels.

A further approach could be direct importation of less carbon-intensive technologies provided by the CDM. This latter outcome is possible but not likely, as already outlined above.

Economic theory provides guidance about the structure of a possible climate change policy for China.[13] Since greenhouse gases are emitted by a vast number of highly heterogeneous sources, minimising the cost of abating a given amount of emissions requires that all sources clean up amounts that cause their marginal cost of abatement to be equated. To achieve this, the standard economic policy prescription would be a market-based instrument, such as a tax on emissions or a tradable permit system for emission rights. These types of market-based incentives for environmental pollution are already being undertaken in China through pollution charges and permit trading in sulphur dioxide. Cooper (2005) has advocated a carbon tax for China. Garbaccio et al. (1999) and McKibbin and Wilcoxen (2004) find that a price signal would be effective in changing China's future emission profiles. Given the advantages and disadvantages of the standard economic instruments, McKibbin and Wilcoxen (2002a, 2002b) show that it is possible to combine the attractive features of both systems into a single approach. They also show that it is possible to develop a system that is common in philosophy across industrialised and developing economies but in which developing economies do not incur the short-term costs to the economy in the form of higher energy prices until they have reached a capacity to pay. McKibbin and Wilcoxen (2002) have argued for a hybrid approach in which the short-term and long-term prices of carbon are changed in order to give incentives to move away from carbon-emitting energy sources. The implications of this hybrid approach for China are discussed in detail in McKibbin (2006a, 2006b).

Sensitivity of energy projections to growth assumptions in China

In this section, emission projections are presented from the G-cubed multi-country model[14] to show how sensitive the projections are to assumptions about the sources of economic growth in China. Two scenarios are considered: one in which all sectors have the same productivity growth and one in which sectors experience differential productivity growth similar to the experience of the United States in the past 30 years.

A summary of the approach is provided here but further details on the technique used in the G-cubed model can be found in McKibbin et al. (2004). In the following discussion, the source of economic growth is labour-augmenting technical change and population growth. The population growth assumptions are the same across both scenarios and are based on the 2004 United Nations population projections

(Mid scenario). In order to simplify the discussion, labour-augmenting technical change is referred to as 'productivity growth' throughout the remainder of this chapter.

In the G-cubed model, productivity growth by sector and by country is assumed to be driven by a productivity catch-up model. The United States is assumed to be the technological leader in each sector. Other countries are allocated an initial productivity gap by sector and a rate at which this gap is closed. For industrial countries and China, this is assumed to be closed at the rate of 2 per cent per annum. For other developing countries, it is assumed to be closed at 1 per cent per annum, reflecting the empirical literature. In this chapter, Chinese productivity is assumed to be 20 per cent of productivity in the equivalent sector in the United States. In the first scenario, the United States is assumed to have the same productivity growth across all sectors. This is the typical assumption in models where aggregate GDP drives energy use and therefore emissions. This scenario is labelled 'uniform productivity growth'. The implications for growth are shown in Figure 17.6. Productivity growth in all Chinese sectors is the same given the same initial gaps to the United States and the same catch-up rate across sectors.

In the second scenario, it is assumed that the differential productivity growth across sectors in the United States is similar to that experienced in the past 30 years. The growth rates are adjusted so that the aggregate GDP growth rate for

Figure 17.6 **Labour-augmentative technical change for uniform productivity scenario, 2002–2100** (all sectors)

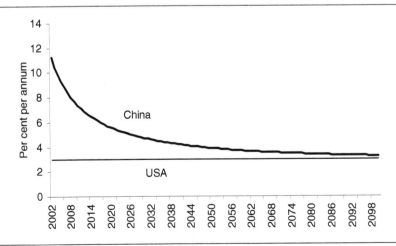

Source: G-cubed model version 63E.

the United States is similar to GDP growth generated in the first scenario, and the main difference between the scenarios is the composition of growth. It is not possible to target GDP growth exactly.

Figures 17.6 and 17.7 show the productivity growth assumptions for each sector in the United States and the implications for the equivalent sector in China under the assumptions of the same initial gaps and rates of convergence. Although the initial productivity gaps are the same, note that in Figure 17.7, different sectors in China experience different rates of productivity growth. This is important because capital accumulation is endogenous in the G-cubed model, responding to changes in real and expected rates of return to capital.

The results from the G-cubed model for Chinese carbon dioxide emissions and GDP growth under two scenarios are shown in Figures 17.8 and 17.9 for the period from 2003 to 2030. By 2020, emissions under the uniform productivity scenario are 20 per cent higher than under the differential productivity growth scenario, even though GDP growth is slightly higher under the latter. Part of the difference is due to differential sectoral demand for energy as an input as well as considerably different relative energy prices under the two scenarios. These results suggest that future projections of carbon emissions and energy use in China need to be interpreted carefully.

Despite this warning on the importance of structural change in energy projections, it is difficult to see a major shift in trends away from coal under current energy prices. Interestingly, there is also little change in the real price of oil or any fossil fuels throughout the projection period in the *International Energy Outlook* results presented earlier, yet there are significant changes in the projections from the G-cubed model, depending on assumptions about the sources of growth.

Under most scenarios, the emergence of China as a key supplier and producer of energy is one of the most important issues in the debate over global energy use for the foreseeable future. This is also critical for environmental issues in China, Asia and globally.

Sensitivity of carbon emissions to price changes

The above scenarios considered differences in emission projections due to different growth assumptions. Due to the endogeniety of relative prices in the modelling framework used, some of the differences in energy use and emissions are due to changing relative prices due to changes in demand and supply of energy and other goods in the global economy. In this section, the focus is on the sensitivity of emission projections to relative carbon prices, by considering a carbon tax in China.

Figure 17.7 Labour-augmentative technical change by sector in differential productivity scenario, 2002–2100

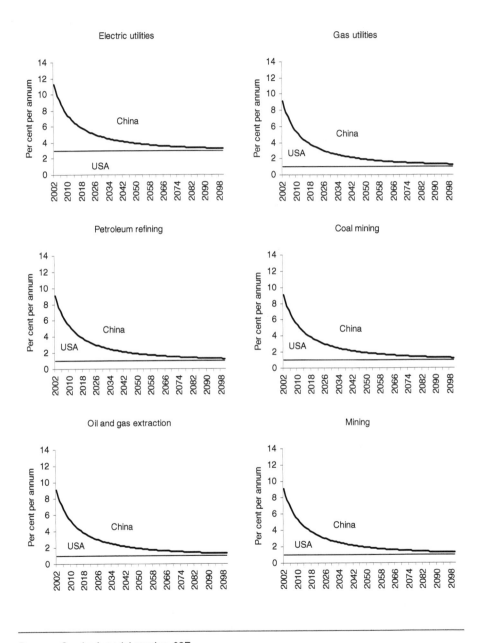

Source: G-cubed model version 63E.

Figure 17.7 **Labour-augmentative technical change by sector in differential productivity scenario, 2002–2100,** continued

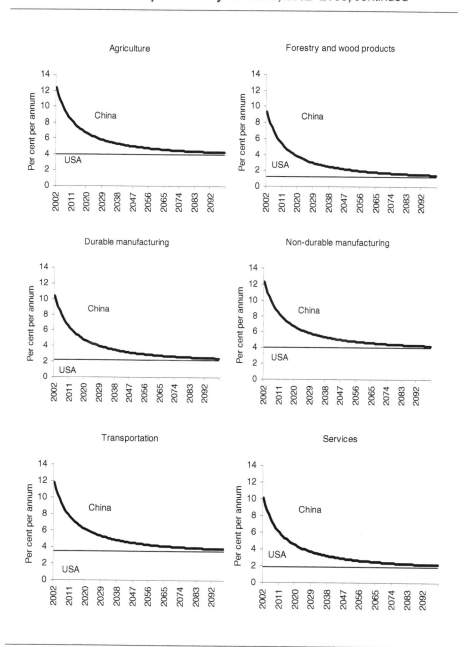

Source: G-cubed model version 63E.

Growth, energy use and gas emissions in China

This result can also be translated approximately into the responsiveness of Chinese emissions to a conventional permit-trading system in China or a McKibbin and Wilcoxen hybrid system, except that there will be differential income and wealth effects of the latter system due to revenue going to the permit holders rather than to the government via a tax.

Figures 17.10 and 17.11 contain results from the G-cubed model of a tax of US$10 (in 2002 constant prices) per tonne of carbon, for the United States and China. Results are shown from 2007 to 2055. The short-term response of emissions in China is much larger than in the United States. The initial price of energy in China is much lower than in the United States so the tax (on a per unit basis) causes a much larger proportional rise in the price of carbon-intensive energy in China than in the United States. The response in the short term reflects substitution and conservation by households and industry as well as a significant contraction in economic activity in China relative to the baseline. GDP falls by 0.9 per cent relative to the baseline in the initial year, compared with 0.2 per cent in the United States. Over time, substitution in production and the use of energy allows a larger carbon reduction with less impact on GDP. GDP initially falls in both countries and in the longer term it is higher in China due to efficiency gains from more efficient use of

Figure 17.8 **Projection of Chinese carbon emissions, 2002–2026**

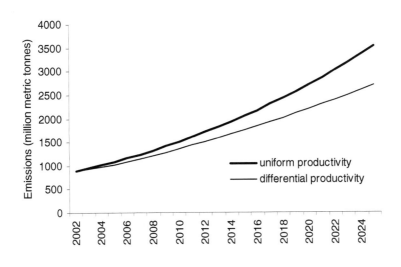

Source: G-cubed model version 63E.

Figure 17.9 **Projection of Chinese real GDP growth, 2002–2026** (per cent per annum)

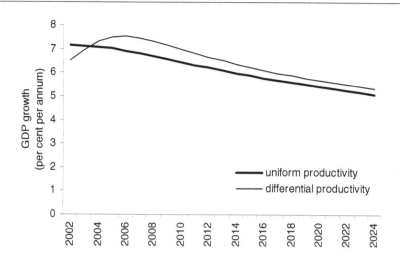

Source: G-cubed model version 63E.

energy. These results indicate that in the G-cubed model energy prices—in particular, the price of carbon—are important in changing the future emissions profile.

Conclusion

China currently faces a number of important problems related to energy use. At the forefront is the issue of how to deal with the desire for sustained economic growth at the same time as tackling serious environmental issues caused by energy generation. This issue is likely to become more important in coming years, especially as energy demand soars, environmental problems worsen and incomes rise. It is likely, under current global energy price structures, that future energy in China will be generated largely by the use of coal. Under current technologies in China, this is likely to have serious environmental consequences. Current plans to increase the use of nuclear and renewable energy such as hydroelectric and wind power are impressive but will likely have little impact in a rapidly expanding energy sector unless there is a significant change in the expected relative price of carbon. Other technologies—such as carbon sequestration, which is showing great potential—are also an option, although this technology will be more economically viable more quickly with a change in Chinese and global carbon prices.

For some time, China has been taking action on local environmental issues. This has been particularly true in dealing with air and water quality as well as sulphur dioxide emissions. Action is already under way to reduce emissions of sulphur dioxide by moving away from high-sulphur coal, by closing small, high-sulphur coalmines, with direct controls on sulphur dioxide emissions, implementation of pilot schemes for sulphur dioxide emission charges and pilot schemes for sulphur dioxide emissions trading. These are having an impact on emissions of sulphur, although the impact on acid rain in China and across Northeast Asia has been less clear.[15]

I have argued (McKibbin 2006a) that black carbon and its direct health, economic and environmental consequences are promising areas for close attention and direct policy intervention within China. This is not an issue of technological change at the power utilities as might usually be the focus of energy policy. A reduction in the emissions of black carbon will require a technology shift in the way households generate energy for heating and cooking and in the way farmers clear their land after harvest. Black carbon is a good candidate for consideration under the Asia Pacific Partnership for Clean Development and Climate (APPCDC) announced on 28 July 2005, which includes the United States, Japan, Australia, South Korea, China and India.

A critical issue facing China and the global community directly related to energy use in China is the emission of carbon dioxide. China and most other countries are yet to take effective action on reducing greenhouse gas emissions. Even if rapid action were possible, the lags between emissions and climate change are so long that benefits are unlikely for many decades. Although some researchers believe that global responses, such as through the CDM in the Kyoto Protocol, are a way to proceed,[16] it is doubtful that much can be achieved through this approach alone. A strong case can be made for responses to be developed within China, Korea, Japan and other economies in the Asia Pacific region for dealing with carbon dioxide emissions. This has already begun to emerge within the APPCDC. The current idea within this group of countries of technology transfer without a carbon price signal is unlikely to be as effective as a way forward as a system based on clear long-term price signals that give incentives for reducing carbon dioxide emissions. One estimate of the sensitivity of carbon emissions to price changes has been presented in this paper. Within the APPCDC framework, there is potential to experiment with hybrid market–government control schemes such as the McKibbin–Wilcoxen blueprint, in which important institutions are created to begin a long process of reduced carbonisation of the Chinese economy. This would allow China to continue to grow but would put in place a pricing mechanism for future carbon emissions as an

Figure 17.10 **Response of emissions to a carbon tax in each country, 2007–2058** (US$10 per tonne of carbon)

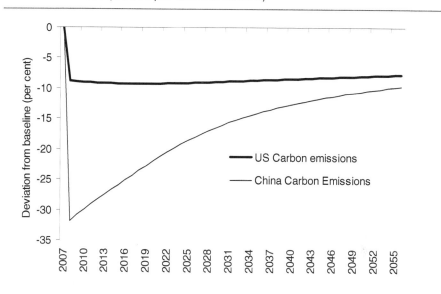

Source: G-cubed model version 63E.

Figure 17.11 **Response of GDP to a carbon tax in each country, 2007–2055** (US$10 per tonne of carbon)

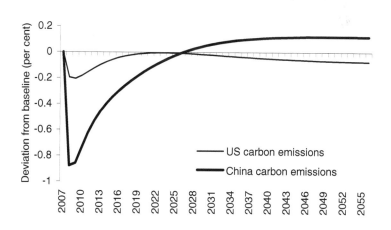

Source: G-cubed model version 63E.

incentive to shift Chinese energy systems gradually to low carbon-emitting technologies. The creation of institutions for environmental management based on market incentives together with appropriate pricing of consequences of current energy generation technologies are important for long-range energy planning in China.

China and other countries in the Asia Pacific region are at a critical juncture in determining the nature of energy use in the global economy and the potential global environmental impact of a rapidly growing China. Addressing this problem effectively is not easy, as shown by the reality that many of the potential solutions to environmental problems related to energy use are not yet implemented in other Asia Pacific economies. The form of future energy systems and the problem of reducing global carbon dioxide emissions cannot be resolved seriously without the complete participation of China in any strategies. But these strategies need to be determined domestically within a framework of multilateral cooperation rather than being imposed from the outside. The preliminary results in this chapter suggest that, given appropriate use of markets and pricing energy—in particular, carbon pricing—China can sustain high economic growth with less environmental damage from energy use and a smaller contribution to global carbon dioxide emissions than an extrapolation of recent trends would predict.

Acknowledgments

This chapter extends earlier research funded by the China Economic Research and Advisory Program (CERAP). The author thanks Yan Yang for excellent research assistance. The views expressed in the paper are those of the author and should not be interpreted as reflecting the views of the institutions with which the author is affiliated, including the trustees, officers or other staff of the ANU, the Lowy Institute and the Brookings Institution.

Notes

1 All data, unless specifically indicated otherwise, are sourced from Energy Information Agency, 2006b. *International Energy Outlook 2006*, Department of Energy, Washington DC.
2 These issues are discussed more extensively in McKibbin 2006. See also China Council for International Cooperation on Environment and Development 2001; Panayotou and Zheng 2000; Streets 2004; and Wang and Smith 1999.
3 See Jiang 2002; and Zhang 1998.
4 There are many other environmental problems in China caused by a large population and rapid economic growth, such as water and air quality problems caused by deforestation and desertification. China's demand for resources also has a large impact on the environment of other countries. These important problems are not the subject of this paper, but for an overview see Liu and Diamond 2005.
5 China's *Environmental Protection Law* was promulgated in 1979 — a nationwide levy system on

pollution began in 1982. The collection of fees for sulphur dioxide pollution from coal began in 1992. See Jiang 2003 for an overview.

[6] See Jiang 2003; and Panayatou 1998 for an overview of China's environmental problems.

[7] 2004 UNDP Human Development Report.

[8] DOE 2005.

[9] See National Bureau of Statistics of China, *China Statistical Yearbooks* for 1990–2005.

[10] See McKibbin and Wilcoxen 2002 for a summary of the negotiations and critique of the approach.

[11] Earlier estimates of the cost of Kyoto can be found in Weyant 1999. Direct comparisons of the COP3 and COP7 versions of the protocol can be found in Bohringer 2001; Buchner et al. 2001; Kemfert 2001; Löschel and Zhang 2002; and McKibbin and Wilcoxen 2004.

[12] See Intergovernmental Panel on Climate Change 2001.

[13] See McKibbin and Wilcoxen 2002a for a survey; and Pezzey 2003 for a comparison of taxes and permits.

[14] See McKibbin and Wilcoxen 1998, and documentation at http://www.gcubed.com

[15] Nakada and Ueta 2004 point out that there are likely to be gains for other economies in the region, such as Japan and Korea, to cooperate with China in controlling sulphur emissions since these economies are also directly affected by acid rain emanating from China.

[16] See Ueta et al. 2005.

[17] Full details of the model, including a list of equations and parameters, can be found online at www.gcubed.com

[18] These issues include: Reaganomics in the 1980s; German reunification in the early 1990s; fiscal consolidation in Europe in the mid 1990s; the formation of the North American Free Trade Agreement (NAFTA); the East Asian financial crisis; and the productivity boom in the United States.

[19] See Blanchard and Fischer 1989; and Obstfeld and Rogoff 1996.

Appendix 17.1: the G-cubed model for projecting energy use and greenhouse emissions in China

The G-Cubed model is an intertemporal general equilibrium model of the world economy. The theoretical structure is outlined in McKibbin and Wilcoxen (1998).[17] A number of studies—summarised in McKibbin and Vines (2000)—show that the G-cubed modelling approach has been useful in assessing a range of issues across a number of countries since the mid 1980s.[18] Some of the principal features of the model are as follows.

The model is based on explicit intertemporal optimisation by the agents (consumers and firms) in each economy.[19] In contrast with static CGE models, time and dynamics are of fundamental importance in the G-cubed model. The MSG-cubed model is known as a Dynamic Stochastic General Equilibrium (DSGE) model in the macroeconomics literature and as a Dynamic Intertemporal General Equilibrium (DIGE) model in the computable general equilibrium literature.

In order to track the macro time series, the behaviour of agents is modified to allow for short-term deviations from optimal behaviour due either to myopia or to restrictions on the ability of households and firms to borrow at the risk-free bond rate on government debt. For households and firms, deviations from intertemporal optimising behaviour take the form of rules of thumb, which are consistent with an optimising agent that does not update predictions based on new information about future events. These rules of thumb are chosen to generate the same steady-state behaviour as optimising agents so that in the long term there is only a single intertemporal optimising equilibrium of the model. In the short term, behaviour is assumed to be a weighted average of the optimising and the rule-of-thumb assumptions. Therefore, aggregate consumption is a weighted average of consumption based on wealth (current asset valuation and expected future after-tax labour income) and consumption based on current disposable income. Similarly, aggregate investment is a weighted average of investment based on Tobin's 'q' (a market valuation of the expected future change in the marginal product of capital relative to the cost) and investment based on a backward-looking version of 'Q'.

There is an explicit treatment of the holding of financial assets, including money. Money is introduced into the model through a restriction that households require money to purchase goods.

The model also allows for short-term nominal wage rigidity (by different degrees in different countries) and therefore allows for significant periods of unemployment depending on the labour-market institutions in each country. This assumption, when taken together with the explicit role for money, is what gives the model its macroeconomic characteristics. (Here again, the model's assumptions differ from the standard market-clearing assumption in most CGE models.)

The model distinguishes between the stickiness of physical capital within sectors and within countries and the flexibility of financial capital, which immediately flows to where expected returns are highest. This important distinction leads to a critical difference between the quantity of physical capital that is available at any time to produce goods and services, and the valuation of that capital as a result of decisions about the allocation of financial capital.

As a result of this structure, the G-cubed model contains rich dynamic behaviour, driven on the one hand by asset accumulation and, on the other, by wage adjustment to a neoclassical steady state. It embodies a wide range of assumptions about individual behaviour and empirical regularities in a general equilibrium framework. The interdependencies are solved using a computer algorithm that solves the rational expectations of equilibrium of the global economy. It is important to stress that the term 'general equilibrium' is used to signify that as many interactions as possible are captured, not that all economies are in a full market-clearing equilibrium at each point in time. Although it is assumed that market forces eventually drive the world economy to a neoclassical steady-state growth equilibrium, unemployment does emerge for long periods due to wage stickiness, to an extent that differs between countries due to differences in labour-market institutions.

Appendix Table A17.1 **Overview of the G-cubed model (version 63E)**

Regions
- United States
- Japan
- Australia
- Europe
- Rest of the OECD
- China
- Oil-exporting developing countries
- Eastern Europe and the former Soviet Union
- Other developing countries

Sectors

Energy:
- Electric utilities
- Gas utilities
- Petroleum refining
- Coalmining
- Crude oil and gas extraction

Non-energy:
- Mining
- Agriculture, fishing and hunting
- Forestry/timber products
- Durable manufacturing
- Non-durable manufacturing
- Transportation
- Services Capital-producing sector

References

Acemoglu, D., 2005. 'Constitutions, politics, and economics: a review essay on Persson and Tabellini's *The Economic Effects of Constitutions*', *Journal of Economic Literature*, XLIII(4):1025–49.

Albuquerque, R., Loayza, N. and Servén, L., 2003. *World market integration through the lens of foreign direct investors*, Policy Research Working Paper Series 2030, World Bank, Washington, DC.

Alesina, A. and Rodrik, D., 1994. 'Distributive politics and economic growth', *Quarterly Journal of Economics*, 109(2):465–90.

Allen, F., Qian, J. and Qian, M., 2006. *China's financial system: past, present and Future*, Working Paper, University of Pennsylvania.

Almanac of China's Finance and Banking, 1995, 2003, 2004, 2005.

Anderson, K., 1990. *Changing Comparative Advantages in China*, OECD, Paris.

——, 1997. 'On the complexities of China's WTO accession', *The World Economy*, 20(6):749–72.

Arrow, K., Bolin, B., Costanza, R., Dasgupta, P. Folke, C. Holling, C.S..Jansson, B.L Levin, S. Maler, K.G. Pimental, D., 1995. 'Economic growth, carrying capacity, and the environment', *Science*, 268:519–28.

Asian Development Bank, 2002. 'Research on Poverty', Unpublished Report, Manila.

Auerbach, A.J. and Chun, Y.J., 2003. Generational accounting in Korea, unpublished draft.

References

Auerbach, A.J., Gokhale, J. and Kotlikoff, L.J., 1991. 'Generational accounts: a meaningful alternative to deficit accounting', in D. Bradford (ed.), *Tax Policy and The Economy*, Vol. 5, MIT Press, Cambridge:55–110.

——, 1994. 'Generational accounting: a meaningful way to evaluate fiscal policy', *The Journal of Economic Perspectives*, Winter:73–94.

Bagnoli, P., McKibbin, W. and Wilcoxen, P., 1996. 'Future projections and structural change', in N. Nakicenovic, W. Nordhaus, R. Richels and F. Toth (eds), *Climate Change: integrating economics and policy*, CP 96-1, International Institute for Applied Systems Analysis, Vienna:181–206.

Bai, C.E., Du, Y.J., Tao, Z.G. and Tong, Y.T., 2003. *Local protectionism and regional specialization: evidence from China's industries*, William Davidson Working Paper 565, University of Michigan Business School

Balassa, B., 1965. 'Trade liberalisation and "revealed comparative advantage"', *The Manchester School of Economic and Social Studies*, 33:99–123.

Ball, A., Hansard, A., Curtotti, R. and Schneider, K., 2003. *China's Changing Coal Industry—Implications and Outlook*, eReport 03.3, Australian Bureau of Agriculture and Research Economics (ABARE), Canberra.

Banister, J., 2004. 'Manufacturing employment and compensation in China', *Foreign Labor Statistics*, December, US Department of Labor, Bureau of Labor Statistics. Available from www.bls.gov/fls/Chinareport.pdf (accessed 20 July 2005).

——, 2005. 'Manufacturing earnings and compensation in China', *Monthly Labour Review*, 128(8):22–44.

Bank for International Settlements, 1999. *Strengthening the banking system in China: issues and experiences*, BIS Policy Papers No. 7, October, Basel.

Bank of China, 2006. *Global Offering Prospectus*, May, Hong Kong.

Banks, J., Disney, R. and Smith, Z., 1999. *What can we learn about pension reform from generational accounting for the UK?*, Working Paper Series No. W99/16, The Institute for Fiscal Studies, London.

Barbier, B., 1994. 'Natural capital and the economics of environment and development', in Jansson, A.M., Hammer, M., Folker, C., and Costanza, R., (eds), *Investing in Natural Capital: the ecological economics approach to sustainability*, Island Press, Washington D.C.

Bardhan, P. and Mookherjee, D., 2005. 'Decentralizing antipoverty program delivery in developing countries', *Journal of Public Economics*, 89(4):675–704.

Barlett, B., 1994. 'The high cost of turning green', *Wall Street Journal*, 14:18.

Barro, R.J. and Jong-Wha Lee., 2000. 'International data on educational attainment: updates and implications', CID Working Paper, No. 42.

Bates, R., 2005. *Markets and States in Tropical Africa: the political basis of agricultural policies*, University of California Press.

Beck, P.J. and Maher, M.W., 1986. 'A comparison of bribery and bidding in thin markets', *Economics Letter*, 20:1–5.

Becker, G., 1964. *Human Capital*, Columbia University Press, New York.

Becker, G.S., Murphy, K. and Tammura, R., 1990. 'Human capital, fertility and economic growth', *Journal of Political Economy*, 98:s12–s37.

Beckerman, W., 1992. 'Economic growth and the environment: whose growth? Whose environment?', *World Development*, 20:481–96.

Bell, S. and McGillivray, D., 2000. *Environmental Law* (Fifth Edn), Blackstone Press Limited, London.

Benabou, R., 1996. *Inequality and growth*, NBER Working Paper 5658, National Bureau of Economic Research, Cambridge.

Benjamin D., Brandt L. and Giles J 2005. 'The evolution of income inequality in rural China', *Economic Development and Cultural Change*, 53(4):769–824

Bergsten, C.F., (ed.), 2005. *The United States and the World Economy: foreign economic policy for the next decade*, Institute for International Economics, Washington, D.C.

Bergsten, C.F., 2006. 'Clash of the titans', *Newsweek*, 24 April.

Bergsten, C.F., Bates, G., Lardy, N.R., Mitchell, D., 2006. *China: the balance sheet*, Public Affairs, New York.

Berloffa, G. Segnana, M.L., 2004. 'Trade, inequality and pro-poor growth: two perspectives, one message?', Contributo a 'Economic Growth and Distribution: on the Nature and Causes of the Wealth of Nations, Lucca, 16–18 June 2004.

Bernanke, B., 2005. The global saving glut and the US current account deficit, Presented at the Sandridge Lecture, Virginia Economics Association, Richmond, 10 March.

Bhagawati, J., 1993. 'The case for free trade', *Scientific American*:42–9.

Birnie, P.W. and Boyle, A.E., 2002. *International Law and the Environment* (2nd Ed.), Oxford University Press, Oxford.

Blanchard, O. and Fischer, S., 1989. *Lectures on Macroeconomics*, MIT Press, Cambridge, Mass.

Blanchard, O.J., Giavazzi, F. and Filipa, S.A., 2005 *The US current account and the dollar*, NBER Working Paper 11137, National Bureau of Economic Research, Cambridge.

Bloom, D.E. and Williamson, J.G., 1997. 'Demographic transitions, human resource development and economic miracles in emerging Asia', in J. Sachs and D.

Bloom (eds), *Emerging Asia*, Asian Development Bank, Manila.

Bloom, D.E., Canning, D. and Sevilla, J., 2002. *The Demographic Dividend: a new perspective on the economic consequences of population change*, RAND, Santa Monica.

Bohringer, C., 2001. *Climate policies from Kyoto to Bonn: from little to nothing?*, ZEW Discussion Paper No. 01-49, Mannheim.

Borjas, G.J., 1985. 'Assimilation, changes in cohort quality, and the earnings of immigrants', *Journal of Labor Economics*, 3:463–89.

——, 1995. 'Assimilation and changes in cohort quality revisited: what happened to immigrant earnings in the 1980s?', *Journal of Labor Economics*, 13(2):201–45.

BP, 2004. *Statistical Review of World Energy*. Available from http://www.bp.com/statisticalreview2004

——, 2005. *Statistical Review of World Energy 2005*.

Brown, L.R., 2006. *Plan B 2.0 Rescuing a Planet Under Stress and a Civilization in Trouble*, W.W. Norton & Company, New York. Also available from http://www.earth-policy.org/Books/PB2/pb2ch12.pdf (accessed 28 June 2006).

Buchner, B., Carraro, C. and Cersosimo, I., 2002. 'Economic consequences of the US withdrawal from the Kyoto/Bonn Protocol', *Climate Policy*, 2:273–92.

Bureau of Labor Statistics, 2005. *National Compensation Survey: employer costs for employee compensation*, March. Available from www.bls.gov/ncs/home.htm#news (accessed 15 November 2005).

Cai, F., (ed.), 2006. *Green Book of Population and Labour — Demographic Transition and Its Social and Economic Consequences*, Social Sciences Academic Press, Beijing.

——, and Wang, D., 2005. 'China's demographic transition: implications for growth', in R. Garnaut and L. Song (eds), *The China Boom and Its Discontents*, Asia Pacific Press, Canberra.

——, 2005. 'Preparing for labour shortage in China's development in 21st century', *The Chinese Journal of Population Science*, (6).

——, Du, Y. and Wang, M., 2003. *The Political Economy of Labor Migration*, Shanghai Sanlian Press, Shanghai.

——, Yang, D. and Meiyan, W. (eds.), (forthcoming). *An Overview on China's Labour Market, in National Development and Restructuring Commission*.

——, Zhang, X. and Fan, S., 2002. 'Emergence of urban poverty and inequality in China: evidence from household survey', *China Economic Review*, 13:430–43.

——, Du, Y. and Wang, M., 2001. 'Household registration system and employment protection', *Journal of Economic Research*, 12:41–9.

Caijing Magazine, 2004. (123).

——, 2005a. 3 October.

——, 2005b. (136).

——, 2006. 'Nongchanpin chukou "kending men"' [Agricultural product export 'positive listing'], (11), 29 May.

Capital Markets Consultative Group, 2003. *Foreign Direct Investment in Emerging Market Countries*.

Castles, I. and Henderson, D., 2003. 'The IPCC emission scenarios: an economic-statistical critique', *Energy & Environment*, 14(2&3):159–85.

Chan, M.M. and Tyers, R., 2006. *Global demographic change and labour force growth: projections to 2020*, Centre for Economic Policy Research Discussion Paper, Research School of Social Sciences, The Australian National University, December.

Chang, G.G., 2001. *The Coming Collapse of China*, Random House, New York.

Chattopadhyay, R. and Duflo, E., 2004. 'Women as policy makers: evidence from a randomized policy experiment in India', Econometrica, 72(5):1409–43.

Chenery, H.B., 1960. 'Patterns of industrial growth', *American Economic Review*, 50(4)(September):624–54.

——, 1961. 'Comparative advantage and development policy', *American Economic Review*, 51(1)(March):18–51.

Cheng, G., 1997. *Jiaru Shimao Zuzhi dui Woguo Nongye Yingxiang de Fenxi* [*Studies on the impact of joining the WTO on China's agriculture*], Brief Research Report No. 6, Institute of Agricultural Economics of the Chinese Academy of Agricultural Sciences.

Cheng, L.K. and Kwan, Y.K., 1999. 'What are the determinants of the location of foreign direct investment? The Chinese experience', *Journal of Economics*, 51 (2):379–400.

Cheng, Y.F. and Wen, Y.Z., 2002. 'Shui lai wei tamen tigong baozhang? Nongminggong shebao wenti yinren guangzhu' (Who will provide security for them? Migrant workers' social security deserves attention), *Xinhua News Agency*, 21 June.

China Coal News, 2006. 'China's total output of coal in 2005 exceeds 2.1 billion tonnes', 9 January.

China Coal, 2002. 'Report about coalmine safety governance', *Zhongguo Meitan* (*China Coal*), 4. Available from http://www.zgmt.com.cn/2002/zgmt2002/zgmt4/

MKAQ4mkaq.htm (accessed 28 June 2006).

China Construction Bank, 2005. *Global Offering Prospectus*, October, Hong Kong.

China Council for International Cooperation on Environment and Development, 2001. *Report of Environmental Working Group*, Beijing.

China Daily, 2003. 'Ministry sounds warning on trade barriers against China', 11 June.

——, 2004. 'China–ASEAN agricultural trade on fast track', 9 August.

China Department of Energy, 2004. *An Energy Overview of the People's Republic of China*. Available from http://www.fe.doe.gov/international/EastAsia_and_Oceania/chinover.html

China Finance Yearbook Committee, 2003. *China Finance Yearbook 2003*.

China General Administration of Customs, 2005. *Zhongguo Haiguan Tongji Yuebao (China Customs Statistical Monthly Report)*, various issues, Zhongguo Haiguan Chubanshe, Beijing.

China Health Yearbook Committee, 2003. *China Health Yearbook*, People's Medical Publishing House.

China Money, 2005. (46), August.

China News, 2001. 'Coal will still be China's main energy in 21st century.' Available from http://www.china.org.cn/chinese/EC-c/29235.htm (accessed 28 June 2006).

China Securities News, 2005. 7 September.

——, 2006. 6 June.

China Tax Yearbook Committee, 2003. *China Tax Yearbook 2003*, China Tax Press.

China Urban Poverty Research Group, 2003. *Urban Poverty: new challenge for China's development*, Chinese Economics Press, Beijing.

Chinese Academy of Preventive Medicine, 2001. *Recommended Nutrition Intake for Chinese Households* (in Chinese), Publishing House of the Chinese Light Industry, Beijing.

Chinese Academy of Social Sciences, 2001. *China Urban Labour Survey (CULS)*, Institute of Population and Labour Economics, Chinese Academy of Social Sciences.

Chinese Academy of Social Sciences, 2002. *China Income Distribution Survey (CIDS)*, Institute of Economics, Chinese Academy of Social Sciences.

Chiswick, B.R., 1978. 'The effect of Americanization on the earnings of foreign-born men', *Journal of Political Economy*, 86(5):897–921.

Chou, W.L., 2000. 'Exchange rate variability and China's exports', *Journal of Comparative Economics*, 28:61–79.

Chow, G.C., 1993. 'Capital formation and economic growth in China', *The Quarterly Journal of Economics*, August:809–42.

Chu, J., 2001. 'Prenatal sex determination and sex-selective abortion in rural Central China', *Population and Development Review*, 27(2):259–81.

Citigroup, 2002. *Greater China Insights*, 14 June, Hong Kong.

Cole, M., Elliott, R. and Azhar, A., 2000. The determinants of trade in pollution intensive industries: North–South evidence, Mimeo, University of Birmingham, United Kingdom.

Commission of the European Communities, 2002. *Inventory of public aid granted to different energy sources*, Commission Staff Working Paper CEC(2002)1275. Available from http://europa.eu.int/comm/dgs/energy_transport/state_aid/doc/energy_inventory_en.pdf (accessed 28 June 2006).

Coondoo, D. and Dinda, S., 2002. 'Causality between income and emission: a country group-specific econometric analysis', *Ecological Economics*, 40(3):351–67.

Cooper, R., 1971. 'Currency devaluation in developing countries', *Essays in International Finance*, No. 86, Princeton University, Princeton, N.J.

——, 2005. A carbon tax in China?, Paper prepared for the Climate Policy Center, Washington, DC.

Copeland, B. and Taylor, M., 1995. 'Trade and transboundary pollution', *American Economic Review*, 85(4):716–37.

Crockett, A., 1998. From banking crisis to solid macroeconomic growth: lessons for Japan from other industrial countries, Speech given at the IMF–Kobe University Symposium, Kobe, 14 July.

Dasgupta, S., Laplante, B., Wang, H. and Wheeler, D., 2002. 'Confronting the environmental Kuznets curve', *Journal of Economic Perspectives*, 16(1):147–68.

De Bruyn, S. 1999. *Economic growth and the environment: an empirical analysis*, Kluyer Academic Publishers, Dordrect.

de Bruyn, S. and Heintz, R., 1998. 'The environmental Kuznets curve hypothesis', in *Handbook of Environmental Economics*, Blackwell Publishing Co., Oxford:656–77.

Demeny, P., 2003. *Population policy: a concise summary*, Policy Research Division Working Paper No. 173, Population Council.

Démurger, S., Sachs, J.D., Woo, W.T., Bao, S., Chang, G. and Mellinger, A., 2002. *Geography, economic policy, and regional development in China*, NBER Working Paper.

Deustche Bank 2006. *Emerging Markets Monthly*, March 10, London.

Dinda, S., 2004. 'Environmental Kuznets curve hypothesis: a survey', *Ecological Economics*, 49:431–55.

Dong, F. and Jensen, H., 2004. *The challenge of conforming to sanitary and phytosanitary measures for China's agricultural exports*, MATRIC Working Paper 04-MWP 8, March. Available from www.matric.iastate.edu

Department of Trade and Industry, 2002. *Energy: its Impact on the Environment and Society (2002)*, URN 05/1274.

——, 2005. 'Energy statistics: Coal', the information will be continuously updated, the newest version can be found in: http://www.dti.gov.uk/energy/statistics/source/coal/page18529.html (accessed 21 June 2006).

——, 2006. 'Quarterly Energy Prices Tables - URN No: 06/276b/tab', the information will be continuously updated, the newest version can be found in: http://www.dti.gov.uk/energy/statistics/publications/prices/ (accessed 28 June 2006).

Dziobeck, C. and Pazarbasioglu, C., 1997. 'Lessons and elements of best practice', in Davis, W.A. J. Ebrill, L. and Lingren C.J., (eds), *Systemic Bank Restructuring and Macroeconomic Policy*, Washington, DC.

Eberstadt, N., 2004. China's 'triple bind': demography, economics and health in an ageing low-income society, Presentation at the CSIS/CASS Conference on Preparing for China's Aging Challenge, abridged version, 25 May. Available from www.csis.org/gai/dc04/eberstadt.pdf

Edwards, S., 1993. 'Openness, trade liberalization and growth in developing countries', *Journal of Economic Literature*, XXXI(September):1358–93.

——, 1998. 'Openness, productivity and growth: what do we really know?', *Economic Journal*, 108(September):383–1398.

Ekins, P., 1997. 'The Kuznets curve for the environment and economic growth: examining the evidence', *Environment and Planning*, 29:805–30.

——, 2000. *Economic Growth and Environmental Sustainability: the prospects for growth*, Routledge, London.

Energy Information Agency, 1949–2004. *Coal Production*. Available from http://www.eia.doe.gov/emeu/aer/txt/ptb0702.html (accessed 28 June 2006).

——, 2001. *International Energy Outlook 2001*, US Department of Energy, Washington, DC.

——, 2002. *International Energy Outlook 2002*, US Department of Energy, Washington, DC.

——, 2004. *International Energy Outlook 2004*, US Department of Energy, Washington, DC.

——, 2005a. *International Energy Outlook 2005*, US Department of Energy, Washington, DC.

——, 2005b. *Germany Country Analysis Brief* (updated November 2005), US Department of Energy, Washington, DC. Available from http://www.eia.doe.gov/emeu/cabs/germany.html#coal (accessed 28 June 2006).

——, 2006a. *Annual Energy Outlook 2006 with Projections to 2030*, US Department of Energy, Washington, DC. Available from http://www.eia.doe.gov/oiaf/aeo/ (accessed 28 June 2006).

——, 2006b. *International Energy Outlook 2006*, US Department of Energy, Washington, DC.

——, 2006c. *UK Country Analysis Brief — Natural Gas* (updated May 2006). Available from http://www.eia.doe.gov/emeu/cabs/United_Kingdom/NaturalGas.html (accessed 28 June 2006).

European Environment Agency, 2000. *Environmental Taxes: recent development in tools for integration, Denmark*. Available from http://reports.eea.eu.int/Environmental_Issues_No_18/en/envissue18.pdf (accessed 28 June 2006).

Fan, G., 2003. 'China's non-performing loans and national comprehensive liability', *Asian Economic Papers*, 2(1)(Winter):145–52.

Fearnside, P.M., 2004. 'Greenhouse gas emissions from hydroelectric dams: controversies provide a springboard for rethinking a supposedly "clean" energy source — an editorial comment', *Climatic Change*, 66:1–8.

Fedderke, J.W. and Liu, W., 2002. 'Modeling the determinants of capital flows and capital flight: with an application to South African data from 1960 to 1995', *Economic Modeling*:419–44.

Fei, J.C.H. and Ranis, G., 1963, 'Innovation, capital accumulation and economic development', *American Economic Review*, Vol. 51, No. 4, pp. 533–65.

——, 1964a. *Development of the Labour Surplus Economy: theory and policy*, Yale University Press: New Haven.

——, 1964b. 'Capital-labor ratios in theory and in history: reply', *American Economic Review*, Vol. 54, No. 6, 1063–69

——, 1966, 'Agrarialism, dualism and economic development', in Adelman, I. and Thorbecke, E., (eds), *The Theory and Design of Economic Development*, Johns Hopkins Press: Baltimore, Maryland, pp. 3–43

Feng, W. and Mason, A., 2005. Demographic dividend and prospects for economic development in China, UN Expert Group Meeting on Social and Economic Implications of Changing Population Age Structures, Mexico City, 21 August–2 September.

Feng, X. and Guo, Y., 2001. 'Coal combustion and environmental protection in new century', *China Coal News*, 2 April.

Financial News, 2005a. 20 October.

——, 2005b. 7 September.

——, 2005c. 9 September.

Fleisher, B. and Yang, D., 2003. 'Labour laws and regulations in China', *China Economic Review*, 14:426–33.

Foster, A. and Rosenzwig, M., 2001. Democratization, decentralization and the distribution of local public goods in a poor rural economy, Mimeo, Department of Economics, Brown University.

France.com, 2006. *France to Close Last Coal Mine — And Two Centuries of Sooty History*. Available from http://www.france.com/docs/424.html (accessed 28 June 2006).

Frankel, A.J. and Romer, D., 1999. 'Does trade cause growth?', *American Economic Review*, 89(3):379–99.

Fukao, M., 1991. 'Exchange rate movements and capital-asset ratios of banks: on the concept of structural position', *The Bank of Japan Monetary and Economic Studies*, 9(2), September, Tokyo.

——, 2002. *Financial sector profitability and double-gearing*, NBER Working Paper No. 9368, National Bureau of Economic Research, Cambridge.

Fung, B., George, J., Hohl, S. and Ma, G., 2004. *Public asset management companies in East Asia*, Financial Stability Institute Occasional Paper No. 3, February, Basel.

Gale, F., 2005. *China's agricultural imports boomed during 2003–04*, Electronic Outlook Report from the Economic Research Service WRS-05-04, US Department of Agriculture. Available from www.ers.usda.gov

Gan, L., Xu, L. and Yao, Y., 2005a. Health shocks, village governance, and farmers' long-term income capabilities: evidence from rural China, Memo, CCER, Peking University.

——, 2005b. Local governance, finance, and consumption smoothing, Memo, the World Bank Research Group.

Garbaccio, R.F., Ho, M.S. and Jorgenson, D.W., 1999. 'Controlling carbon emissions in China', *Environment and Development Economics*, 4(4):493–518.

Garcia-Herrero, A., Gavila, S. and Santabarbara, D., 2005. *China's banking reform: an assessment of its evolution and possible impact*, Bancode Espana Occasional Papers No. 0502.

Garnaut, R., 2002. 'Catching up with America', in Garnaut, R. and Song, L., (eds),

———, *China 2002: WTO entry and world recessions*, Asia Pacific Press, The Australian National University, Canberra.

———, 2006. 'The sustainability of rapid growth in China', *Australian Journal of International Affairs*, (forthcoming).

———, Clunies, R. A., 1983. *The Taxation of Mineral Rent,* The Clarendon Press, Oxford.

———, and Ma, G., 1993. 'How rich is China: evidence from food economy', *Australian Journal of Chinese Affairs*, 30(July):121–48.

———, and Huang, Y., 1994. How rich is China: more evidence, Seminar paper at The Australian National University.

———, and Huang, Y., 2005. 'The risks of investment-led growth', in Ross Garnaut and Ligang Song (eds), *The China Boom and its Discontents*, Asia Pacific Press, The Australian National University, Canberra:1–18

———, Song, L. Tenev, S. and Yao, Y., 2005. *China's Ownership Transformation: Process, Outcomes, Prospects*, The World Bank and International Finance Corporation, Washington D.C.

———, L. Song, and Y. Yao, 2006, 'Impact and significance of SOE restructuring in China', The China Journal, No. 55 (January), pp. 35–66

——— and Song, L., 2006. 'Rapid industrialisation and market for energy and minerals: China in East Asian context', *Nankai Economic Studies*, 127(1):5–22

Gastanaga, V.M., Nugent, J.B. and Pashamova, B., 1998. 'Host country reform and DDI inflows: how much difference do they make?', *World Development*, 26(7):1299–314.

Gibson, J., Huang, J. and Rozelle, S., 2003. 'Improving estimates of inequality and poverty from urban China's household income and expenditure survey', *Review of Income and Wealth*, 49(1):53–68.

Giles, J., Park, A. and Cai, F., 2006. 'How has economic restructuring affected China's urban workers?', *The China Quarterly*, 185:61–95.

Globerman, S. and Shapiro, D., 2002. 'Global foreign direct investment flows: the role of governance infrastructure', Conference on Multinationals, Growth and Governance, April 24–5, Ontario.

Goldsmith, R., 1969. *Financial Structure and Economic Development*, Yale University Press, New Haven.

Goldstein, M. and Lardy, N., 2003. 'Two stage currency reform for China', *Asian Wall Street Journal*, A9, 12 September.

———, 2006. 'A new way to deal with the renminbi', *Financial Times*, 20 January.

——, M., 2005. Renminbi controversies, Paper presented at the Cato Institute Conference on Monetary Institutions and Economic Development, 3 November, revised December 2005. Available at from www.iie.com (accessed 15 January 2006).

Greenspan, A., 2004. 'Alan Greenspan on the Economic Implications of Ageing', *Population and Development Review*, 30(4), December:779–83.

Grilli, E. and Yang, M.C., 1988. 'Primary commodity prices, manufactured goods prices and the terms of trade of developing countries: what the long run shows', *World Bank Economic Review*, 2(1), January.

Grossman, G. and Krueger, A., 1991. *Environmental impacts of the North American Free Trade Agreement*, NBER Working Paper 3914.

——, 1995. 'Economic growth and the environment', *Quarterly Journal of Economics*, 110(2):353–77.

Guo, Z. and Bernstein, T., 2004. 'The impact of *elections* on the village structure of power: the relations between the village committees and the party branches', Journal of Contemporary China, 13(39):257–75.

Gupta, S. and Goldar, B., 2003. 'Do stock markets penalize environment-friendly behavior? Evidence from India, Mimeo', Institute of Economic Growth, Dehli

Gyntelberg, J., Ma, G. and Remolona, E., 2005. 'Corporate bond markets in Asia', *BIS Quarterly Review*, December:83–93.

Hagemann, R.P. and Christoph, J., 1997. 'Fiscal reform in Sweden: what generational accounting tells us', *Contemporary Economic Policy*, 15(3)(July):1–12.

Haigh, N., 1990. *Environmental Policy and Britain* (2nd Ed.), Longman, Essex.

Han, T., Wailes, E.J. and Cramer, G.L., 1995. 'Rural and urban data collection in the People's Republic of China', in *Proceedings of WCC-101 Symposium*, China Market Data and Information Systems, Washington, DC.

Hawkins, J. and Turner, P., 1999. 'Banking restructuring in practice: an overview', in *Bank restructuring in practice*, BIS Policy Paper No. 6, August, Basel:6–105.

Hayami, Y., 1997. *Development Economics: from the poverty to the wealth of nations*, Clarendon Press, Oxford.

Heckman, J.J., 2002. *China's investment in human capital*, NBER Working Paper No. 9296.

Heller, P. and Symansky, S., 1997. *Implications for savings of aging in the Asian 'Tigers'*, IMF Working Paper WP/97/136, October.

Hertel, T.W. (ed.), 1997. *Global Trade Analysis Using the GTAP Model*, Cambridge University Press, New York. Available from http://www.agecon.purdue.edu/gtap

Heston, A., Summers, R. and Aten, B., 2002. *Penn World Table* (Version 6.1), Center for International Comparisons, University of Pennsylvania. Available from http://ptw.econ.upenn.edu/

Hillman, A.L. and Katz, E., 1987. 'Hierarchical structure and the social costs of bribes and transfers', *Journal of Public Economics*, 34(2)(November):129–42.

Ho, L.S., 2006. A sustainable currency regime for East Asia: WCU, Paper presented at conference on New Monetary and Exchange-Rate Arrangement for East Asia, Bellagio, Italy, 22–27 May.

Hoff, K. and Stiglitz, J., 2004. 'After the big bank? Obstacles to the emergence of the rule of law in post-communist societies', *American Economic Review*, 94(3):753–63.

Hsiao, C. and Shen, Y., 2002. Foreign direct investment and economic growth — the importance of institutions and urbanization.

Hu, R., 2005. 'Economic development and the implementation of village elections in rural *China*', Journal of Contemporary China, 14(44):427–44.

Huang, Y., 2004. A labor shortage in China', *Asian Wall Street Journal*. A7, August 6–8.

Huang, J. and Chen, C., 1999. *Effects of trade liberalisation on agriculture in China*, Working Paper, United Nations ESCAP CGPRT Centre.

Huang, J., 1998. 'The impact of joining the WTO on China's grain market', *International Trade*, (20):10–13.

Huang, M. and Shaw, D., 2002. 'Economic growth and the environmental Kuznets curve in Taiwan: a simultaneity model analysis', in M. Boldrin et al. (eds), *Long-Run Growth and Economic Development: from theory to empirics*, Edward Elgar, Aldershot, UK.

Hufbauer, G. and Wong, Y., 2004. *China bashing 2004*, Institute for International Economics Policy Brief 04-5, Institute for International Economics, Washington, DC.

Humphrey, W.S. and Stanislaw, J., 1979, 'Economic growth and energy consumption in the UK, 1700–1975', *Energy Policy* (March):29–42.

Huntington, S.P., 1986. *Political Order in Societies*, Yale University Press, New Haven.

Hussain, A., 2002. 'Demographic transition in China and its implications', *World Development*, 30(10):1823–34.

Ianchovichina, E. and McDougall, R., 2000. *Theoretical structure of dynamic GTAP*, GTAP Technical Paper No. 17, Purdue University, December. Available from http://www.agecon.purdue.edu/gtap/GTAP-Dyn

Institute of Population and Labour Economics, 2001, 2002 and 2005. *China Urban Labour Survey*, Chinese Academy of Social Sciences.

Intergovernmental Panel on Climate Change, 2001. *Climate Change 2001*, 3 vols, Cambridge University Press, Cambridge.

International Energy Agency, 2004. *Analysis of the Impact of High Oil Prices on the Global Economy*, May, Paris.

International Finance Company, 2000. *China's emerging private enterprises*, IFC Report.

International Monetary Fund, 2002. *IMF International Financial Statistics Yearbook 2002*, International Monetary Fund, Washington, DC.

——, 2004a. 'The IMF on policies responding to demographic change', *Population and Development Review*, 30(4)(December):783–89.

——, 2004b. *World Economic Outlook*, September, Washington D.C.

Jackson, R. and Howe, N., 2004. The greying of the Middle Kingdom, Presentation at the CSIS/CASS Conference on Preparing for China's Aging Challenge, abridged version, 25 May. Available from www.csis.org/gai/dc04/eberstadt.pdf

Jackson, R., 2005. *Building Human Capital in an Aging Mexico: a report of the US–Mexico Binational Council*, CSIS Press, Washington, DC.

James, E., 2001. How can China solve its old age security problem? The interaction between pension, SOE and financial market reform, Paper prepared for Conference on Financial Sector Reform in China, Harvard University, September.

Jansson, A.M., Hammer, M., Folker, C., and Costanza, R., (eds) 1994. *Investing in Natural Capital: the ecological economics approach to sustainability*, Island Press, Washington D.C.

Jiang, T. and McKibbin, W., 2002. 'Assessment of China's pollution levy system: an equilibrium pollution approach', *Environment and Development Economics*, 7, Cambridge University Press:75–105.

Jiang, T., 2003. *Economic Instruments of Pollution Control in an Imperfect World*, Edward Elgar, Cheltenham, UK.

Jiang, Y., Ruoen, R. and Woo, W.T., 2006. A generational accounts analysis of China's fiscal situation: que sera sera, the future's not ours to see?, Manuscript, University of California.

Jingtang, P., 2002. 'The present situation of retirement age of male and female in the world', *Gansu Social Science*, (1).

Johnson, S.P. and Corcelle, G., 1997. *Environmental Policy of the European Communities* (Second Edn), Kluwer Law International, London.

Junsen, Z., Yaohui, Z., Park, A. and Xiaoqing, S., 2005. 'Economic returns to schooling in urban China, 1988 to 2001', *Journal of Comparative Economics*, 33:730–52.

Keay, M., 2003. 'The view from Europe—and elsewhere', *Oxford Energy Forum*, (52).

Kemfert, C., 2001. 'Economic effects of alternative climate policy strategies', *Environmental Science and Policy*, 5(5):367–84.

Kennedy, J., Rozelle, S. and Shi, Y., 2004. 'Elected leaders and collective land: farmers' evaluation of v*illage* leaders' performance in rural China', *Journal of Chinese Political Science*, 9(1):1–22.

Kinugasa, T. and Mason, A., 2005. The effects of adult longevity on saving, Mimeo, University of Hawai'i at Manoa.

Kotlikoff, L.J., 1993. 'From deficit delusion to generational accounting, *Harvard Business Review*, 71(3)(May–June):104–5.

Krueger, A.O., 1974. 'The political economy of the rent-seeking society', *American Economic Review*, 64(3):291–303.

——, 1998. 'Why trade liberalization is good for growth', *Economic Journal*, 108(September):1513–22.

Krugman, P., 1994a. 'The myth of Asia's miracle', *Foreign Affairs, 73(6)*, November–December.

——, 1994b. 'Trade, jobs, and wages', *Scientific American*, April:22–7.

Kunrong, S. and Wenjie, S., 2004. 'Investment efficiency, capital formation and macroeconomic fluctuation', *Social Science in China*, 6:52–64.

Kuznets, S., 1955. 'Economic growth and income inequality', *American Economic Review*, 45(1):1–28.

La Porta, R., Lopez-de-Silanes, F., Shleifer, A. and Vishny, R.W., 1997. 'Legal determinants of external finance', *Journal of Finance*, 52:1131–50.

——, 1998. 'Law and finance', *Journal of Political Economy*, 106:1113–55.

Lardy, N., 1998. *China's Unfinished Economic Revolution*, Brookings Institution Press, Washington, DC.

——, 2002. *Integrating China into the Global Economy*, Brookings Institution Press, Washington, DC.

Leamer, E., 1984. *Sources of International Comparative Advantage: theory and evidence*, MIT Press, Cambridge, Massachusetts.

Leff, N.H., 1964. 'Economic development through bureaucratic corruption', *The American Behavioral Scientist*, 8(2)(November):8–14.

Levine, R. and Renelt, D., 1992. 'A sensitivity analysis of cross-country growth regressions', *American Economic Review*, 82:942–63.

Levine, R. and Zervos, S., 1998. 'Stock markets, banks, and economic growth', *American Economic Review*, 88:537–58.

Levine, R., 2003a. 'Bank-based or market-based financial systems: which is better?', *Journal of Financial Intermediation*.

——, 2003b. Denying foreign bank entry: implications for bank interest margins, Mimeo, University of Minnesota.

——, Loayza, N. and Beck, T., 2000. 'Financial intermediation and growth: causality and causes', *Journal of Monetary Economics*, 46:31–77.

Lewis, W.A., 1952. 'World production, prices and trade, 1870–1960', *Manchester School of Economic and Social Sciences*, 20(2)(May):105–38.

——, 1954. 'Economic development with unlimited supplies of labour,' *Manchester School of Economics and Social Studies*, XXII, 2:139–91.

——, 1954. 'Economic development with unlimited supplies of labor', *Manchester School*, Vol. 22:139–191

Li, J., 2003. 'Coal industry is not a *XiYang Gongye* (Setting Sun)', *Meitan Jingji Yanjiu (Coal Economics Research)*, 3.

Liang, J. and McKitrick, R., 2002. Income growth and air quality in Toronto: 1973–1997, Mimeo, Economics Department, University of Guelph.

Lien, D.H.D., 1986. 'A note on competitive bribery games', *Economic Letters*, 22:337–41.

Ligang, S. 1996. *Changing Global Comparative Advantage: evidence from Asia and the Pacific*, Addison-Wesley Longman Australia, Melbourne.

Lin, Y. and Li, Y., 2002. 'Export and China's economic growth: an analysis from the perspective of demand', *CCER Working Paper*, Peking University.

Lin, J.Y. and Li, Y., 2003. 'Export and economic growth in China: a demand-oriented analysis', *China Economic Quarterly*, 2(4).

Lin, J.Y. and Tan, G., 1999. 'Policy burdens, accountability and the soft budget constraint', *American Economic Review: Papers and Proceedings*, 89(2)(May):426–31.

Lin, J.Y., 2003. 'Development strategy, viability and economic convergence', *Economic Development and Cultural Change*, 51:277–308.

——, 2004. *The People's Republic of China's future development and economic relations with Asia and Latin America*, Latin America/Caribbean and Asia/Pacific Economics and Business Association Working Paper No. 21, December.

——, Fang, C. and Zhou, L., 1994 (Chinese edition). *China's Miracle: development strategy and economic reform*, Shanghai Sanlian Press, Shanghai.

——, 1998. 'Competition, policy burdens and state-owned enterprises reform', *American Economic Review*, 88(2):422–27.

Lin, J.Y., Liu, M., Pan, S. and Zhang, P., 2006. Factor endowments, development strategy and economic institutions in developing countries, Mimeo, Peking University.

Lin, J.Y., Liu, M., Qian, Y. and Zhang, P., 2006. Technology choice and economic performance in the developing countries, Mimeo, Peking University.

Lin, J.Y., Sun, X. and Jiang, Y., 2006. *The optimal financial structure for economic development*, Working Paper, Peking University.

Lindbeck, A., 1979. *Inflation and Unemployment in Open Economies*, Amsterdam.

List, J. and Gallet, C., 1999. 'The environmental Kuznets curve: does one size fit all?', *Ecological Economics*, 31:409–23.

Liu, J. and Diamond, J., 2005. 'China's environment in a globalizing world', *Nature*:1179–86.

Liu, J., van Leeuwen, N., Vo, T.T., Tyers, R. and Hertel, T.W., 1998. *Disaggregating labor payments by skill level in GTAP*, Technical Paper No. 11, September, Center for Global Trade Analysis, Department of Agricultural Economics, Purdue University, West Lafayette.

Liu, Y., Wang, X. and Yao, Y., 2001. *The Chinese Village: inside and out*, Hebei Renmin Press, Shijiazhuang.

Lopez, R., 1994. 'The environment as a factor of production: the effects of economic growth and trade liberalization', *Journal of Environmental Economics and Management*, 27:163–184.

Loschel, A. and Zhang, Z.X., 2002. 'The economic and environmental implications of the US repudiation of the Kyoto Protocol and the subsequent deals in Bonn and Marrakech', *Nota Di Lavoro*, 23.2002, April, Fondazione Enie Enrico Mattei, Venice.

Lucas, Jr., R.E., 1988. 'On the mechanism of economic development', *Journal of Monetary Economics*, 22:3–22.

Lui, F.T., 1985. 'An equilibrium queuing model of bribery', *Journal of Political Economy*, August, 93(4):760–81.

Ma, G. and Fung, B., 2002. *China's asset management corporations*, BIS Working Paper No. 115, August, Basel.

Ma, G. and McCauley, R., 2006. Do China's capital controls still bind?, Paper presented at the conference China and Emerging Asia: reorganising the global economy, Seoul, and the conference New Monetary and Exchange Rate Arrangements for East Asia, Bellagio, May.

McCauley, R.N., 2003. 'Unifying government bond markets in East Asia', *BIS Quarterly Review*, December:90–8.

McFarland, J., Herzog, H. and Jacoby, H., 2004. *The Future of Coal Consumption in a Carbon Constrained World*. Available from http://uregina.ca/ghgt7/PDF/papers/nonpeer/139.pdf (accessed 28 June 2006).

McGinley, P.C., 1992. 'Regulation of the environmental impact of coal mining in the USA', *Natural Resources Forum*, 16(4).

McKibbin, W. and Wilcoxen, P., 1998. 'The theoretical and empirical structure of the G-cubed model', *Economic Modelling*, 16(1):123–48.

McKibbin, W., 2006a. Global energy and environmental impacts of an expanding China, Paper prepared for the China Economic Research and Advisory Program (CERAP) as part of the study 'China and the global economy, 2010', in *China and the World Economy*, Blackwell.

——, 2006b. China and the global environment, Paper prepared for the conference China and Emerging Asia: reorganizing the global economy, Seoul, South Korea, 11–12 May.

McKibbin, W., Pearce, D. and Stegman, A., 2004. *Long run projections for climate change scenarios*, the Lowy Institute for International Policy Working Paper in International Economics.

McKibbin, W.J. and Vines, D., 2000. 'Modeling reality: the need for both intertemporal optimization and stickiness in models for policymaking', *Oxford Review of Economic Policy*, 16(4):106–37 (32).

McKibbin, W.J. and Wilcoxen, P.J., 2002a. *Climate Change Policy After Kyoto: a blueprint for a realistic approach*, the Brookings Institution, Washington, DC.

——, 2002b. 'The role of economics in climate change policy', *Journal of Economic Perspectives*, 16(2):107–30.

——, 2004. 'Estimates of the costs of Kyoto–Marrakesh versus the McKibbin–Wilcoxen blueprint', *Energy Policy*, 32(4):467–79.

McKinnon, R., 1973. *Money and Capital in Economic Development*, Brookings Institution, Washington, DC.

McKinnon, R., 2005. *Exchange Rates Under the East Asian Dollar Standard: living with conflicted virtue*, MIT Press (Chinese translation, 2005; Japanese translation, forthcoming).

McKinnon, R., 2006. China's exchange rate trap: Japan redux?, Conference paper, American Economic Association Meetings, Boston, 7 January.

Maddison, A., 1998. *Chinese Economic Performance in the Long Run*, OECD Development Centre, Paris.

Mankiw, G., 2003. *Macroeconomics* (5th Ed.), Worth Publishers, New York.

Martin, W., 1993. 'The fallacy of composition and developing country exports of manufactures', *The World Economy*, 23:979–1003.

Mayer, J., 2003. *The fallacy of composition: a review of the literature*, UNCTAD Discussion Paper No. 166, February.

Meadows, D.H. Meadows, D.L. Randers, J. and Behrens III, W.W., 1972. *The Limits to Growth*, New York University Books.

Meng, X., 2004. 'Economic restructuring and income inequality in urban China', *Review of Income and Wealth*, Vol. 50, No. 3:357–79.

Meng, X. and Zhang, J., 2001. 'The two-tier labor market in urban China: occupational and wage differentials between urban residents and rural migrants in Shanghai', *Journal of Comparative Economics*, 29(3):485–504.

Meng, X., Gregory, R.G. and Wang, Y., 2005. 'Poverty, inequality, and growth in urban China, 1986–2000', *Journal of Comparative Economics*, 33(4):710–29.

Meng, X., 2000. *China's Labour Market Reform*, Cambridge University Press, Cambridge.

Merton, R.C., 1995. 'A functional perspective of financial intermediation', *Financial Management*, 24:23–41.

Milanovic, B. and Ying, Y., 2001. *Democracy and income inequality: an empirical analysis*, World Bank Policy Research Working Paper Series 2561, Washington D.C.

Minami, R., 1973. *The Turning Point in Economic Development: Japan's Experience*, Kinokinyu Bookstore Co. Ltd, Tokyo.

Mingyong, L., Helian, X. and Qun, B., 2003. *Export and Economic Growth in China: theories, models and empirical research*, Shanghai Sanlian Press.

Ministry of Civil Affairs, 1998. *1997 Civil Affairs Statistical Report*. Available from http://www.mca.gov.cn

Ministry of Commerce of China, 2005. *Challenges for Agricultural Trade*, 27 February. Available from http://english.mofcom.gov.cn

Ministry of Education of China and National Bureau of Statistics of China, 2003. *China Education Expenditure Statistical Yearbook 2002*, China Statistics Press, Beijing.

Ministry of Health, Labour and Welfare of Japan, 2006. *Introduction of the Positive List System for Agricultural Chemical Residues in Foods*, May, Department of Food Safety, Ministry of Health, Labour and Welfare. Available from http://www.mhlw.go.jp/english/topics/foodsafety/positivelist060228/introduction.html

Ministry of Labor and Social Security of China, 2003. *China Labor and Social*

Security Yearbook 2003, China Labor and Social Security Press.

Mo, Y.K., 1999. 'A review of recent banking reforms in China', in *Strengthening the banking system in China: issues and experiences*, BIS Policy Papers No. 7, October:90–109.

Moody's Investors' Service, 2005a. *Bank System Outlook for China: reform on track, but more needed*, June, Hong Kong.

——, 2005b. *Reform of China's State Banks: moving beyond IPOs; positive rating actions likely*, November, Hong Kong.

Murphy, K.M., Shleifer, A. and Vishny, R.W., 1993. 'Why is rent-seeking so costly to growth?', *American Economic Review*, 83(2)(May):409–14.

Mussa, M., 2005. 'Sustaining global growth while reducing external imbalances', in C. Fred Bergsten (ed.), *The United States and the World Economy: foreign economic policy for the next decade*.

Nakada, M. and Ueta, K., 2004. *Sulfur emissions control in China: domestic or regional cooperative strategies?*, 21COE Discussion Paper 41, Kyoto University.

Nakaso, H., 2001. *The financial crisis in Japan during the 1990s: how the Bank of Japan responded and the lessons learnt*, BIS Papers No. 6, October.

National Bureau of Statistics of China, 1982. *China Statistical Yearbook 1981*, Hong Kong Economic Information Agency, Beijing.

——, 1985. *China Statistical Yearbook 1985*, Statistical Publishing House, Beijing.

——, 1993. *China Statistical Yearbook 1993*, China Statistics Press, Beijing.

——, 1994. *China Statistical Yearbook 1994*, China Statistics Press, Beijing.

——, 1995. *China Statistical Yearbook 1995*, China Statistics Press, Beijing.

——, 1996. *China Statistical Yearbook 1996*, China Statistics Press, Beijing.

——, 1997. *China Statistical Yearbook 1997*, China Statistics Press, Beijing.

——, 1998. *China Statistical Yearbook 1998*, China Statistics Press, Beijing.

——, 1999. *China Statistical Yearbook 1999*, China Statistics Press, Beijing.

——, 2000. *China Statistical Yearbook 2000*, China Statistics Press, Beijing.

——, 2001a. *China Statistical Yearbook 2001*, China Statistics Press, Beijing.

——, 2001b. *Tabulation on the 2000 Population Census of the People's Republic of China*, Population Census Office under the State Council and Department of Population, Social, Science and Technology Statistics, China Statistics Press, Beijing.

——, 2002. *China Statistical Yearbook 2002*, China Statistics Publishing House, Beijing.

——, 2003a. *China Statistical Yearbook 2003*, China Statistics Press, Beijing.

——, 2003b. *China Labor Statistical Yearbook 2003*, China Statistics Press, Beijing.

——, 2003c. *China Population Statistics Yearbook 2003*, Department of Population, Social, Science and Technology Statistics, China Statistics Press, Beijing.

——, 2003d. *International Statistical Yearbook*, China Statistics Press, Beijing.

——, 2004. *China Statistical Yearbook 2004*, China Statistics Publishing House, Beijing.

——, 2005a. *China Statistical Yearbook 2005*, China Statistics Press, Beijing.

——, 2005b. *Plan of Environmental Legislation in the 11th Five Years (2006–10)*. Available from http://www.sepa.gov.cn/eic/649086798147878912/20051202/13436.shtml (accessed 7 May 2006).

——, 2005c. *China Compendium Statistics 1949–2004*, China Statistics Press, Beijing.

——, 2006a. *China Statistical Abstract 2006*, China Statistics Press, Beijing.

——, 2006b. *China Statistical Monthly*, various issues, China Statistics Press, Beijing.

——, 2006c. *Table of GDP at Current Prices*. Available from www.stats.gov.cn/tjdt/zygg/P020060109431083446682.doc (accessed 9 January 2006)

——, 2006d. *The Statistical Communiqué on the 2005 National Economic and Social Development*, 28 February.

Naughton, B., 2003. 'How much can regional integration do to unify China's markets?', in N. Hope, D. Yang and M.Y. Li (eds), *How Far Across the River? Chinese Policy Reform at the Millennium*, Stanford University Press:204–32.

North, D.C. and Thomas, R.P., 1973. *The Rise of the Western World: a new economic history*, Cambridge University Press, Cambridge.

North, D.C., 1981. *Structure and Change in Economic History*, W.W. Norton and Company, New York.

——, 1990. *Institutions, Institutional Change, and Economic Performance*, Cambridge University Press, New York.

O'Connor, J., 1973. *The Fiscal Crisis of the State*, St Martin's Press, New York.

Obstfeld, M. and Rogoff, K., 1996. *Foundations of International Macroeconomics*, MIT Press, Cambridge, Mass.

——, 2005. 'The unsustainable US current account position revisited', in R. Clarida (ed.), *G7 current account imbalances: sustainability and adjustment*, National Bureau of Economic Research Working Paper 10869, November.

OECD, 2006. *Challenges for China's Public Spending: toward greater effectiveness and equity*, OECD, Paris.

——. Public debt and state revenue data. Available from http://stats.oecd.org/wbos/viewhtml.aspx?QueryName=2&QueryType=View&Lang=en

Ohlin, B., 1933. *Interregional and International Trade*, Harvard University Press, Cambridge, Massachusetts.

Oi, J. and Rozelle, S., 2000. 'Elections and power: the locus of decision-making in Chinese villages', *China Quarterly*, 162:513–39.

Otto, J. and Barberis, D., 1994. *Environmental legislation in mining and the need for EIA and pollution control*, CEPMLP Professional Paper, University of Dundee, Dundee.

Panayotou, T. and Zheng, 2000. *The Cost of Environmental Damage in China: assessment and valuation framework*, China Council for International Cooperation on Environment and Development.

Panayotou, T., 1993. *Empirical tests and policy analysis of environmental degradation at different stages of economic development*, ILO Technology and Employment Programme Working Paper WP238, Geneva.

——, 2000. *Economic growth and the environment*, CID Working Paper No. 56, July, Center for International Development, Harvard University.

Pearson, P., 1994. 'Energy, externalities and environmental quality: will development curve the ills it creates?', *Energy Studies Review*, 6(3):199–215.

Peng, X., 2005. Population ageing, economic growth and population policy options in China: a CGE analysis, Doctoral thesis, Monash University.

People's Bank of China, (various years) *Quarterly Statistical Bulletin*.

People's Daily, 2006. 'Ten features in China's 11th five-year plan', People's Daily Online. Available from http://english.people.com.cn/200603/08/eng20060308_248947.html *(accessed 28 April 2006)*.

Perrings, C., 1987. *Economy and Environment: a theoretical essay on the interdependence of economic and environmental systems*, Cambridge University Press.

Pezzey, J., 2003. 'Emission taxes and tradable permits: a comparison of views on long run efficiency', *Environmental and Resource Economics*, 26(2):329–42.

Pizer, W.A., 1997. *Prices vs. Quantities Revisited: the case of climate change*, Resources for the Future Discussion Paper 98-02, Resources for the Future, Washington, DC.

Porter, M.E. and Linda, C.V.D., 1995. 'Toward a new conception of the environment competitiveness relationship', *Journal of Economic Perspectives*, 9(4):97–118.

Prodhan, M., Suryahadi, A., Sumarto, S. and Pritchett, L., 2001. Measurements of poverty in Indonesia: 1996, 1999 and beyond (unpublished manuscript).

Prestowitz, C., 2005. *Three Billion New Capitalists: the great shift of wealth and power to the East*, Basic Books, New York.

Qiao, H., 2005. Exchange rates and trade balances under the dollar standard, August, Stanford University.

Rajan, R.G. and Zingales, L., 2002. Banks and markets: the changing character of European finance, Mimeo, University of Chicago.

Ramakrishnan, R.T.S. and Thakor, A., 1984. 'Information reliability and a theory of financial intermediation', *Review of Economic Studies*, 51:415–32.

Ranis G. and Fei J., 1961, 'A theory of economic development, *American Economic Review*, Vol. 51, No. 4: 533–65.

Ravallion, M., 1994. *Poverty Comparisons*, Harwood Academic Publishers, Chur.

Ren, R. and Chen, K., 1995. *China's GDP in US dollars based on purchasing power parity*, Policy Research Working Paper No. 1415, the World Bank.

Ren, R., Yunyun, J., Nannan, X. and Li, L., 2004. 'Generation account approach and its application on the pension system in China', *Jin Ji Yan Jiu (Economic Research Journal)*, 39(9)(September):118–28.

Retherford, R., Choe, M.K., Chen, J., Li, X. and Cui, H., 2005. 'How far has fertility in China really declined?', *Population and Development Review*, 31(1):57–84.

Ricardo, D., 1817. *The Principles of Political Economy and Taxation*, John Murray, London.

Riskin, C., Zhao, R. and Li, S., 2002. *China's Retreat from Equality*, University of Michigan Press, Ann Arbor.

Roberts, K., 1997. 'China's "tidal wave" of migrant labor: what can we learn from Mexican undocumented migration to the United States', *International Migration Review*, 31(2):249–93.

Roberts, M.J. and Spence, A.M., 1976. 'Effluent charges and licenses under uncertainty', *Journal of Public Economics*, 5:193–208.

Rodriguez, F. and Rodrik, D., 2002. 'Trade policy and economic growth: a skeptic's guide to the cross-national evidence', NBER Working Paper 7801, National Bureau of Economic Research, Cambridge.

Rogoff, K. and Reinhart, C., 2003. *FDI to Africa: the role of price stability and currency instability*, IMF Working Paper.

Romer, P., 1986. 'Increasing returns and long-run growth', *Journal of Political Economy*, 94(5)(October):1002–37.

——, 1990. 'Endogenous technological change', *Journal of Political Economy*, 98:s71–s102.

——, 1994. 'New goods, old theory, and the welfare costs of trade restrictions', *Journal of Development Economics*, 43(1)(February):5–38.

Rothbard, M., 1995. *Making Economic Sense*, Ludwig von Mises Institute,

Auburn:271–3.

Schultz, T., 1962. 'Reflections on investment in man', *Journal of Political Economy*, 70:1–8.

——, 1963. *The Economic Value of Education*, Columbia University Press, New York.

——, 1964. *Transforming Traditional Agriculture*, Yale University Press, New Haven.

Securities Times, 2005. 17 December.

Selden, T. and Song, D., 1994. 'Environmental quality and development: is there a Kuznets curve for air pollution emissions?', *Journal of Environmental Economics and Management*, 27:147–62.

Shafik, N. and Bandyopadhyay, S., 1992. *Economic growth and environmental quality: time series and cross-country evidence*, Background Paper for the World Development Report, World Bank, Washington, DC.

Shafik, N., 1994. 'Economic development and environmental quality: an econometric analysis', *Oxford Economic Papers*, 46:757–73.

Shang, H., 2001. 'Coal industry status as primary energy cannot be challenged', *China Coal News*, 26 April.

Sharping, T., 2003. *Birth Control in China 1949–2000: population policy and demographic development*, RoutledgeCurzon, London.

Sheng, A., 1999. *Bank Restructuring: lessons from the 1980s*, World Bank, Washington, DC.

Shi, X., 1999. 'Analysis, consideration and proposals considering the policy of closing mines and restricting the total yield', *The Journal of Coal Economic Research*, (6):19–26.

Shimkus, J., 2005. Press release from the office of Congressman John Shimkus, 14 September. Available from http://www.house.gov/shimkus/press/prfuturegenalliancecomments.htm (accessed 28 June 2006).

Singer, H.W., 1998. 'Beyond terms of trade: convergence/divergence and creative destruction', *Zagreb International Review of Economics and Business*, 1(1)(May):13–25.

Smulders, S., 1999. 'Endogenous growth theory and the environment', in Van der Bergh J., (ed), *Handbook of Environmental and Resource Economics*, Edward Elgar:610–21.

Solinger, D.J., 1999. 'Citizenship issues in China's internal migration: comparisons with Germany and Japan', *Political Science Quarterly*, 113(3):455–78.

——, 2001. 'Why we cannot count the "unemployed"', *China Quarterly*, (167):671–88.

Solow, R.M., 1956. 'A contribution to the theory of economic growth', *Quarterly Journal of Economics*, 70:65–94.

Song, H., 2004. *Public Finance in Chinese Villages*, Finance and Economics Press, Beijing.

Southern Weekend Magazine, 2005. 19 April.

Stagl, S., 1999. Delinking economic growth from environmental degradation? A literature survey on the environmental Kuznets curve hypothesis, Mimeo, Vienna University of Economics and Business Administration.

State Administration of Foreign Exchange of China, 2006. *Table of Exchange Rates of RMB*. Available from www.safe.gov.cn/0430/tjsj.jsp?c_t=3 (accessed 27 February 2006).

State Council of China, 1998. *The global and domestic impact of China joining the World Trade Organisation*, Project Report, Development Research Centre, State Council of China.

——, 2000. *China Development Studies: the selected research report of the Development Research Centre of the State Council*, Development Research Centre of the State Council of China, China Development Press.

——, 2006. State Council meets to deploy trial on sustainable development in the coal industry. Available from http://gov.people.com.cn/GB/46742/4315534.html (accessed 26 May 2006).

State Environmental Protection Administration, 2001. *Report of the State of Environment in 2001*, State Environmental Protection Agency, Beijing. Available from http://www.zhb.gov.cn/english/SOE/soechina2001/index.htm (accessed 28 June 2006).

——, 2004a. *Report on the State of the Environment in China: 2003*, State Environmental Protection Agency, Beijing.

——, 2004b. State Public Release of Environment Protection 1996-2004. Available from http://www.zhb.gov.cn/eic/649368268829622272/index.shtml (accessed 28 June 2006).

——, 2005. 'Plan of Environmental Legislation in the 11th Five Years Plan (2006-10)'. Available from http://www.sepa.gov.cn/eic/649086798147878912/20051202/13436.shtml (assessed 07 May 2006)

Stern, D., 1998. 'Progress on the environmental Kuznets curve?', *Environment and Development Economics*, 3:175–98.

Stern, D., Common, M. and Barbier, E., 1996. 'Economic growth and environmental degradation: the environmental Kuznets curve and sustainable development', *World Development*, 24:1151–60.

Streets, D.G., 2004. Black smoke in China and its climate effects, Paper presented to the Asian Economic Panel, Columbia University, October.

Swan, T.W., 1956. 'Economic growth and capital accumulation', *Economic Record*, 32:334–61.

Tang, X., 2005. 'Non-performing loans, tax revenues and entry of the banking sector', *Economic Research Journal*, 40(7):28–34.

The 21st Century Economic Report, 2005a. 11 August.

——, 2005b. 24 August.

The Asian Wall Street Journal, 2005. 20 June.

——, 2006. 27 January.

Tietenbery, T., 2002. *Environmental and Natural Resource Economics* (Fifth Edn), Addison Wesley Longman, New York.

Tong, J. and Woo, W.T., 2006. The potential fiscal havoc from China's state banks, Manuscript, University of California.

Tyers, R. and Golley, J., 2006. *China's growth to 2030: the roles of demographic change and investment premia*, Presented at the conference on WTO, China and the Asian Economies IV: Economic Integration and Development, University of International Business and Economics, Beijing, China, 24–25 June 2006, Working Papers in Economics and Econometrics No. 461, The Australian National University, Canberra.

Tyers, R. and Shi, Q., (forthcoming). *Global demographic change, labour force growth and economic performance*, Working Papers in Economics and Econometrics No. 462, The Australian National University, Canberra, in E. Ianchovichina, T. Walmsley and T.W. Hertel, *GTAP-Dynamic: an intertemporal model of the world*, Cambridge University Press.

Tyers, R., 2005. Ageing and slower population growth: effects on global economic performance, Presented at the Experts Meeting on Long Term Scenarios for Asia's Growth and Trade, Asian Development Bank, 10–11 November.

——, Bain, I. and Vedi, J., 2006. *The global implications of freer skilled migration*, Working Papers in Economics and Econometrics, The Australian National University, Canberra.

——, Shi, Q. and Chan, M.M., 2005. *Global demographic change and economic performance: implications for the food sector*, September, Report for the Rural Industries Research and Development Corporation, Canberra.

Ueta, K., Inada, Y., Fujikawa, K., Mori, A., Na, S., Hayashi, T. and Shimoda, M., 2005. *Win-win strategy for Japan and China in climate change policy*, Report to the International Collaborations Project on Sustainable Societies.

UK Department of Trade and Industry, 2002. *Energy: its impact on the environment and society (2002)*, URN 05/1274.

———, 2005. *Energy Statistics: coal*, URN No. 05/87a10. The information is updated continuously and the newest version is available from http://www.dti.gov.uk/energy/statistics/source/coal/page18529.html (accessed 21 June 2006).

———, 2006. *Quarterly Energy Prices Tables*, URN No. 06/276b/tab. The information is updated continuously and the newest version is available from http://www.dti.gov.uk/energy/statistics/publications/prices/ (accessed 28 June 2006).

United Nations Statistics Division. Commodity Trade Statistics Database, COMTRADE. Available from http://unstats.un.org/unsd/comtrade/default.aspx

United Nations, 2002. *Berlin II Guidelines for Mining and Sustainable Development*. Available from http://www.mineralresourcesforum.org/workshops/Berlin/docs/Guidelines.pdf (accessed 28 June 2006).

———, 2003. *World Population Prospects: the 2002 revision*, UN Population Division, Department of Economic and Social Affairs, Washington, DC. Available from www.un.org/esa/population/publications/wpp2002

———, 2004. 'Status of Ratification', *United Nations Framework Convention on Climate Change (UNFCCC)*. Available from http://unfccc.int/resource/conv/ratlist.pdf (accessed 28 June 2006).

———, 2005. *World Population Prospects: the 2004 revision*, UN Population Division. Available from http://esa.un.org/unpp/

———, 2006. 'Kyoto Protocol Status of Ratification', *United Nations Framework Convention on Climate Change (UNFCCC)*. Available from http://unfccc.int/files/essential_background/kyoto_protocol/application/pdf/kpstats.pdf (accessed 28 June 2006).

US Department of Commerce, (forthcoming). *Bureau of Industry and Security Annual Report for FY 2005*, Department of Commerce, Washington, DC.

———, 2006. *US International Transactions Accounts Data, Table 2. US Trade in Goods*, Bureau of Economic Analysis, International Economic Accounts. Available from www.bea.gov/bea/international/bp_web/simple.cfm?anon=71&table_id=2&area_id=3 (accessed 30 June 2006).

US Department of Energy, 2004. *An Energy Overview of the People's Republic of China*. Available from http://www.fe.doe.gov/international/EastAsia_and_Oceania/chinover.html

US Department of Treasury, 2003. *The use and counterfeiting of United States currency abroad, Part 2*, March, the second report to the Congress by the Secretary of the Treasury, in consultation with the Advanced Counterfeit

Deterrence Steering Committee, pursuant to Section 807 of PL104-132.

US Food and Drug Administration, 2006. *Import refusal reports for OASIS*, June 2005 to May 2006. Available from http://www.fda.gov/ora/oasis/ora_ref_cntry.html

US Government Printing Office, 2000. *Social Security Programs Throughout the World — 1999*, Washington, DC.

Wang, D., Cai, F. and Gao, W., 2006. 'Globalisation and the shortage of rural workers: a macroeconomic perspective', in I. Nielsen, R. Smyth and M. Vicziany (eds), *Globalization and Labour Mobility in China*, MAI Press, Melbourne.

Wang, G., 2006. 'Population projection and analysis', in C. Fang (ed.), *Green Book of Population and Labour—Demographic Transition and Its Social and Economic Consequences*, Social Sciences Academic Press, Beijing.

Wang, J. and Ding, S., 2006. 'A re-estimation of China's agricultural surplus labour — the demonstration and modification of three prevalent methods', *Frontiers of Economics in China*, 1(2):171–81.

Wang, X. and Meng, L., 2001. 'A re-estimation of China's economic growth', *China Economic Review*, (12)4.

Wang, X. and Smith, K., 1999. 'Secondary benefits of greenhouse gas control: health impacts in China', *Environmental Science and Technology*, 33(18):3056–61.

Wang, X., 2000. 'Sustainability of China's economic growth and institutional reform', *Economic Research*, 387(7):3–15.

Wang, Y., Xu, D., Wang, Z. and Zhai, F., 2004. 'Options and impact of China's pension reform: a computable general equilibrium analysis', *Journal of Comparative Economics*, 32:105–27.

Wang, Z., 1997. *The impact of China and Taiwan joining the World Trade Organisation on US and world agricultural trade: a computable general equilibrium analysis*, Economic Research Service Report, Technical Bulletin No. 1858, US Department of Agriculture.

Warhurst, A., 1994. 'The limitations of environmental regulation in mining', in R.G. Eggert (ed.), *Mining and the Environment: international perspectives on public policy*, Resources for the Future, Washington, DC.

Weitzman, M.L., 1974. 'Prices vs. quantities', *Review of Economic Studies*, 41:477–91.

Weyant, J. (ed.), 1999. 'The costs of the Kyoto Protocol: a multi-model evaluation', *The Energy Journal*, Special Issue.

Whalley, J. and Shuming, Z., 2004. *Inequality Change in China and (Hukou) Labour*

Mobility Restrictions, National Bureau of Economic Research Working Paper No. 10683, National Bureau of Economic Research, Cambridge, Mass.

White, L., 1991. *The S&L Debacle: public policy lessons for bank and thrift regulation*, Oxford University Press, New York.

White, W., 2004. *Are changes in financial structure extending safety net?*, BIS Working Paper No. 145, January.

World Bank, 1997a. *China 2020: old age security*, World Bank, Washington, DC.

——, 1997b. *Clear Water, Blue Skies: China's environment in the new century*, World Bank, Washington, DC.

——, 1997c. *China 2020 — Development Challenges in the New Century*, World Bank, Washington, DC.

——, 2002. *World Development Indicators 2002*, World Bank, Washington, DC.

——, 2003. *World Development Indicators*, World Bank, Washington, DC.

——, 2005. *China's Integration of National Product and Factor Markets: economic benefits and policy recommendations, poverty reduction and economic management unit*, East Asia and Pacific Region Report No. 31973-CHA, World Bank, Washington, DC.

——, 2006. *World Development Indicators Database*, 1 July, World Bank, Washington, DC. Available from http://siteresources.worldbank.org/DATASTATISTICS/Resources/

World Coal Institute, 2001. *Sustainable Entrepreneurship—The Way Forward for Coal Industry*. Available from http://www.worldcoal.org/assets_cm/files/PDF/sustainable_entrepreneurship_report.pdf (accessed 28 June 2006).

World Combined Services, 2003. 'UMWA: coal dust testing changes monstrous', *People's Weekly World Newspaper*, 15 May. Available from http://host10.cpusa.org/article/view/3452/1/163/ (accessed 28 June 2006).

World Health Organisation, 2001. *Environment and People's Health*, World Health Organisation and UNDP, Geneva.

——, 2004. *Environmental Health Country Profile — China*, August, World Health Organisation, Geneva.

World Trade Organisation, 2005a. *Online Statistics, Trade Profiles*. Available from stat.wto.org/CountryProfile/WSDBCountryPFHome.aspx?Language=E (accessed 22 November 2005).

——, 2005b. *WTO Online Statistics, Time Series*. Available from stat.wto.org/StatisticalProgram/WSDBStatProgramHome.aspx?Language=E (accessed 28 November 2005)

——, 2006. *Country Profiles*. Available from http://stat.wto.org?CountryProfiles.htm

(accessed 25 January 2006).

Wu, H., 2004. *Power Plant, I Sob for You*, China Environment Science, Beijing.

Wu, H.X., 1997. *Measuring China's GDP*, Briefing Paper Series No. 8, Department of Foreign Affairs and Trade, Australia.

Wu, L., Kaneko, S. and Matsuoko, S., 2003. 'Driving forces behind the stagnancy of China's energy related CO_2 emissions from 1996 to 1999: the relative importance of structural change, intensity change and scale change', *Energy Policy*.

Xiang, B., 2003. *Migration and Health in China: problems, obstacles and solutions*, Asian MetaCentre Research Paper Series No. 17, National University of Singapore.

Xiao, G., 2005. 'Non-performing debts in Chinese enterprises: patterns, causes and implications for banking reform', *Asian Economic Papers*, 4(3):61–113.

Xiao, Y., 2002. 'Yi nian sunshi 4.5 yi, "zhiyebing" rang Beijing tong xia shashou' (450 million lost a year, occupational diseases force Beijing to act), 11 April. Available from www.21dnn.com.cn.

Xinhua Net, 2005a. 'Suggestions on 11th Five-Year Plan by the Central Commission of Chinese Communist Party', *Xinhua News Agency*, 18 October. Available from http://news.xinhuanet.com/politics/2005-10/18/content_3640318.htm (accessed 28 June 2006).

——, 2005b. 'Family planning becomes a controversial topic', *Xinhua News Agency*. Available from http://www.cpirc.org.cn/en/enews20051230htm (accessed 30 December 2005).

Yang, J. and Schreifels, J., 2003. 'Implementing SO_2 emissions in China', *OECD Global Forum on Sustainable Development: emissions trading*, OECD, Paris.

Yifu, L. and Yongjun, L., 2002. *Export and China's economic growth: an analysis from the perspective of demand*, CCER Working Paper, Peking University.

Young, A., 2000a. 'The razor's edge: distortions and incremental reform in the People's Republic of China', *Quarterly Journal of Economics*, 115(4):1091–135.

——, 2000b. *Gold into base metals: productivity growth in the People's Republic of China during the reform period*, NBER Working Paper W7856, National Bureau of Economic Research, Cambridge.

Zhang, G. and Zhao, Z., 2006. 'Re-examining China's fertility puzzle: data collection and quality over the last two decades', *Population and Development Review*, 32(2):293–321.

Zhang, J., Guiying, W. and Jipeng, Z., 2004. 'An estimation on China's provincial physical capital stock: 1952–2000', *Economic Research*, 10:35–44.

Zhang, K.H., 2001. 'How does foreign direct investment affect economic growth in China?', *Economics of Transition*, Vol.9:679–93.

Zhang, L., Huang, J. and Rozelle, S., 2002. 'Employment, emerging labour markets and the role of education in rural China', *China Economic Review*, 13:313–28.

Zhang, P., 2006. Factor endowments, industrial structure, technology choice and economic development, Ph.D. dissertation, Peking University.

Zhang, X. and Fan, S., 2000. *Public investment and regional inequality in rural China*, EPTD Discussion Paper 71.

Zhang, X. and Tan, K.-Y., 2004. *Blunt to Sharpened Razor: incremental reform and distortions in the product and capital markets in China*, International Food Policy Research Institute DSGD Discussion Paper No. 13, August.

Zhang, X., Fan, S., Zhang, L. and Huang, J., 2004. 'Local governance and public goods provision in rural China', *Journal of Public Economics*, 88(12):2857–71.

Zhang, Z., 1996. *The exchange value of the renminbi and China's balance of trade: an empirical study*, NBER Working Paper 5771.

——, 1998. *The Economics of Energy Policy in China: implications for global climate change*, Edward Elgar, Cheltenham, UK.

Zhao, Y., 2002. 'Causes and consequences of return migration: recent evidence from China', *Journal of Comparative Economics*, 30(2):376–94.

Zheng, J., 2006. *China maintained its stable and rapid growth in the first half of 2006*, 18 July, National Bureau of Statistics. Available from http://www.stats.gov.cn/

Zhong, Y. and Chen, J., 2002. 'To vote or not to vote: an analysis of peasants' participation in Chinese village elections', *Comparative Political Studies*, 35(6):686–712.

Zhou, X., 2004. Some issues concerning the reform of the state-owned commercial banks, Speech given at the IIF Spring Membership Conference, Shanghai, 16 April. Available from www.pbc.gov.cn

Zhu, R., 2003. 'Technical barriers hamper China trade', *The Bulletin*, July.

Made in the USA
Lexington, KY
10 July 2012